SCOTT FORESMAN • ADDISON WESLEY

# Mathematics


## Authors

**Randall I. Charles**
**Warren Crown**
**Francis (Skip) Fennell**

**Janet H. Caldwell**
**Mary Cavanagh**
**Dinah Chancellor**
**Alma B. Ramirez**

**Jeanne F. Ramos**
**Kay Sammons**
**Jane F. Schielack**

**William Tate**
**Mary Thompson**
**John A. Van de Walle**

## Consulting Mathematicians

**Edward J. Barbeau**
Professor of Mathematics
University of Toronto
Toronto, Ontario, Canada

**David M. Bressoud**
DeWitt Wallace Professor of Mathematics
Macalester College
Saint Paul, Minnesota

**Gary Lippman**
Professor of Mathematics and Computer Science
California State University Hayward
Hayward, California

*Editorial Offices:* Glenview, Illinois • Parsippany, New Jersey • New York, New York

*Sales Offices:* Parsippany, New Jersey • Duluth, Georgia • Glenview, Illinois
Coppell, Texas • Ontario, California • Mesa, Arizona

## Reading Consultants

**Peter Afflerbach**
Professor and Director of
The Reading Center
University of Maryland
College Park, Maryland

**Donald J. Leu**
John and Maria Neag
Endowed Chair in Literacy and Technology
University of Connecticut
Storrs, Connecticut

## Reviewers

**Donna McCollum Derby**
Teacher
Kernersville Elementary School
Kernersville, North Carolina

**Terri Geaudreau**
Title I Math Facilitator
Bemiss Elementary
Spokane, Washington

**Sister Helen Lucille Habig, RSM**
Assistant Superintendent of
Catholic Schools
Archdiocese of Cincinnati
Cincinnati, Ohio

**Kim Hill**
Teacher
Hayes Grade Center
Ada, Oklahoma

**Martha Knight**
Teacher
Oak Mountain Elementary
Birmingham, Alabama

**Catherine Kuhns**
Teacher
Country Hills Elementary
Coral Springs, Florida

**Susan Mayberger**
Supervisor of English as a Second
Language/Director of Migrant Education
Omaha Public Schools
Omaha, Nebraska

**Judy Peede**
Elementary Lead Math Teacher
Wake County Schools
Raleigh, North Carolina

**Lynda M. Penry, EdD**
Teacher
Wright Elementary
Ft. Walton Beach, Florida

**Jolyn D. Raleigh**
District Math Curriculum Specialist K–2
Granite School District
Salt Lake City, Utah

**Vickie H. Smith**
Assistant Principal
Phoenix Academic Magnet
Elementary School
Alexandria, Louisiana

**Ann Watts**
Mathematics Specialist
East Baton Rouge Parish School System
Baton Rouge, Louisiana

ISBN: 0-328-03015-5



6 7 8 9 10 V064 09 08 07 06 05 04

CHAPTER 1

# Position and Sorting

## Section A Position and Location



## Section B Sorting and Classifying

### Additional Resources

# Chapter 4 Numbers Through 10

## Section A Understanding Numbers 6 Through 10

## Section B Using Numbers 6 Through 10

### Additional Resources

# Numbers Through 31

## Section A Numbers 11 Through 20



## Section B Numbers Through 31



## Section C Using Numbers Through 31



### Additional Resources

- Math Story, 5A
- Home-School Connection, 101
- Practice Game, 102
- Chapter 5 Test, 129

CHAPTER 10

# Understanding Addition

## Section A Joining Groups

## Section B Addition Sentences

### Additional Resources

# Understanding Subtraction

### Additional Resources

CHAPTER 12

# Counting and Number Patterns to 100

Section A

## Numbers to 100



Section B

## Skip Counting

### Additional Resources

# My name is ______________________________

## Matching One-to-One

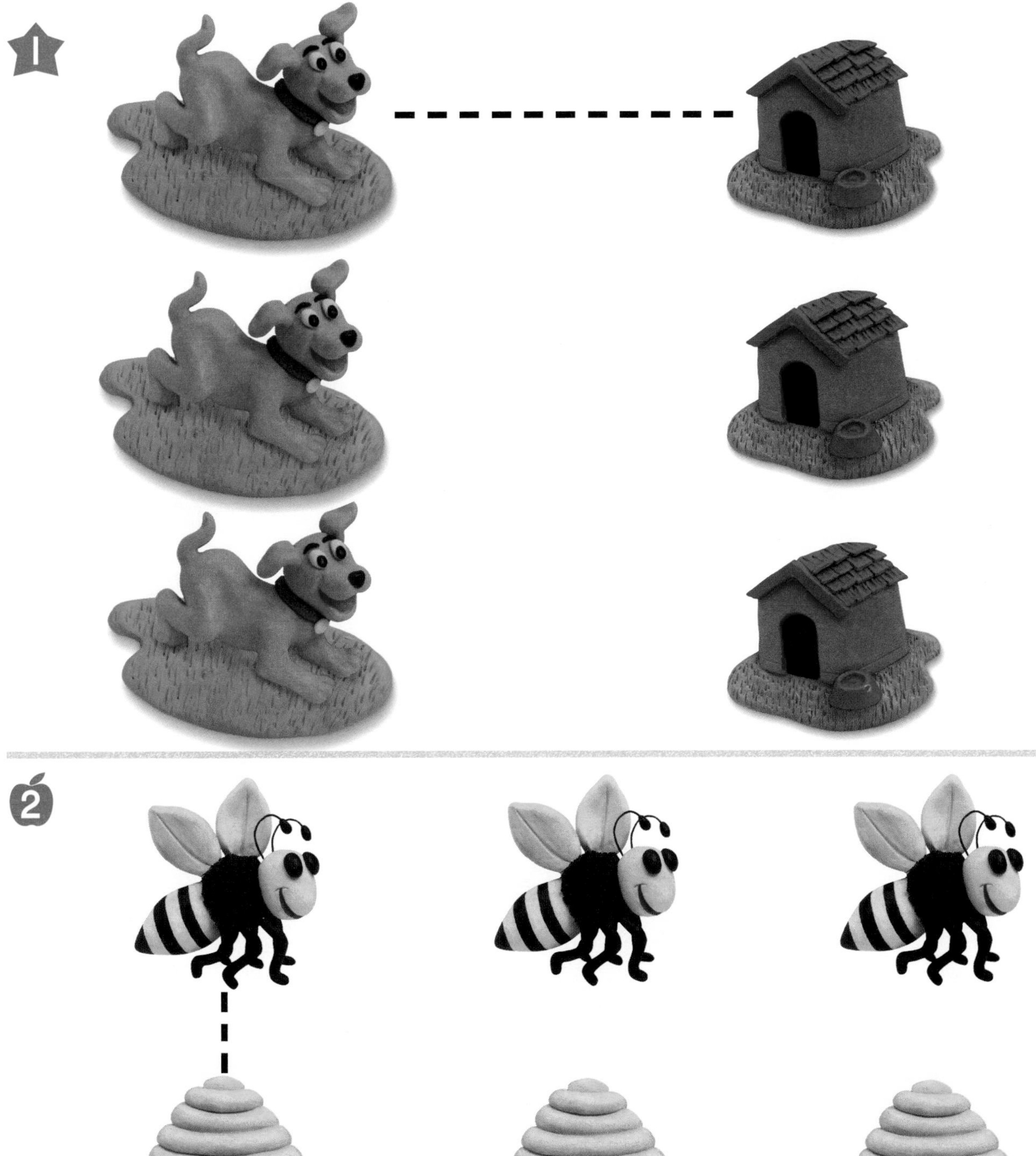

**Directions** Have children write their name on the line at the top of the page. Then have them draw a line to match each dog to a dog house and each bee to a beehive.

# Does Not Belong

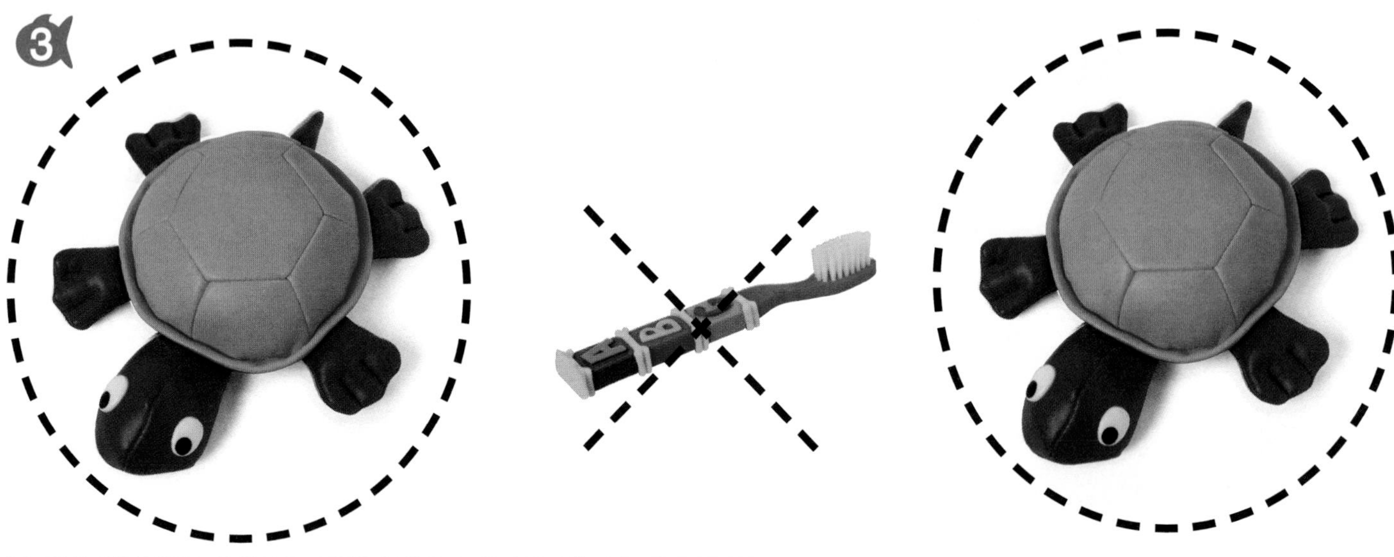

**Directions** In each row have children circle the objects that are the same and mark an *X* on the object that does not belong.

**Home Activity** Talk with your child about the pictures on these two pages. Have your child tell you how he or she completed the pages.

Name ______________________________

**Directions** Have children color the cherries red, the balloon blue, the sun yellow, and the leaf green.

**Directions** Have children trace and color the shapes at the top of the page. Then have children color the circles yellow, the squares blue, and the triangles green.

**Home Activity** Talk with your child about the pictures on these two pages. Have your child tell you how he or she completed the pages.

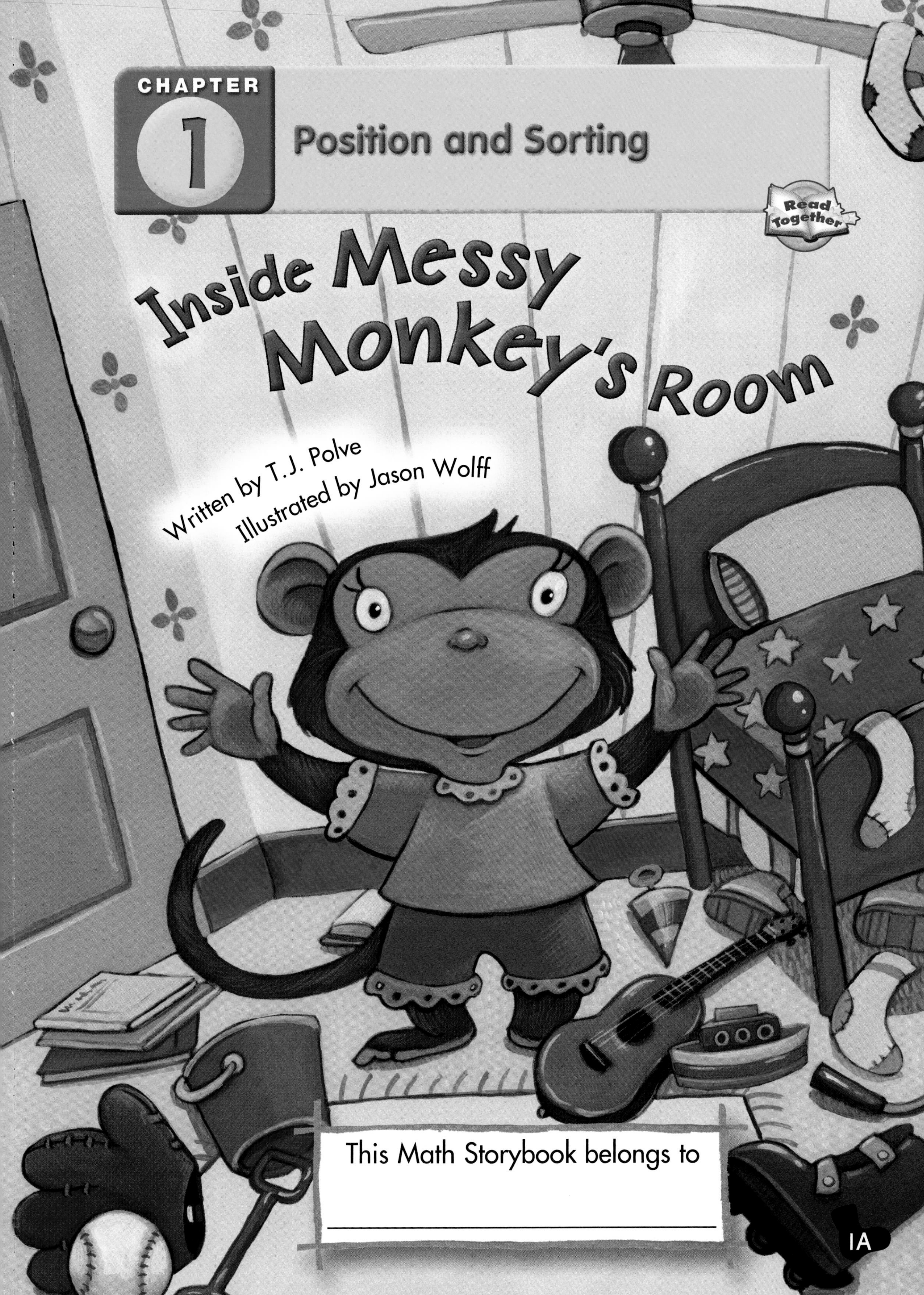
CHAPTER
1
Position and Sorting
Read Together
Inside Messy Monkey's Room
Written by T.J. Polve
Illustrated by Jason Wolff
This Math Storybook belongs to

Messy Monkey's room is a mess.
Oh, yes!

On the floor.
Under her bed.
By the door.
Over her head.

A mess?
Oh, yes!

If Messy Monkey wants to play,
she has to clean up right away!

She makes a pile here.
She makes a pile there.
She makes lots of piles
everywhere.

She puts away
her balls and blocks.
She puts away
her shoes and socks.

She looks to the left.
She looks to the right.
All her mess is out of sight.

Hip, hip, hooray!
Now it's time to go and play!

# Home-School Connection

Dear Family,

Today my class started Chapter 1, **Position and Sorting.** I will learn how to tell where things are. I will also learn how to sort objects into groups. Here are some of the math words I will be learning and some things we can do to help me with my math.

Love,

_______________________

## Math Activity to Do at Home

Play "Opposites." Stand inside the kitchen and say, "I am standing inside the kitchen." Then help your child act out the opposite and say, "I am standing outside the kitchen." Use objects to act out other opposites, such as *over* and *under, top* and *bottom.*

## Books to Read Together

Reading math stories reinforces concepts. Look for these titles in your local library:

***The Berenstain Bears: Inside, Outside, Upside Down***
By Stan and Jan Berenstain
(Random House, 1997)

***Sorting (Math Counts)***
By Henry Pluckrose
(Children's Press, 1995)

**Take It to the NET**
**More Activities**
www.scottforesman.com

## My New Math Words

**sort** A sorting rule might say, "Sort these objects by size. Put all the small books on the top shelf. Put all the big books on the bottom shelf."

5

6

7

8

**Directions** Have children mark an *X* on the item in each row that is different from the other two items.

**Home Activity** At a grocery store, ask your child to point out two items that are the same and one item that is different. Have your child tell you why the items are the same or different.

CHAPTER
2
Graphing and Patterns
Read Together
Scaredy Skunk's Dance
Written by
Theresa Volpe
Illustrated by
Donna Catanese
This Math Storybook belongs to
2A

Look! It's time
for the dance.
But Scaredy Skunk
won't take a chance.

## Home-School Connection

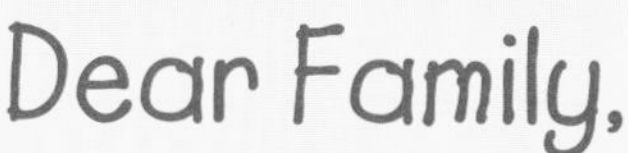


Today my class started Chapter 2, **Graphing and Patterns.** I will learn how to read a graph. I will also learn how to recognize different kinds of patterns. Here are some of the math words I will be learning and some things we can do to help me with my math.

Love,

______________________

### Math Activity to Do at Home

Go on a Color Hunt. Help your child write his or her three favorite colors on a sheet of paper. Then look for those colors around the house, putting a check mark next to each color when you find it. Count the check marks. Which color did you find most often? Least often?

### Books to Read Together

Reading math stories reinforces concepts. Look for these titles in your local library:

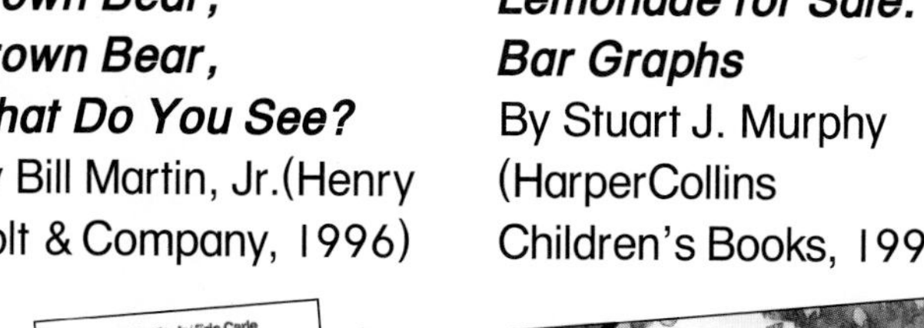

***Brown Bear, Brown Bear, What Do You See?***
By Bill Martin, Jr.(Henry Holt & Company, 1996)

***Lemonade for Sale: Bar Graphs***
By Stuart J. Murphy (HarperCollins Children's Books, 1998)

### My New Math Words

**real graph**

**picture graph**

Our Class

Boys

Girls

**bar graph**

Our Pets

Dogs

Cats

Birds

**pattern** There are many kinds of patterns. Here is a repeating sound pattern: clap, clap, stomp; clap, clap, stomp; clap, clap, stomp.

Name________________________________

# Dancing Footprints

### What You Need

paper bag
red and blue markers

## How to Play

1. Work with a partner to help Scaredy Skunk get to the dance.
2. Take turns choosing a marker from the bag. Does the color you chose come next in the pattern?
3. If it does, put it on the next space. If it doesn't, put it back in the bag.
4. Keep taking turns to continue the pattern.
5. When you get to FINISH, dance, dance, dance with Scaredy Skunk and his friends!

Name ___________________________

# As Many, More, and Fewer

1

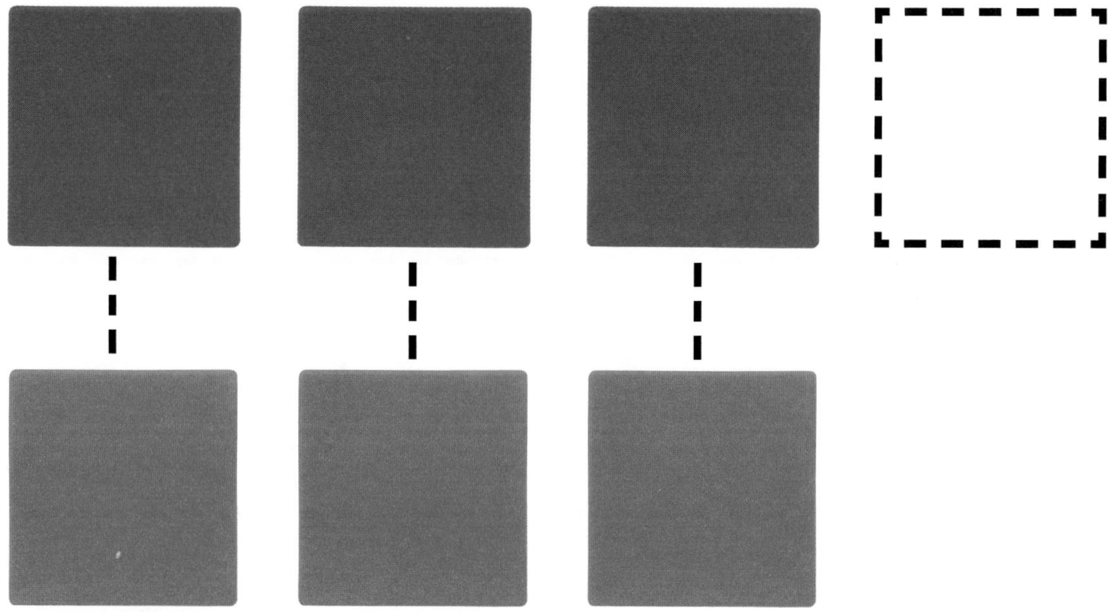

2

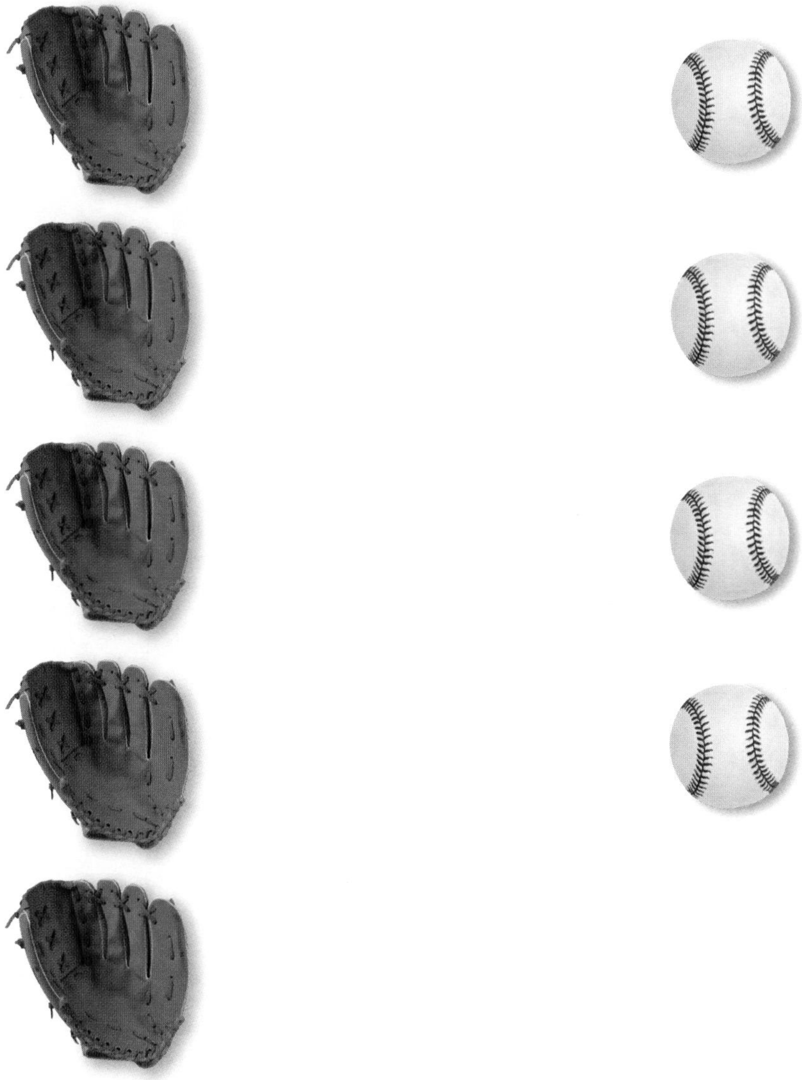

**Directions** Exercise 1: Have children draw lines from the blue to the red tiles. Ask them to show more by tracing the extra tile and coloring it blue. Then have children draw a red tile to show as many red tiles as blue ones. Exercise 2: Have children draw a line from each mitt to a ball and then draw a ball so that each mitt has a ball.

3

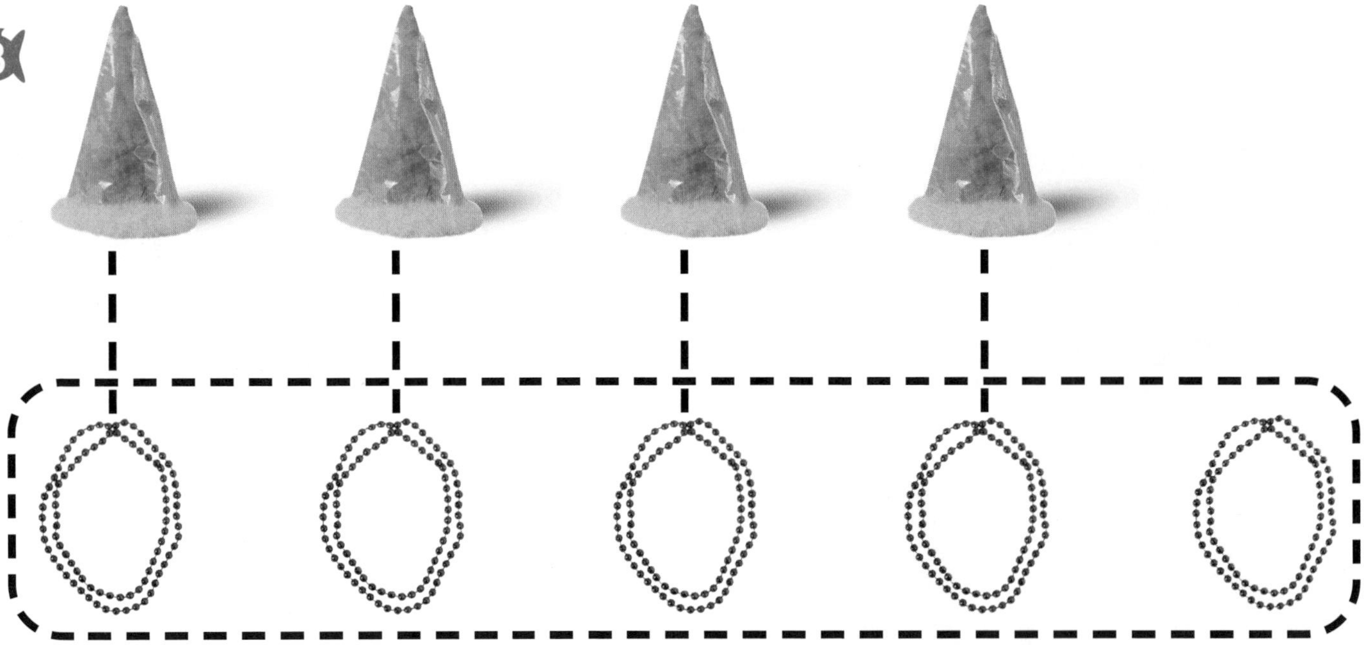

4

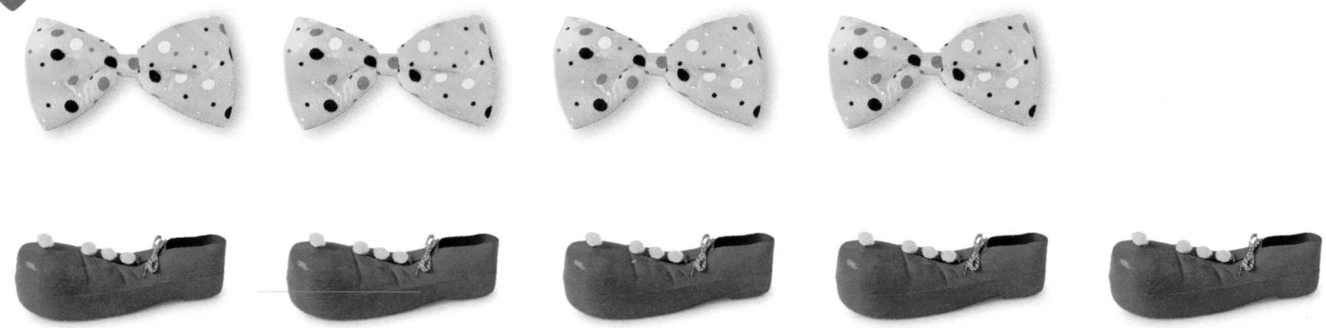

5

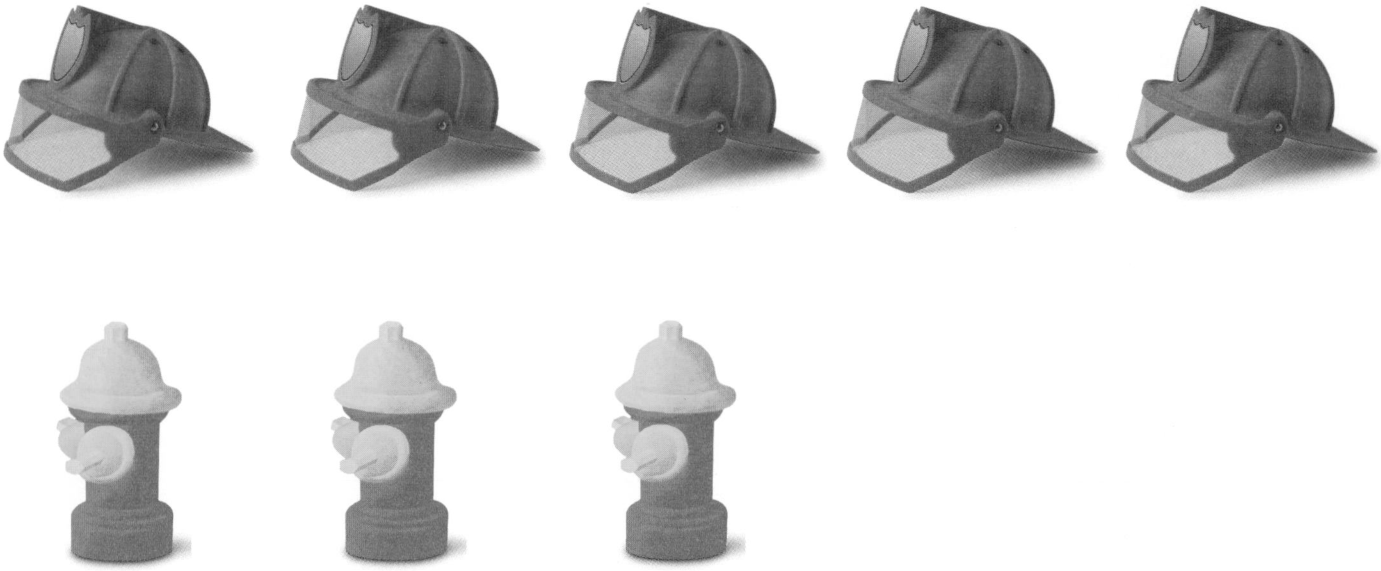

**Directions** In each exercise have children draw a line from each item in the top row to each item in the bottom row and circle the row with more.

**Home Activity** Give your child 4 cups and 3 saucers. Have your child tell you which group has more.

Name ____________________

## Real Graphs

## Which Has More?

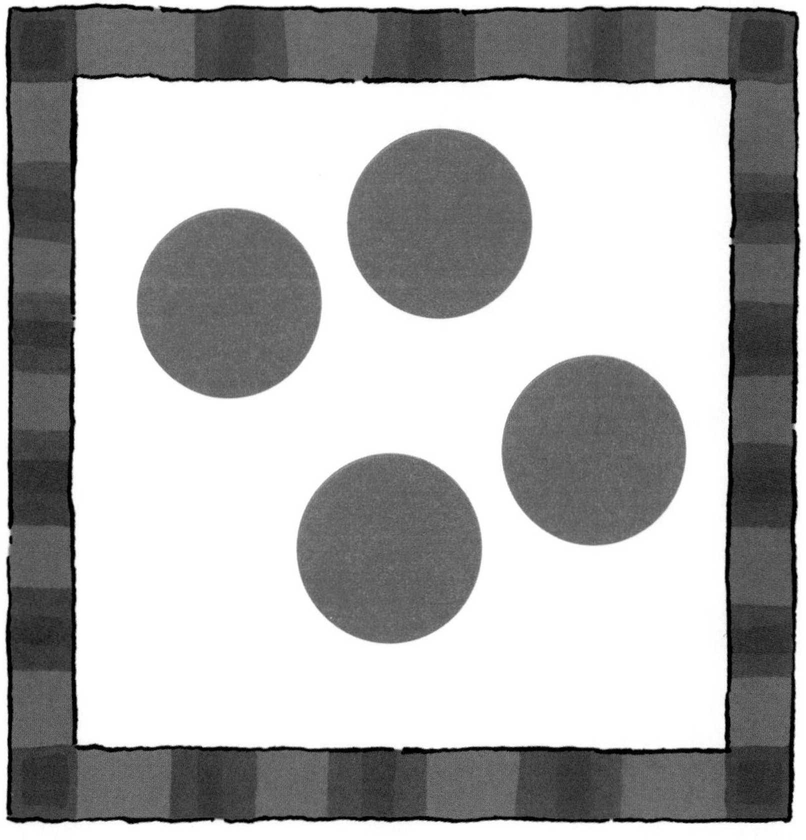

**Directions** Have children place matching counters on the workmats. Then have them move the counters to the graph and color the columns to show the counters. Have them circle the column that has more.

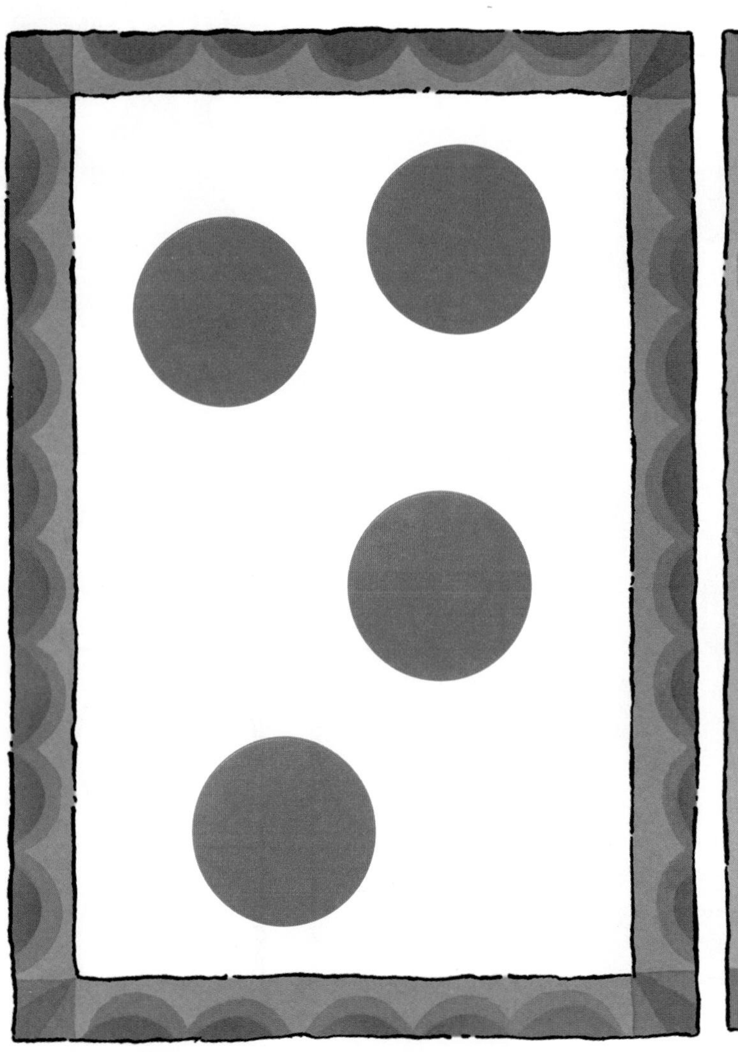
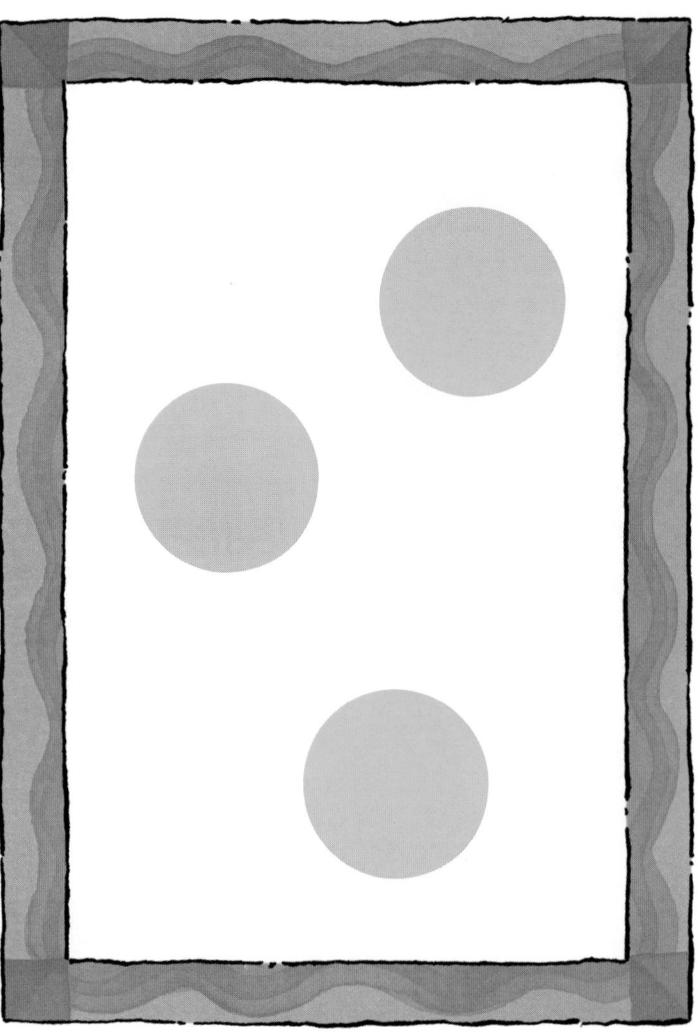

## Which Has Fewer?

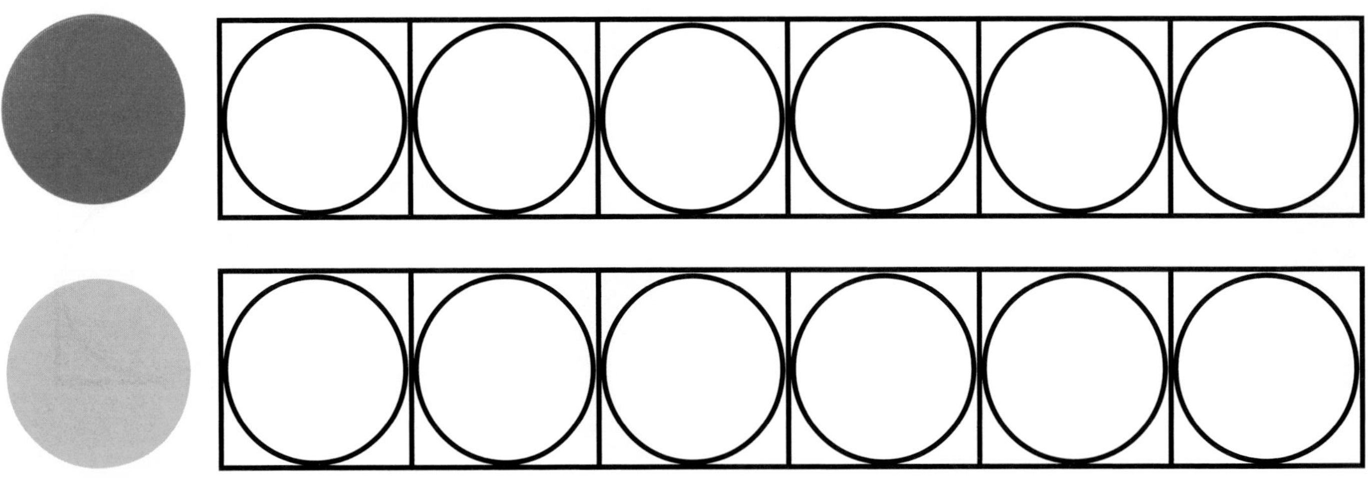

**Directions** Have children place matching counters on the workmats. Then have them move the counters to the graph and color the rows to show the counters. Have them circle the row that has fewer counters.

**Home Activity** Gather toys such as stuffed animals and trucks. Have your child sort the toys into two groups and place them in two rows, one below the other. Ask your child which row has more, or if both rows have the same number.

Name ______________________________

## Are There More Girls or Boys?

|  |  |  |  |  |  |  |
|---|---|---|---|---|---|---|
|  |  |  |  |  |  |  |

**Directions** Have children look at the boys and girls in the scene. Have them color a picture on the graph for each boy and each girl.

# Toys on the Shelves

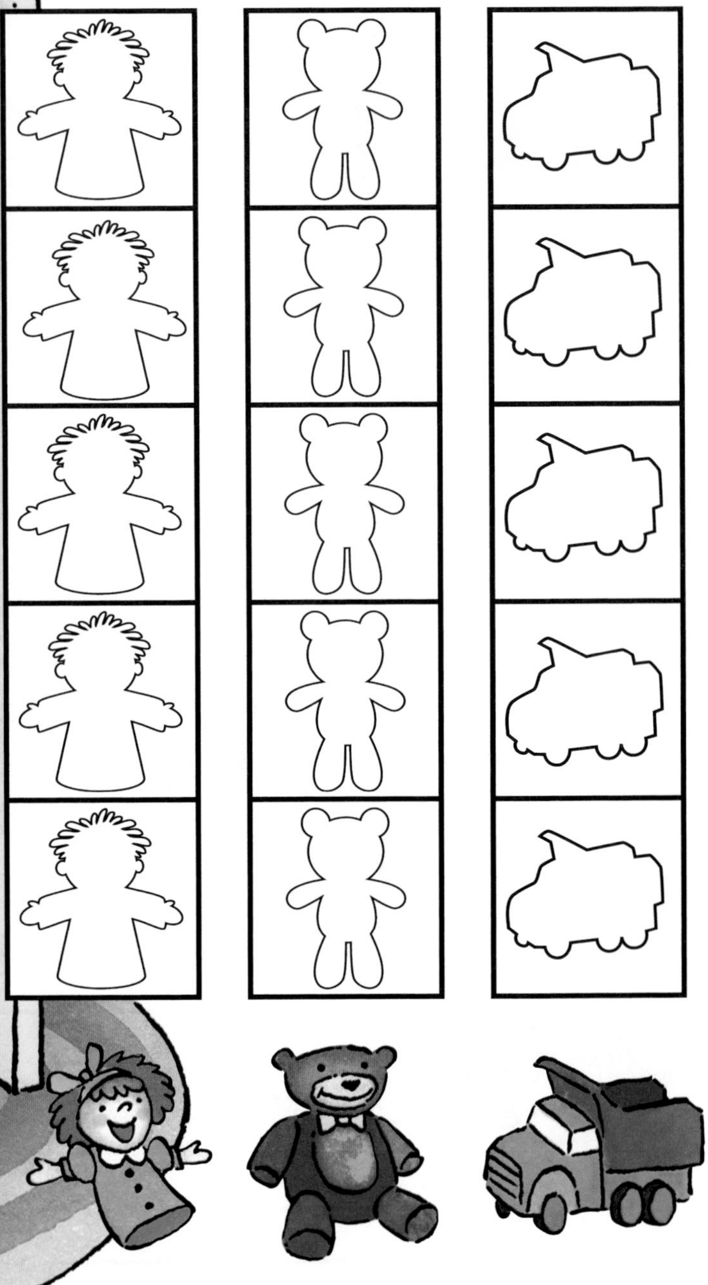

**Directions** Have children look at the puppets, teddy bears, and trucks on the shelves. Have them color a picture on the graph for each toy.

**Home Activity** Ask your child to place 3 pennies in one row and 2 nickels in another row on a sheet of paper. Ask your child to tell you which row has more coins, and to tell you how he or she knows.

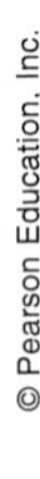

Name ______________________

**Directions** Have children survey some classmates to decide which snack they like better. Have them color a square on the graph for each response. Then have children answer the survey question by circling the fruit that more children like better.

## Which Center Do We Like Better?

| | | | | | | |
|---|---|---|---|---|---|---|
|  (blocks) | | | | | | |
|  (painting) | | | | | | |

**Directions** Have children survey some classmates to decide which activity center they like better: block building or painting. Have them color a square for each response and then tell which activity center more children like.

**Home Activity** Talk with your child about the graph. Have your child tell you which activity center the class likes better. Then ask your child to tell you which activity center he or she likes better.

Name ______________________________

# Sound and Movement Patterns

## Algebra

1

2

3

4

**Directions** In each exercise have children circle the picture that comes next in the pattern.

5

6

7

8

**Directions** In each exercise have children circle the instrument that comes next in the pattern.

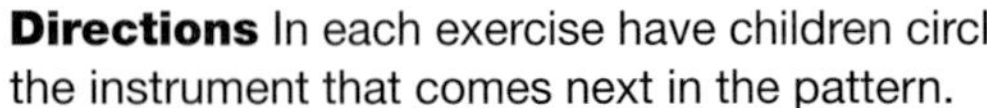

**Home Activity** Ask your child to act out one of the patterns in the pictures on the front side of the page. Have your child make up a new pattern.

Name ______________________________



## Algebra

2

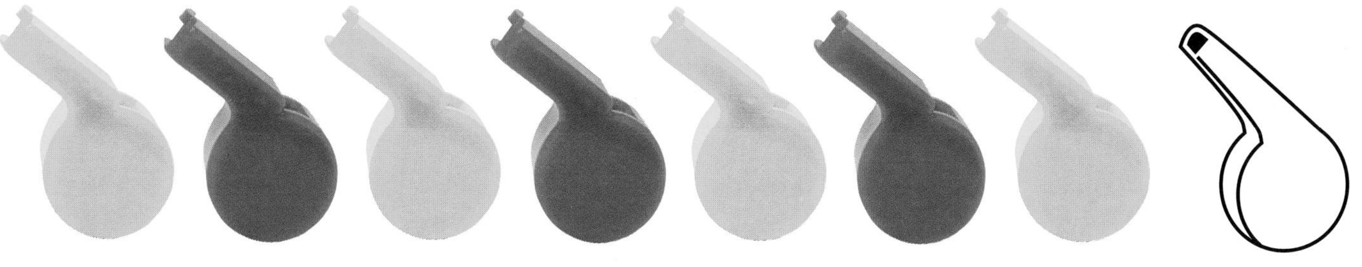

3

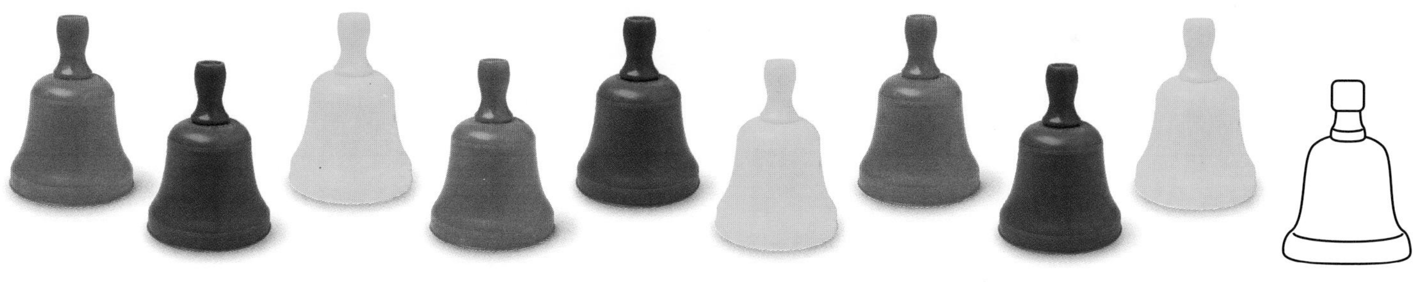

4

**Directions** Have children color the object or objects at the end of each row to show which color or colors come next in the patterns.

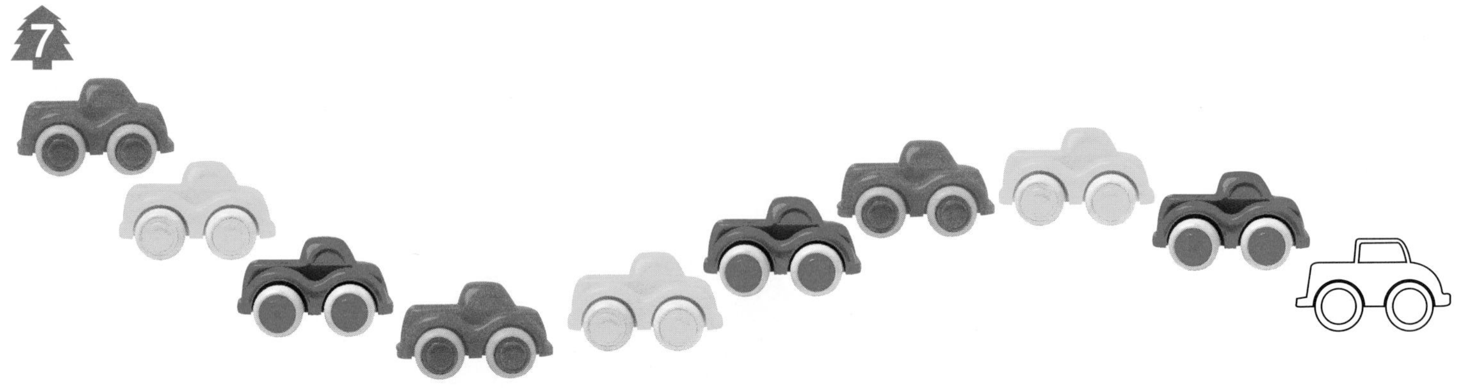

**Directions** Have children color the object or objects at the end of each row to show which color or colors come next in the patterns.

**Home Activity** Gather some buttons. Make a color pattern and have your child tell what comes next. Then have your child make a pattern and you tell what comes next.

Name ________________________________



## Algebra

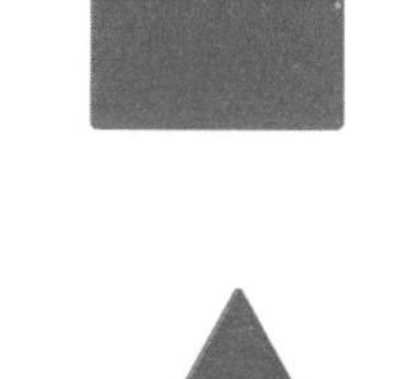

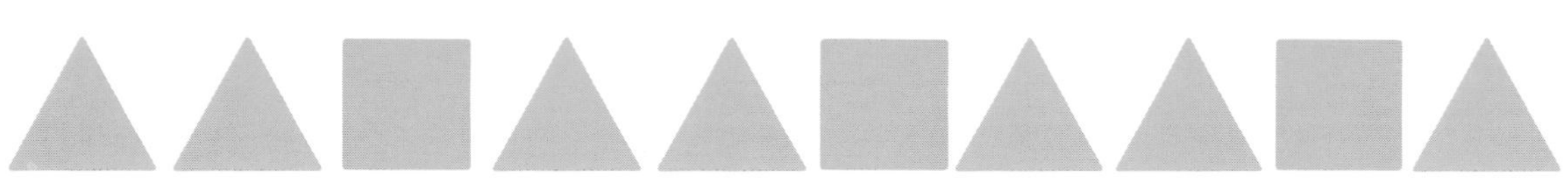

**Directions** In each exercise have children circle the shape that comes next in the pattern.

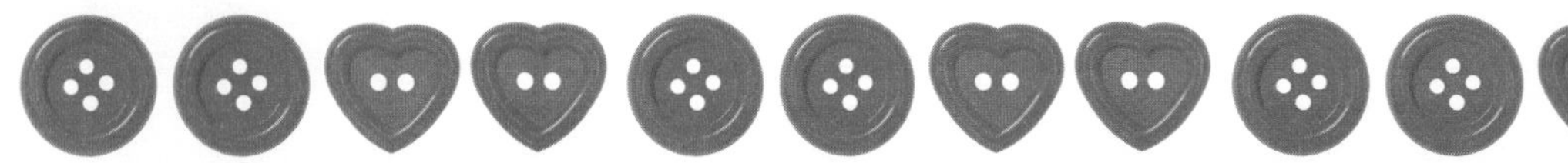

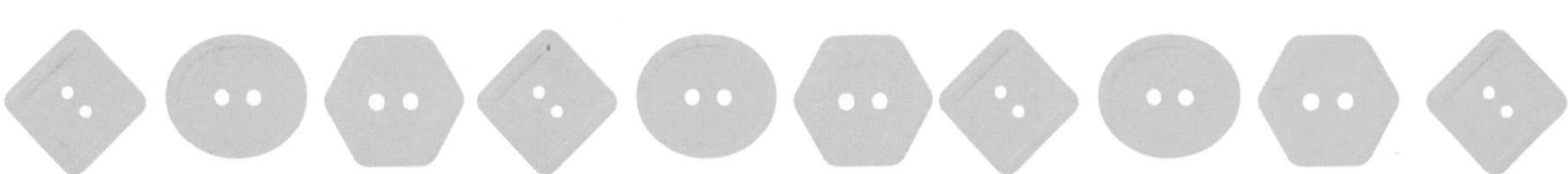

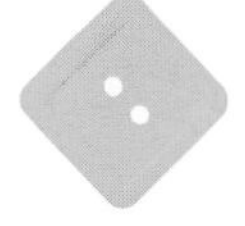

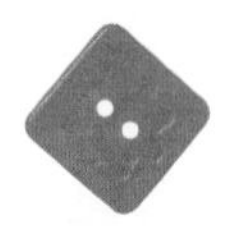

**Directions** Have children circle the shape that comes next in the pattern.

**Home Activity** Have your child use paper plates and napkins to make several shape patterns. Ask him or her to describe the patterns.

Name ______________________________

# Comparing Patterns

## Algebra

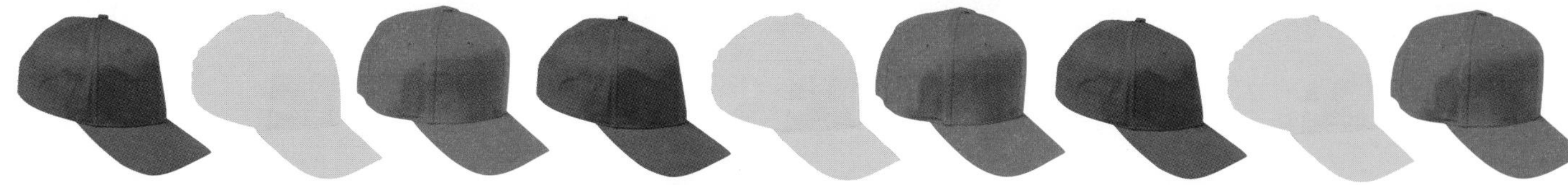

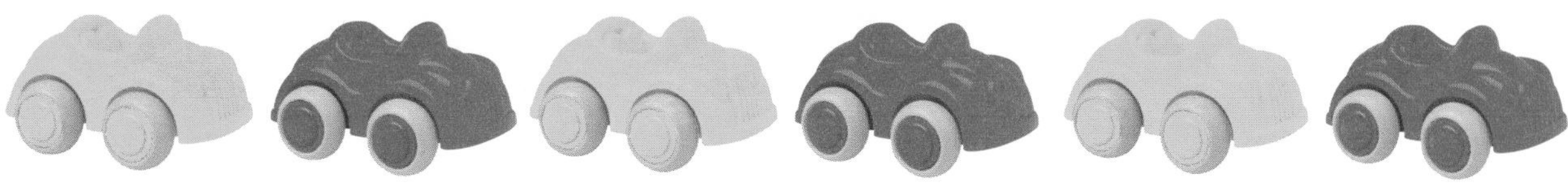

**Directions** Have children look at the cube pattern in Exercise 1. Then have them circle the matching pattern. Have them repeat the activity in Exercise 2. Have children explain their choices.

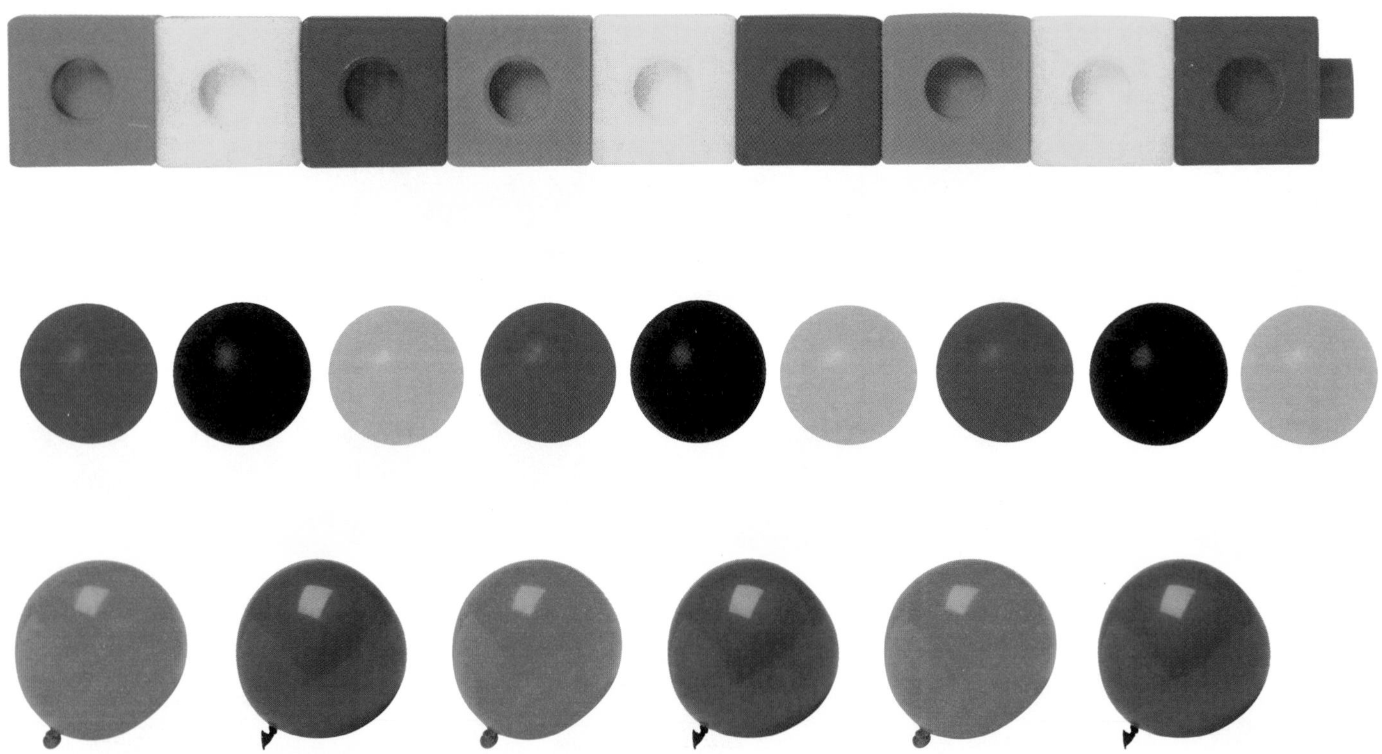

**Directions** Have children circle the pattern that matches the cube pattern at the top of each exercise.

**Home Activity** Have your child use forks and spoons to copy the red and blue cube pattern at the top of the page. Use forks and spoons to make new patterns.

Name ____________________



## Algebra

1

2

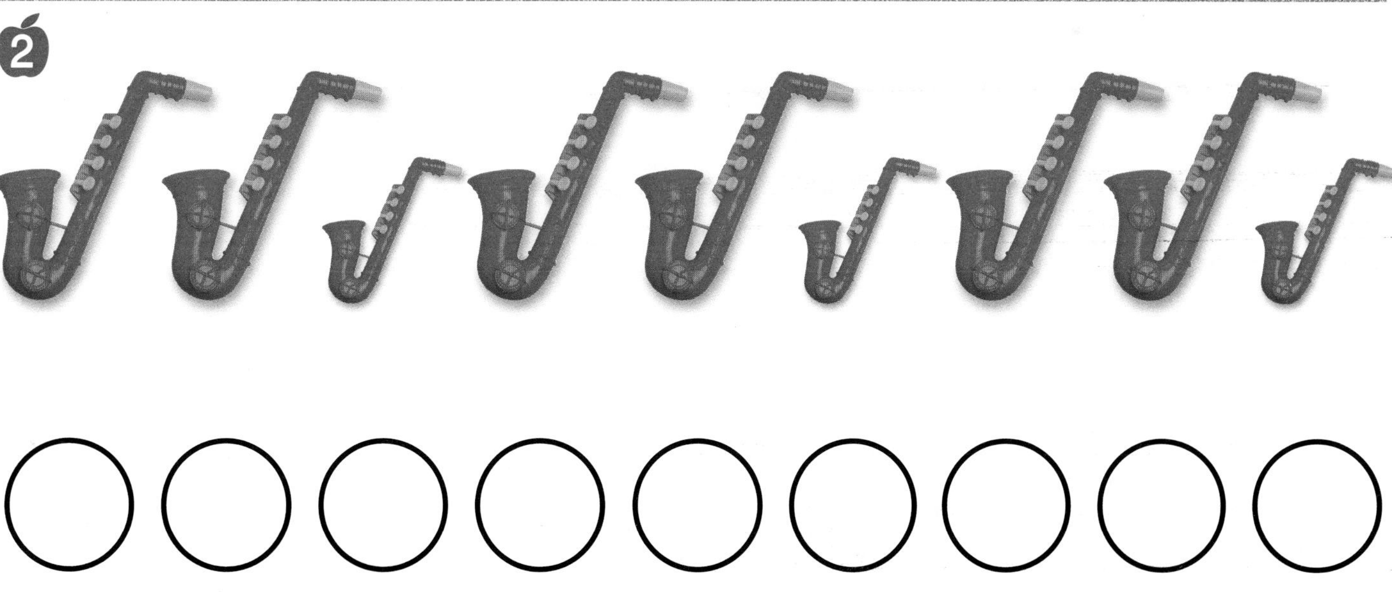

**Directions** For each exercise have children circle where the pattern repeats. Then have children show the pattern in another way by coloring the circles.

3

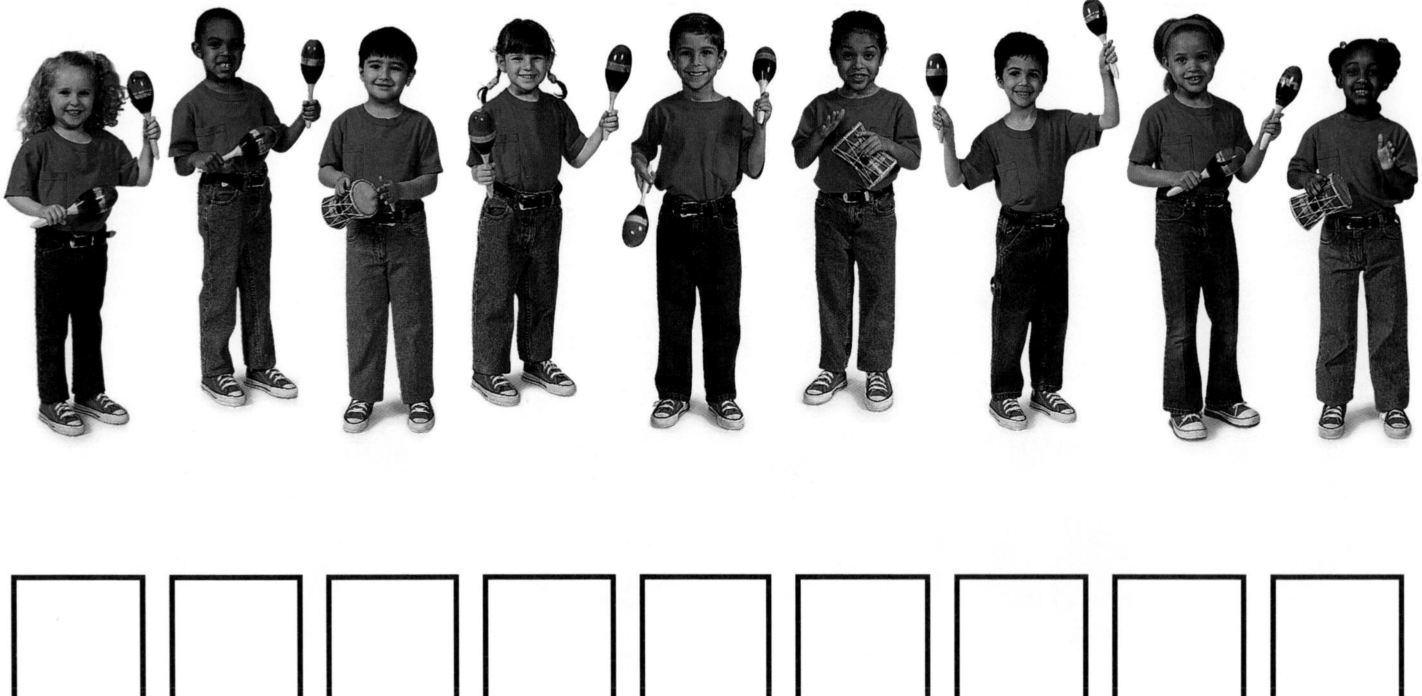

4

**Directions** For each exercise have children circle where the pattern repeats. Then have children show the pattern in another way by coloring the squares.

**Home Activity** Have your child show you the pattern at the top of the page using pennies, nickels, and dimes. Ask him or her to explain the pattern.

Name ______________________________

# Creating Patterns

**Algebra**

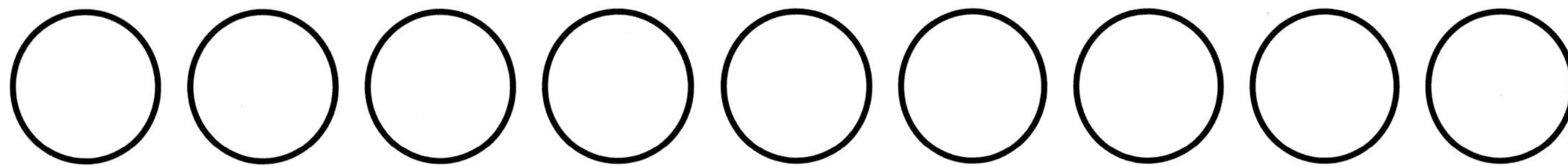

2

3

**Directions** Exercise 1: Have children use two-color counters to make a pattern and then color circles to match their pattern. Exercise 2: Have children use color tiles to make a pattern and then color squares to match their pattern. Exercise 3: Have children make a pattern with counters and tiles and then draw and color the pattern.

4

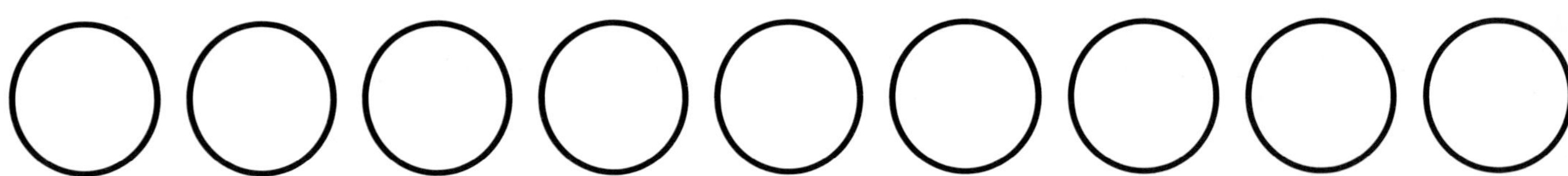

6

**Directions** Exercises 4–5: Have children use two-color counters and color tiles to make patterns and then color circles and squares to match their patterns. Exercise 6: Have children make a pattern with counters and tiles and then draw and color the pattern.

**Home Activity** Have your child make patterns using shoes and socks.

Name ____________________

# Favorite Things

Dorling Kindersley

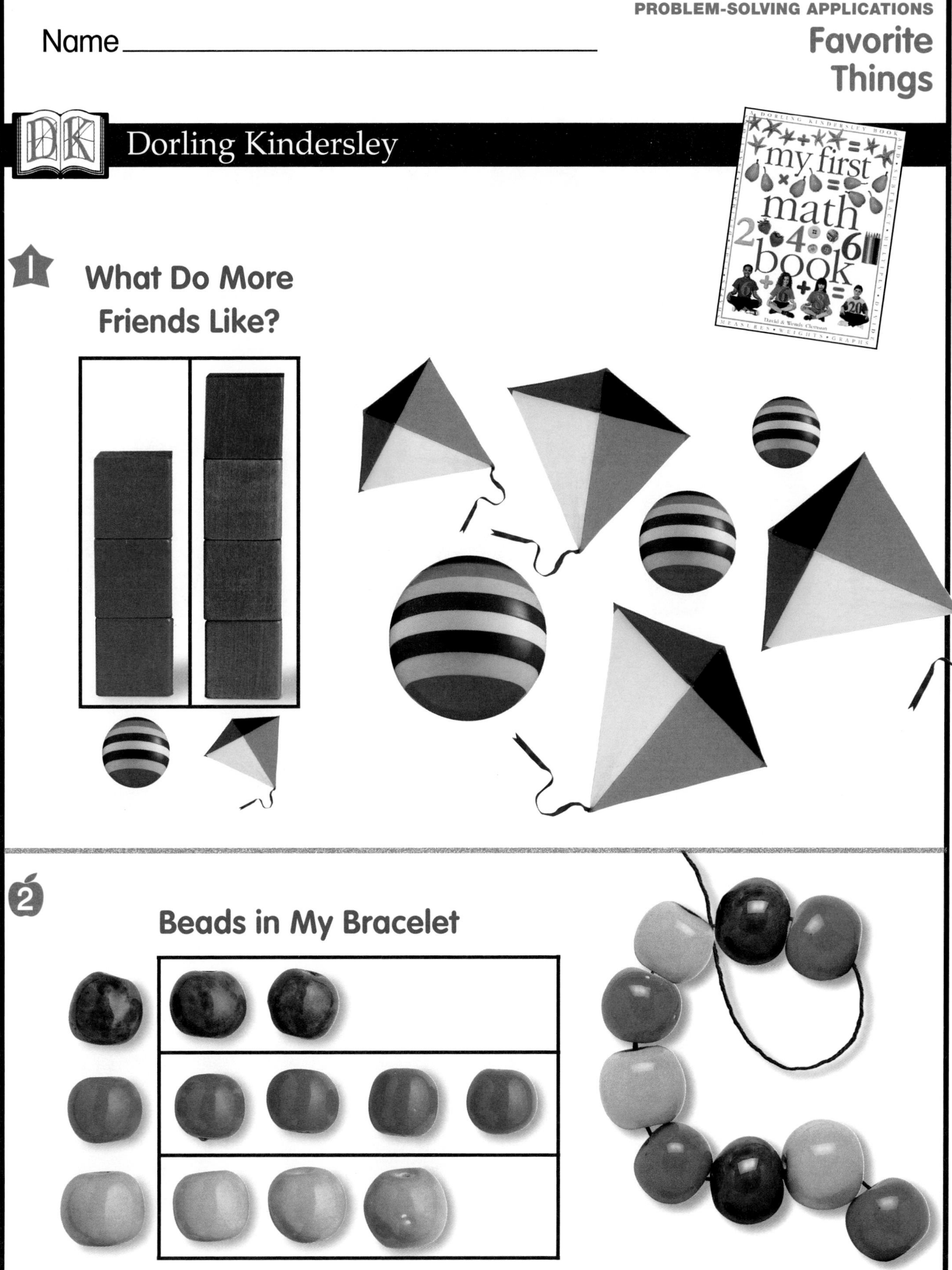


## 1 What Do More Friends Like?

## 2 Beads in My Bracelet

**Directions** Exercise 1: Tell children that Luka made a graph to show what his friends like to do. What do more friends like to do—play ball or fly kites? Have children circle the kite picture. Exercise 2: Tell children that Hanna made a graph to show the beads in her bracelet. Does the bracelet have more red or yellow beads? Have children circle the red bead that labels the row.

3

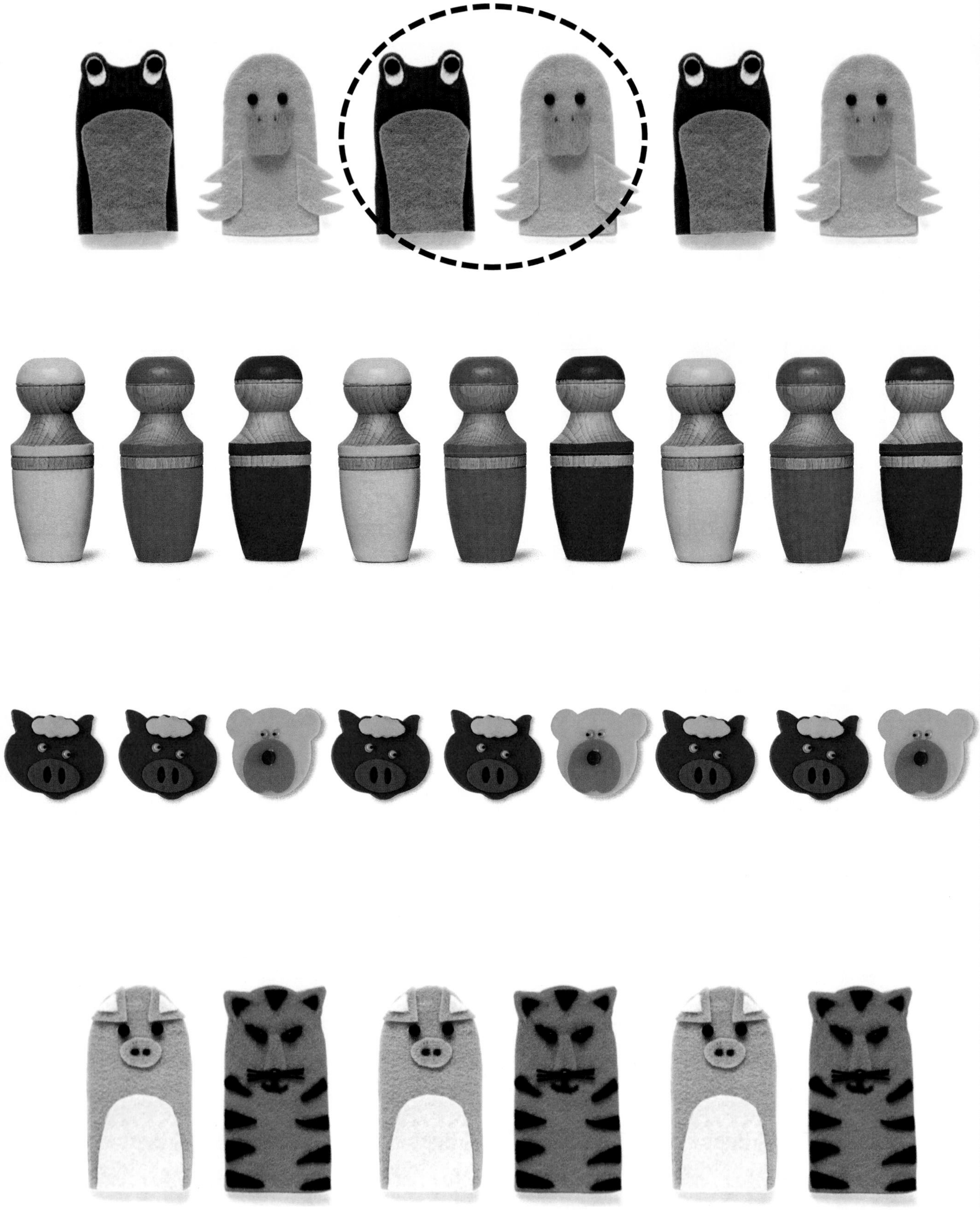

**Directions** Tell children that Nicci likes to make patterns with her toys. Ask children to look at each pattern and decide what pattern Nicci made. Have children circle the repeating part of each pattern.

**Home Activity** Talk with your child about the pictures on these two pages. Have your child tell you how he or she solved problems to complete the pages.

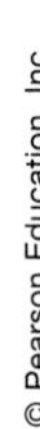

Name ___________________________________

## Which Fruit Do We Like Better?

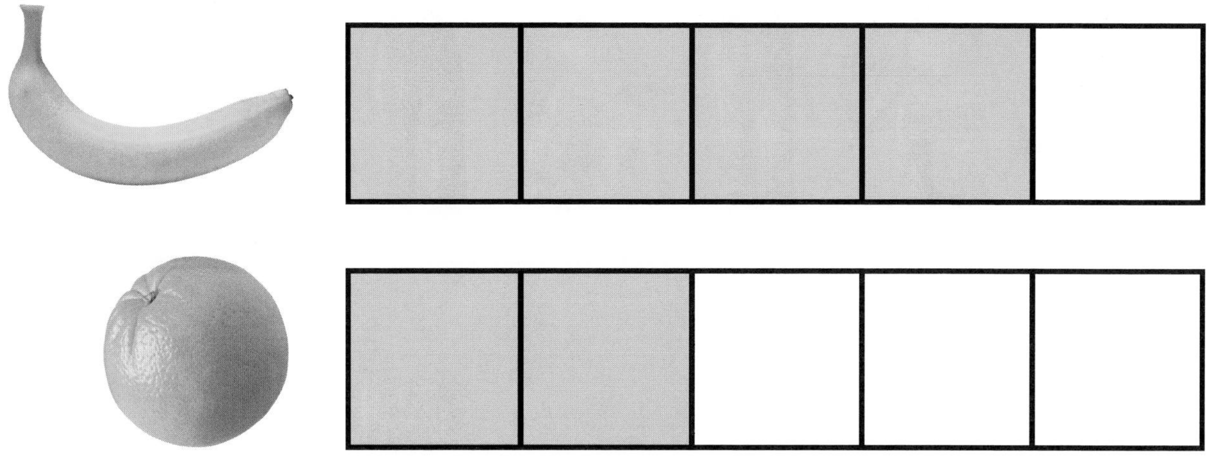

## Which Has Fewer?

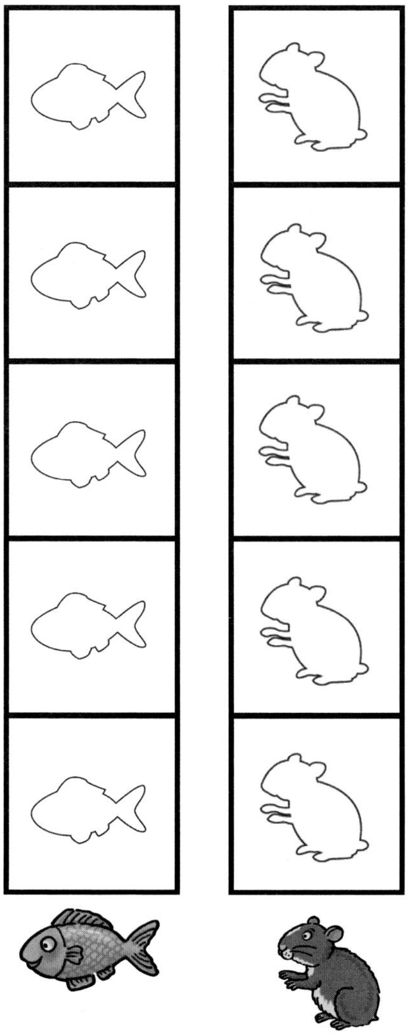

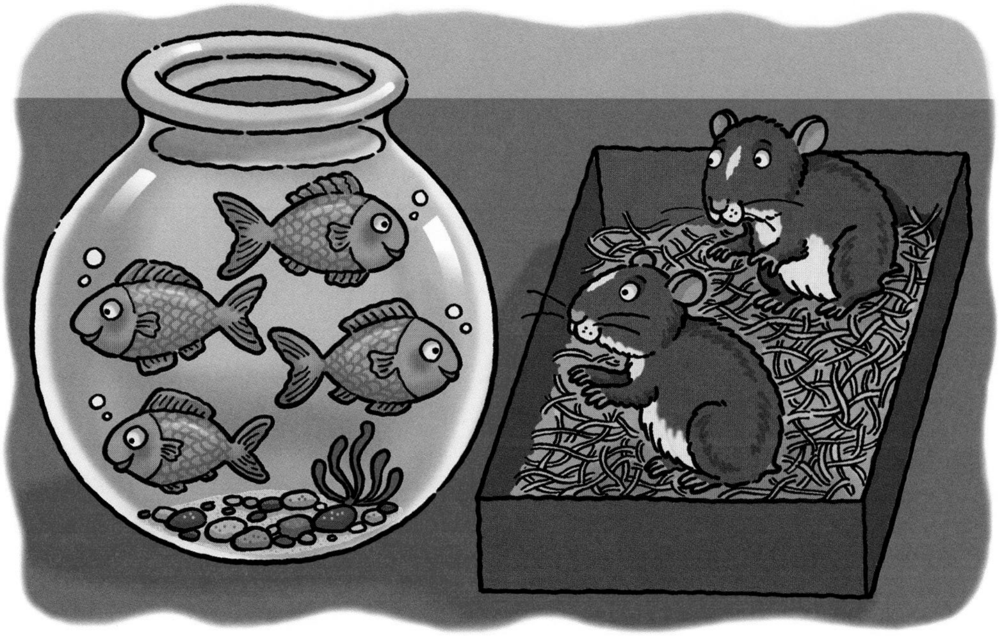

**Directions** Have children: 1. circle the row that shows the fruit more children like; 2. color the graph to show how many goldfish and hamsters and then circle the group with fewer.

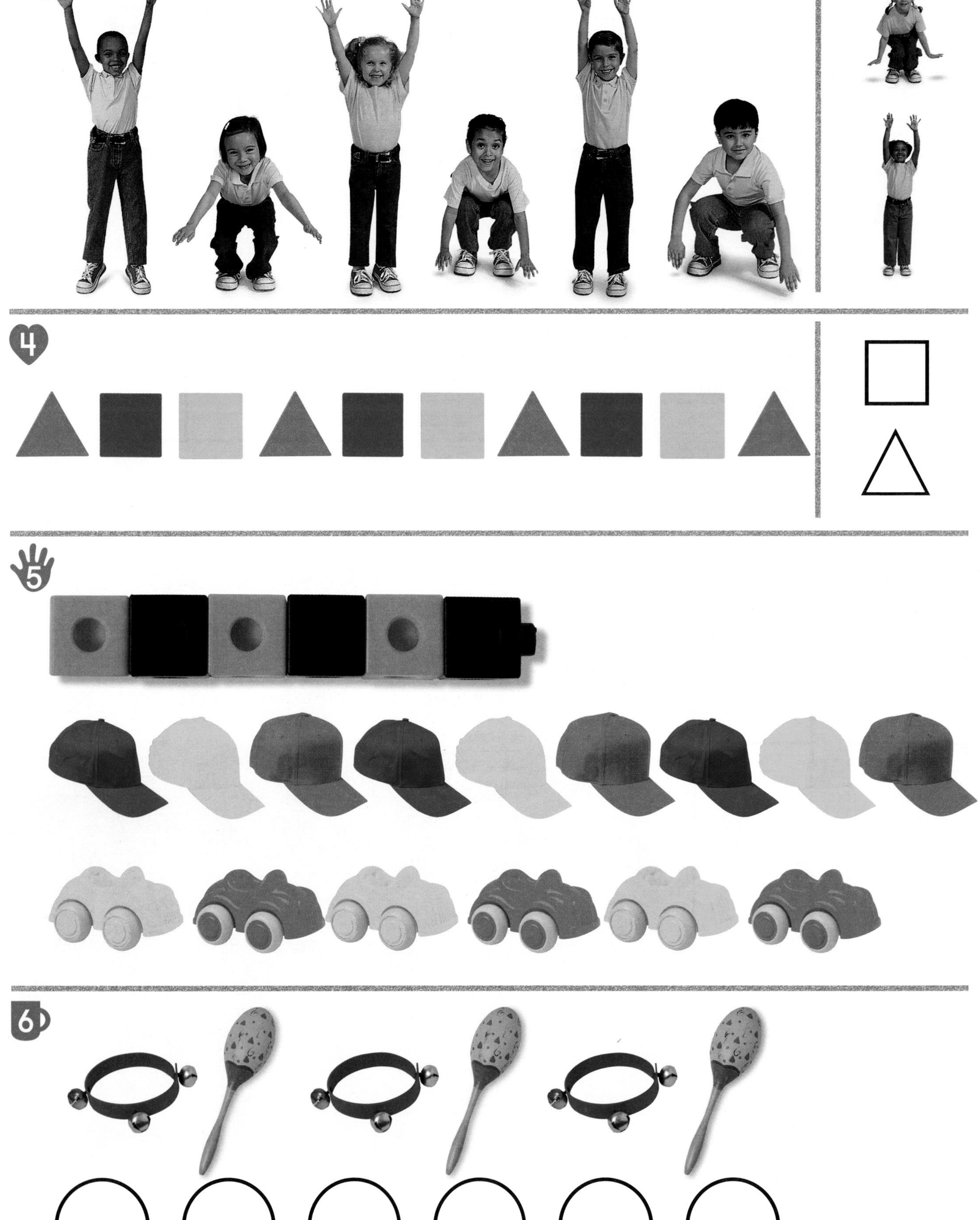


**Directions** Have children: 3. circle the picture that comes next in the pattern; 4. color the shape that comes next in the pattern; 5. circle the pattern that matches the cube pattern; 6. show the pattern in another way by coloring the circles.

Numbers Through 5

# I Went to the Park

Written by Kier Cline • Illustrated by Marisol Sarazin

This Math Storybook belongs to

______________________________

I went to the park and
what did I see?
I saw | green frog
looking at me.

I went to the park and
guess what was there.
I saw **2** brown bunnies
hopping in the air.

I went to the park and
looked in a tree.
I saw **3** gray squirrels as
high as can be.

I went to the park and
to my surprise,
I saw 4 blue birds flying
right by my eyes.

I went to the park and
guess what I found.
I saw 5 yellow ducks
swimming all around.

I went to the park and what did I see?
Will you join in and count along with me?
**I saw 1 frog, 2 bunnies, 3 squirrels,**
**4 birds, and 5 ducks.**
Counting is fun! Do you agree?

3F

## Home-School Connection

Dear Family,

Today my class started Chapter 3, **Numbers Through 5.** I will learn how to count, write, and compare numbers. Here are some of the math words I will be learning and some things we can do to help me with my math.

Love,

_______________________

### Math Activity to Do at Home

Play "Simon Says" with numbers: "Simon says, 'Tap 1 knee; touch 2 ears; clap 3 times; jump 4 times; give me 5.'" Take turns being Simon and remember to give some commands that don't come from Simon!

### Books to Read Together

Reading math stories reinforces concepts. Look for these titles in your local library:

***Counting Caterpillars and other Math Poems***
By Betsy Franco
(Scholastic, 1998)

***Counting Kisses***
By Karen Katz
(Margaret K. McElderry Books, 2001)

### My New Math Words

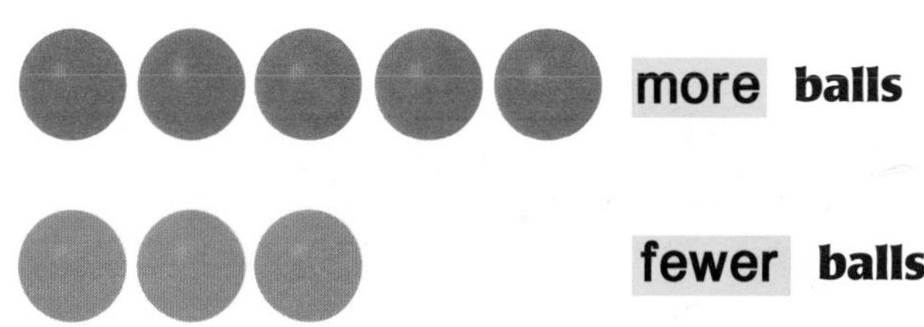

**more** balls

**fewer** balls

5 is **more** than 3. 3 is **less** than 5.

**Take It to the NET**
**More Activities**
www.scottforesman.com

Name ____________________

# Count the Animals

**What You Need**

paper clip

pencil

5 markers

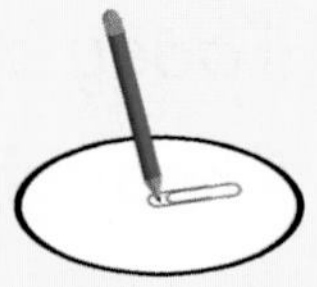

## How to Play

1. Spin the spinner.
2. Say the number.
3. Place a marker on the part of the picture that shows that number.
4. Play until you have covered all 5 groups of animals.

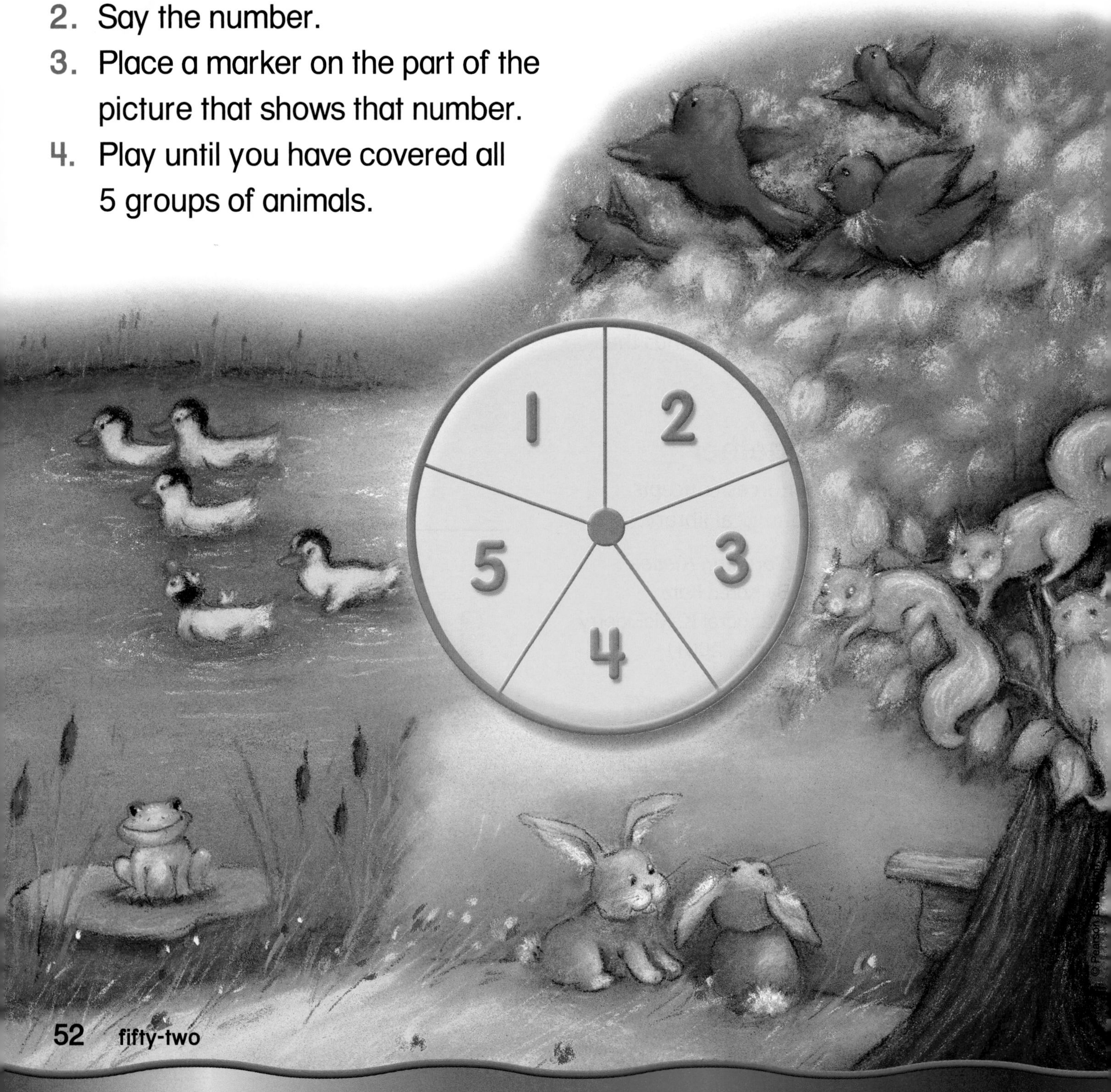

1 2 3 4 5

Name ______________________________

**Directions** Have children count the animals in each group and color one square for each animal in the group. Have them start with the square right by the animal.

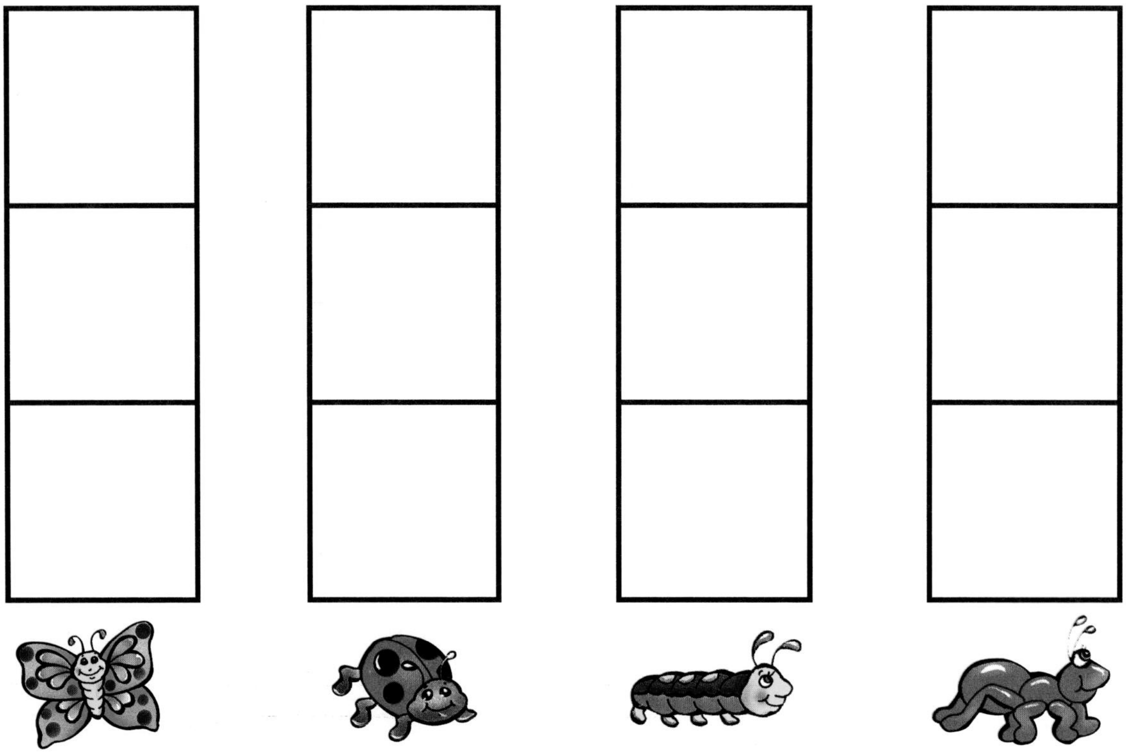

**Directions** Have pairs of children count the insects in each group and color a square for each insect in the group. Then have partners tell number stories about the insect groups.

**Home Activity** Have your child count how many items are in each of these groups: 1 napkin, 2 forks, 3 bowls.

Name ______________________________

# Reading and Writing I, 2, and 3

I
one

2
two

3
three

1

2

3

**Directions** Ask children to show groups of 1, 2, and 3 counters and then draw pictures of the counters. Have children practice writing the numbers 1, 2, and 3, beginning at each black dot.

4

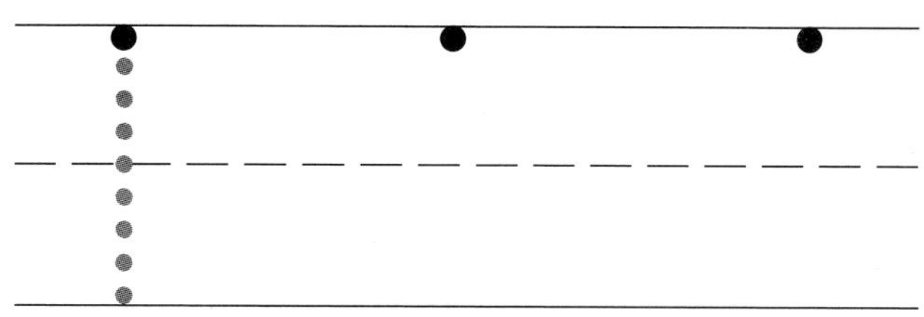

5

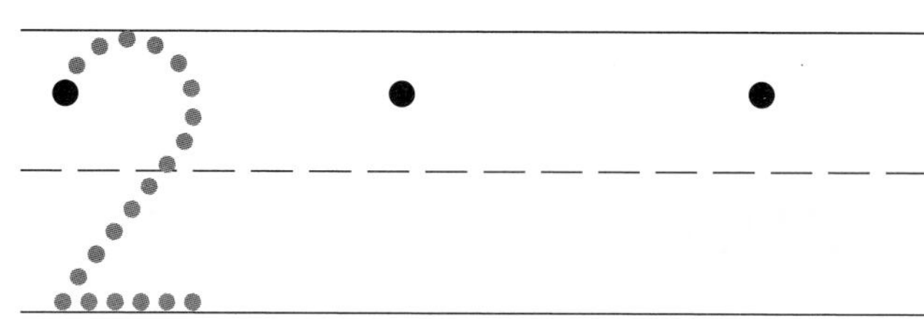

6

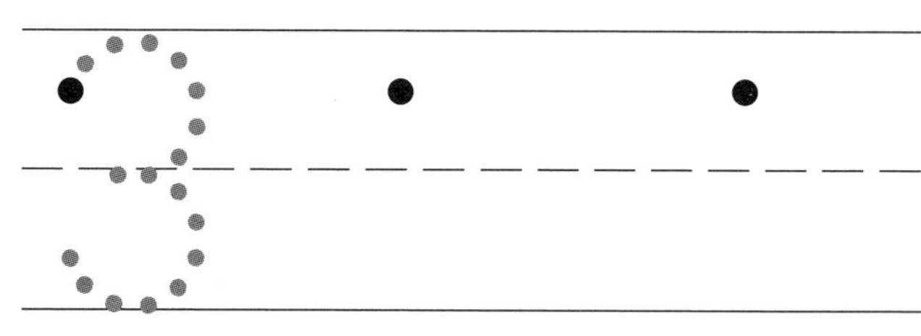

7

8

**Directions** Have children count the animals in each group and practice writing the number.

**Home Activity** Help your child find the numbers 1, 2, and 3 on items such as a clock face, a calendar, small appliances, and food packaging labels.

Name ________________________________

# Counting 4 and 5

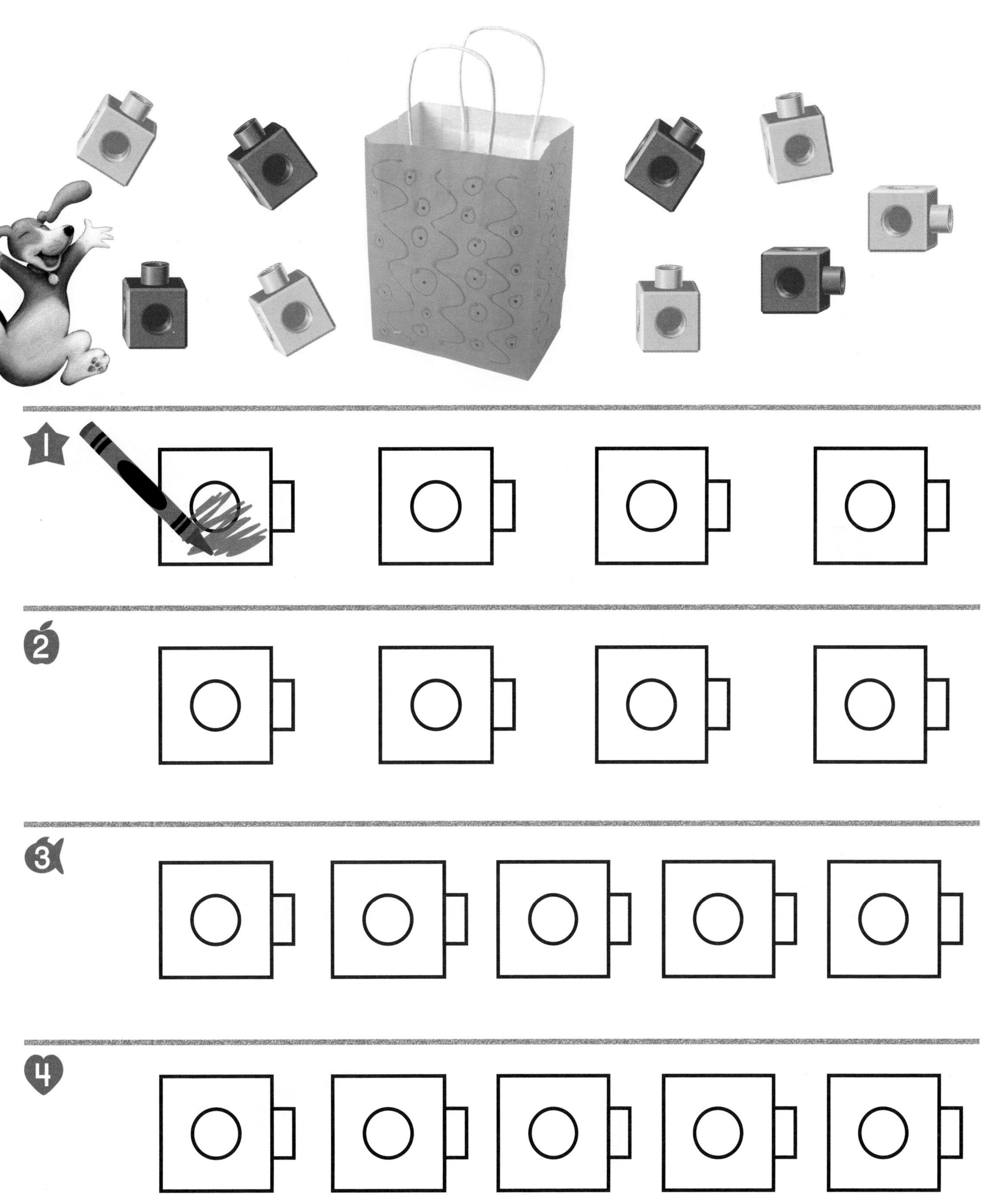

**Directions** Exercises 1–2: Have each child choose 4 cubes of two colors, such as yellow and red. Ask children to color the cubes on the page to match the cubes they chose. Exercises 3–4: Have children choose 5 cubes and repeat the activity.

**Directions** Have children color the groups of 4 apples red and the groups of 5 apples yellow.

**Home Activity** At the grocery store ask your child to help you select groups of 4 or 5 items, such as 4 bananas or 5 apples.

Name ___________________________

# Reading and Writing 4 and 5

4
four

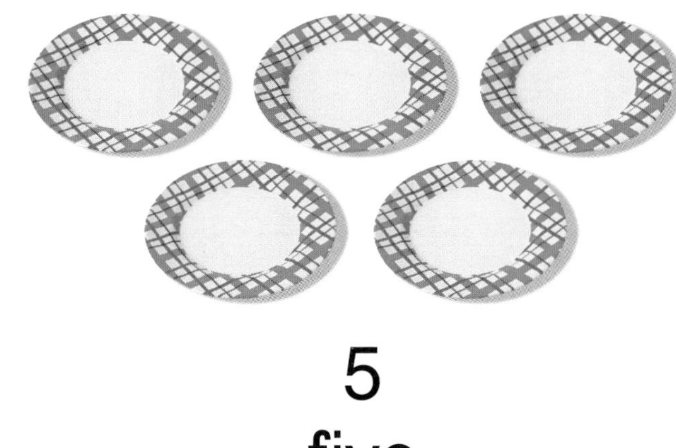

5
five

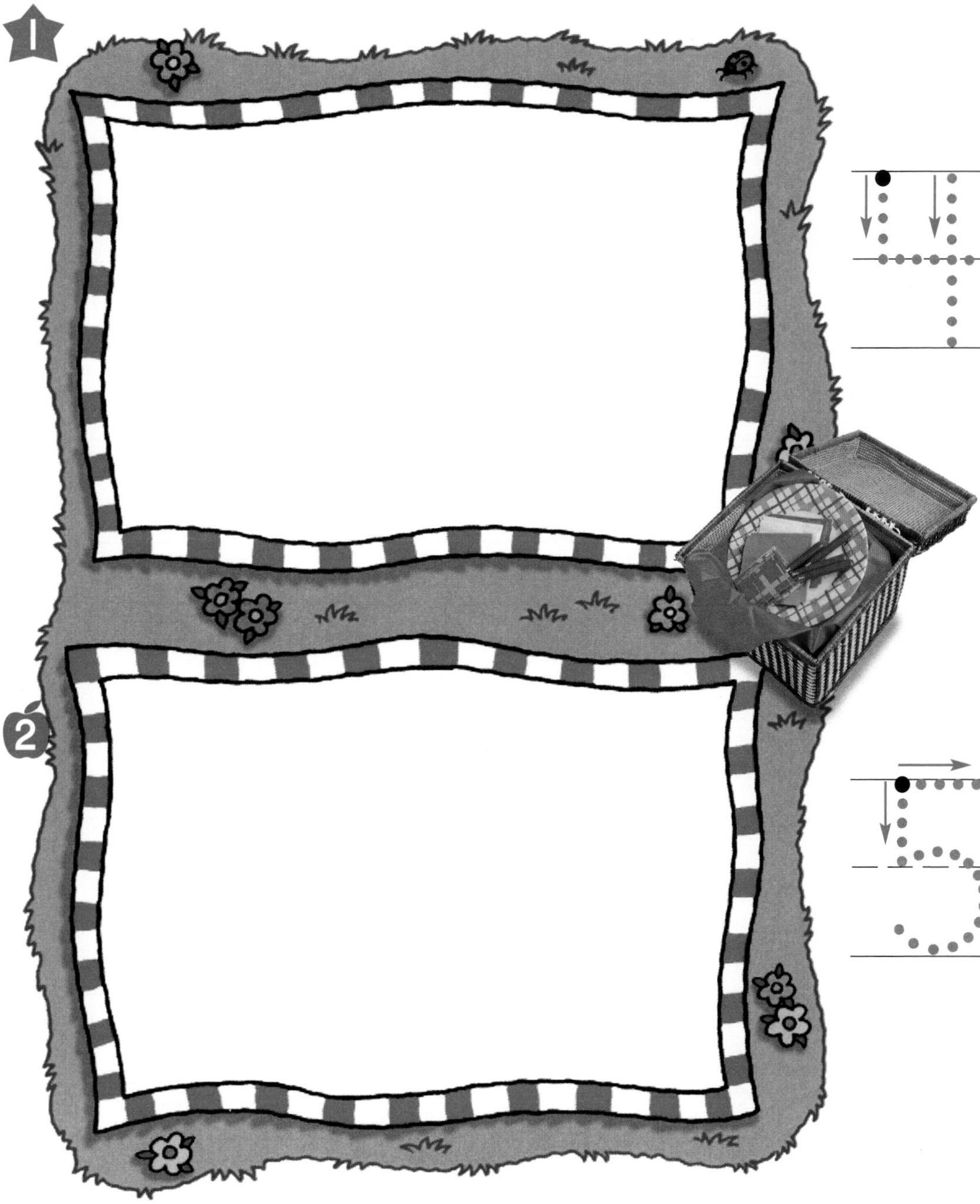

1

2

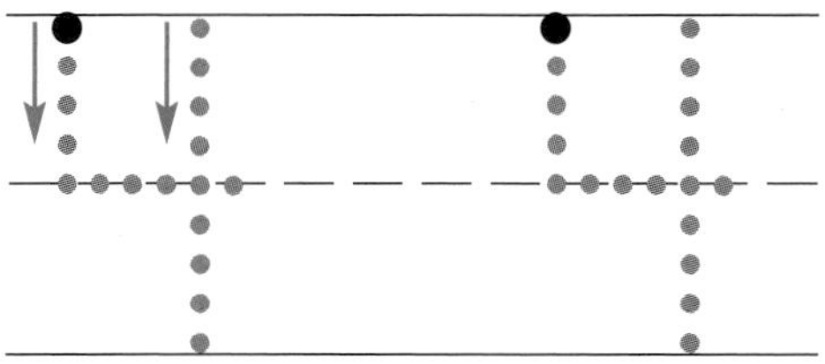

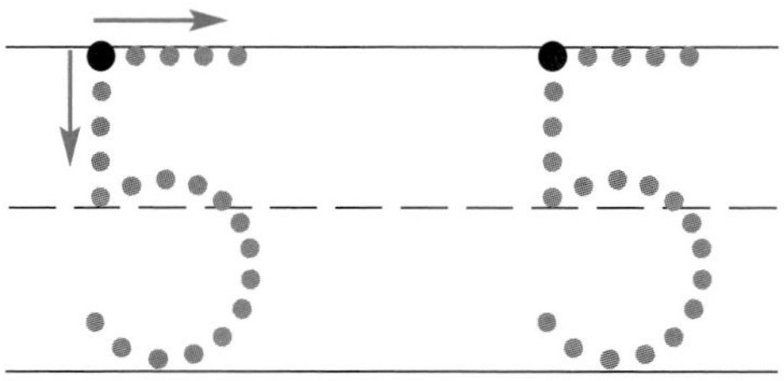

**Directions** Ask children to use counters as plates and place them on the picnic blankets. Then have them draw pictures of their plates and practice writing the numbers 4 and 5, beginning at each black dot.

3

4

4

5

5

6

7

**Directions** Have children count the objects in each group and practice writing the number.

**Home Activity** Have your child show you a group of 4 spoons and label the group by writing the number 4 on a piece of paper.

Name ______________________________

# Reading and Writing 0

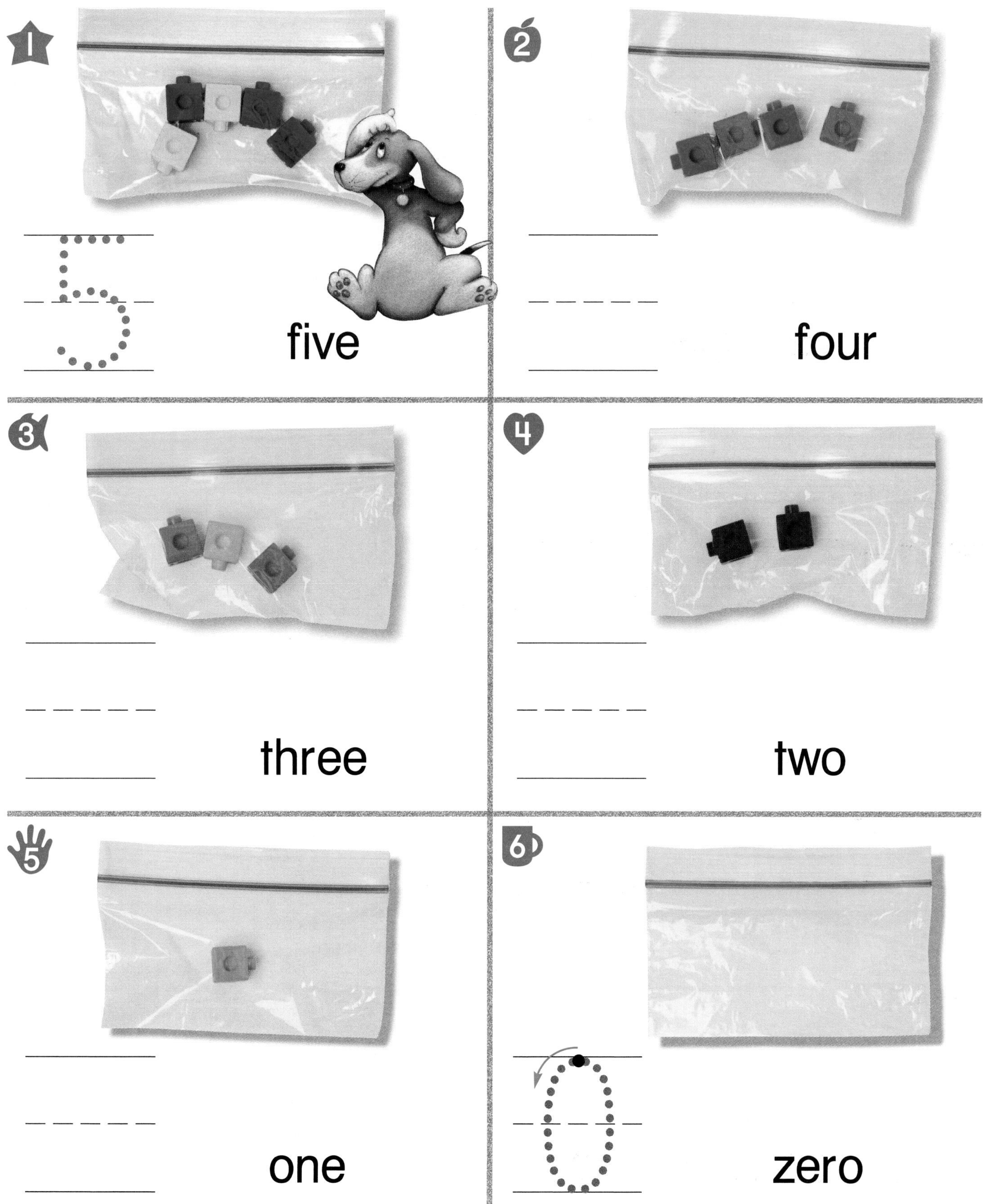


**Directions** Exercises 1–5: Have children look at the pictures, count the cubes, and write how many. For Exercise 6, have children tell how many. Then explain what zero means and have children practice writing 0, beginning at the black dot.

7

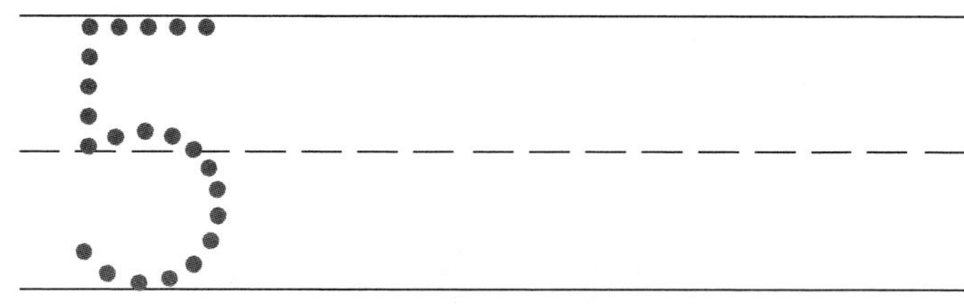

8

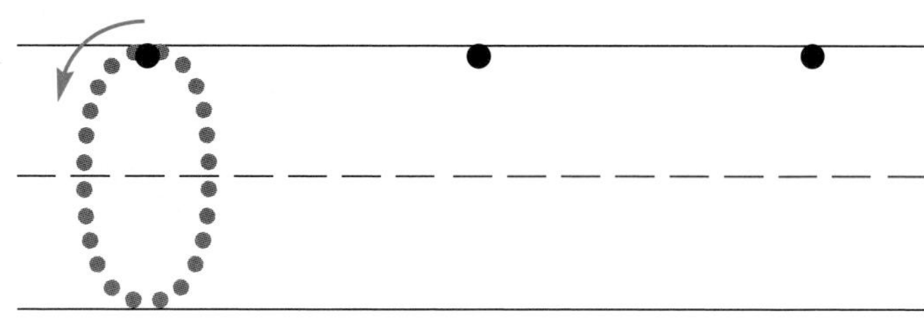

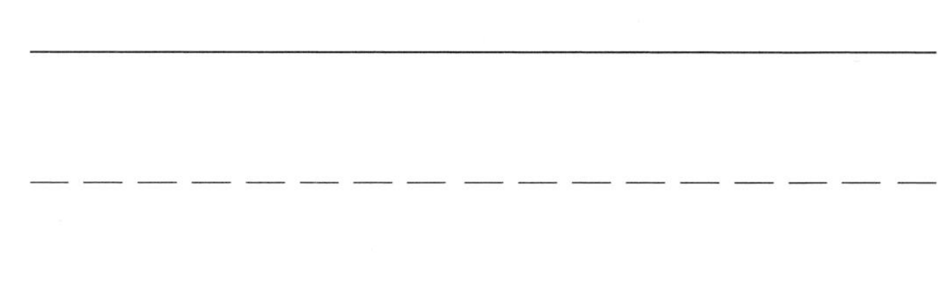

**Directions** Have children count the monkeys in each group and practice writing the number.

**Home Activity** Hold up a few objects in one hand and no objects in your other hand. Ask your child which hand is holding no objects or zero things. Ask your child to tell you about zero.

Name ____________________

# Comparing Numbers Through 5

## Algebra

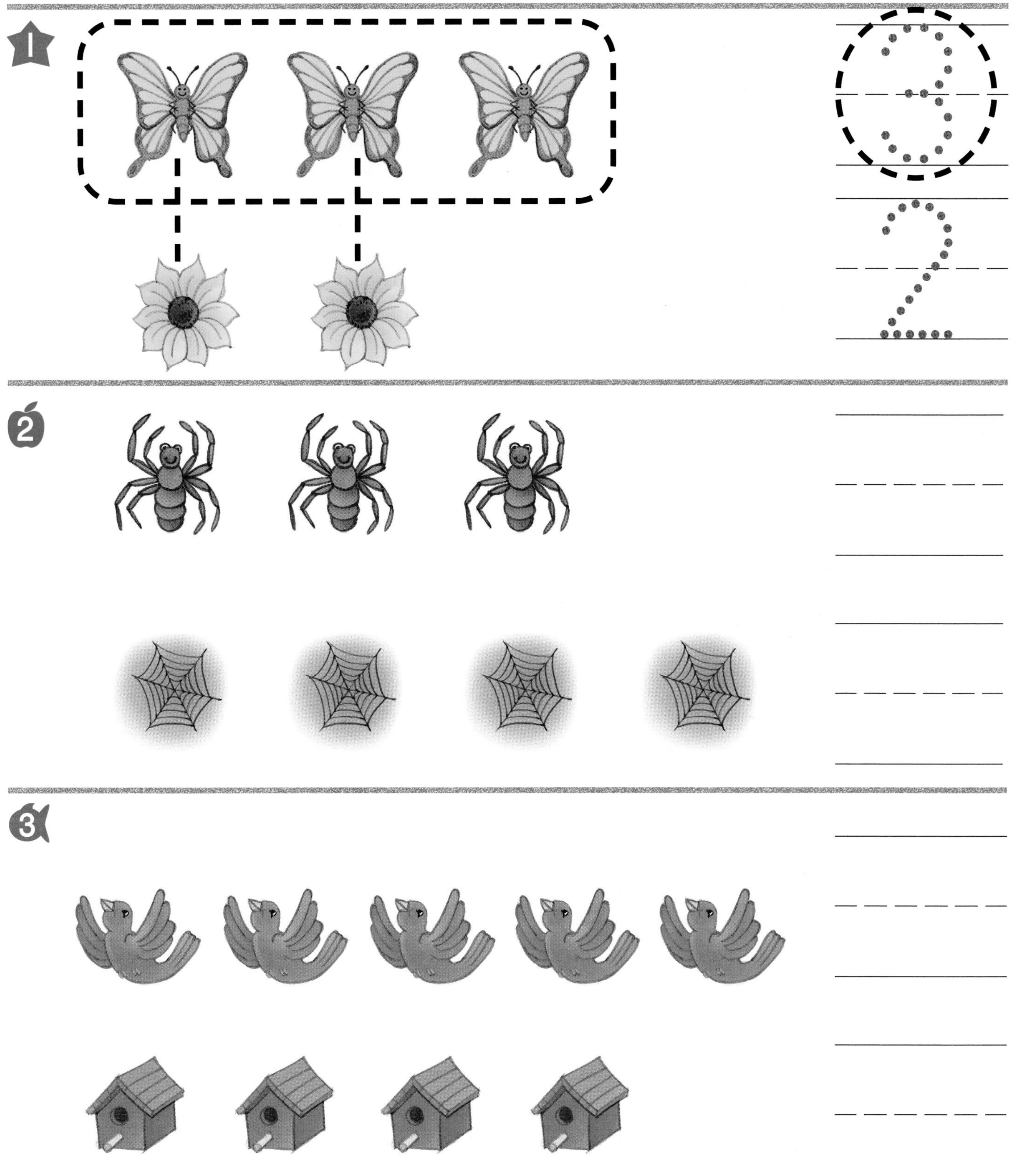


**Directions** Have children draw a line from each item in one group to an item in the other group and circle the group that has more. Then have children count the items, write the corresponding numbers, and circle the number that is more.

4

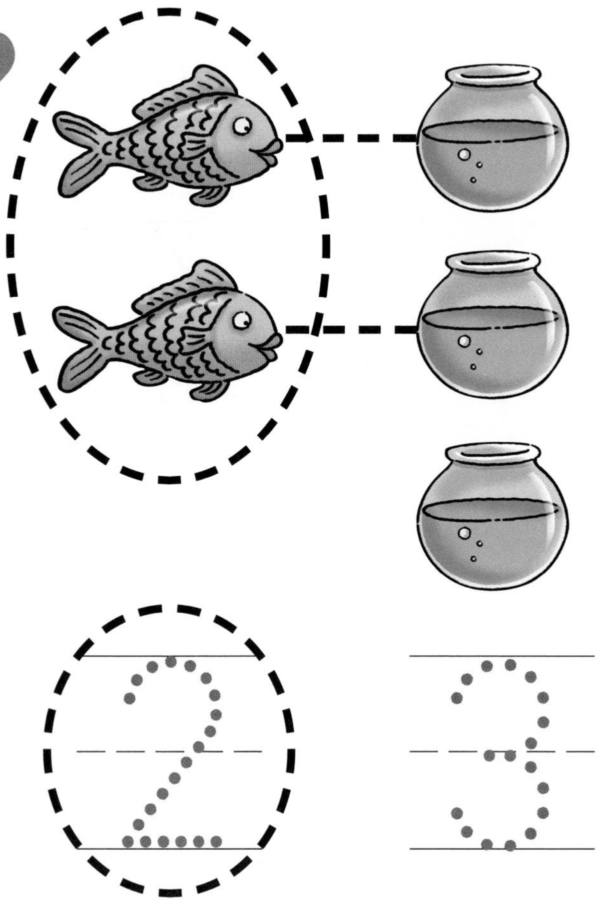

2 3

5

6

7

**Directions** Have children draw a line from each item in one group to an item in the other group and circle the group that has fewer. Then have children count the items, write the corresponding numbers, and circle the number that is less.

**Home Activity** Show your child a group of 3 pennies and a group of 4 pennies. Have your child show you how to decide which group has more.

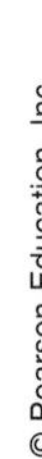

Name ______________________________

# Ordering Numbers 0 Through 5

**Algebra**

0 1 2 3 4 5

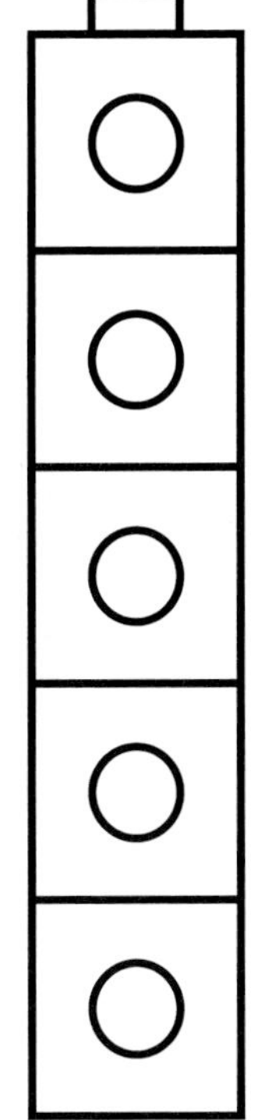

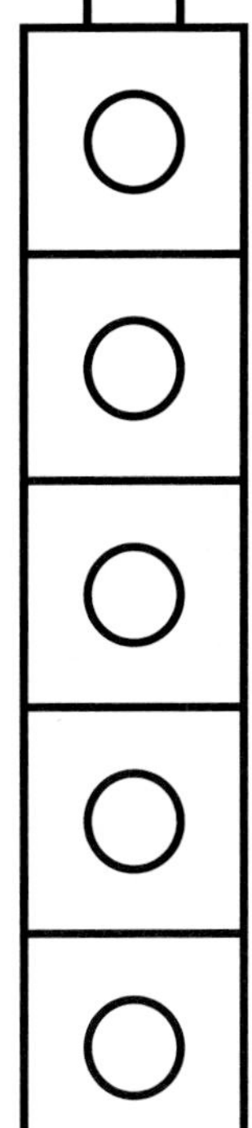

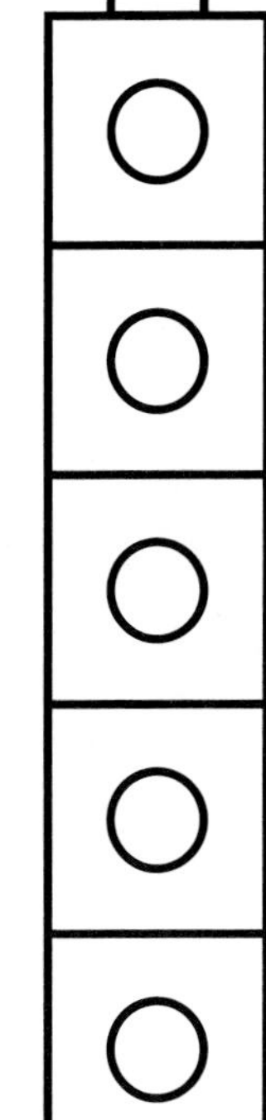

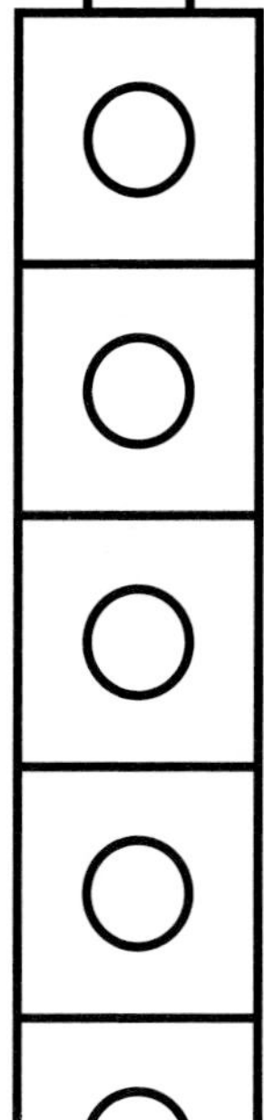

0

**Directions** Have children color cubes and write numbers to show 0 through 5 in order.

5 ___ 3 ___ 1 0

**Directions** Have children tell a number story about a seal holding up 5 beach balls. One by one, the balls fall into the water until zero are left. Have children show what happens by drawing the balls in order and writing the missing numbers.

**Home Activity** Ask your child to take 5 steps and count the steps aloud, starting from 0. Then step backward as they count aloud backward from 5 to 0.

Name ____________________

## Making the Most

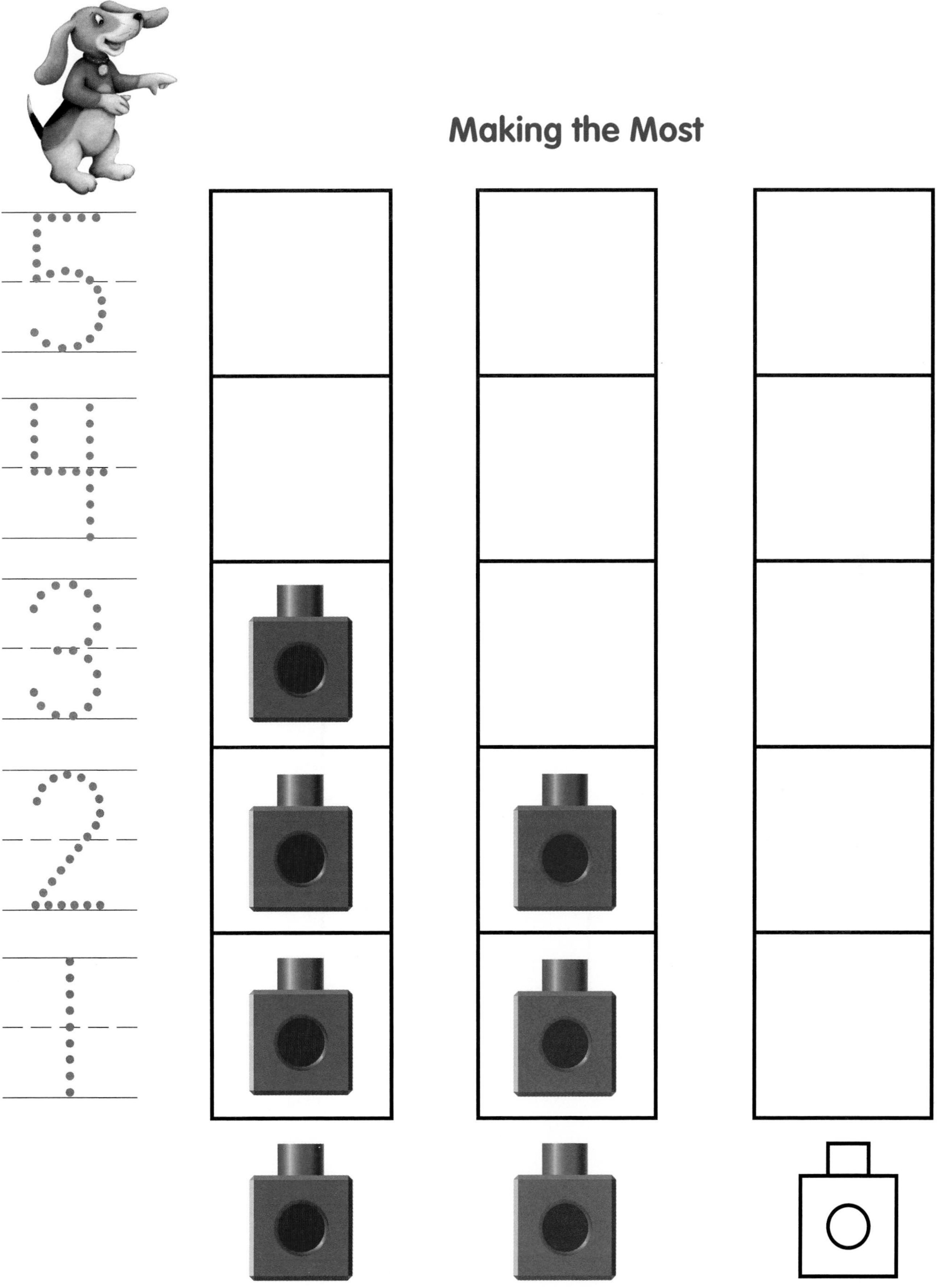


**Directions** In column 3 have children use cubes to show a group with the most cubes. Then have children draw pictures of the cubes in the squares and color the outline of the cube to label the column. To complete the graph, have children trace the numbers on the left side.

# Making the Fewest

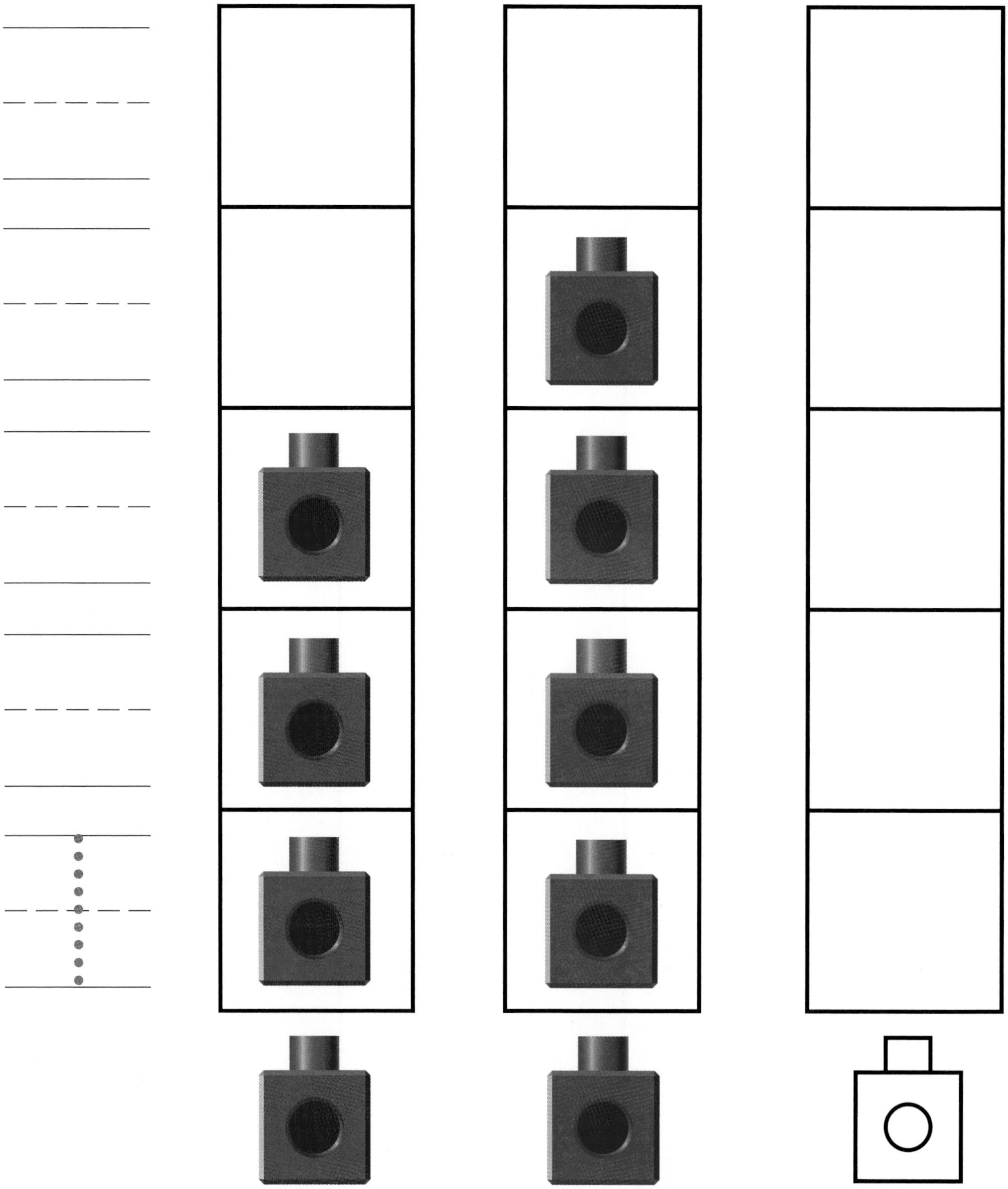

**Directions** In the last column have children use cubes to show a group with the fewest cubes. Then have children draw pictures of the cubes in the squares and color the outline of the cube to label the column. To complete the graph, children write the numbers 1–5 up the left side.

**Home Activity** Have your child make a graph to compare groups of buttons or coins. Then talk about what a graph can show.

Name ______________________________

# Ordinal Numbers Through Fifth

1

2

**Directions** Exercise 1: Have children color the third bee blue, the first bee yellow, the fourth bee green, the second bee red, and the fifth bee orange. Exercise 2: Have children color the ants in a similar way.

3

4

5

6

7

**Directions** Have children circle the first child in row 3, the second child in row 4, the third child in row 5, the fourth child in row 6, and the fifth child in row 7. Check that children understand where each line begins and ends.

**Home Activity** Have your child use the words *first, second, third, fourth,* and *fifth* to describe what he or she does to get ready for school.

Name ____________________



# Mix and Match

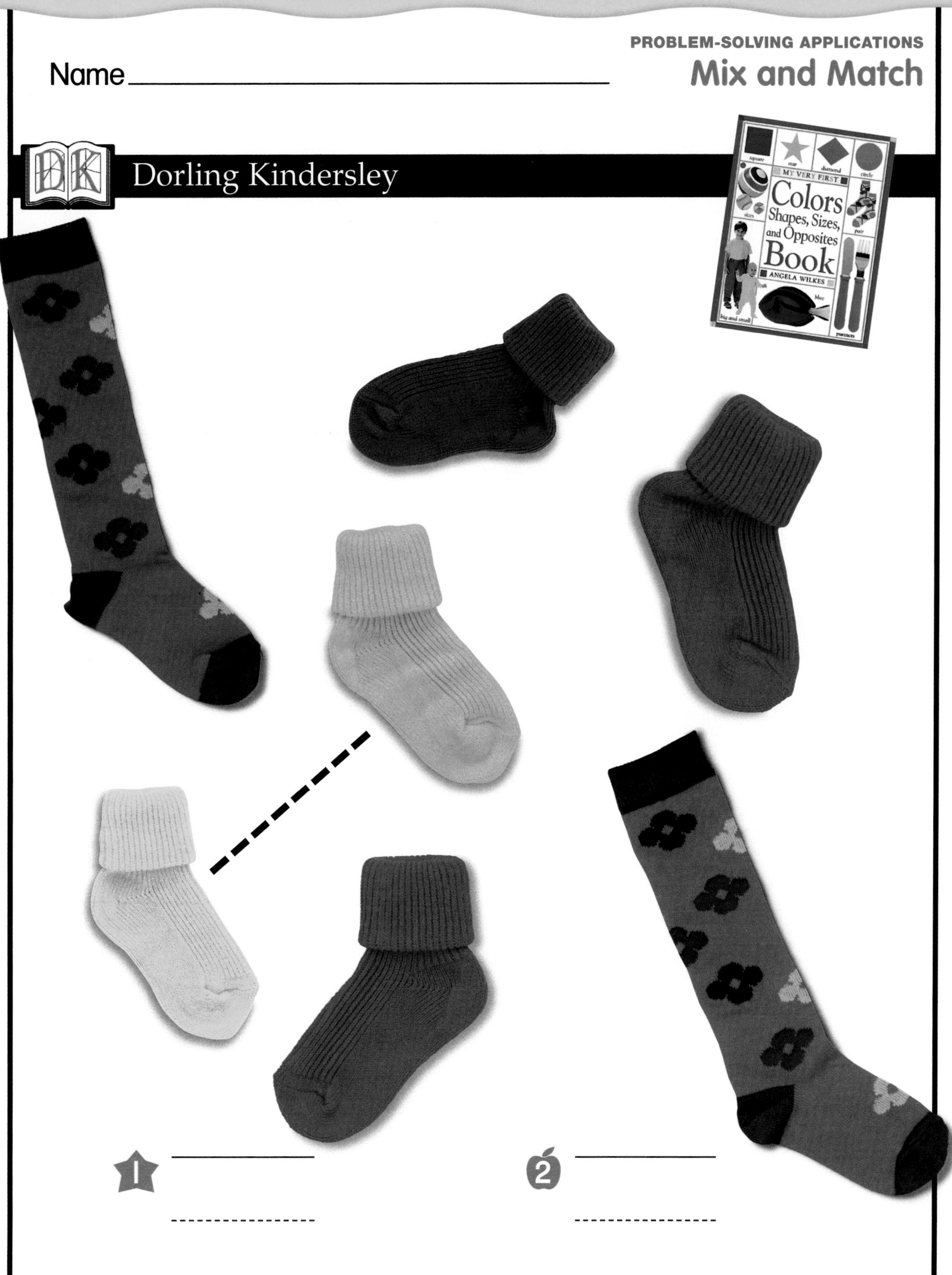


1 ____________

2 ____________

**Directions** Tell children that Kara needs to put her socks away. Ask them to help her find socks that are the same by drawing lines to match the pairs. Does every sock have a match? Then have children: 1. count the socks with a pattern and write the number; 2. count the socks without a pattern and write the number. Ask children to circle the number that is more.

3

4

**Directions** Ask children to name things you can wear on your head and things you can wear on your feet. Have children: 3. count the hats and write the number; 4. count the shoes and write the number. Then have children circle the number that is less.

**Home Activity** Talk with your child about the pictures on these two pages. Have your child tell you how he or she solved problems to complete the pages.

Name ________________________________________

Test

1

2

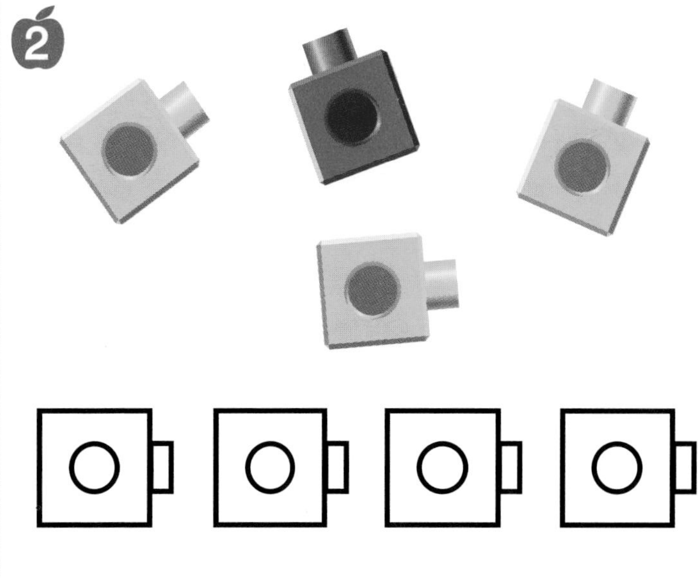

3

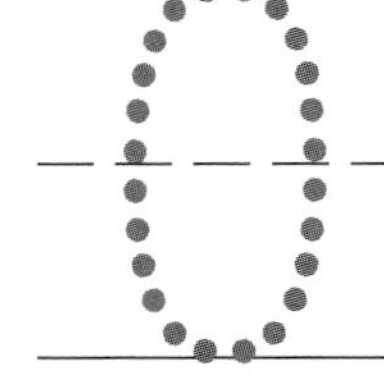

4

**Directions** Have children: 1. color a square for each flower in the group; 2. color the cubes to match the red and yellow cubes; 3. write the numbers 0 to 5 in order; 4. color the second bee from the flower yellow and the fifth bee red.

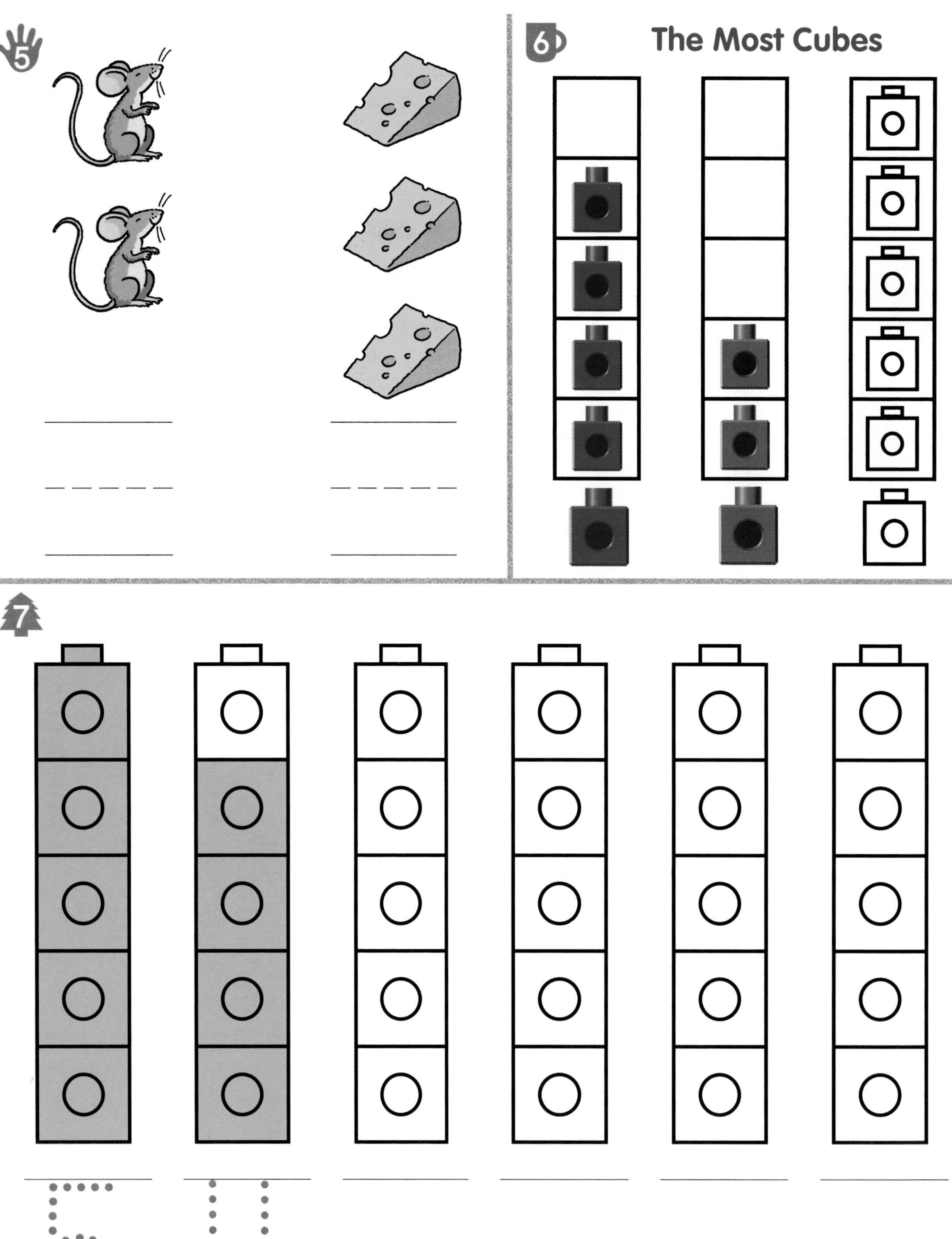


**Directions** Have children: 5. draw a line from each mouse to each piece of cheese, circle the group with fewer, write the numbers, and circle the number that is less; 6. color the cubes in the third column to show a group with the most cubes; 7. color the cubes and write the numbers to show 5 to 0 in order.

CHAPTER 4

## Numbers Through 10

# Ollie Octopus Lost a Shoe

Written by Noelle Ani
Illustrated by Drew Rose

This Math Storybook belongs to

______________________________

Ollie Octopus loves shoes.
Her closet is filled with them.

One day, she could not find
one of her red dancing shoes.

"May I buy 1 red dancing shoe?" Ollie asked Mr. Crabby Crab.

Mr. Crab had just sold his last red dancing shoe.

He tried to sell her
1 soft shell shoe,
2 clam-digging shoes, and
3 fine fishing shoes.

"Not 1 red dancing shoe?" cried Ollie.

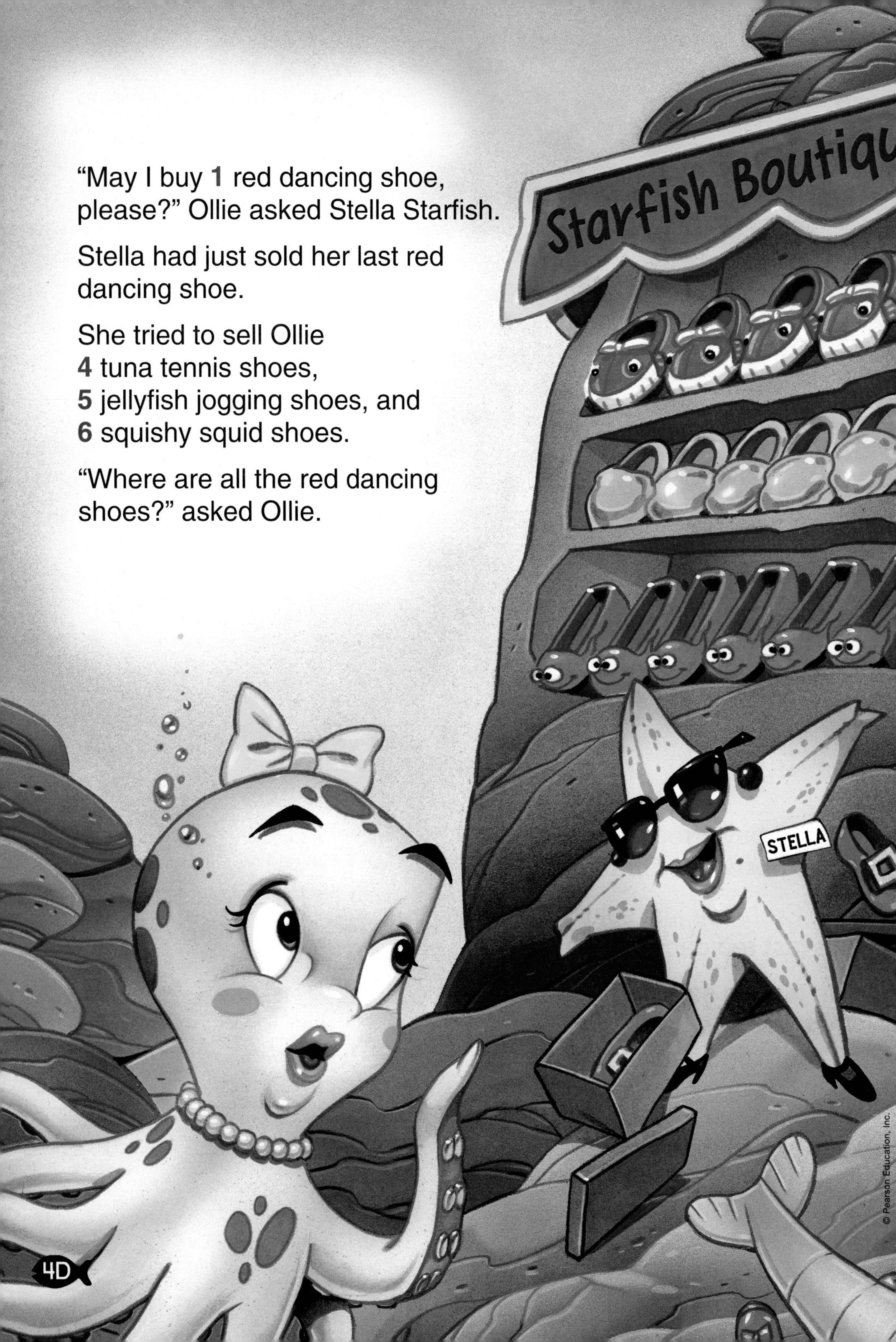


"May I buy **1** red dancing shoe, please?" Ollie asked Stella Starfish.

Stella had just sold her last red dancing shoe.

She tried to sell Ollie
**4** tuna tennis shoes,
**5** jellyfish jogging shoes, and
**6** squishy squid shoes.

"Where are all the red dancing shoes?" asked Ollie.

Ollie swam to the last shoe shop.

In the window Ollie saw
7 diving dolphin shoes,
8 easy eel shoes, and
9 oozing oyster shoes.
But no red dancing shoes.

"Who is buying all the red dancing shoes?" asked Ollie.

Ollie saw Sherri Shrimp swimming out of the shop.

"Sherri Shrimp! It's you!" said Ollie. "You are wearing **10** red dancing shoes.

You are the one who has been buying them!"

Sherri opened her shopping bag. "Surprise! Here is one for you. Now we both have just enough!"

## Home-School Connection

Dear Family,

Today my class started Chapter 4, **Numbers Through 10.** I will learn how to count, write, and compare numbers through 10. Here are some of the math words I will be learning and some things we can do to help me with my math.

Love,

_______________________________

### Math Activity to Do at Home

Make "Bean Cards." Glue 6 beans on one index card, 7 beans on the next card, and so on, through 10. Have your child write the corresponding number on each card. Then ask each other *more, less, most,* and *fewest* questions about the numbers and the groups the numbers represent.

### Books to Read Together

Reading math stories reinforces concepts. Look for these titles in your local library:

***Feast for 10***
By Cathryn Falwell
(Clarion Books, 1993)

***Ten Rosy Roses***
By Eve Merriam
(HarperCollins, 1999)

### My New Math Words

I count **one more** red flower.

I count **one fewer** yellow flower.

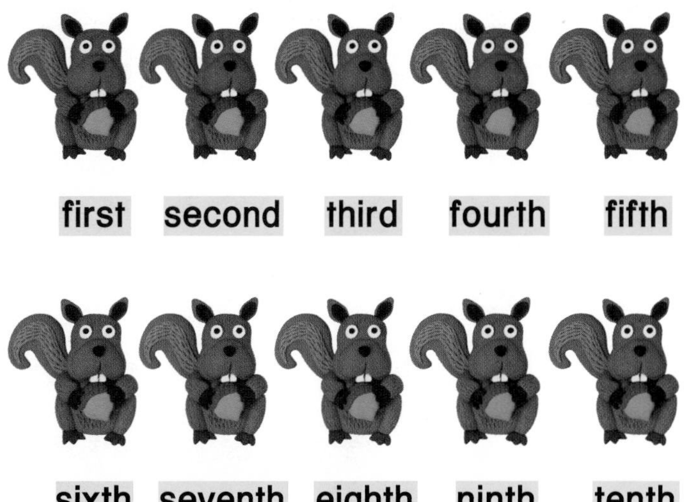

**Take It to the NET**
**More Activities**
www.scottforesman.com

Name ______________________________



# Counting Under the Sea

## What You Need

coin 

1 game marker for each player 

10 paper fish  for each player

## How to Play

1. Play with a partner.
2. Flip a coin. 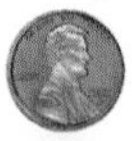
   = move your marker 1 space. 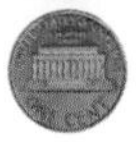
   = move your marker 2 spaces.
3. Say the number you land on. Then put that number of fish into the sea.
4. The first player to place 10 fish into the sea is the winner.

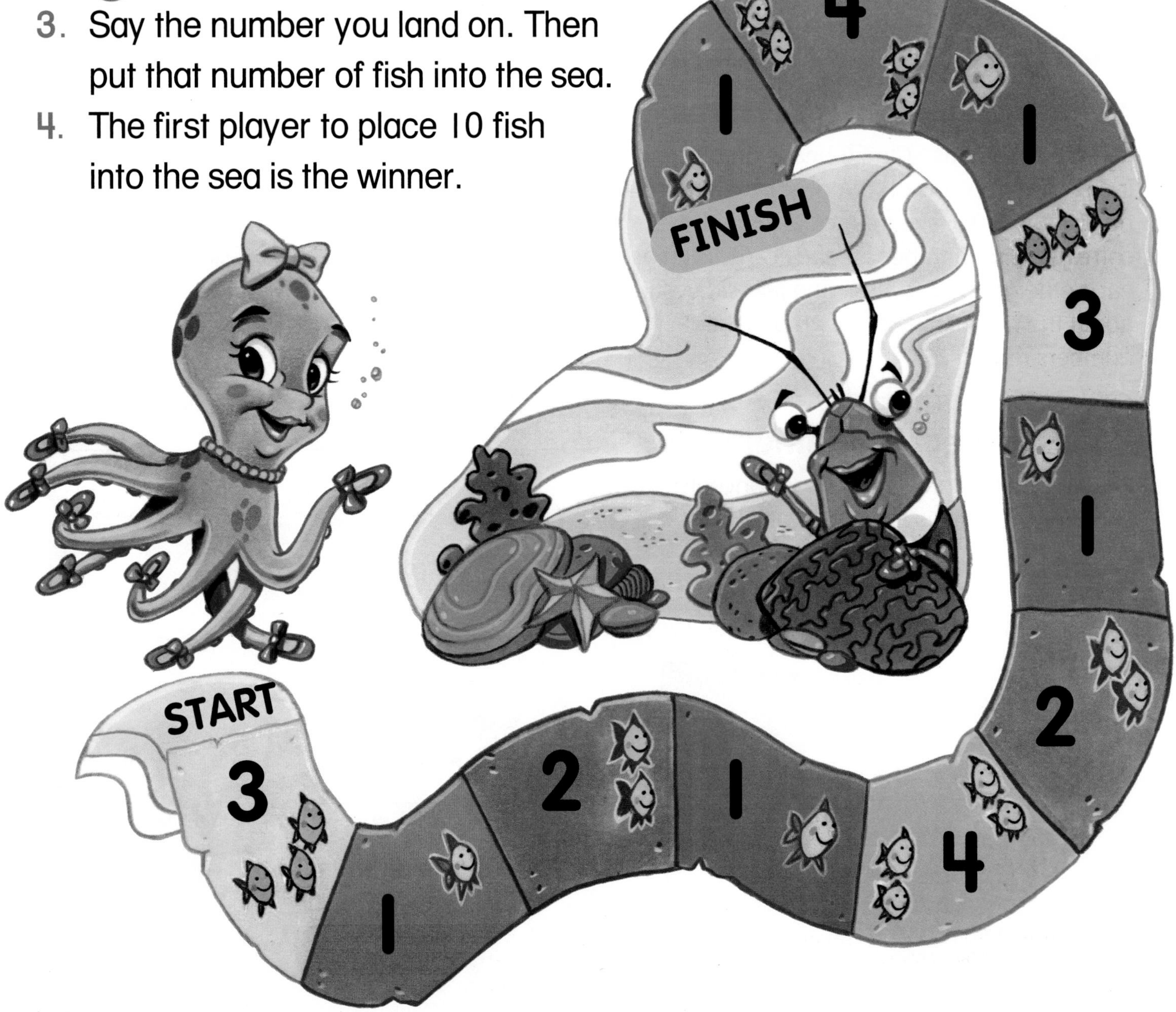

START 3 1 2 1 4 2 1 3 1 4 1 FINISH

Name ____________________

**Directions** Exercise 1: Have children place 5 counters on the five-frame and 1 counter below it. Then have children trace the outlines and color to show the 6 counters. Exercise 2: Have children place 5 counters on the five-frame and 2 counters below it. Then have children draw and color the 7 counters.

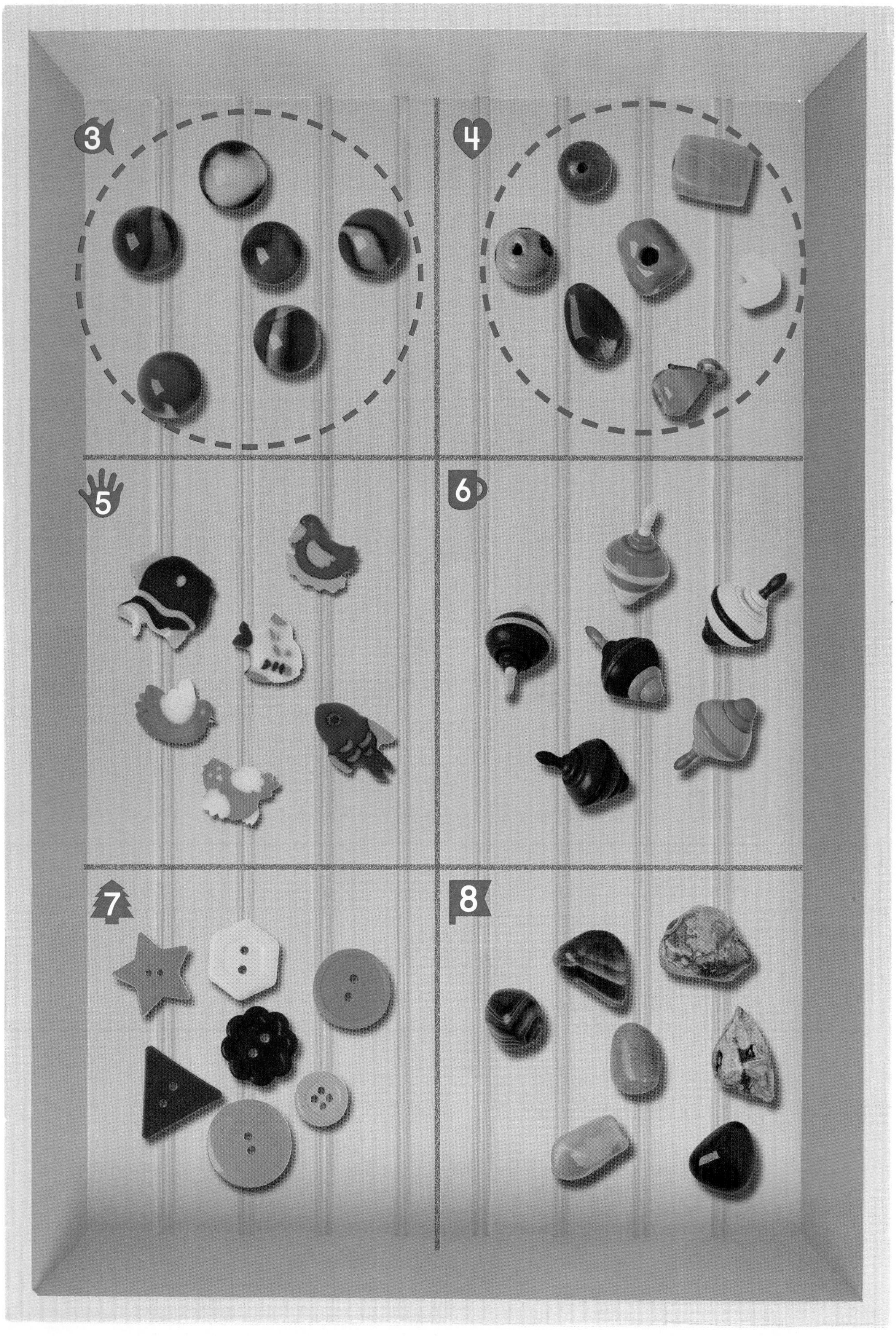

3

4

5

6

7

8

**Directions** Have children count the objects in each group. Have them use a red crayon to circle each group of 6 and a blue crayon to circle each group of 7.

**Home Activity** Have your child find and count groups of 6 things and groups of 7 things in your home.

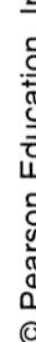

Name ______________________________

# Counting 8

**Directions** Exercise 1: Have children place 5 counters on the five-frame and 3 counters below it. Then have children trace the outlines and color to show the 8 counters. Exercise 2: Have children place 5 counters on the five-frame and 3 counters below it. Then have children draw and color the 8 counters.

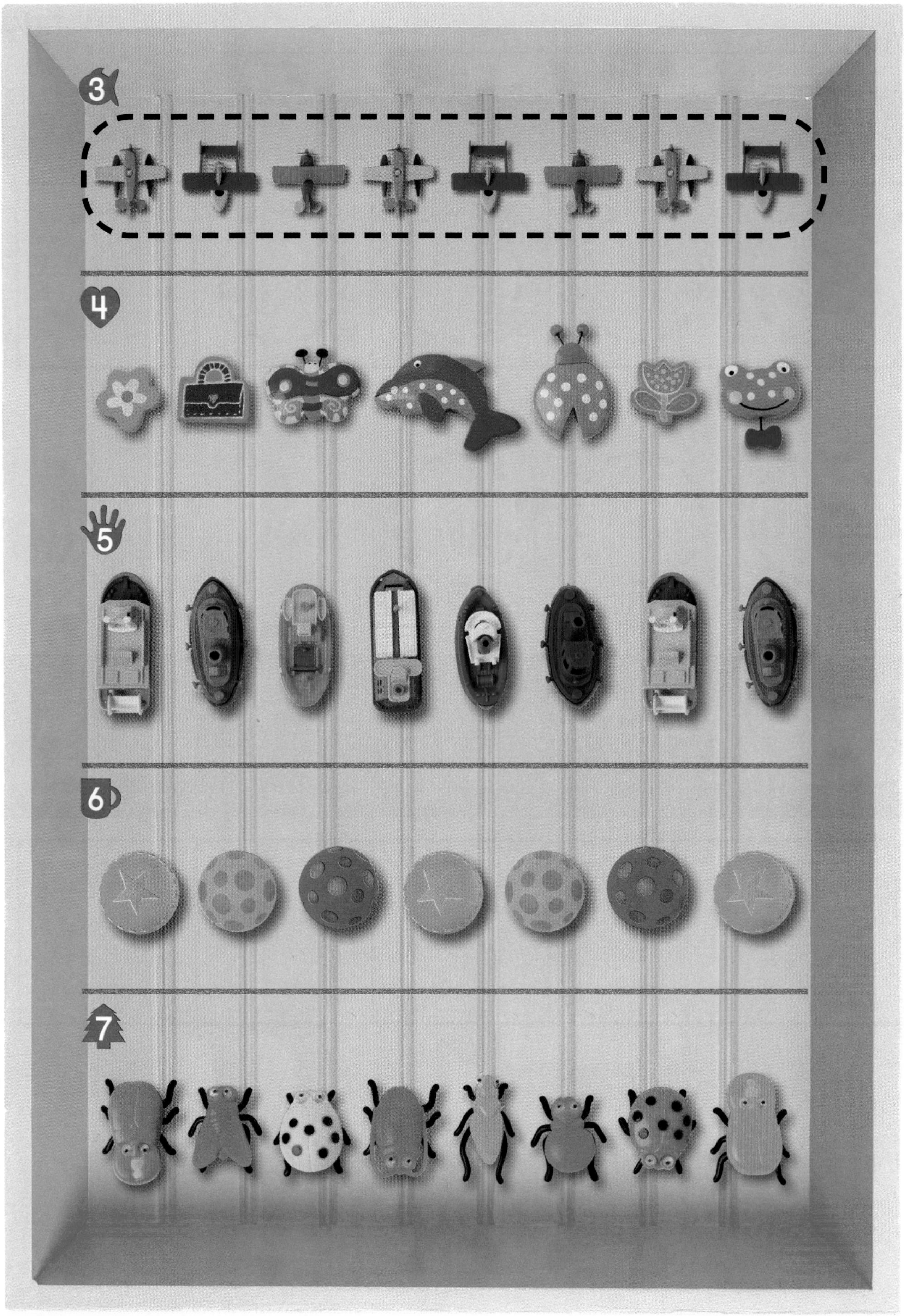

3

4

5

6

7

**Directions** Have children count the objects in each group and circle each group of 8.

**Home Activity** Have your child find and count a group of 8 things in your home.

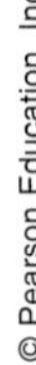

Name ______________________________

# Reading and Writing 6, 7, and 8

6
six

7
seven

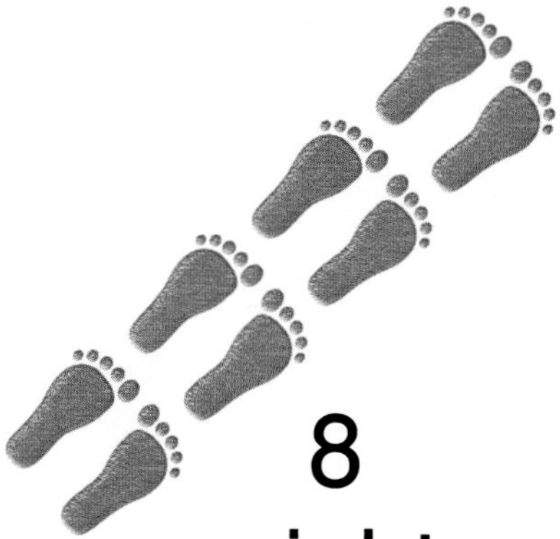

8
eight

1

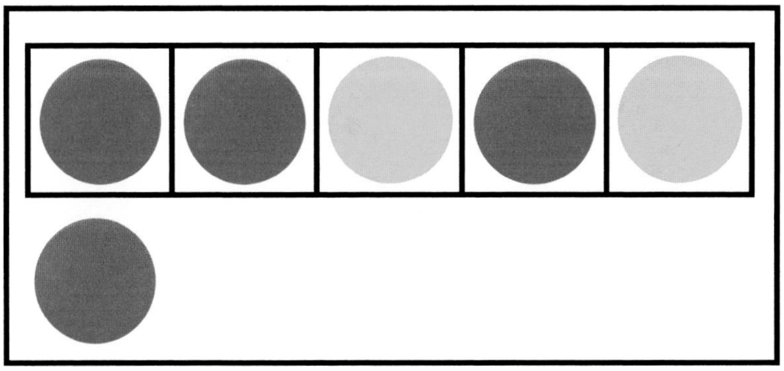

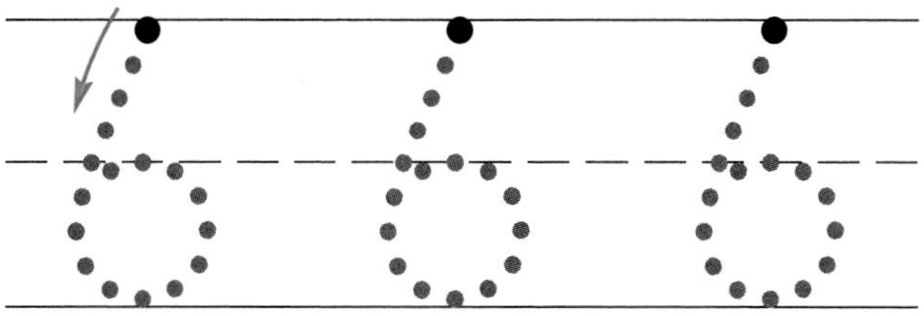

6 6 6

2

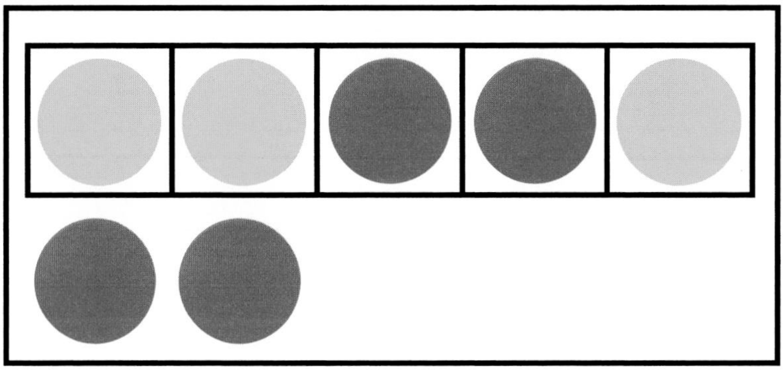

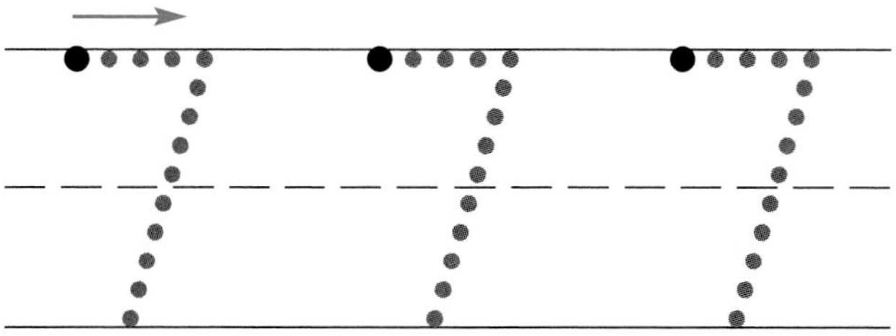

7 7 7

3

8 8 8

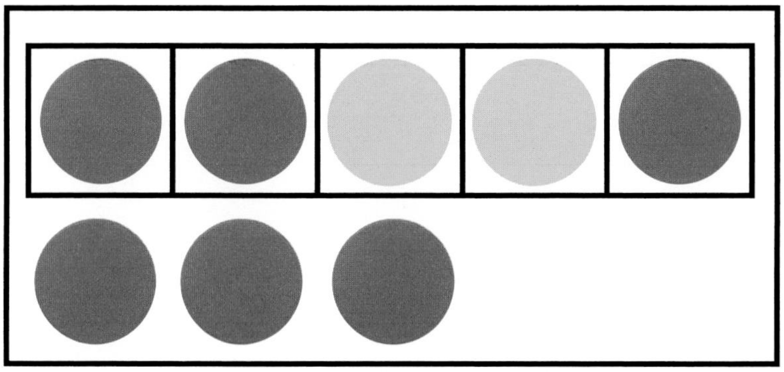

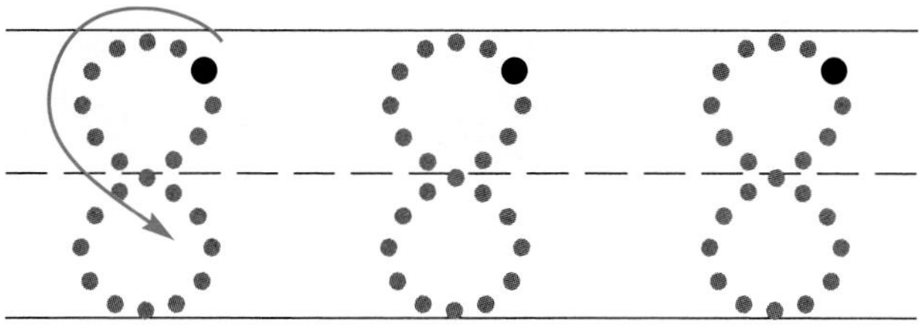

**Directions** In each exercise have children count the counters and practice writing the matching numbers 6, 7, and 8, beginning at each black dot.

4

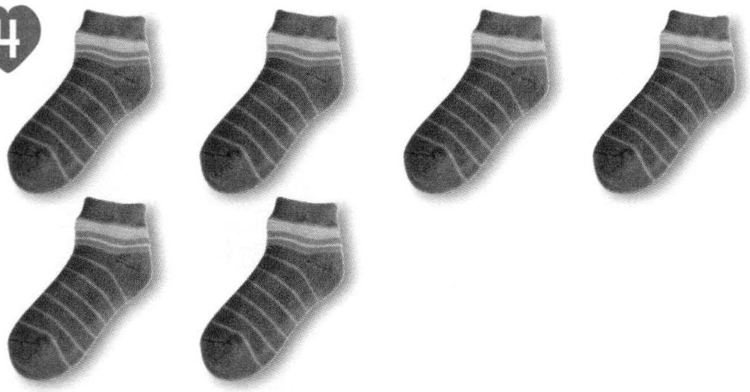

5

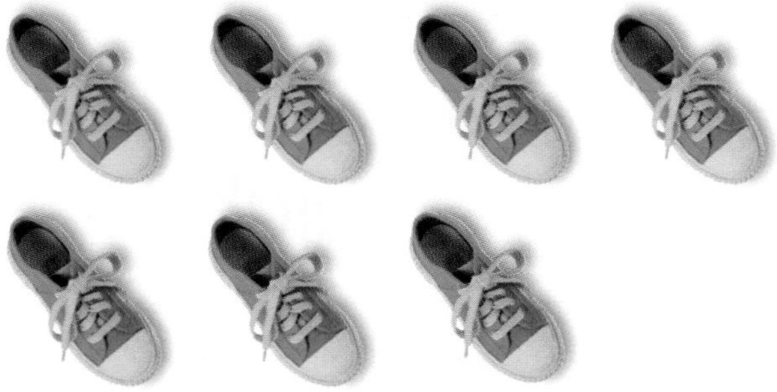

6

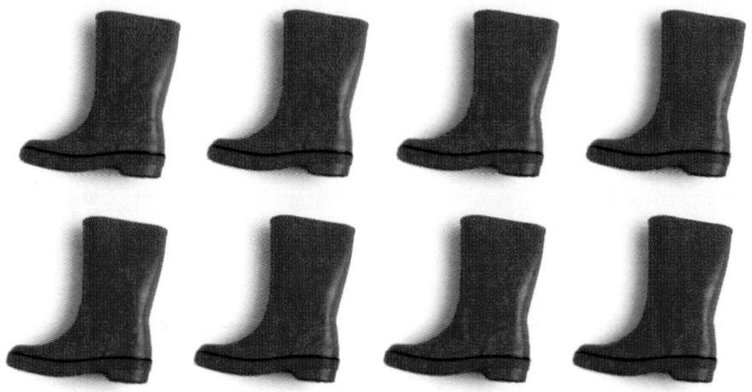

7

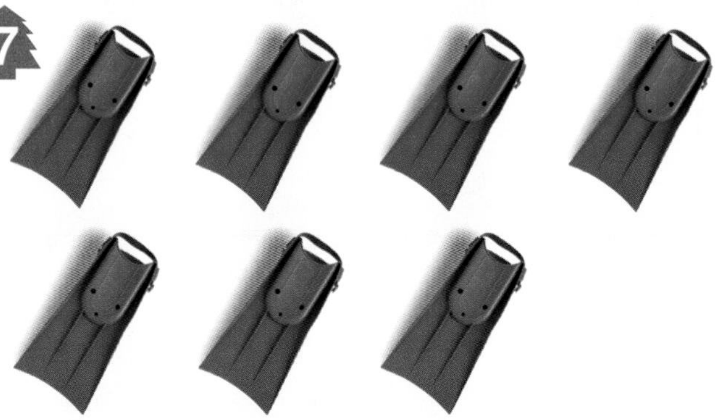

8

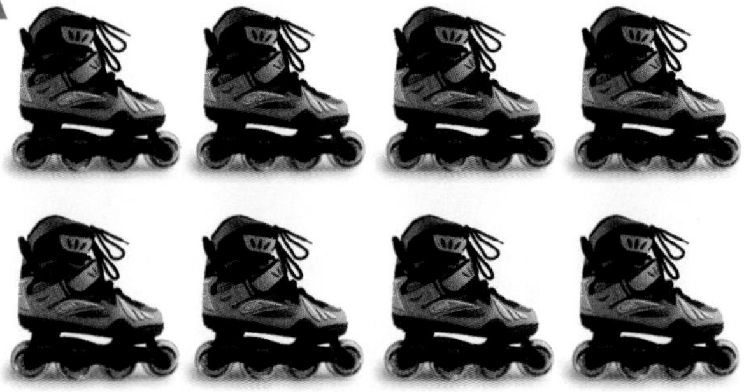

**Directions** Have children count the objects in each group and practice writing the number.

**Home Activity** Have your child show how to write the numbers 6, 7, and 8. Talk about what they know about 6, 7, and 8.

Name ____________________

# Counting 9 and 10

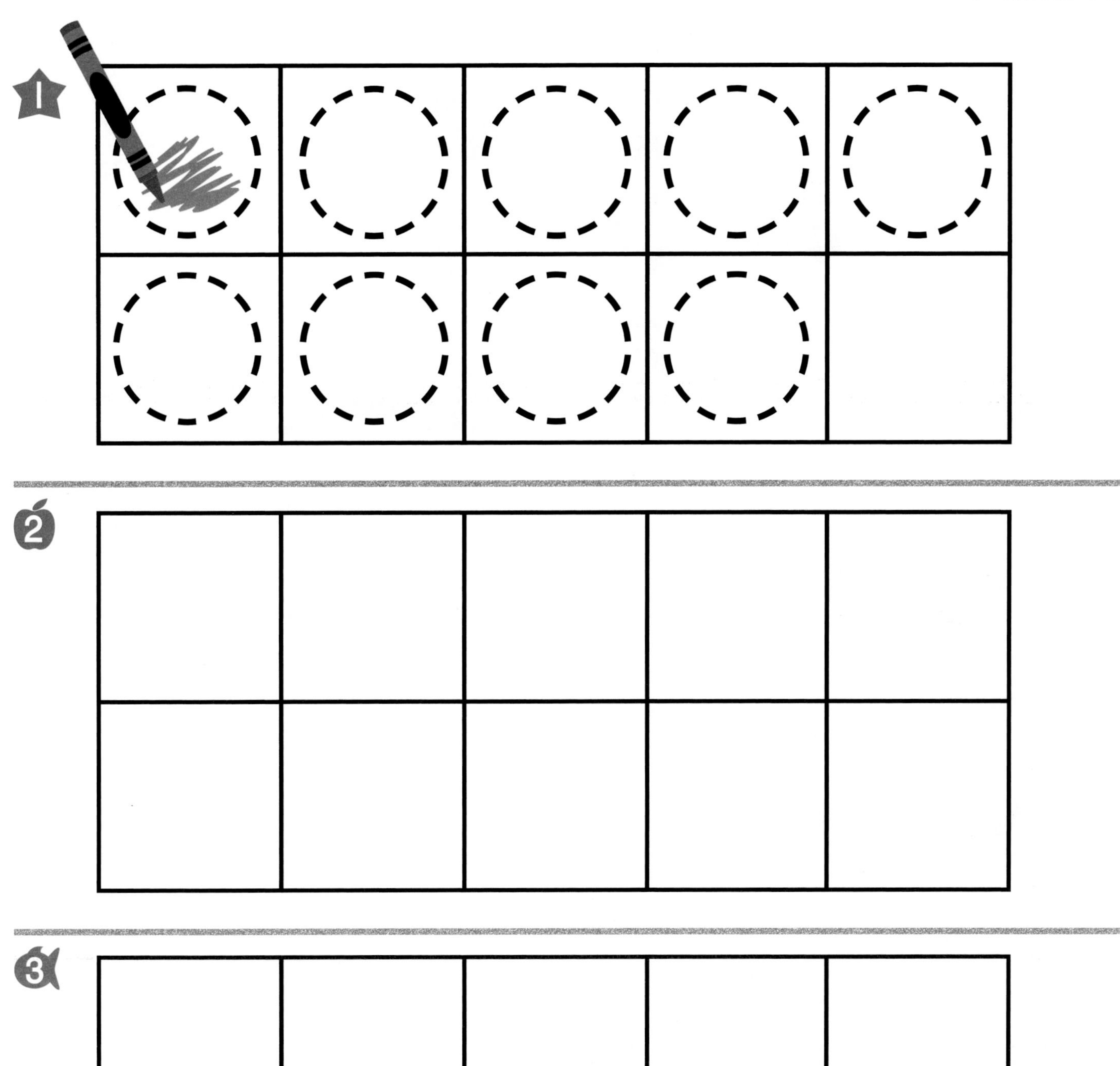

**Directions** Exercise 1: Have children place 9 counters on the ten-frame and then trace the outlines and color to show the counters. Exercise 2: Have children place 9 counters on the ten-frame and then draw and color the counters. Exercise 3: Repeat the activity with 10 counters.

4

**Directions** Have children count how many in each group. Have them use a red crayon to circle each group of 9 and a blue crayon to circle each group of 10.

**Home Activity** Show your child a group of 9 pennies and a group of 10 pennies. Ask your child to count the pennies and tell you which group has 9 and which has 10.

Name ____________________

# Reading and Writing 9 and 10

9
nine

10
ten

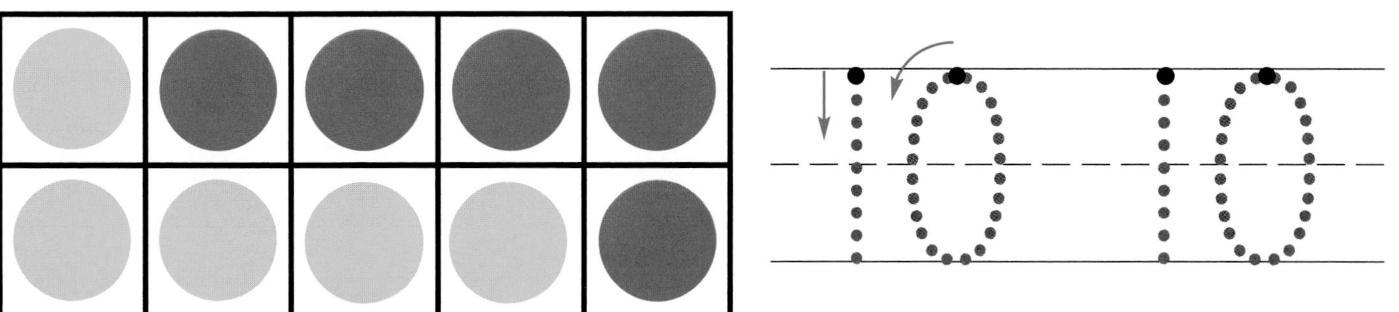

**Directions** Have children count the counters on the ten-frames and practice writing the numbers 9 and 10, beginning at each black dot.

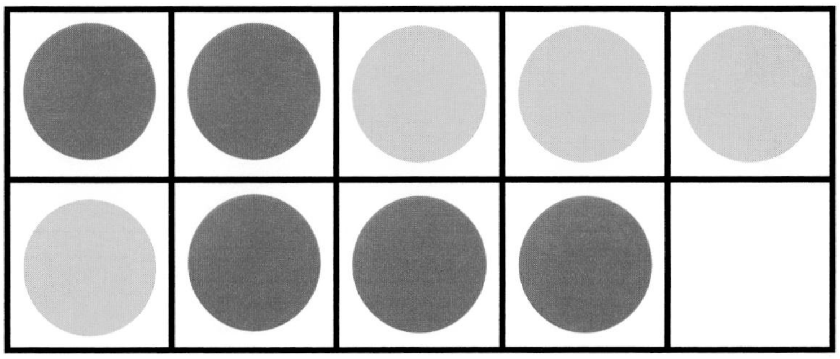

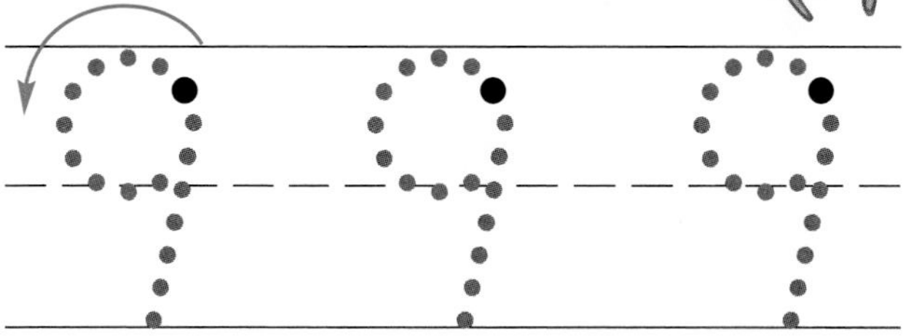

3

9

4

10

5

6

7

**Directions** Have children count the objects in each group and practice writing the number.

**Home Activity** Have your child count groups of 10 objects and write the number 10.

Name ______________________



**Algebra**

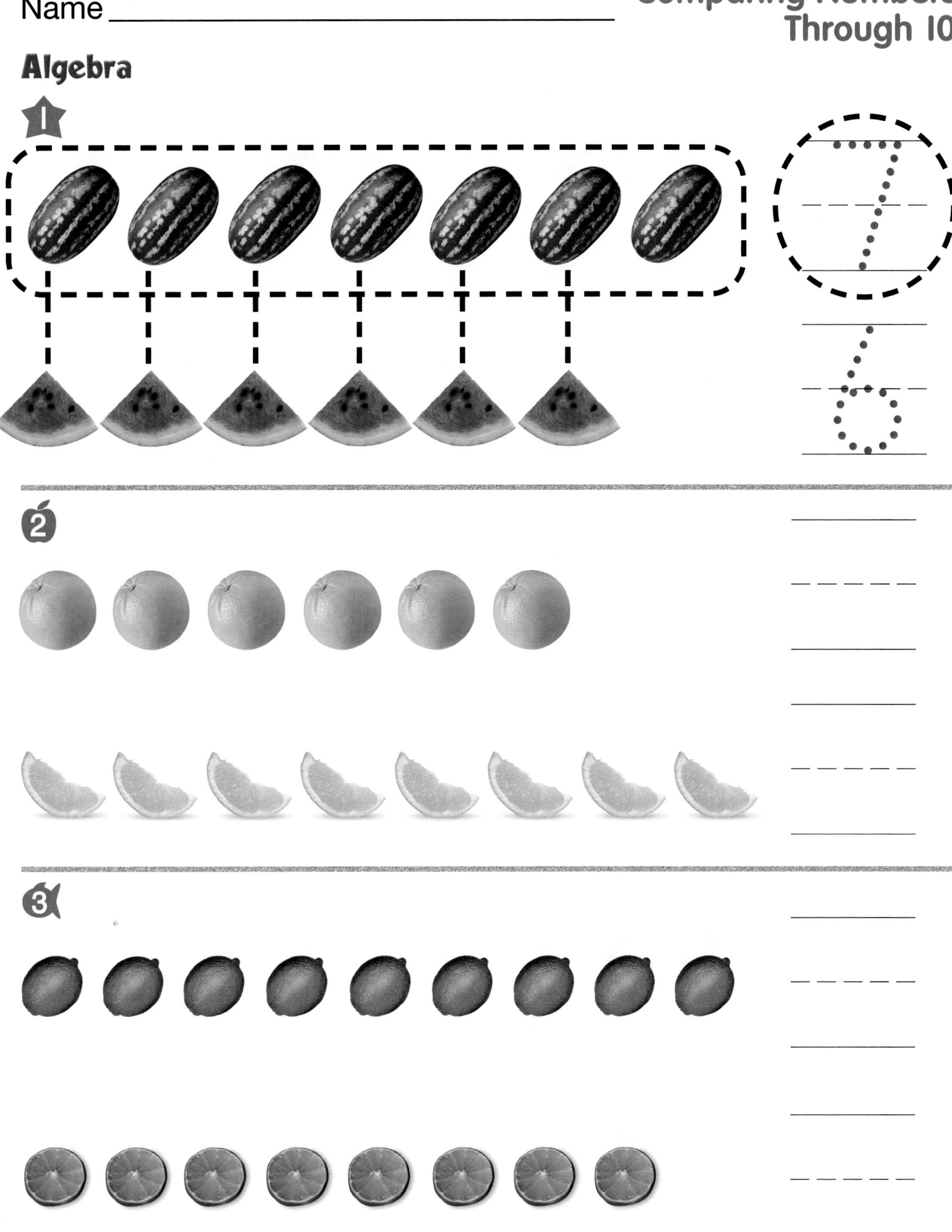

**Directions** Have children draw a line from each item in one group to an item in the other group and circle the group that has more. Then have children count the items, write the corresponding numbers, and circle the greater number.

4

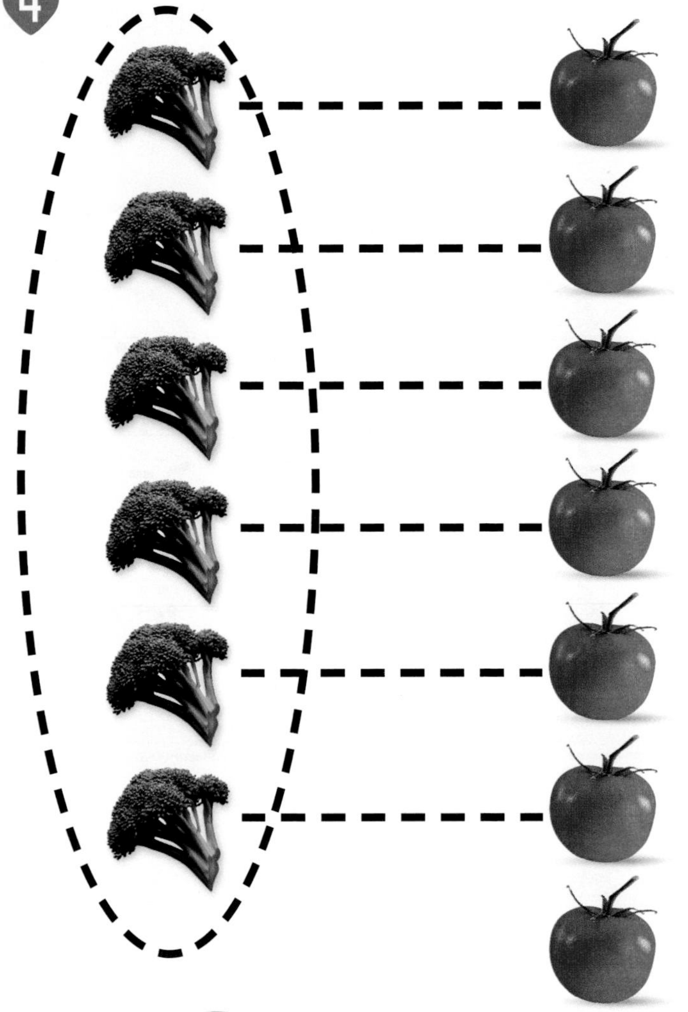

6

7

5

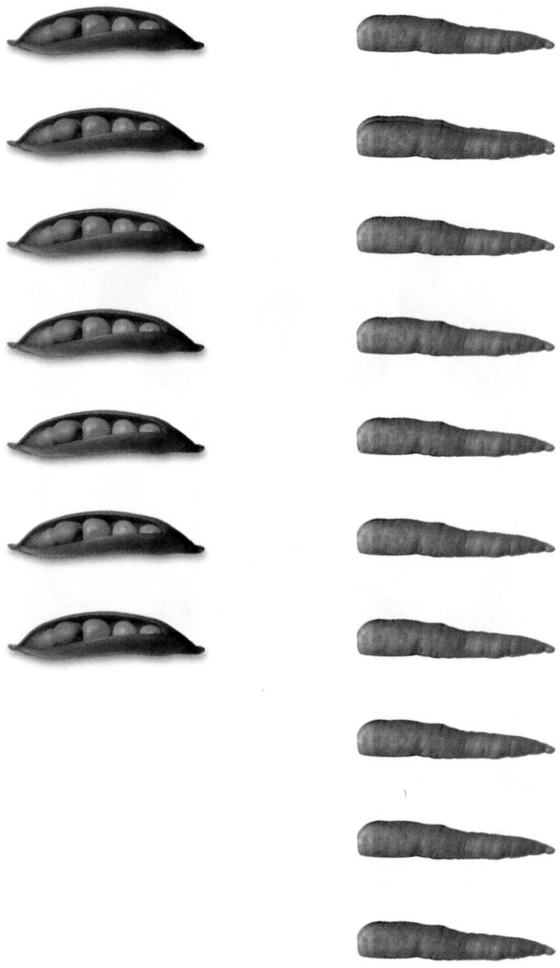

6

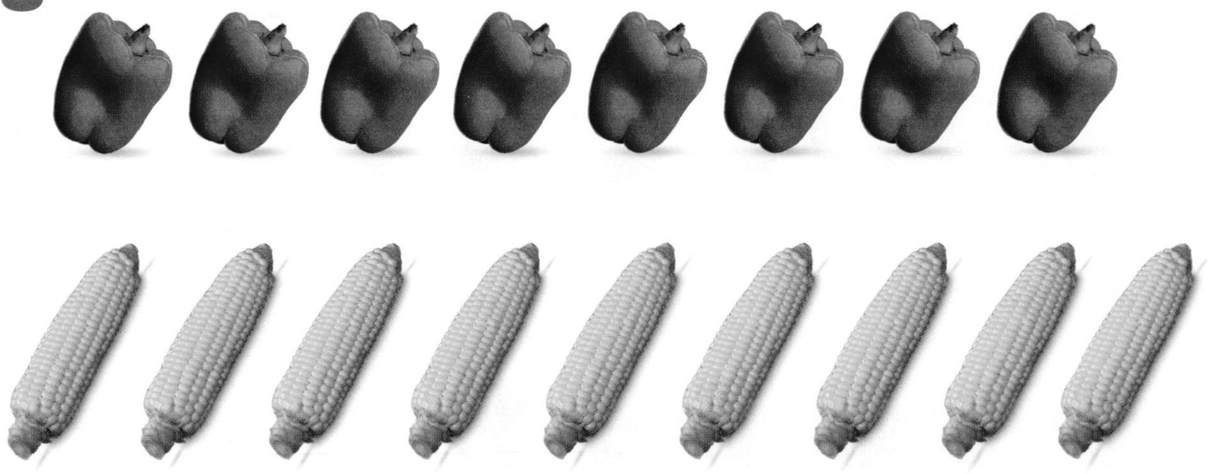

**Directions** Have children draw a line from each item in one group to an item in the other group and circle the group that has fewer. Then have children count the items, write the corresponding numbers, and circle the lesser number.

**Home Activity** Give your child 7 forks and 8 spoons. Have your child show how to decide which group has more.

Name ____________________

# Comparing Numbers to 5 and 10

1 2

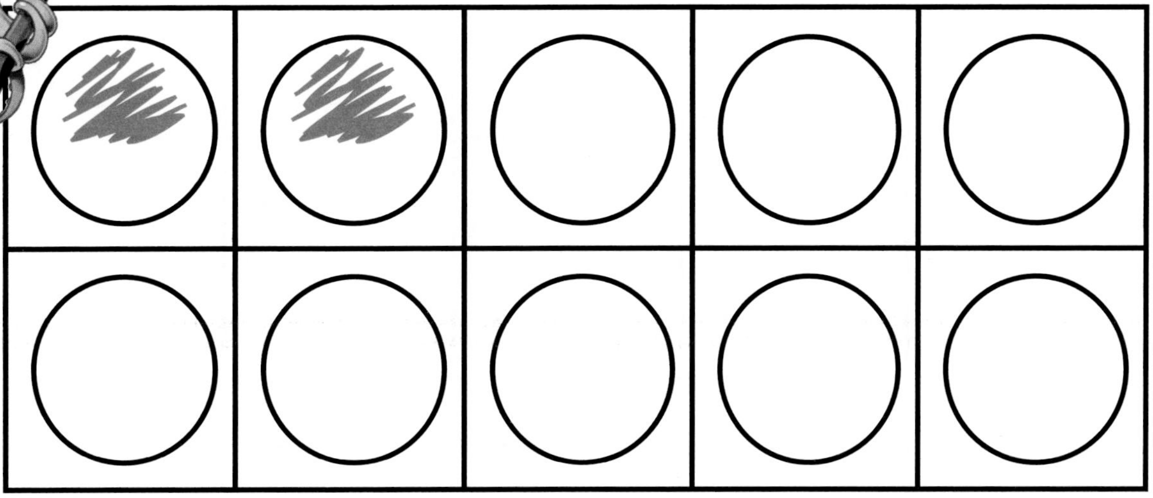

2 7

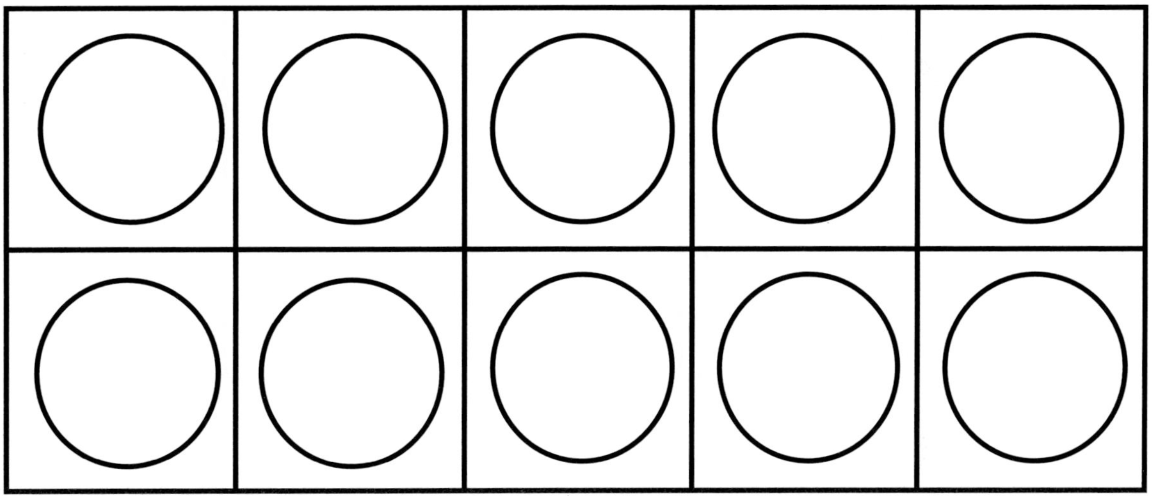

3 4

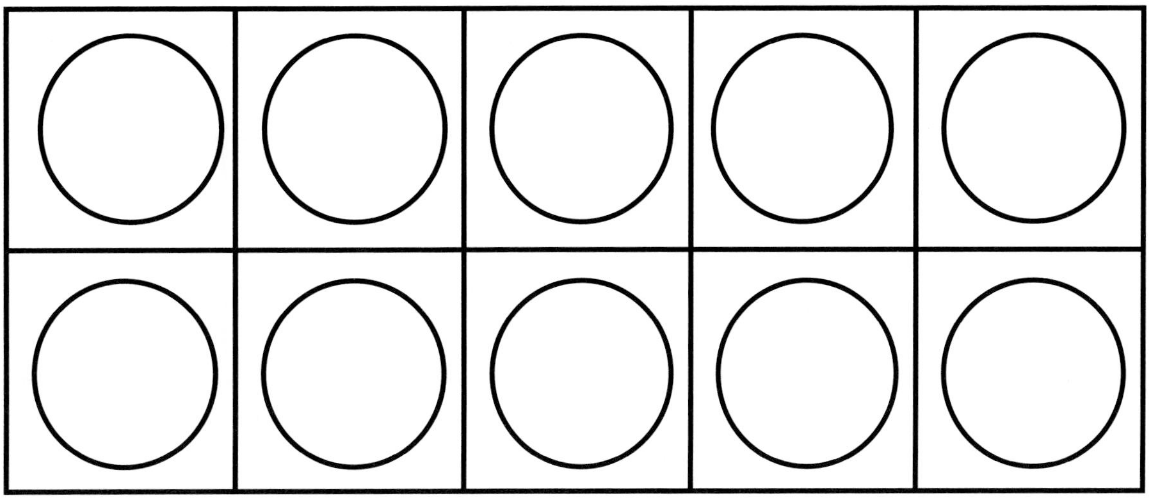

**Directions** Have children write each number and then color counter outlines to show that number. Then have children circle the numbers that are less than 5.

4

8

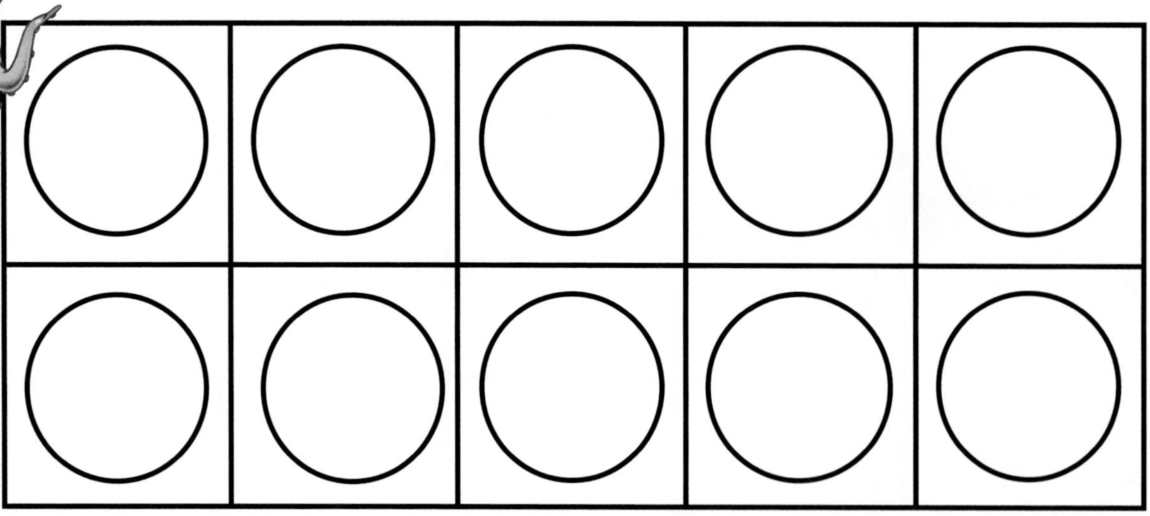

5

3

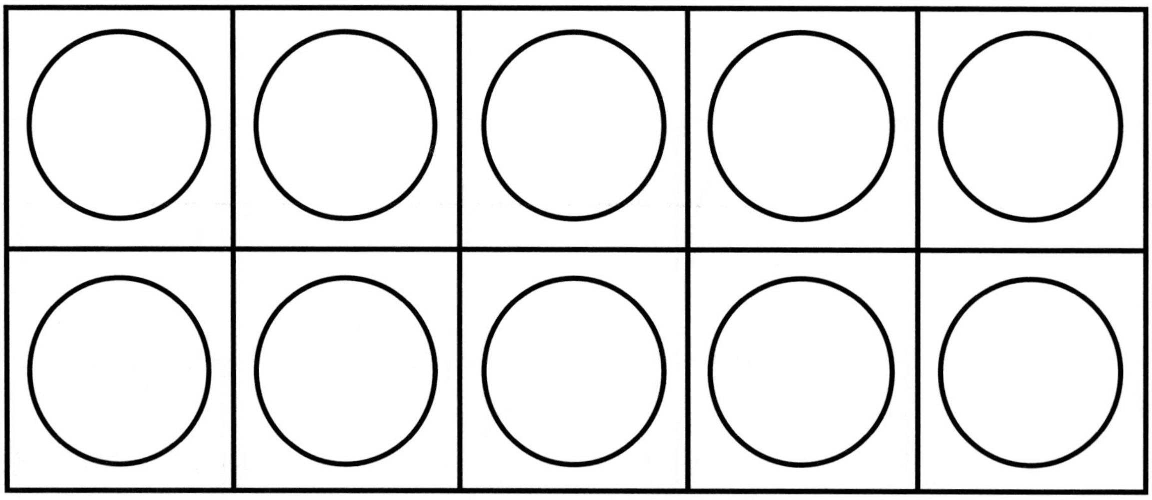

6

9

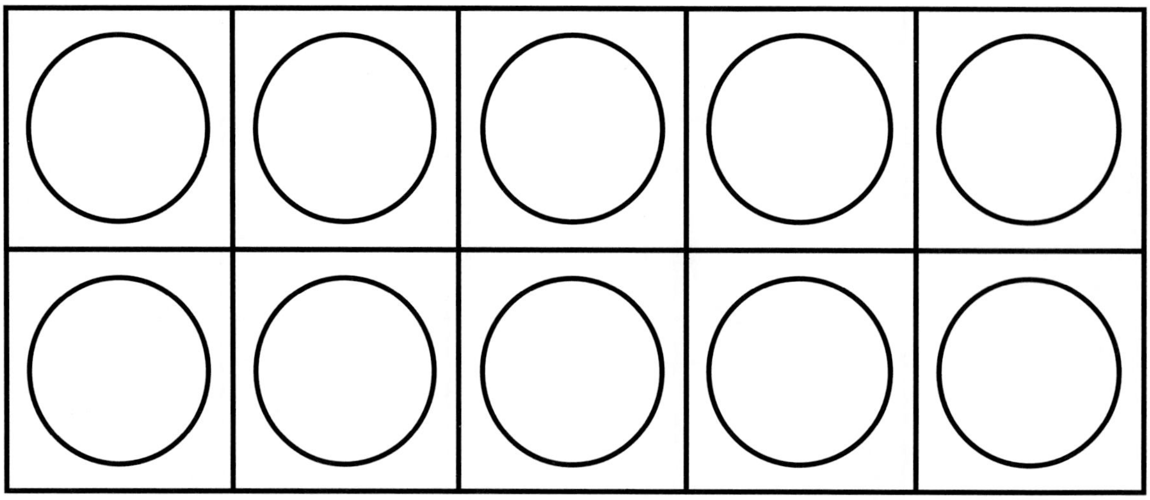

**Directions** Have children write each number and color counter outlines to show that number. Then have children circle the numbers that are more than 5 but less than 10.

**Home Activity** Give your child 8 pennies. Ask your child to count them and tell if the number of pennies is less than 5 or greater than 5. Repeat with other numbers of coins.

Name ____________________

## Ordering Numbers 0 Through 10

**Algebra**

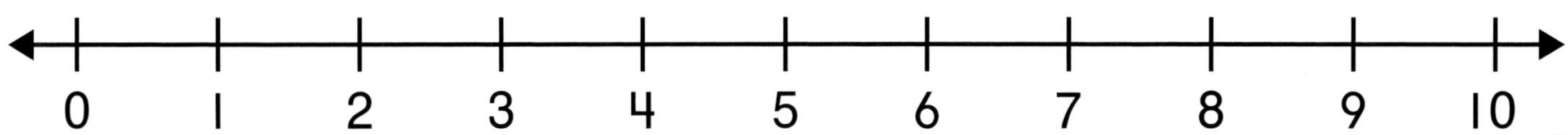


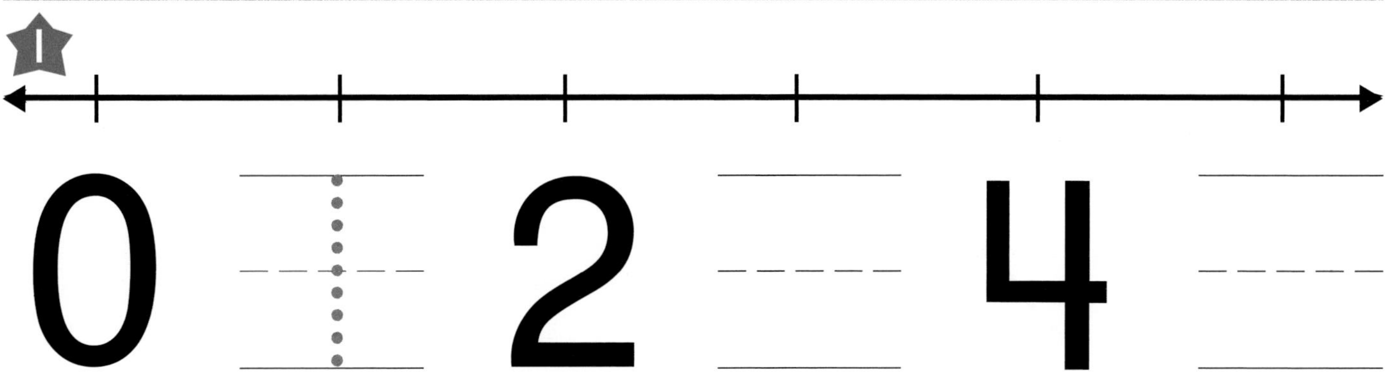


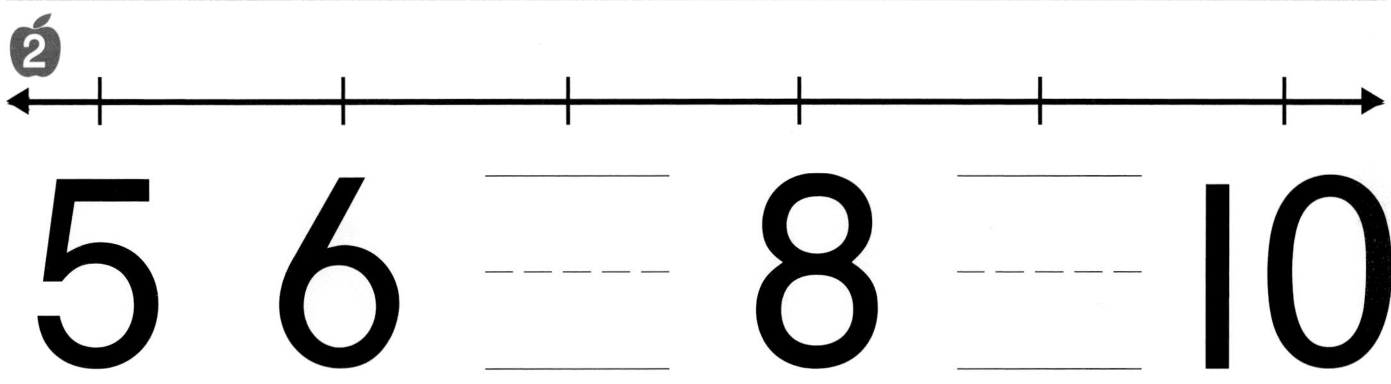


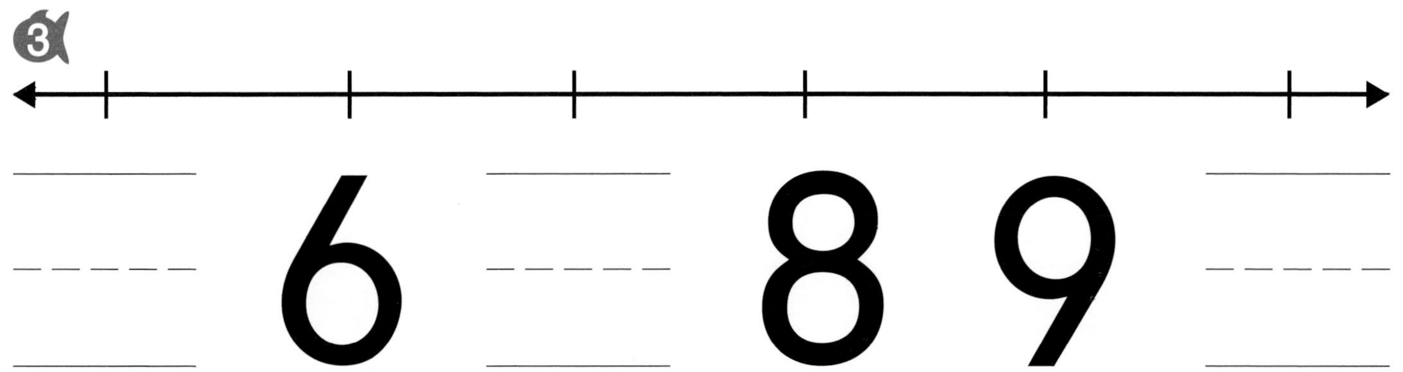


**Directions** In each exercise have children write the missing numbers for the number line.

4

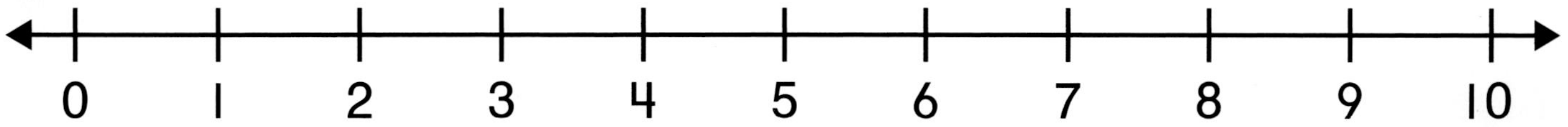

0 1 2 3 4 5 6 7 8 9 10

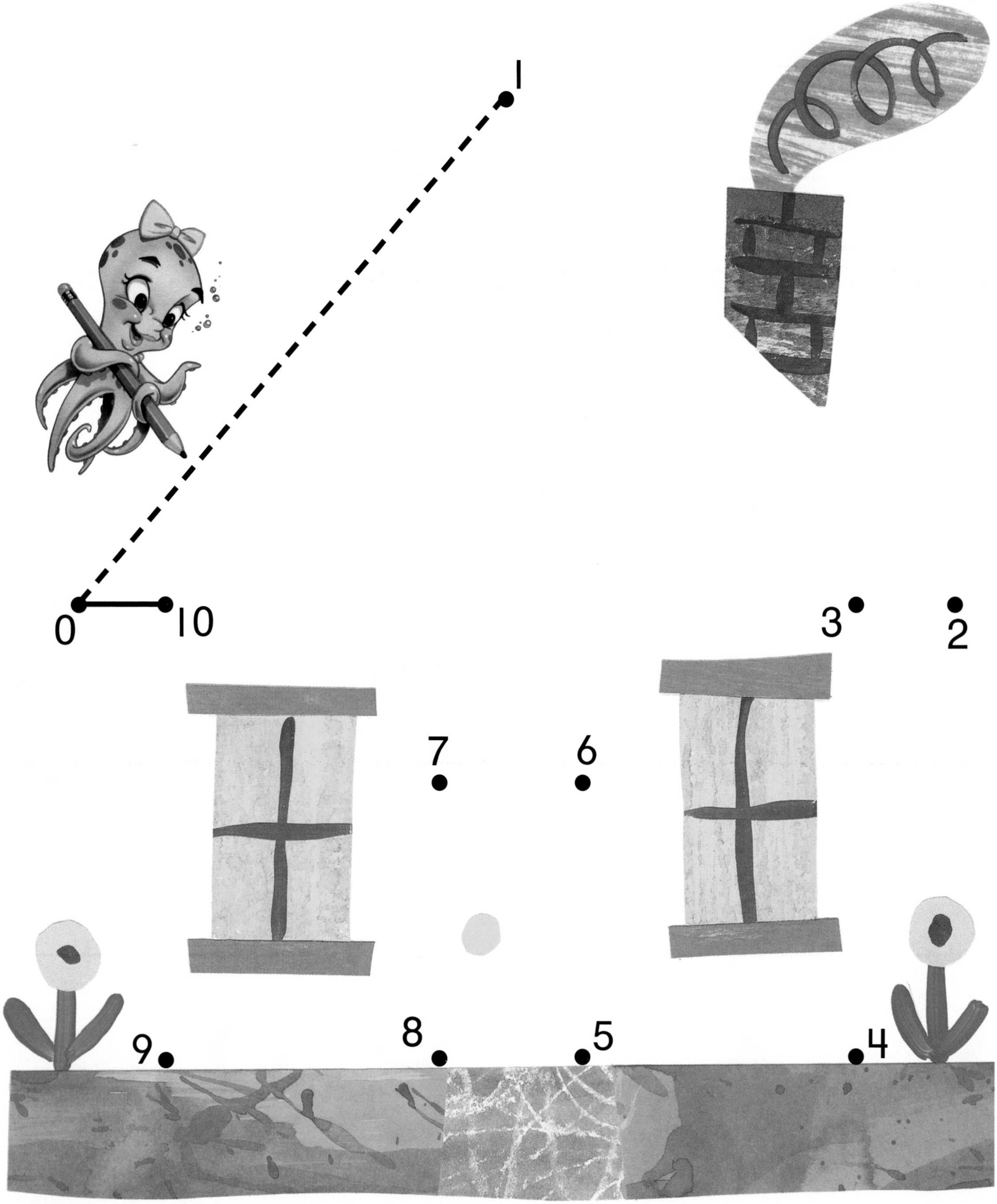

1

0 10 3 2

7 6

9 8 5 4

**Directions** Have children use the numbers in the number line to connect the dots on the page.

**Home Activity** Have your child tell you about the numbers on the line at the top of the page.

Name ____________________

# Ordinal Numbers Through Tenth

1

**Directions** Have children color the monkeys in this way: the eighth monkey blue, the ninth monkey green, the sixth monkey yellow, the tenth monkey orange, and the seventh monkey red.

2

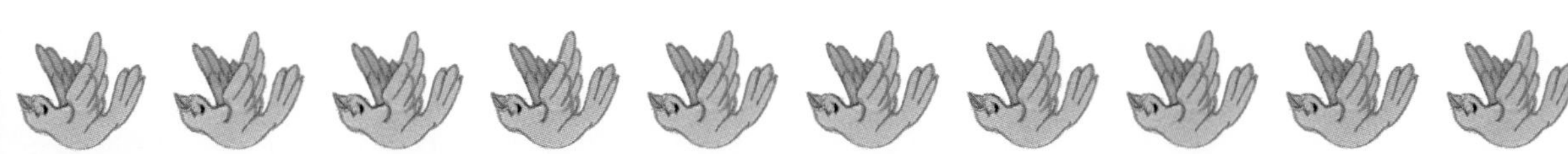

3

4

5

6

**Directions** Have children circle the sixth bird, the ninth raccoon, the seventh penguin, the eighth turtle, and the tenth inchworm.

**Home Activity** When checking out at the grocery store, ask your child to tell you which position you hold in line. Ask which positions the people hold behind you and in front of you.

Name ___________________________



## Look for a Pattern

### Algebra

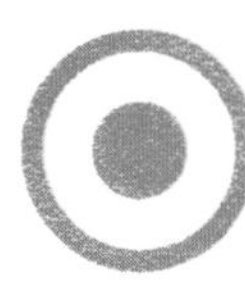

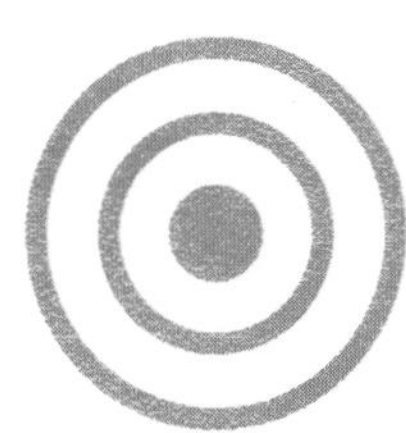

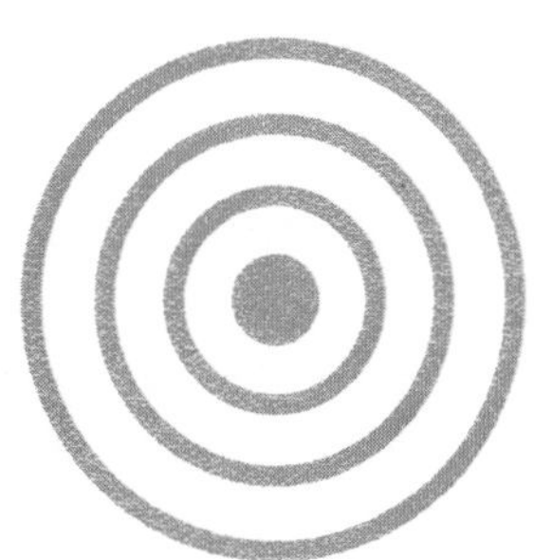

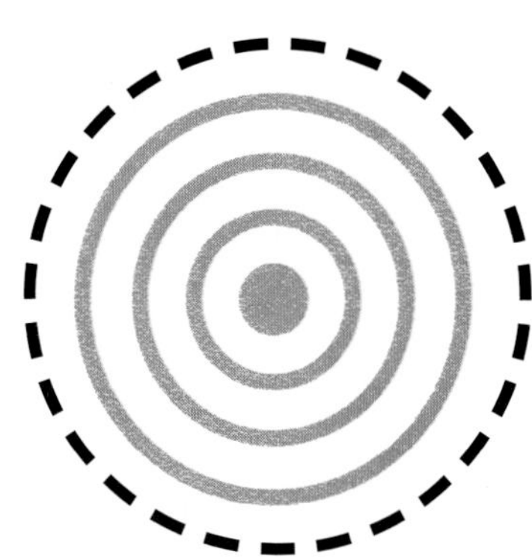

2

XOXOOXOOO

3

○△○○△○○○△

4

**Directions** Exercise 1: Have children identify how the pattern grows and then draw a circle to continue the pattern. Exercises 2–4: Have children identify how the patterns grow and then draw the next elements in each pattern.

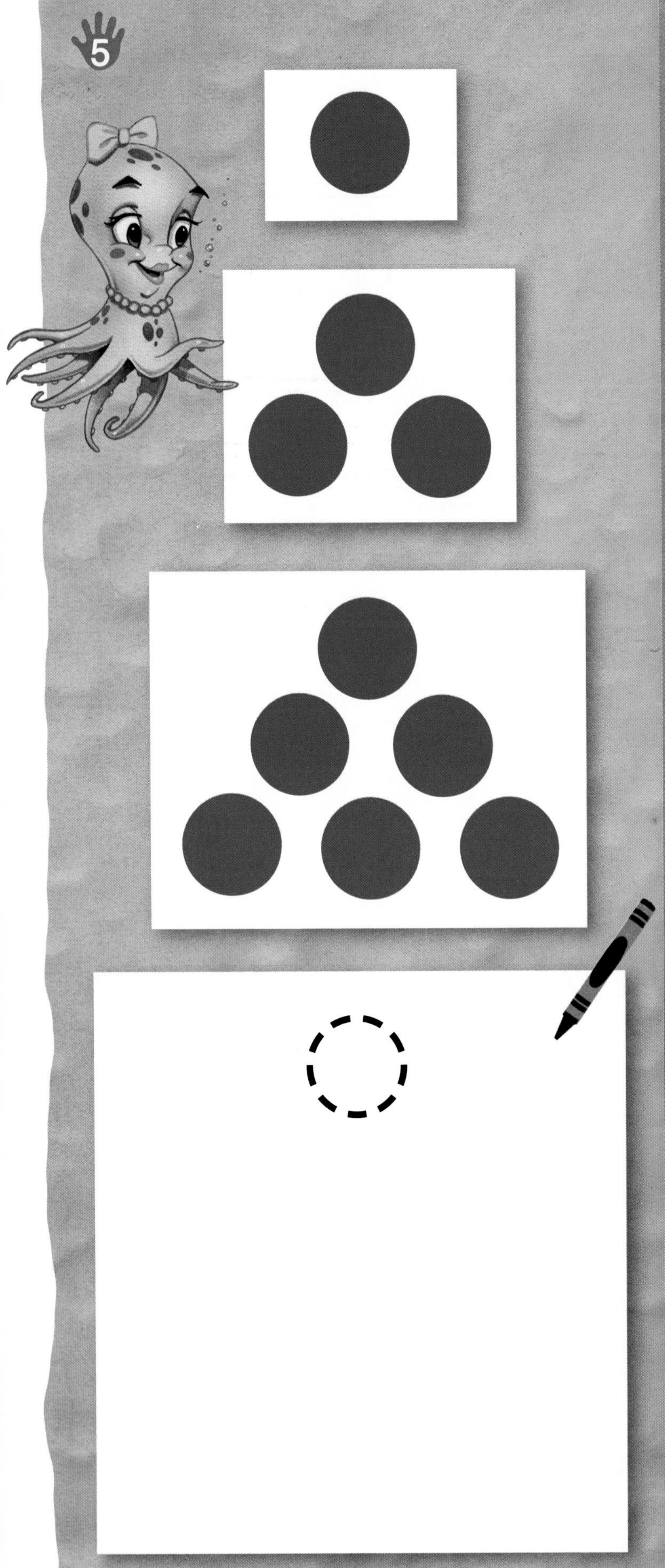

5

6

**Directions** Have children identify how the patterns grow and draw shapes to continue the patterns.

**Home Activity** Ask your child to tell you how the shape patterns grow.

Name ______________________



# Let's Have a Picnic

**Directions** Tell children that six friends are having apples and juice for a picnic lunch. Have children count the apples and juice bottles and record the numbers. Ask children whether there are enough red apples for each friend to have one. Are there enough bottles of juice for each friend to have one?

**Directions** Tell children that the fruit bugs like bananas. Have children find the third bug and tell what it looks like. Then have children circle the third bug. Repeat for the fifth, seventh, and tenth bugs.

**Home Activity** Talk with your child about the pictures on these two pages. Have your child tell you how he or she solved problems to complete the pages.

Name ______________________________ **Test**

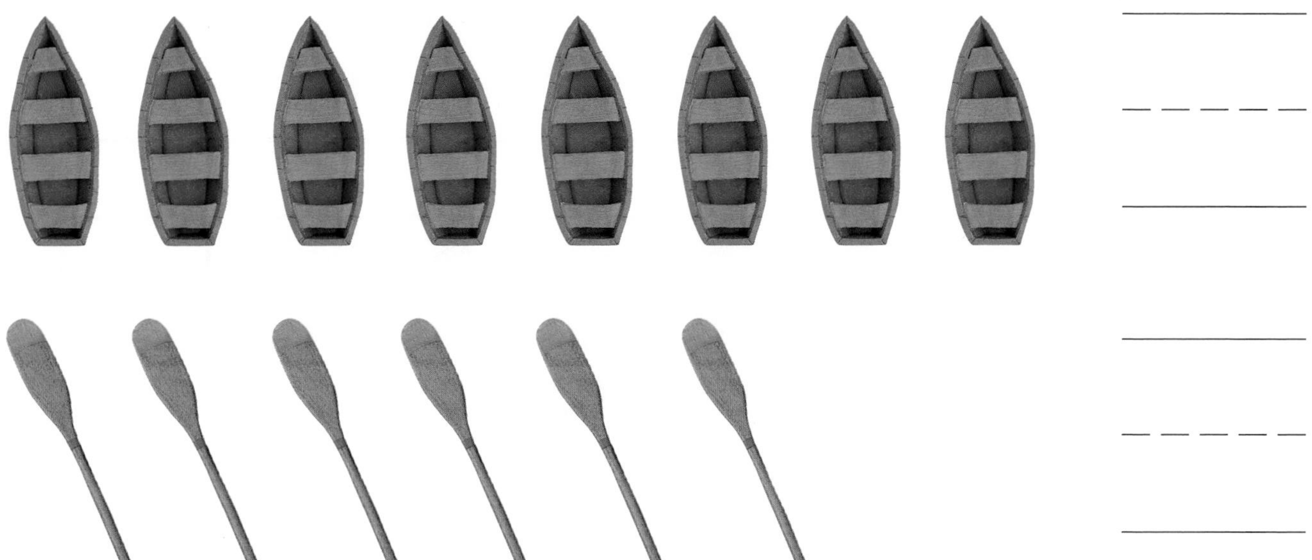

2

**Directions** Have children: 1. draw a line from each oar to a boat, circle the group with more, write the numbers, and circle the number that is greater; 2. color the seventh and ninth cars blue.

3

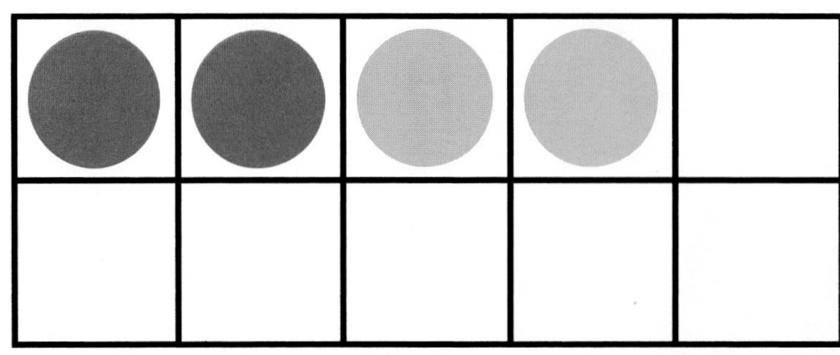

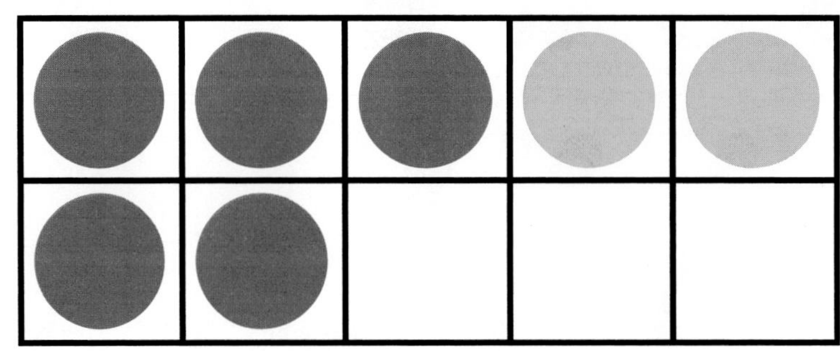

4

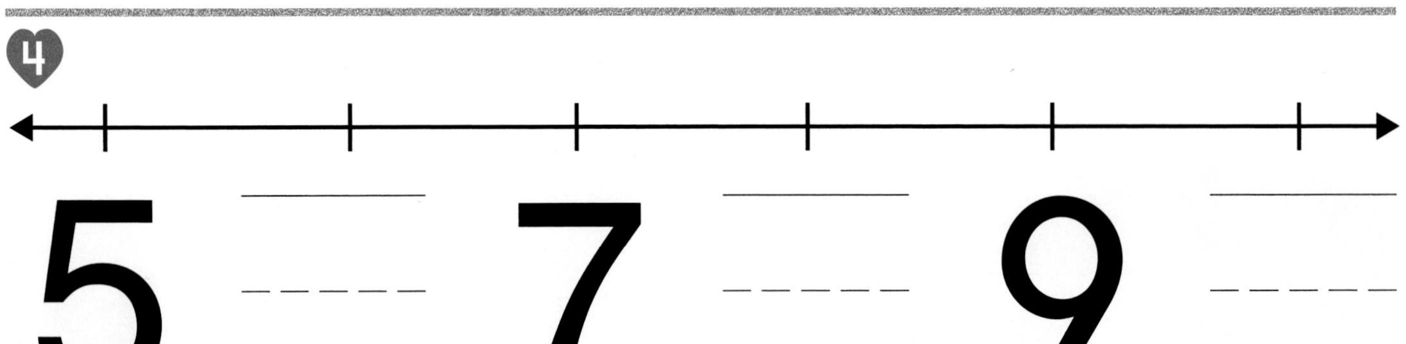


5

X O X X O X X X O

**Directions** Have children: 3. count the counters, write how many, and circle the number that is more than 5; 4. write the missing numbers for the number line; 5. identify how the pattern grows and draw the next elements.

CHAPTER 5

Numbers Through 31

Read Together

# One Fine Day

Written by Lisa D. Thomas

Illustrated by Laura Ovresat

This Math Storybook belongs to

________________________________

One fine day,
the ants came out to play.
How many do you see,
playing beneath my tree?

One fine day,
the grasshoppers came out to play.
How many do you see,
hopping around me?

One fine day,
the butterflies came out to play.
How many do you see,
flying around me?

One fine day,
a ladybug came out to play.

"Hey!" she said.
"Where did everyone go?"

"Surprise!" we all said.

## Home-School Connection

Dear Family,

Today my class started Chapter 5, **Numbers Through 31.** I will learn how to count, write, and compare numbers through 31. I will also learn to skip count by 2s and 5s. Here are some of the math words I will be learning and some things we can do to help me with my math.

Love,

______________________

### Math Activity to Do at Home

Play "Magazine Math." Invite your child to look up page numbers (through 31). Ask, for example, "Can you find Page 10?" Then ask follow-up questions: "Is Page 10 before or after Page 9?" "Which number is one more than 10?" "One less than 9?"

### Books to Read Together

Reading math stories reinforces concepts. Look for these titles in your local library:

***Barn Cat: A Counting Book***
By Carol P. Saul
(Little Brown and Company, 1998)

***Each Orange Had 8 Slices: A Counting Book***
By Paul Giganti, Jr.
(Mulberry Books, 1999)

**Take It to the NET**
**More Activities**
www.scottforesman.com

### My New Math Words

**calendar**

| January | | | | | | |
|---|---|---|---|---|---|---|
| Sunday | Monday | Tuesday | Wednesday | Thursday | Friday | Saturday |
| 1 | 2 | 3 | 4 | 5 | 6 | 7 |
| 8 | 9 | 10 | 11 | 12 | 13 | 14 |

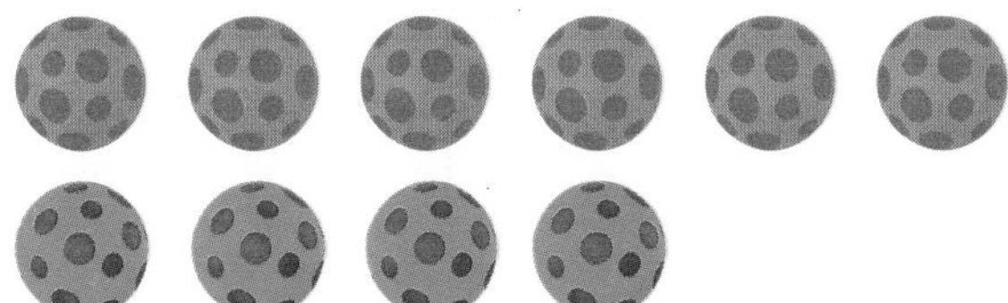

6 is **greater** than 4. 4 is **less** than 6.

**skip counting**

Name ______________________

# Number Memory

**What You Need**

12 paper squares ■

## How to Play

1. Place the squares on the gameboard.
2. Take turns. Take away 2 squares.
3. If you match a number with the picture that shows that number, keep both squares.
4. If the number and the picture do not match, put the squares back where you found them.
5. The person who has the most squares at the end of the game is the winner.

| 1 | | 10 | |
|---|---|---|---|
| | 20 | | 31 |
| 12 | | 5 | |

Name ______________________________



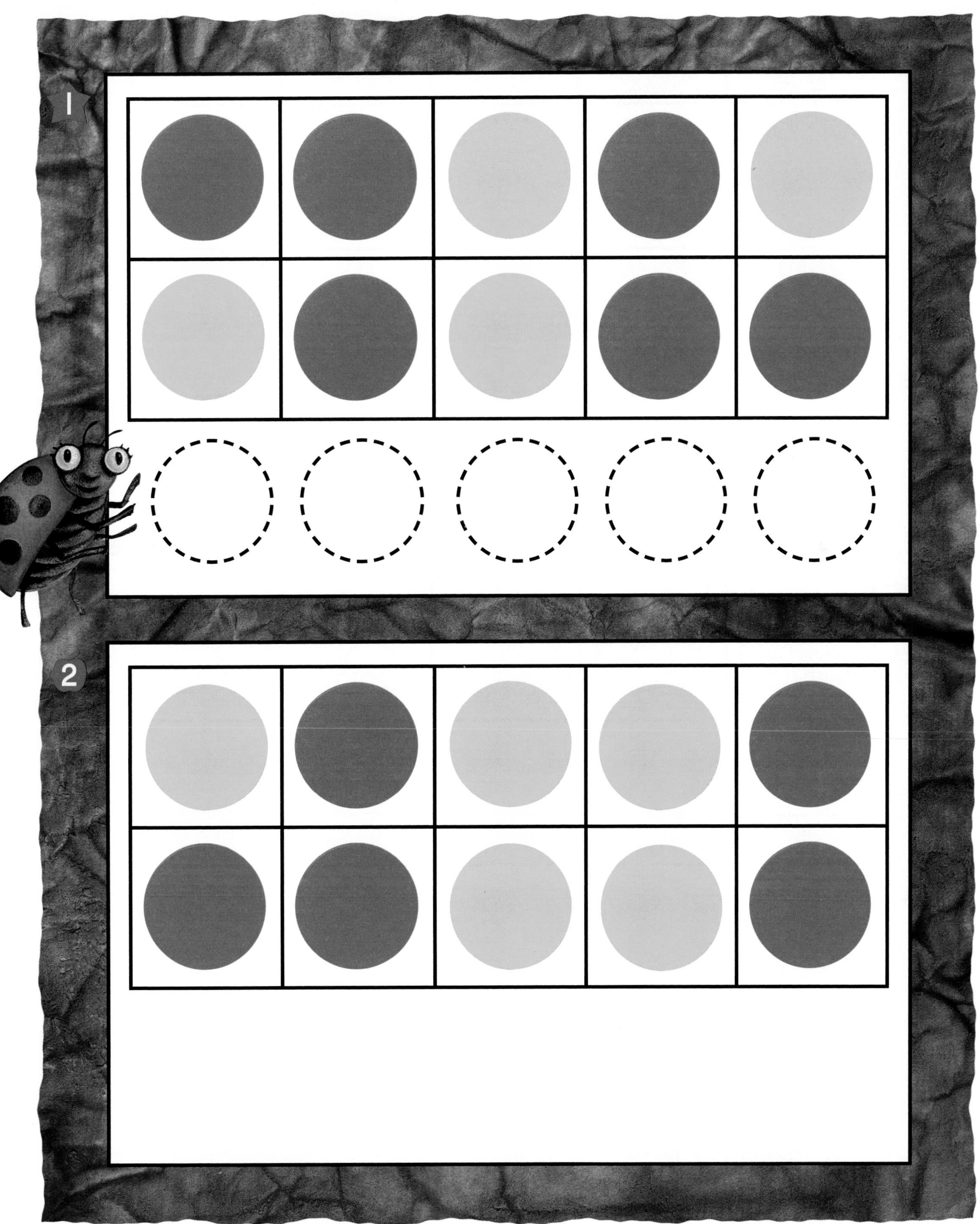


**Directions** Exercise 1: Have children use counters to count and model the numbers 11 through 15. Exercise 2: Have children choose a number from 11 through 15 and use counters to count and model the number. Then have children draw and color enough extra counters to show the number.

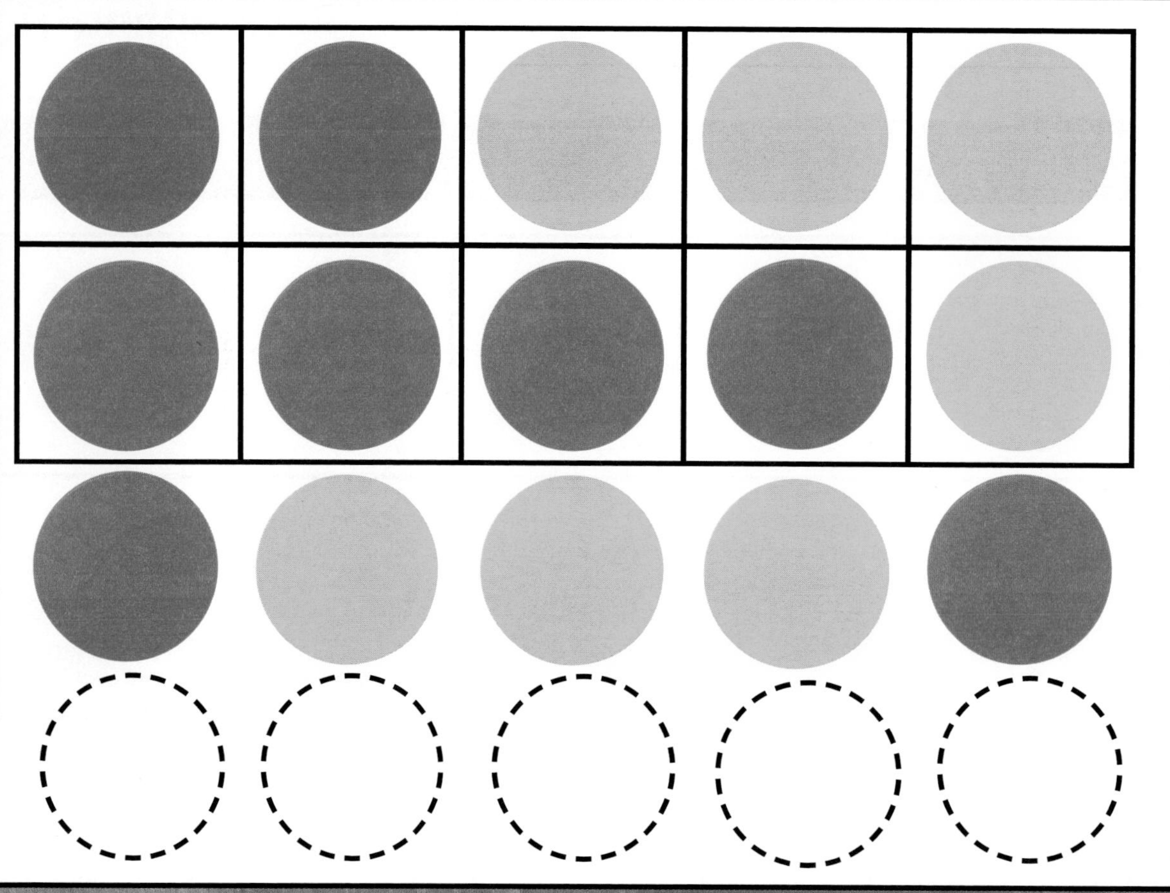


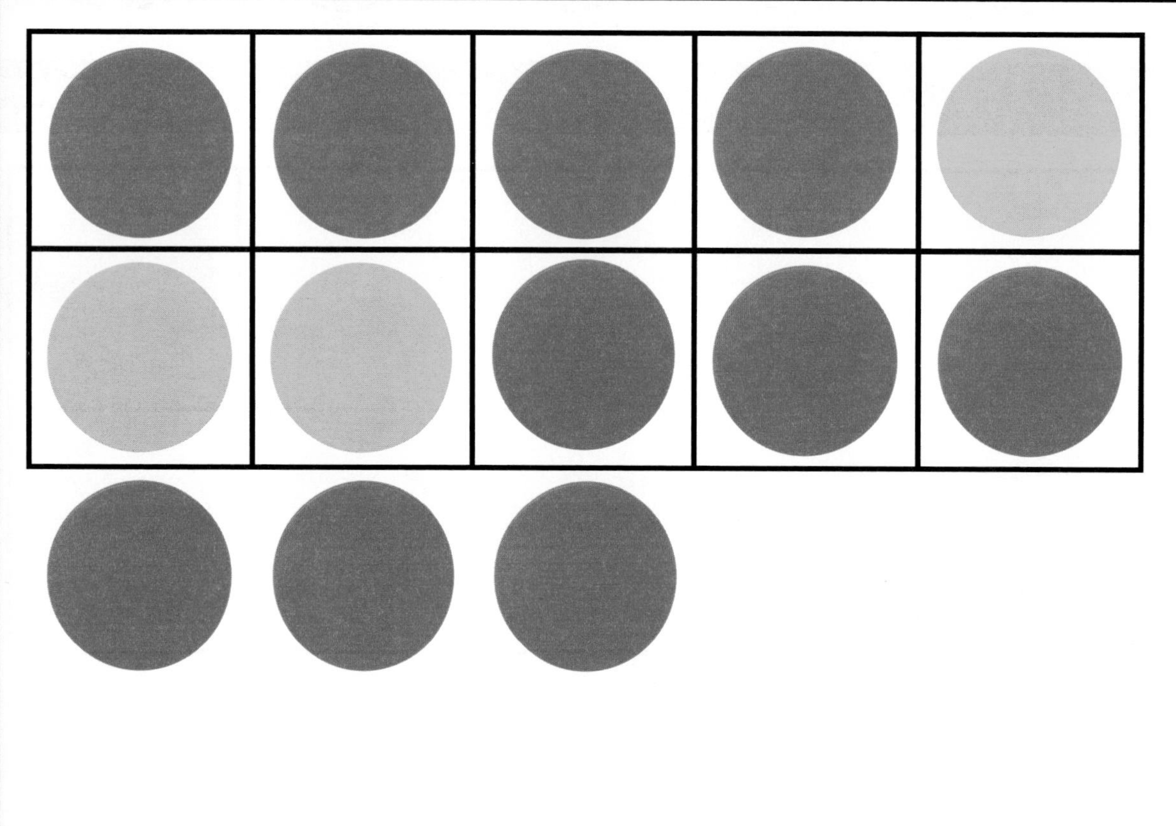


**Directions** Exercise 3: Have children use counters to count and model the numbers 16 through 20. Exercise 4: Have children choose a number from 16 through 20 and use counters to count and model the number. Then have children draw and color enough extra counters to show the number.

**Home Activity** Have your child find groups of 11 to 20 things in your home and count them.

Name ______________________________

# Reading and Writing 11 and 12

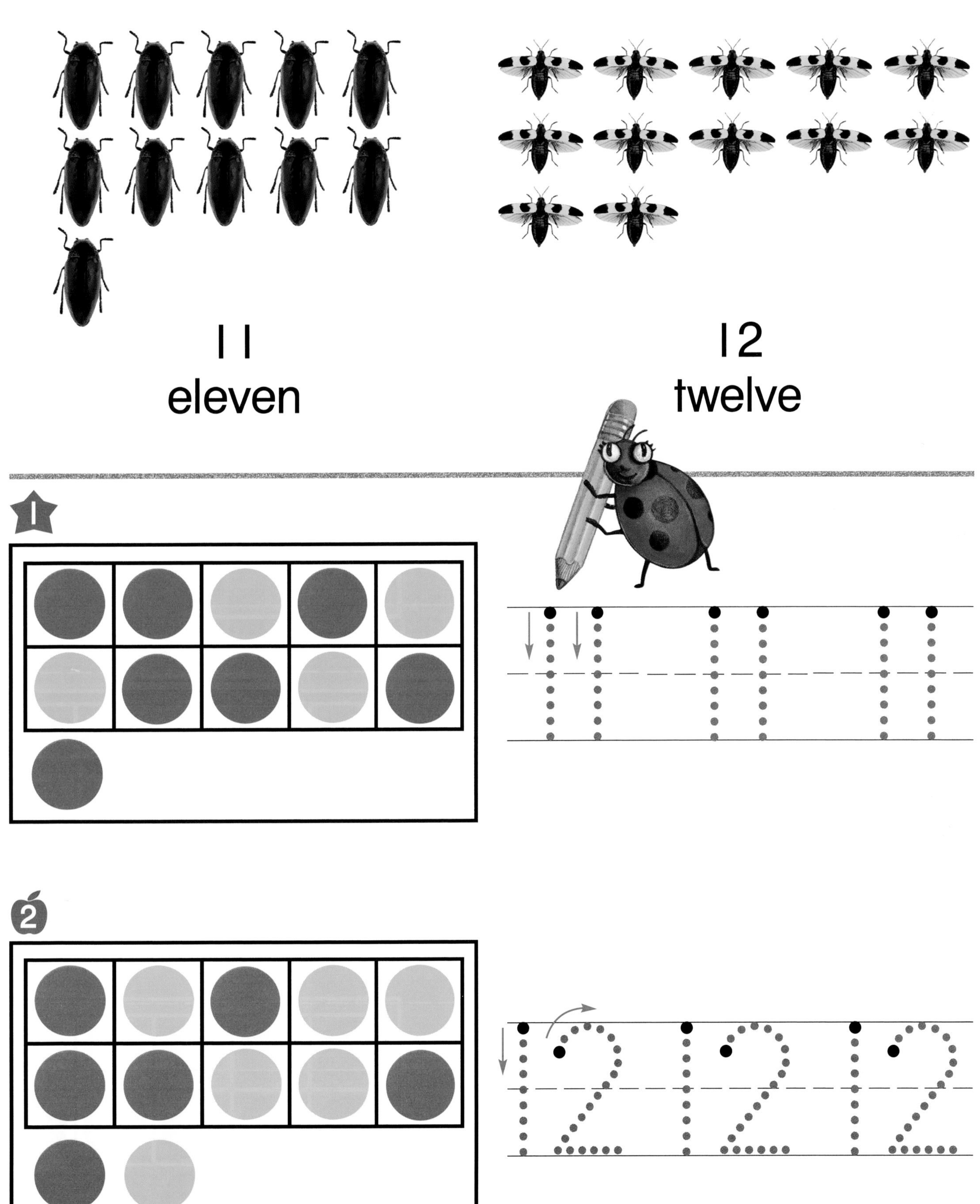


**Directions** Have children count the counters and practice writing the matching numbers 11 and 12, beginning at each black dot.

4

10

5

20

6

30

**Directions** Exercise 4: Have children circle the plate with about 30 cubes on it. Exercise 5: Have children circle the plate with about 10 erasers on it. Exercise 6: Have children circle the plate with about 20 buttons on it.

**Home Activity** Give your child a group of 5 pennies and a group of 10 pennies. Have him or her tell which group has about 10 pennies.

Name ______________________

# Comparing Numbers Through 31

**Algebra**

1

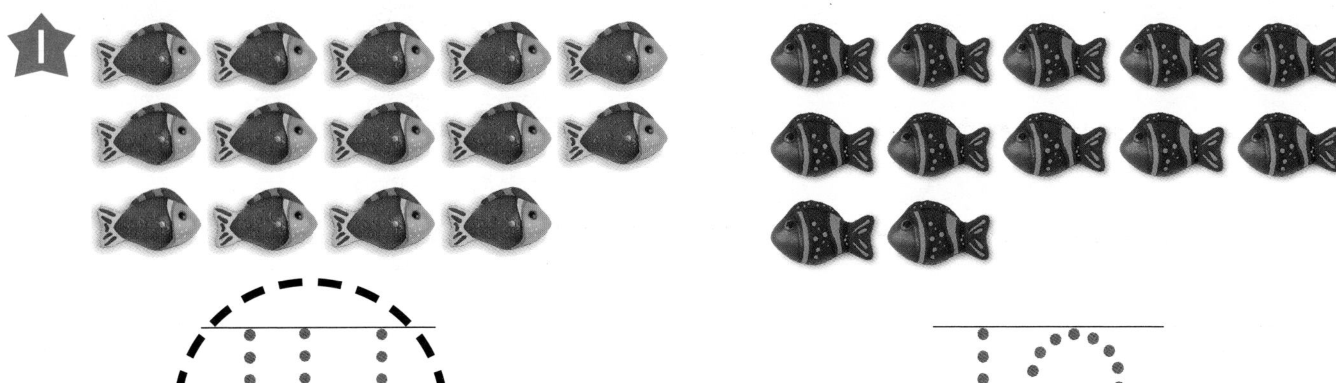

2

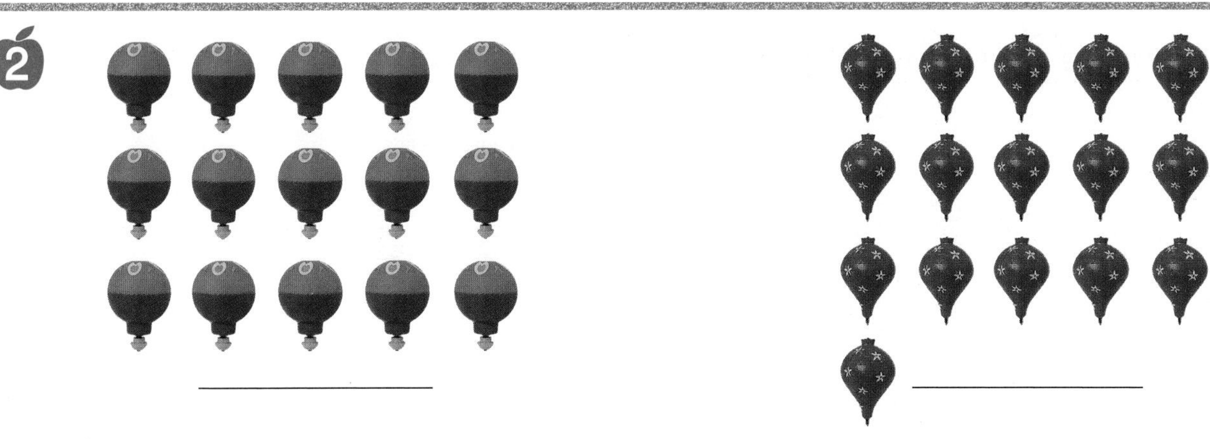

3

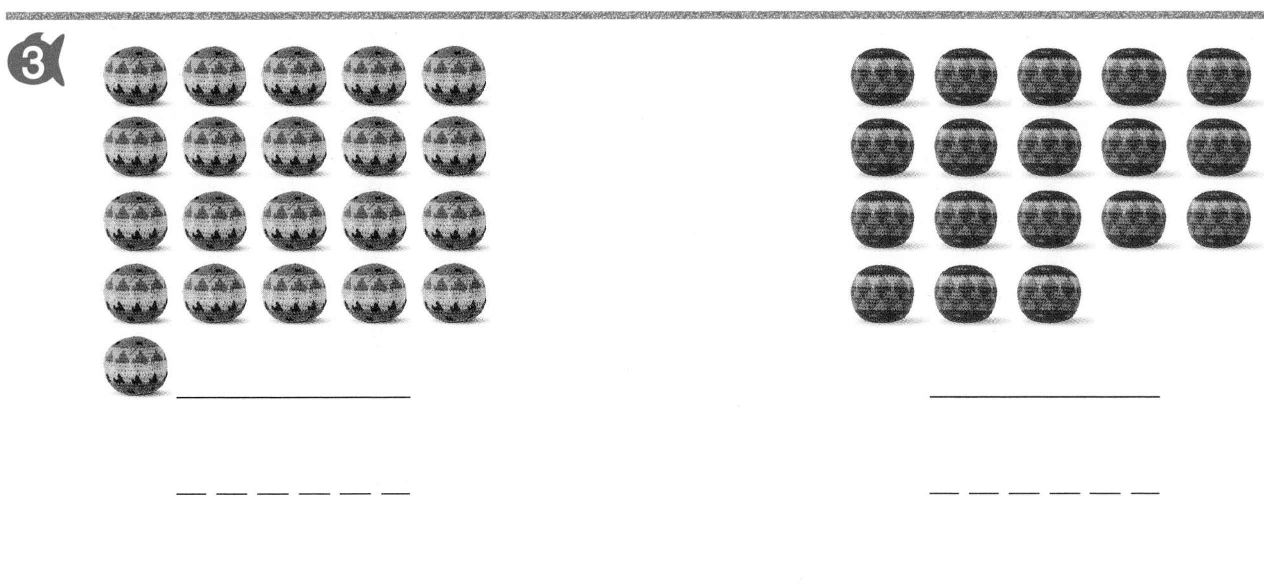

**Directions** For each exercise have children count the objects, write the numbers, and circle the greater number.

4

17  20

5

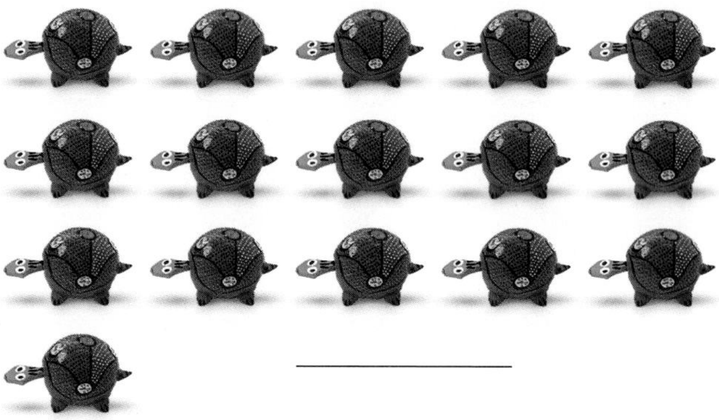

6

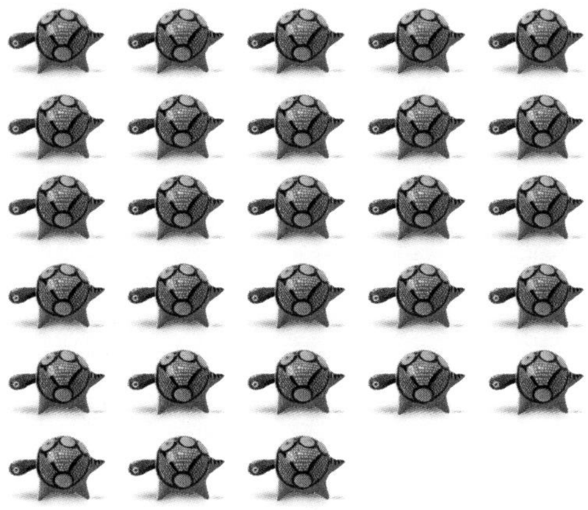

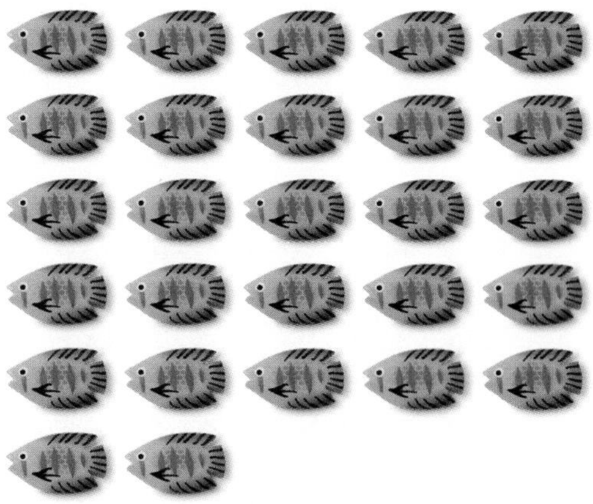

**Directions** For each exercise have children count the objects, write the numbers, and circle the lesser number.

**Home Activity** Show your child a group of 16 pennies and a group of 24 pennies. Ask your child to count the groups and tell which group is greater.

Name ______________________________

# Numbers on a Calendar

**Directions** Have children write the numbers on the calendar. Have them circle the number that comes before 13, mark an *X* on the number that comes after 18, and color the square for the number that comes between 25 and 27.

# November

| Sunday | Monday | Tuesday | Wednesday | Thursday | Friday | Saturday |
|---|---|---|---|---|---|---|
| | | 1 | 2 | 3 | 4 | 5 |
| 6 | 7 | | 9 | | 11 | 12 |
| 13 | | 15 | | 17 | 18 | 19 |
| 20 | 21 | 22 | 23 | | 25 | 26 |
| 27 | | 29 | 30 | | | |

**Directions** Have children write the numbers that come before and after 4, 9, and 15. Then have children write the numbers that come between 17 and 19, 23 and 25, and 27 and 29.

**Home Activity** Show your child a calendar and have him or her point out the numbers that come before and after 10.

Name ______________________________



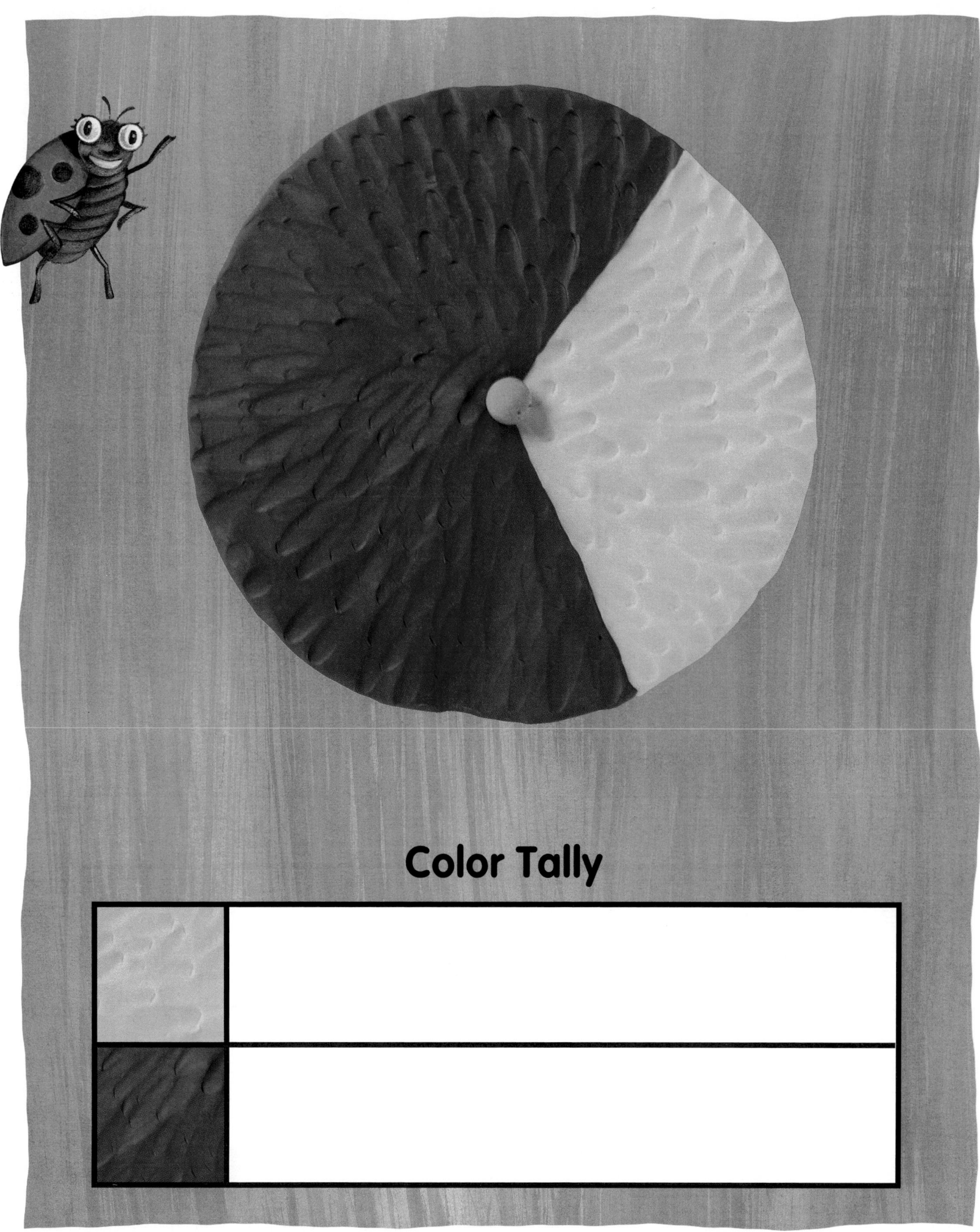


**Directions** Have children place a paper clip on the spinner and hold it in place with an upright pencil. (Point of pencil should be on orange dot.) Ask children to make a tally mark next to the corresponding color in the table after each of 10 spins.

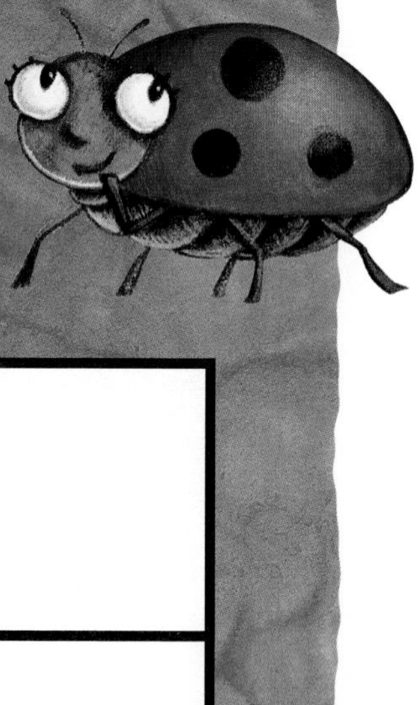

## Color Tally

| | |
|---|---|
| | |
| | |
| | |

**Directions** Have children place a paper clip on the spinner and hold it in place with an upright pencil. (Point of pencil should be on the purple dot.) Ask children to make a tally mark next to the corresponding color in the table after each of 10 spins.

**Home Activity** Have your child spin the spinner and tally the results. Talk about the results with your child.

Name ______________________



# A World of Bugs

**Directions** Have children pretend they are visiting a butterfly garden. Ask questions such as: How many butterflies have the color blue in their wings? How many butterflies have spots? How many have stripes? Then have children count the butterflies and record the number.

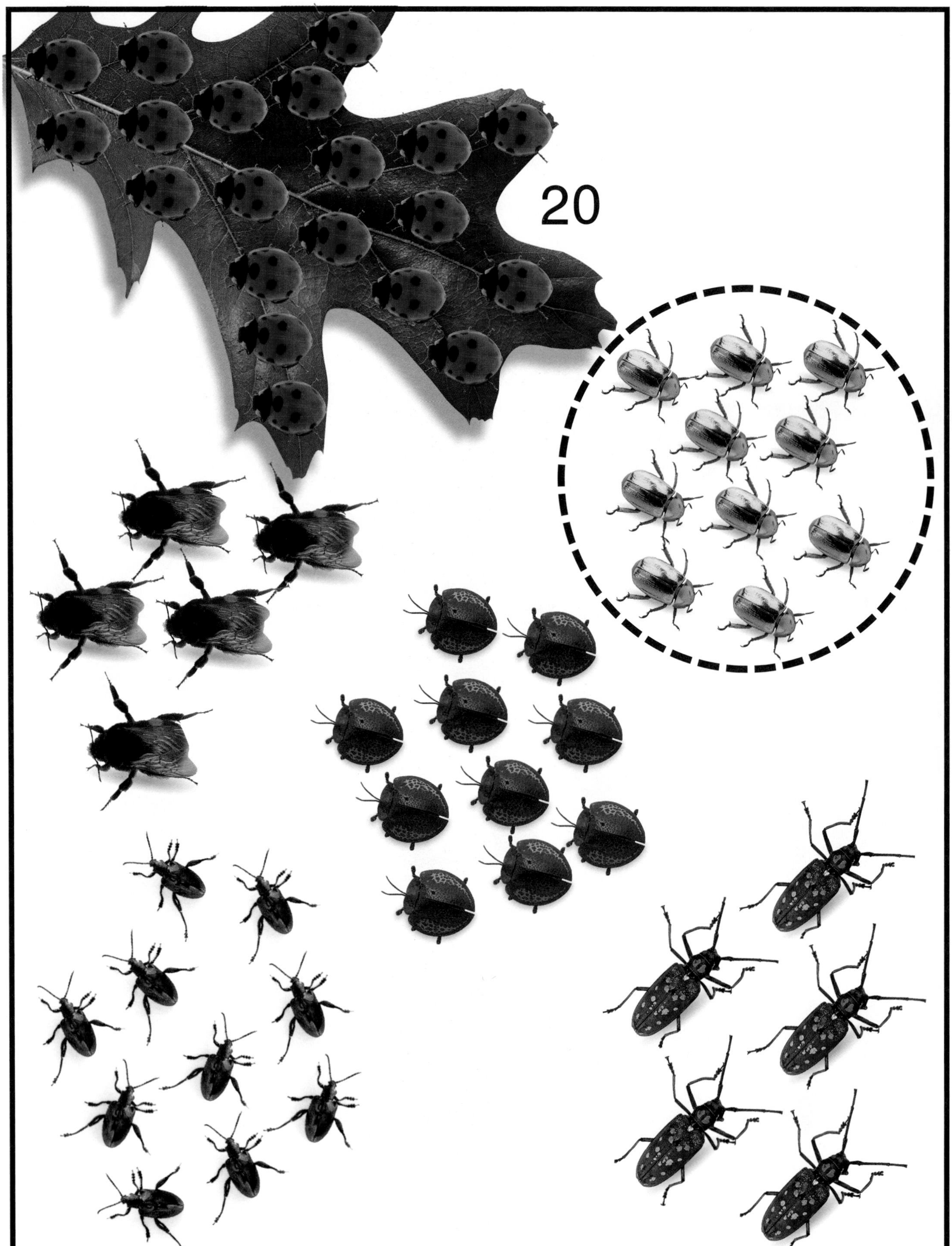

20

**Directions** Ask children how many ladybugs are on the leaf. Then have children look at the other groups and estimate which groups have about 10 bugs. Have them circle these groups.

**Home Activity** Talk with your child about the pictures on these two pages. Have your child tell you how he or she solved problems to complete the pages.

Name ________________________________

Test

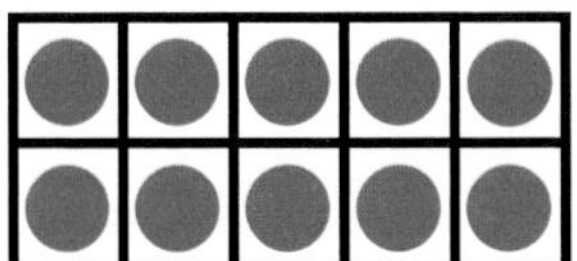

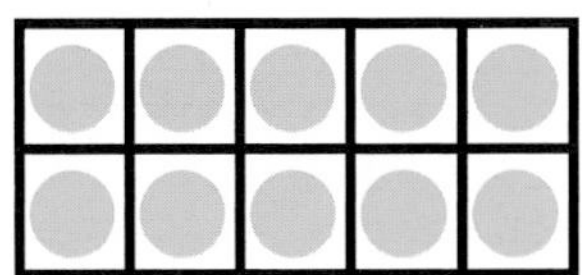

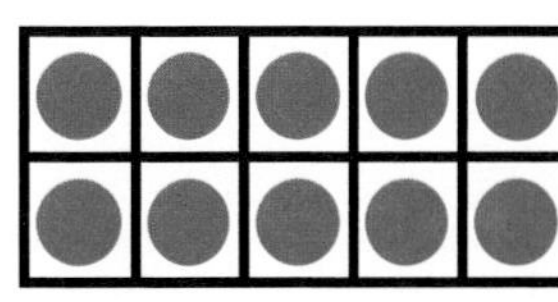

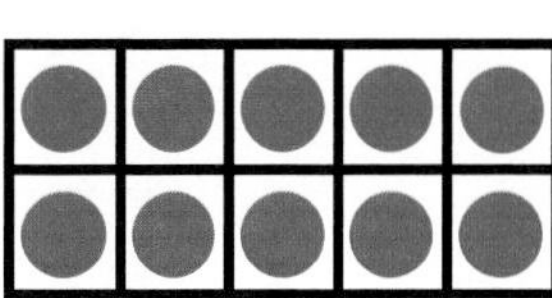

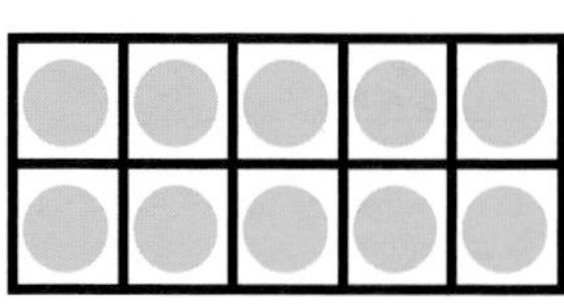

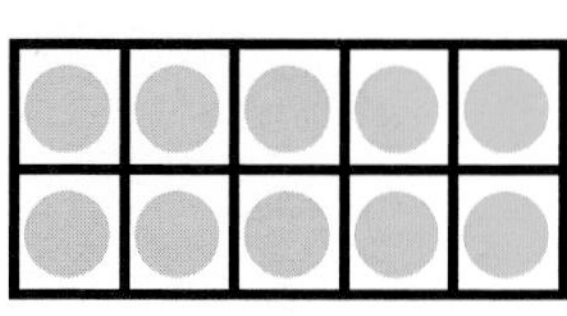

13

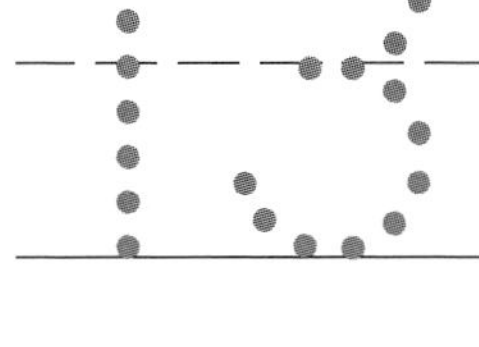

2

10

**Directions** Have children: 1. count the counters and write the numbers; 2. circle the plate with about 20 cubes on it.

3

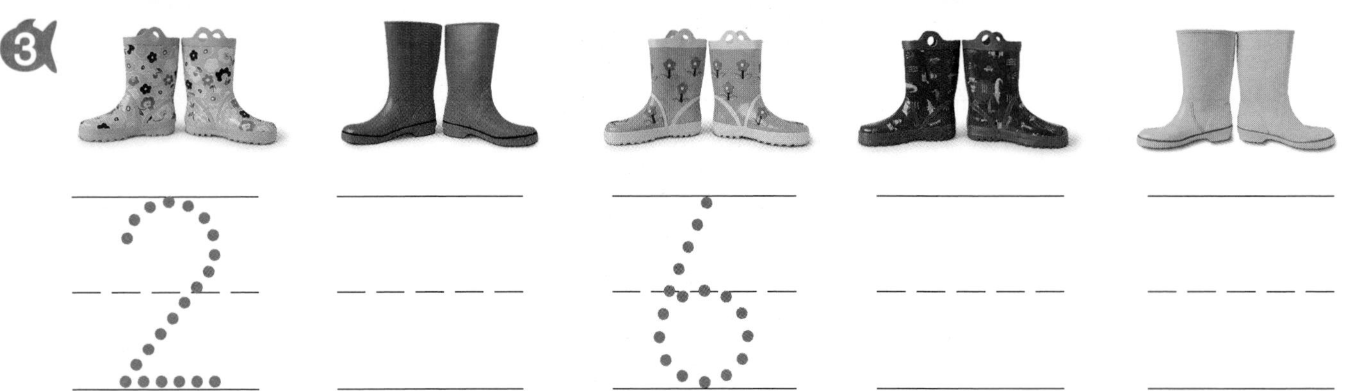

4

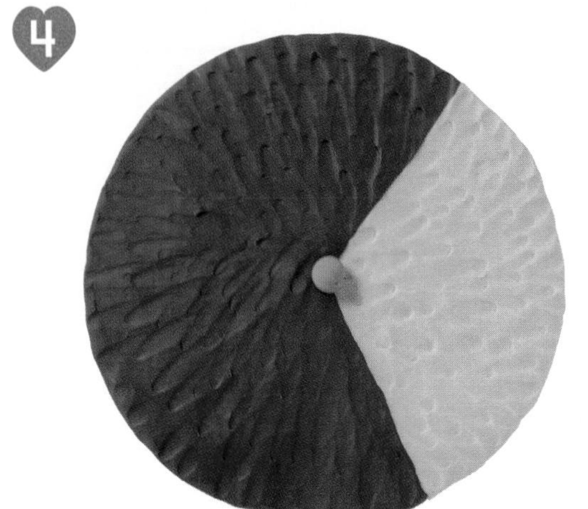

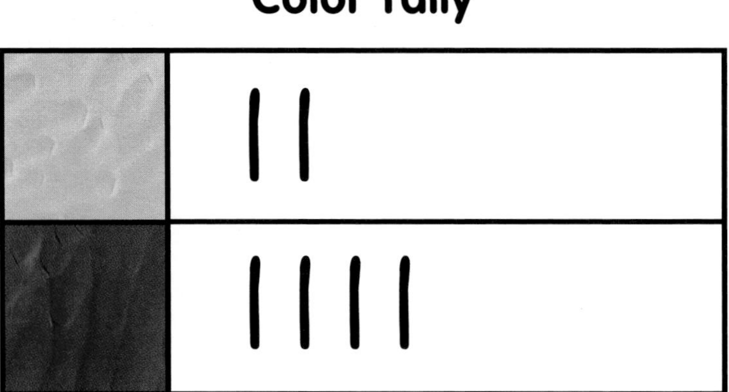


5

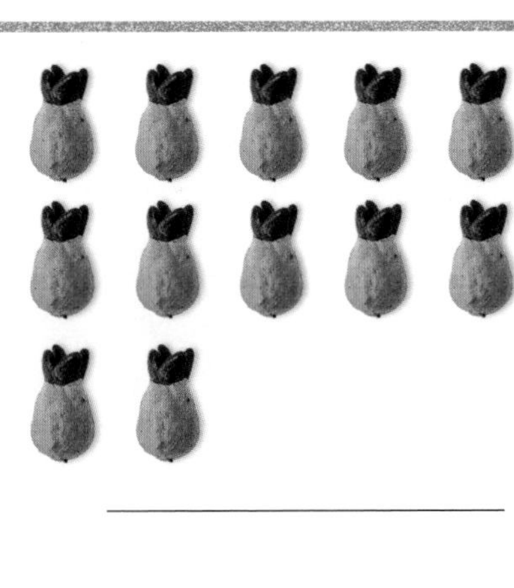

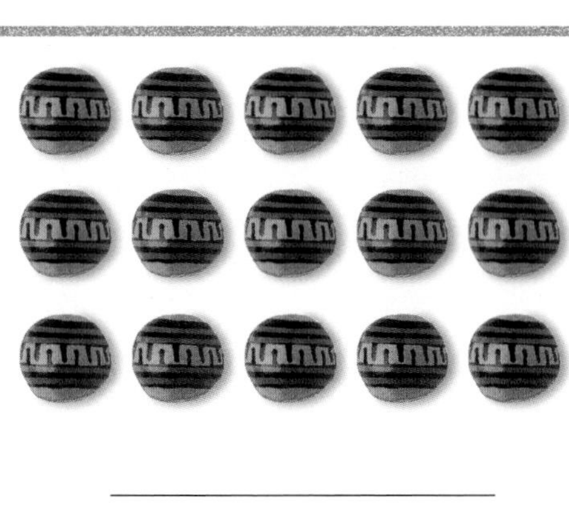

6

| 15 | 16 | 17 | 18 | 19 | 20 | 21 |
|---|---|---|---|---|---|---|

**Directions** Have children: 3. skip count by 2s and record the numbers; 4. look at the table and circle the color with fewer tally marks; 5. count the groups, write the numbers, and circle the greater number; 6. circle the number that comes before 20 and mark an *X* on the number that comes after 15.

CHAPTER 6

Measurement

Read Together

# The Empress and the Tallest Tree

Written by Theresa Volpe

Illustrated by Grace Lin

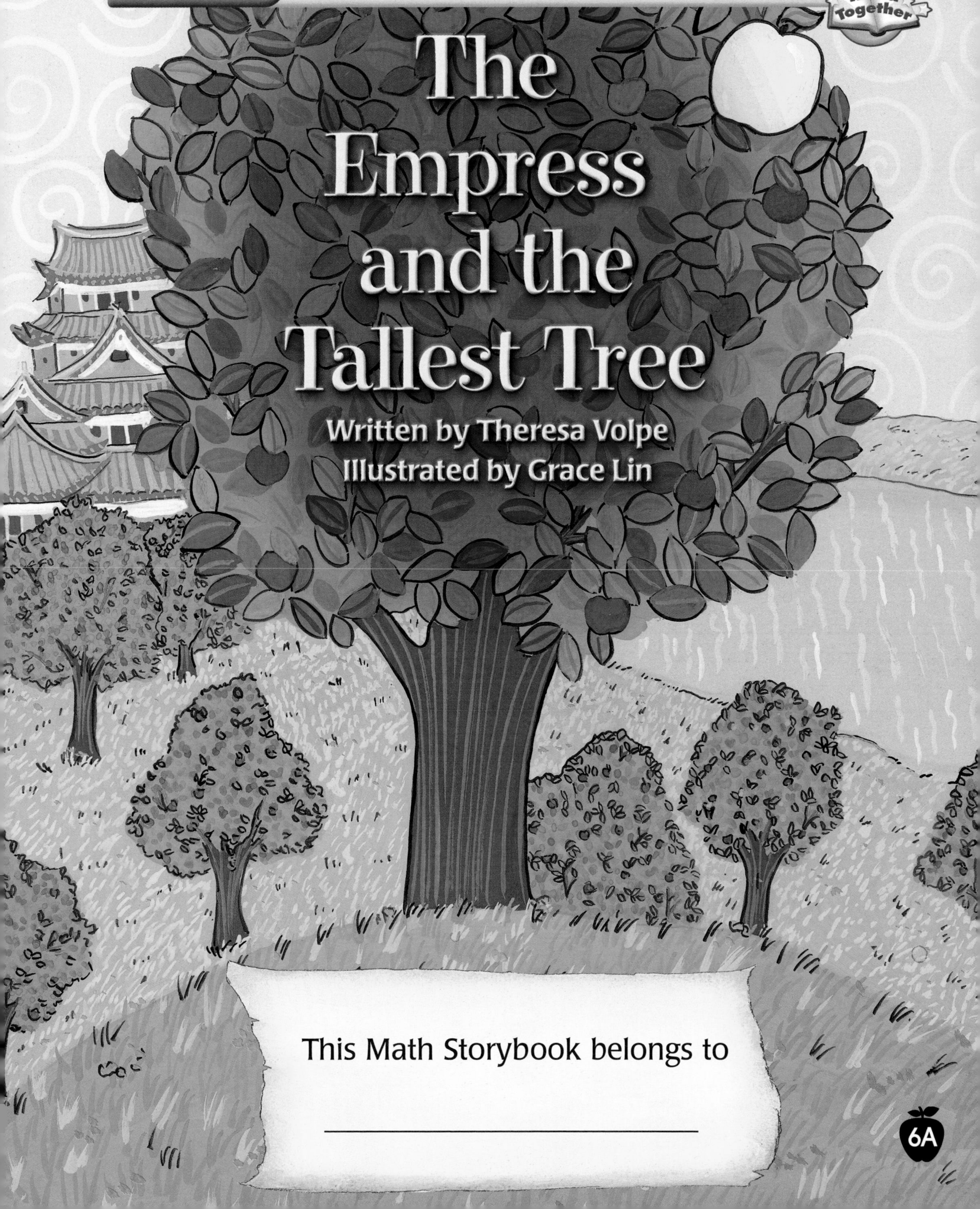

This Math Storybook belongs to

______________________________

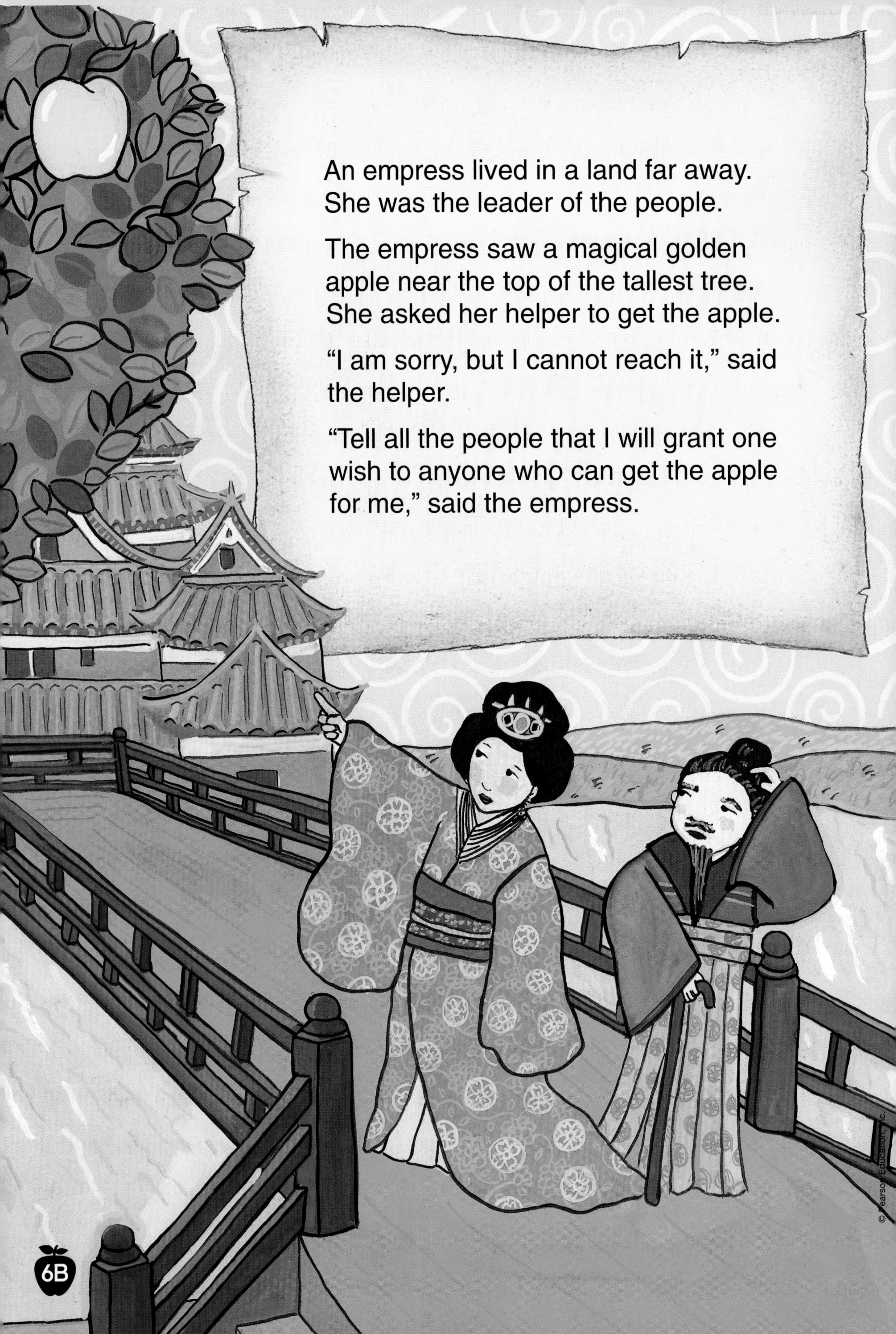

An empress lived in a land far away. She was the leader of the people.

The empress saw a magical golden apple near the top of the tallest tree. She asked her helper to get the apple.

"I am sorry, but I cannot reach it," said the helper.

"Tell all the people that I will grant one wish to anyone who can get the apple for me," said the empress.

Many people tried to get the apple.

A rope maker said he could climb his rope.

A woman said her bird could carry her up to pick the apple.

A girl said, “I can use my paper lanterns to reach the apple.”

The others laughed at her.

The rope maker tried to use his rope to climb the tree. But his rope was too short.

The woman was too heavy for her bird to carry her.

Then the girl put a lantern on her head. Then she put a second lantern under it. And then a third.

Soon there were **30** lanterns on her head.

The others laughed at her. “How are you going to climb the tree with all those lanterns on your head?” they said.

The girl had a monkey. Slowly the monkey climbed the **30** lanterns and grabbed the magical, golden apple.

The girl gave the apple to the empress. The empress was very happy.

"What is your wish?" asked the empress.

"I want every person in our land to hold the apple and make a wish," said the girl.

And everyone did.

# Home-School Connection

Dear Family,

Today my class started Chapter 6, **Measurement.** I will learn how to measure how long things are, how much they weigh, and how much they can hold. Here are some of the math words I will be learning and some things we can do to help me with my math.

Love,

______________________________

## Math Activity to Do at Home

Use a measuring tape to measure your child. Say, "You are ____ feet ___ inches tall." Then go on a "Measurement Hunt," looking for things that are taller and shorter than your child. Make lists of what you find.

## Books to Read Together

Reading math stories reinforces concepts. Look for these titles in your local library:

***The Fattest, Tallest, Biggest Snowman Ever***
By Bettina Ling
(Cartwheel Books, 1997)

***Inch By Inch***
By Leo Lionni
(Mulberry Books, 1995)

Take It to the NET
More Activities
www.scottforesman.com

## My New Math Words

Dad is **taller than** Bobby.

Bobby is **shorter than** Dad.

The alligator **weighs more** than the mouse.

The mouse **weighs less** than the alligator.

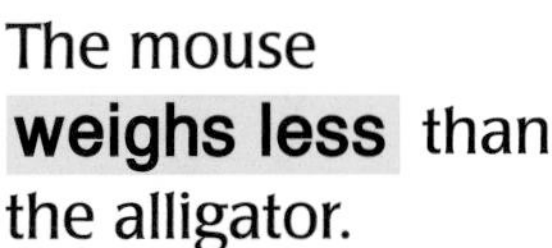

**full** **empty**

Name ____________________

# Race for the Golden Apple

## What You Need

paper clip

pencil
2 game markers
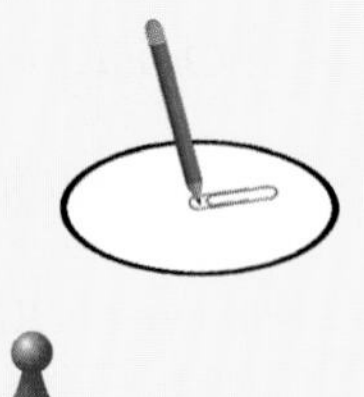

## How to Play

1. Place your markers on START.
2. Take turns spinning the spinner.
3. Move your marker to the next space that has that picture.
4. The first person to get to the last space gets the golden apple!

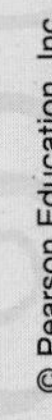

Name ______________________________

# Comparing and Ordering by Size

1

4

**Directions** In each exercise have children circle the larger sign and mark an *X* on the smaller sign.

5

6

7

8

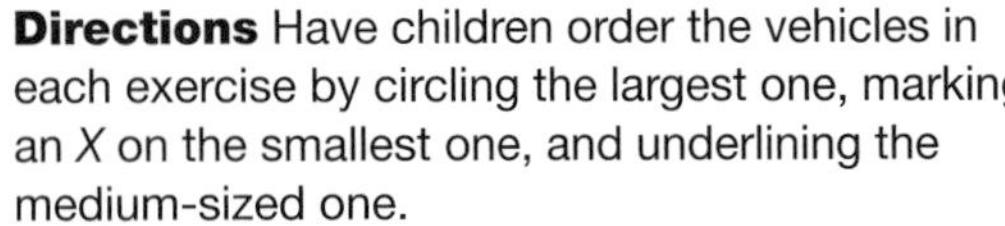

**Directions** Have children order the vehicles in each exercise by circling the largest one, marking an *X* on the smallest one, and underlining the medium-sized one.

**Home Activity** Help your child find three objects of different sizes and tell you which is largest, which is smallest, and which is medium-sized.

Name ____________________

# Comparing by Length

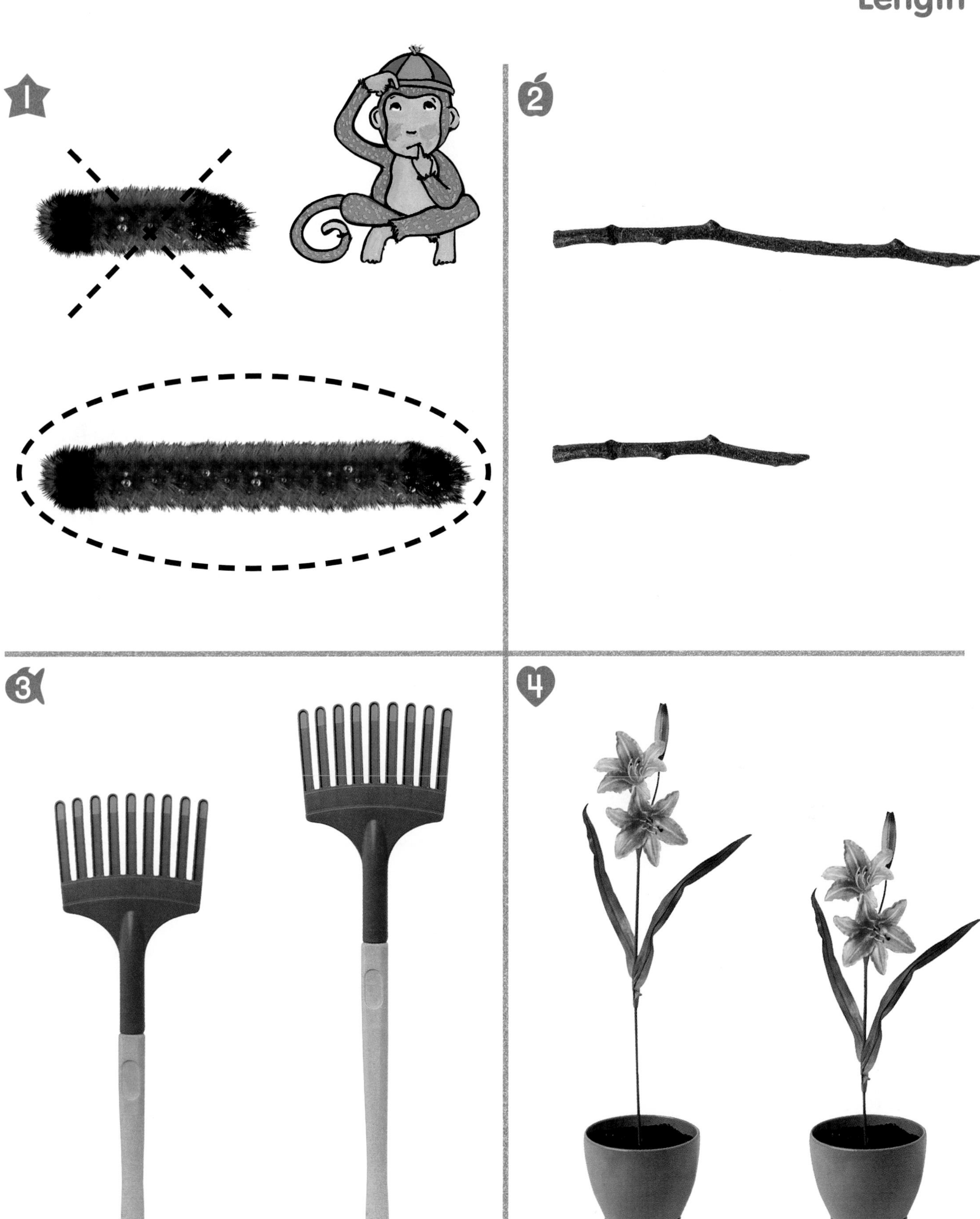

**Directions** In Exercise 1 have children circle the longer caterpillar and mark an *X* on the shorter one. Repeat for the twigs in Exercise 2. In Exercise 3 have children circle the taller rake and mark an *X* on the shorter one. Repeat for the plants in Exercise 4.

**Directions** In Exercise 5 have children draw one or more objects that are shorter than the cube train. In Exercise 6 have children draw one or more objects that are longer than the cube train.

**Home Activity** Set out a serving spoon and a teaspoon. Ask your child to tell you which is longer. Hold the spoons upright on a table. Ask your child which is taller.

Name ______________________________

## Ordering by Length

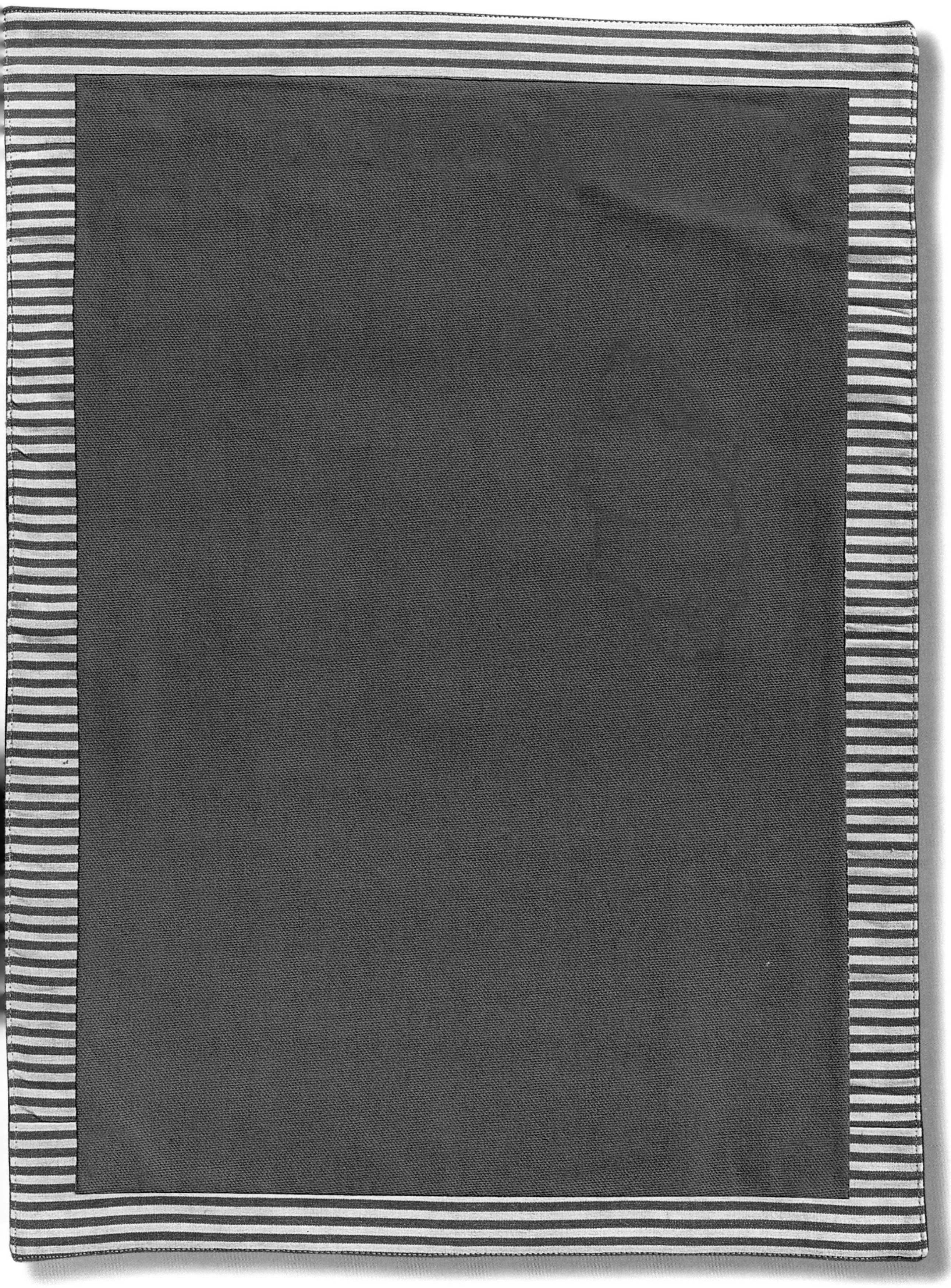

**Directions** Have children cut out the pictures and put them in order from shortest to longest on the place mat. Once they are in order, have children glue the cutouts onto the mat.

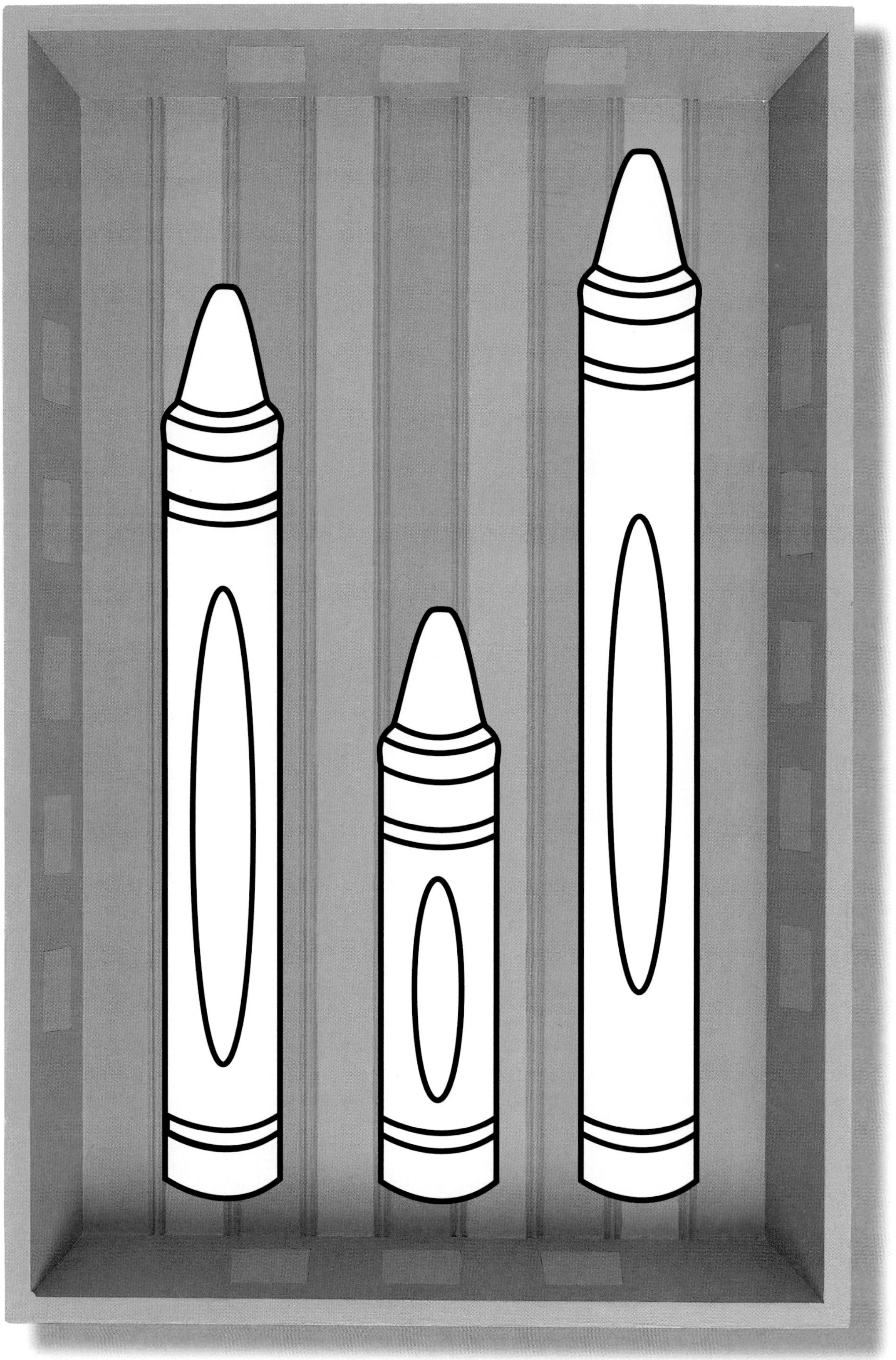

**Directions** Have children put the crayons in order by coloring the tallest red and the shortest blue.

**Home Activity** Have your child show you how to put a knife, fork, and spoon in order from shortest to longest on a tabletop.



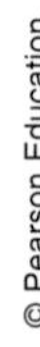

Name ______________________________

# Measuring Length

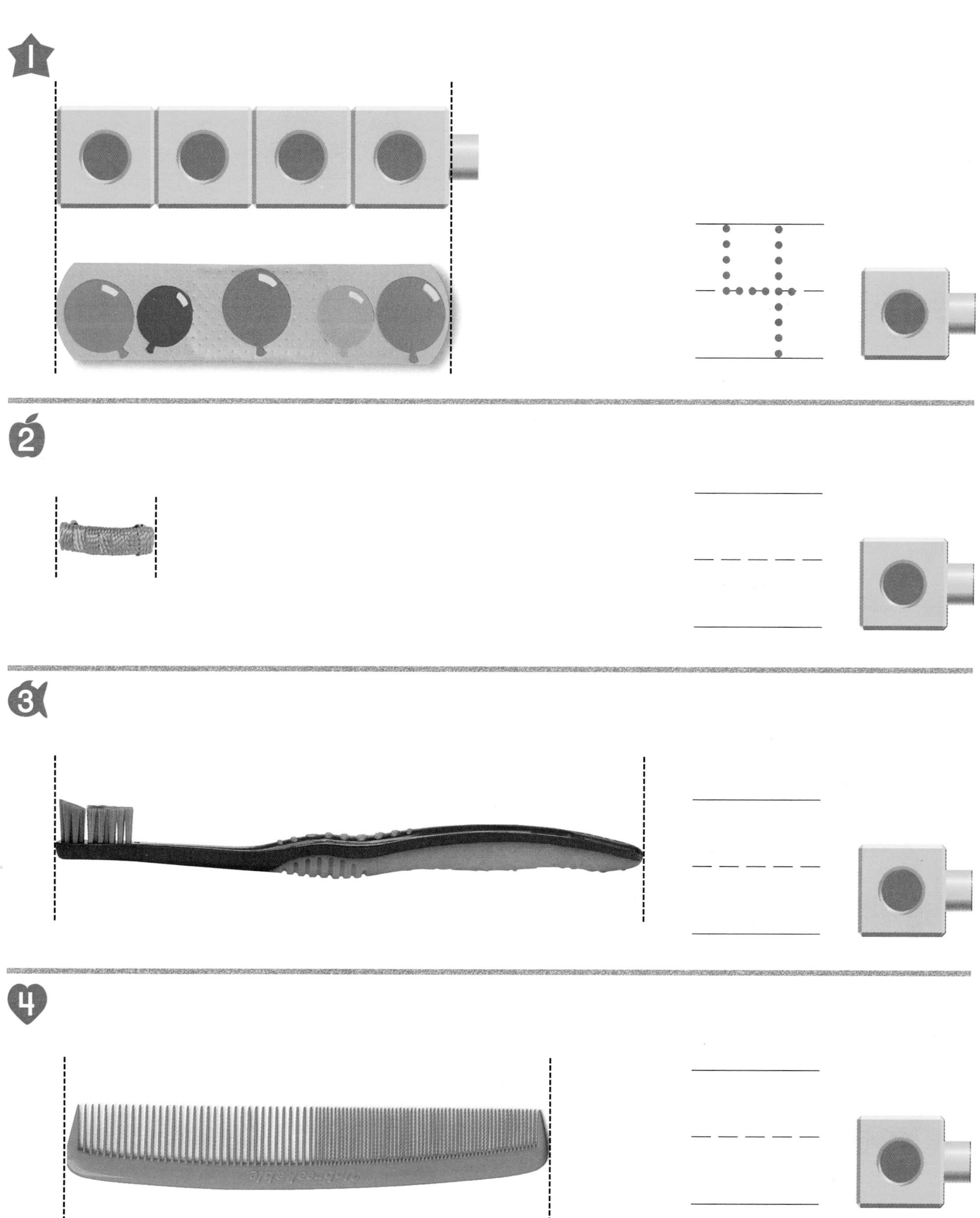

**Directions** Have children use cubes to measure the length of each object. Ask children to record how many cubes long each object is.

5

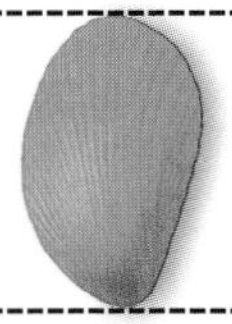

6

7

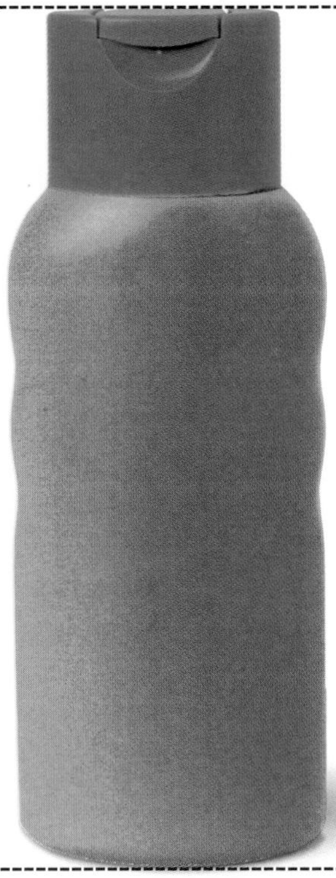

8

9

10

**Directions** Have children use cubes to measure the height of each object and record the number of cubes.

**Home Activity** Have your child measure the length of kitchen utensils using small objects such as toothpicks, paper clips, or twist ties to measure.

Name ________________________

# Estimating and Measuring Length

| Estimate | | Measure |
|---|---|---|
| 1. 2 paper clips |  | 3 paper clips |
| 2. ___ paper clips | 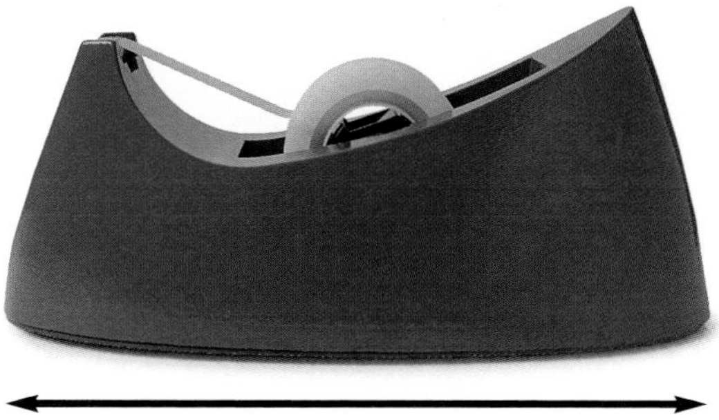 | ___ paper clips |
| 3. ___ paper clips | 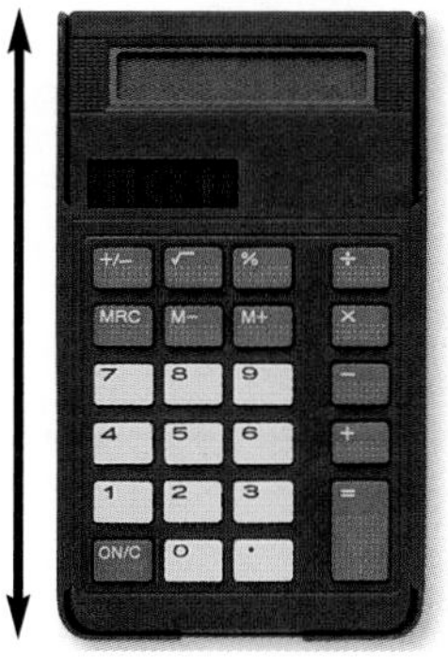 | ___ paper clips |
| 4. ___ paper clips | 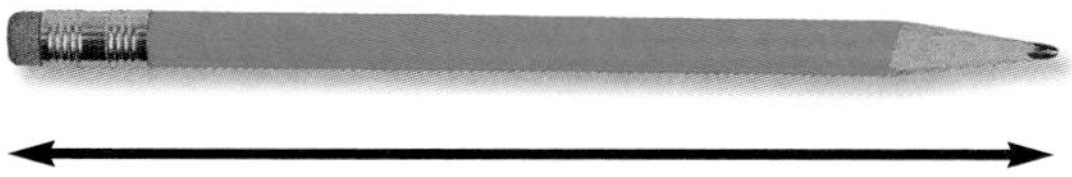 | ___ paper clips |

**Directions** Have children find each object in the classroom, estimate how many paper clips long it is, and record the estimate. Then have children measure and record the actual length.

| Estimate | | Measure |
|---|---|---|
| 5 | 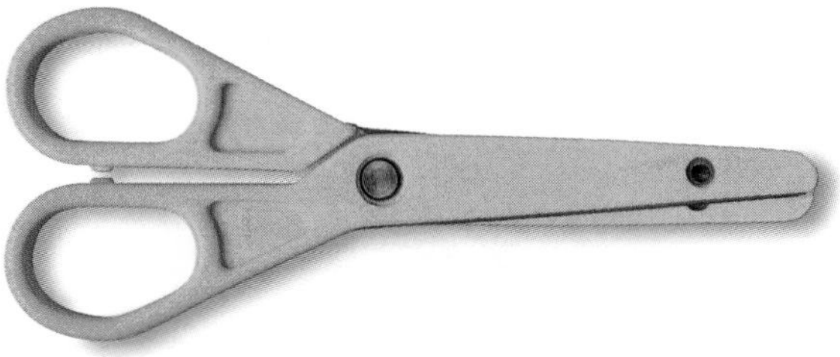 | |
| 6 | 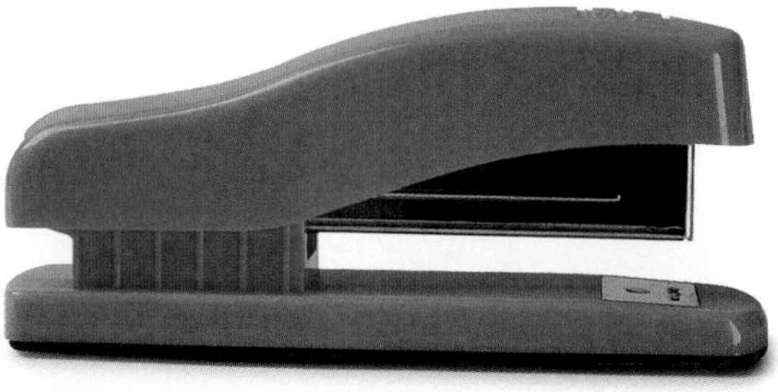 | |
| 7 |  | |
| 8 | | |

**Directions** Have children estimate and record the length of each object in paper clips. Then have children measure and record the actual length.

**Home Activity** Have your child show you how to estimate and measure how long a pencil is, using dried beans or cereal pieces to measure.

Name ______________________

PROBLEM-SOLVING STRATEGY

# Try, Check, and Revise

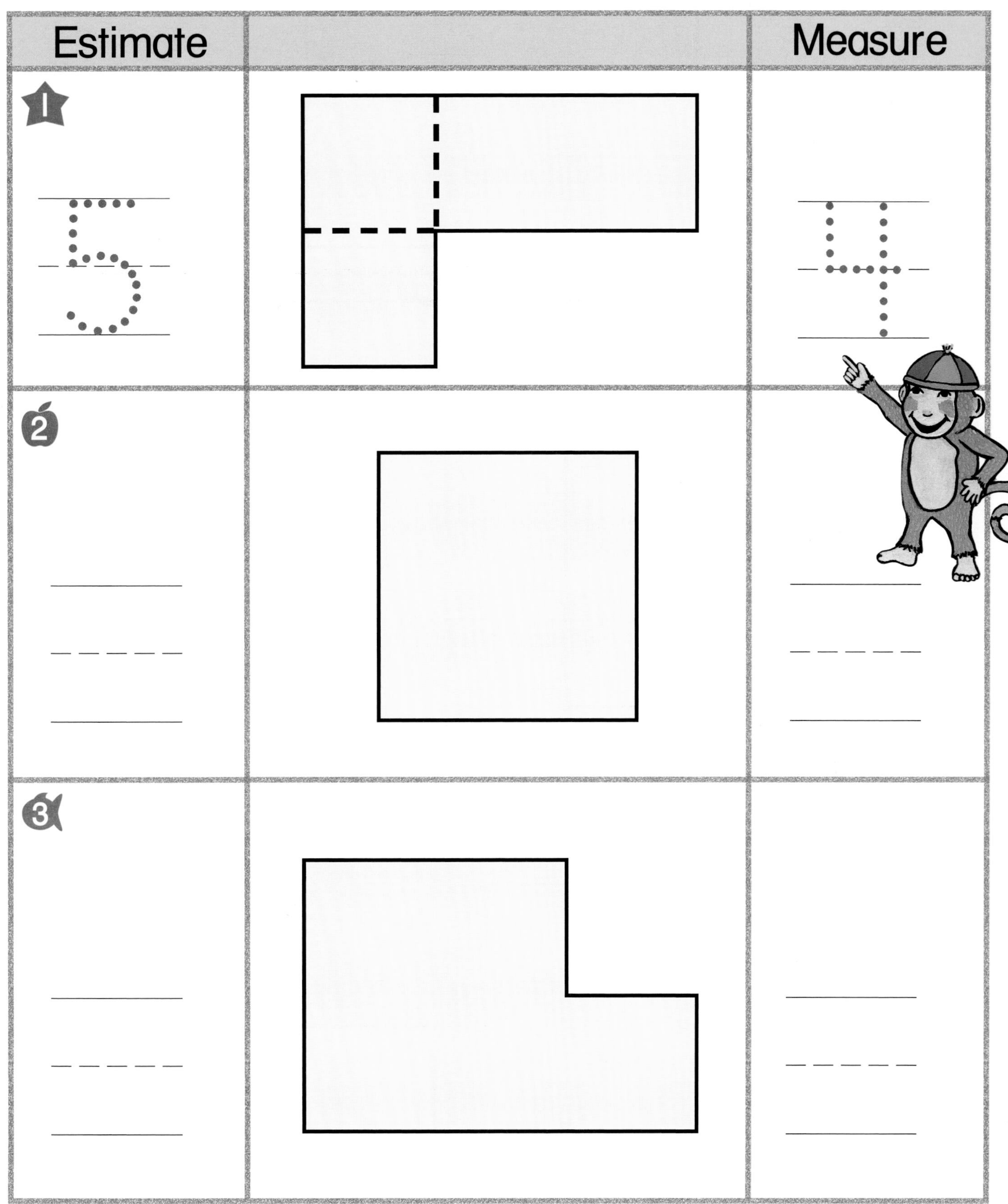


**Directions** Have children estimate how many tiles they will need to cover each shape and record the number. Then have children cover each shape with tiles, count the tiles, and record the number.

| Estimate | | Measure |
|---|---|---|
| 4 | | |
| 5 | 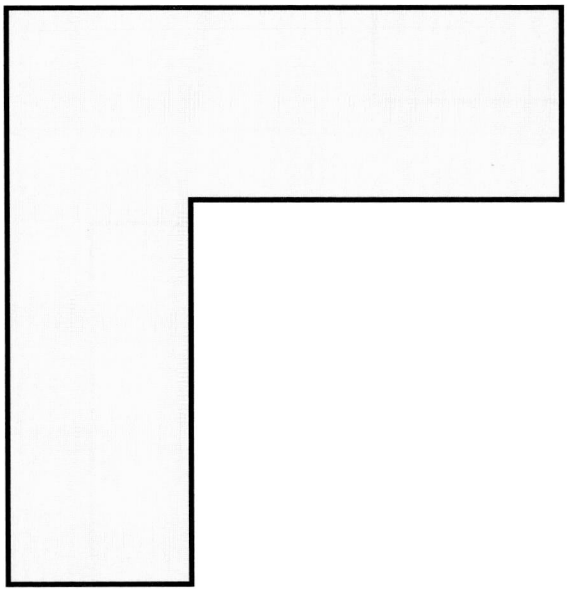 | |
| 6 | 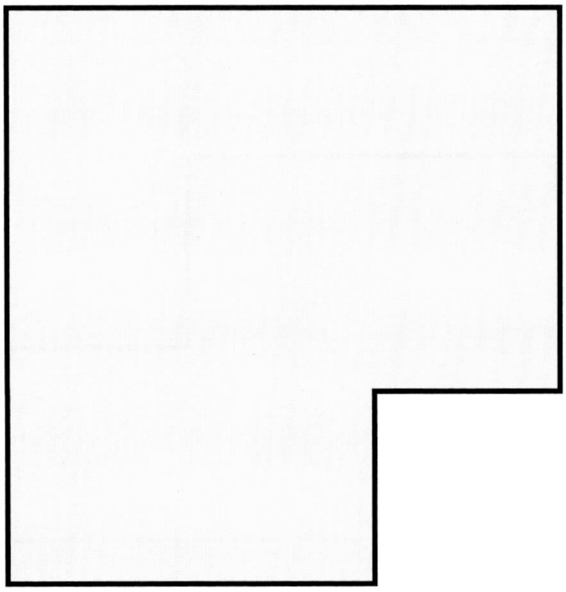 | |

**Directions** For each exercise have children estimate the number of tiles they will need to cover the shape and record the number. Then have children cover the shape with tiles and record the number used.

**Home Activity** Help your child cover the top of a rectangular table with napkins or paper squares. Ask him or her to count the napkins or paper squares and tell how many.

Name ______________________________

# Comparing and Ordering by Capacity

**Directions** In each exercise have children compare the objects by coloring the one that can hold more red and the one that can hold less blue.

7

8

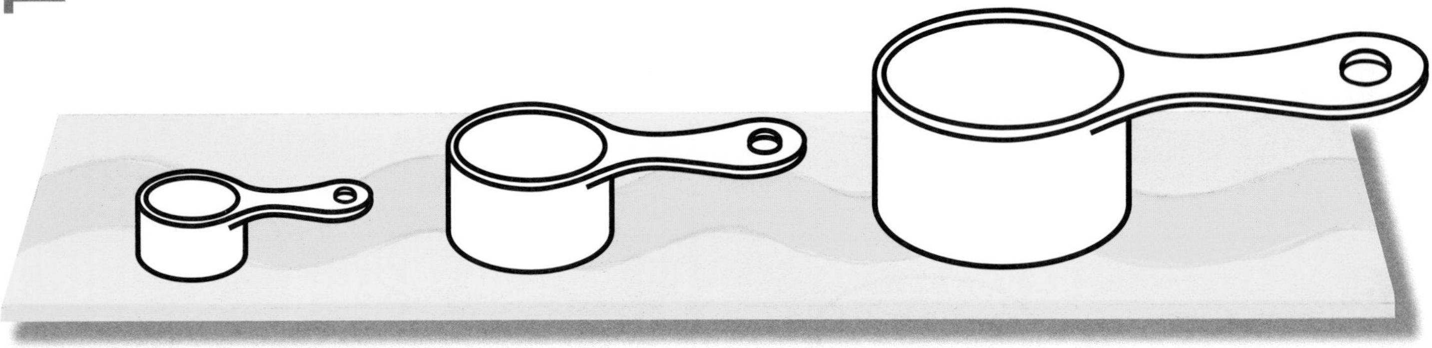

9

10

**Directions** Have children order the containers in each exercise by coloring the one that can hold the most red and the one that can hold the least blue.

**Home Activity** Help your child find three cups of different sizes and experiment to determine which holds the least number of ice cubes.

Name ______________________

# Estimating and Measuring Capacity

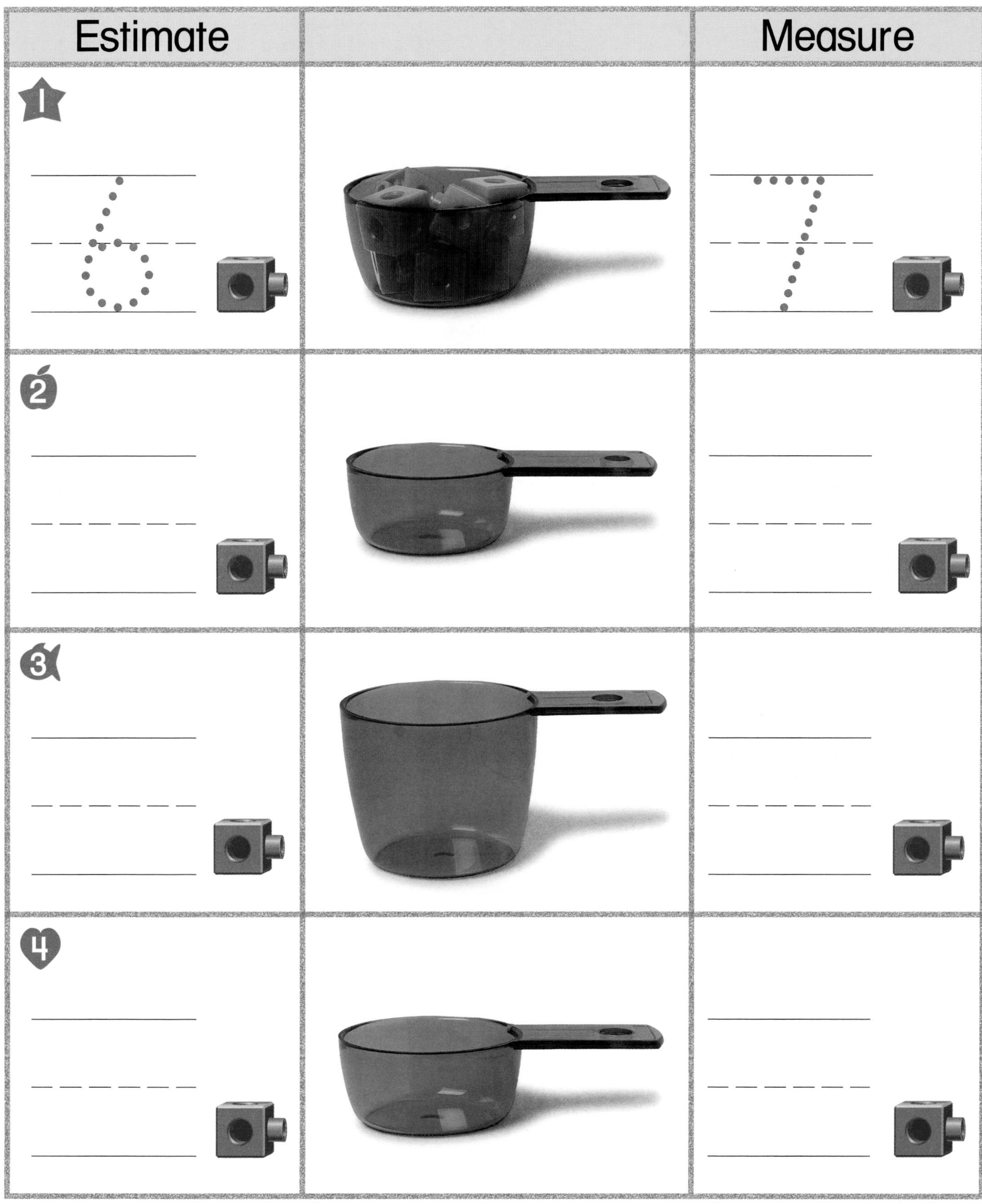


**Directions** If available, use containers like the measuring cups pictured. Have children estimate how many cubes would fill each container and record the number. Then have children fill each container with cubes and record the number used.

| Estimate | | Measure |
|---|---|---|
| 5 | | |
| 6 | | |
| 7 | | |
| 8 | | |

**Directions** Provide containers like those pictured. Have children estimate and record the capacity of each container in cubes. Then have children measure and record the actual capacity.

**Home Activity** Ask your child to estimate how many dried beans or cereal pieces will fill a tablespoon and then fill the tablespoon to find the number.

Name ____________________

# Comparing and Ordering by Weight

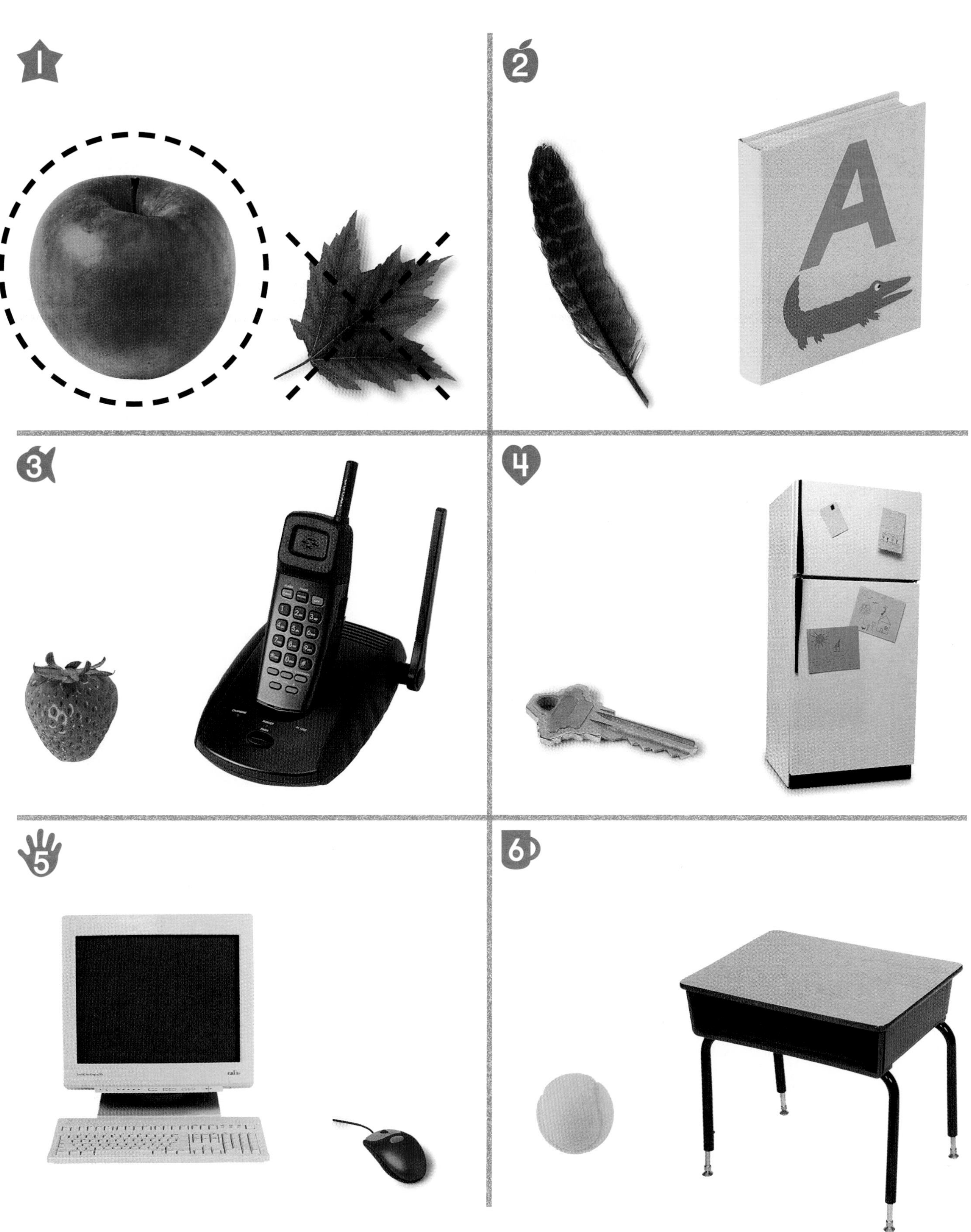

**Directions** In each exercise have children compare the objects by circling the heavier object and marking an *X* on the lighter object.

7

8

9

10

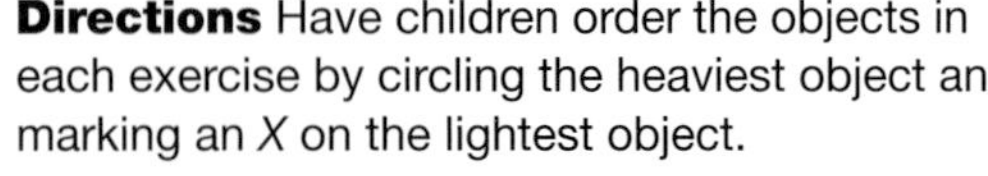
**Directions** Have children order the objects in each exercise by circling the heaviest object and marking an *X* on the lightest object.

**Home Activity** Help your child put three objects of different weights, such as a penny, a small toy, and a thick book, in order from lightest to heaviest.

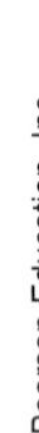

Name ___________________

# Estimating and Measuring Weight

| Estimate | | Measure |
|---|---|---|
| 1   2 | | 3 |
| 2 | | |
| 3 | | |
| 4 | | |

**Directions** Provide small objects like those pictured. Have children estimate the weight of each object in cubes. Then have children use a balance to weigh each object and record the number of cubes.

| Estimate | | Measure |
|---|---|---|
| 5 |  | |
| 6 |  | |
| 7 |  | |
| 8 |  | |

**Directions** Provide objects like those pictured. Have children estimate the weight of each object in cubes, weigh the object, and record the number of cubes.

**Home Activity** Have your child hold an object in each hand and tell you which weighs more or whether the objects weigh about the same.

Name ___________________________________

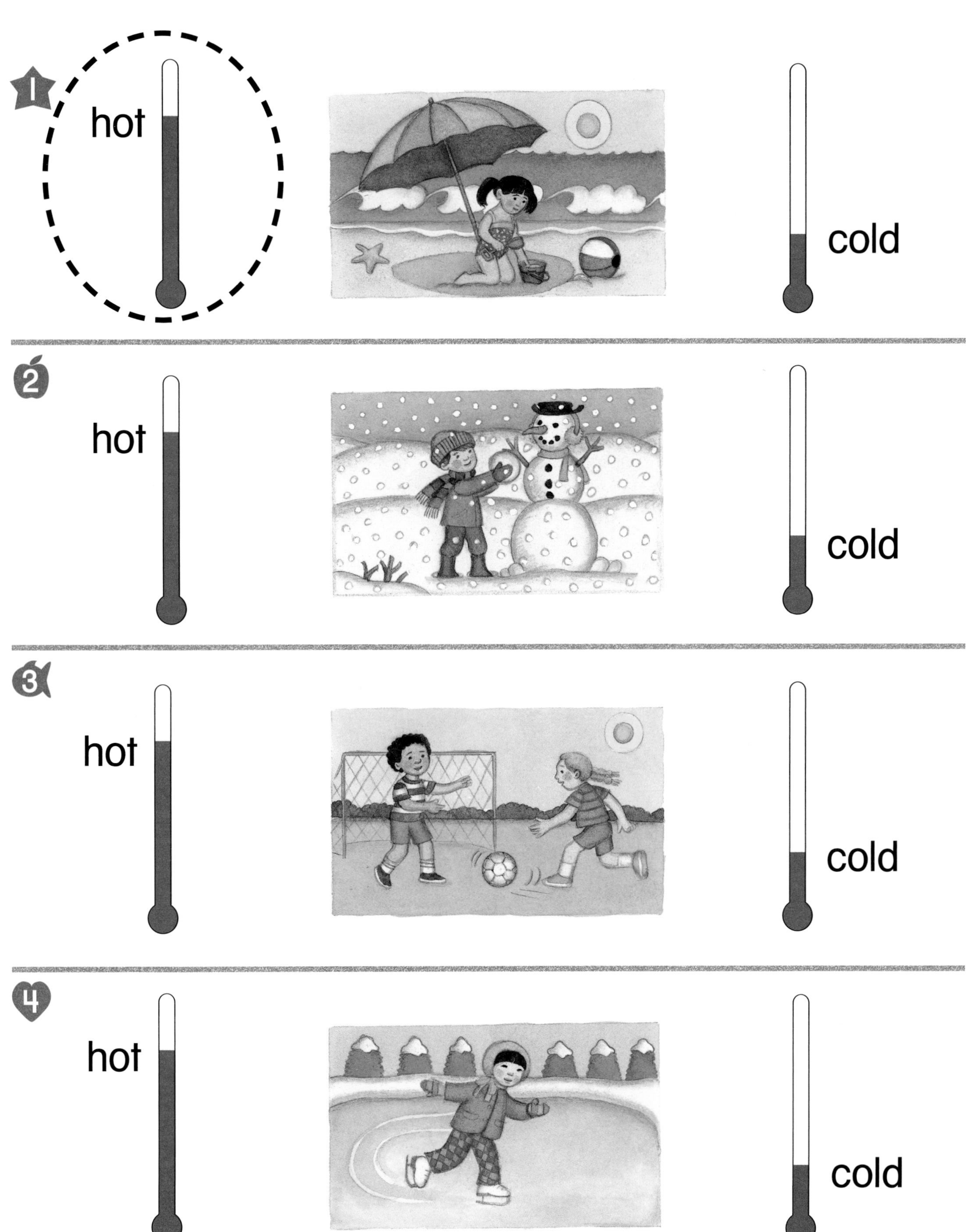


**Directions** In each exercise have children circle the thermometer showing the temperature that might go with picture.

5

hot

cold

6

hot

cold

7

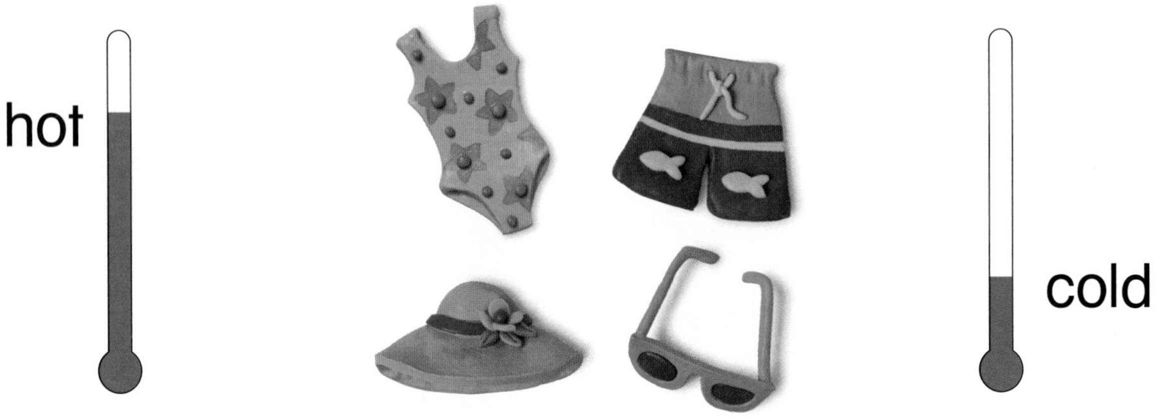

hot

cold

8

hot

cold

**Directions** In each exercise have children circle the thermometer showing the temperature when they might wear the items of clothing.

**Home Activity** Have your child look through magazines for pictures of outdoor scenes showing cold and hot weather.

Name ____________________

Dorling Kindersley

**Directions** Tell children that Amy wants to pour her cereal into the other containers. Which containers will not hold the cereal? Have children mark an *X* on the containers that will hold less than her bowl of cereal does.

**Directions** Tell children that Joey is helping his mother move things. Which things will be harder to move? Have children circle the objects that are heavier than the chair.

**Home Activity** Talk with your child about the pictures on these two pages. Have your child tell you how he or she solved problems to complete the pages.

Name ____________________

**Test**

1

2

3

| Estimate | | Measure |
|---|---|---|
| 4 ______ ______ | | ______ ______ |

**Directions** Have children: 1. circle the tallest child and mark an *X* on the shortest; 2. circle the larger sign and mark an *X* on the smaller sign; 3. circle the longer string of beads and mark an *X* on the shorter one; 4. estimate and measure the ribbon's length in cubes and record the numbers.

5

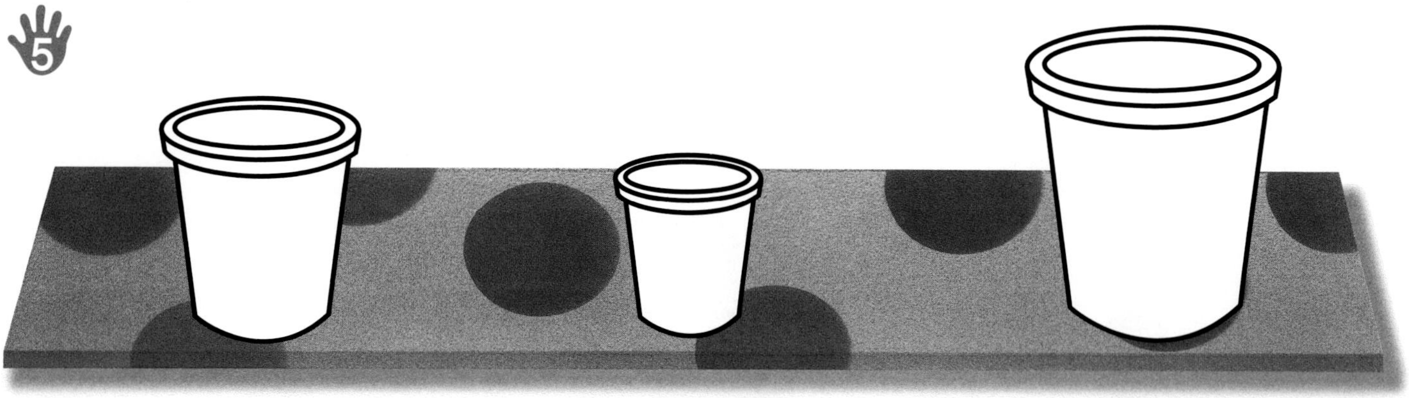

6

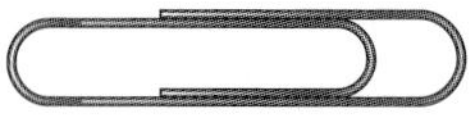

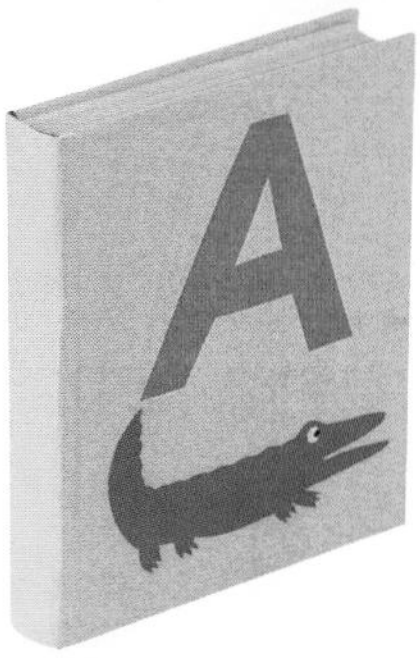

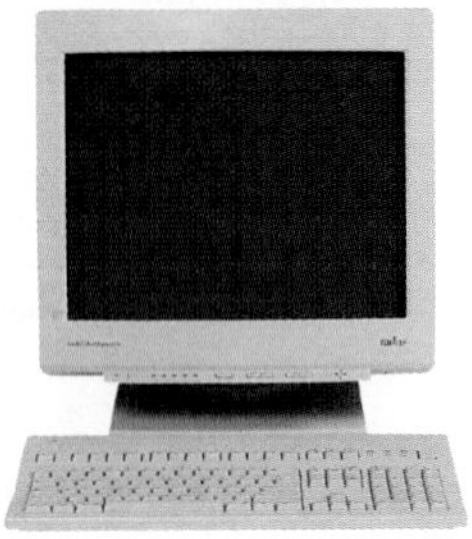

7

hot

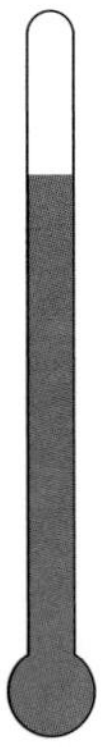

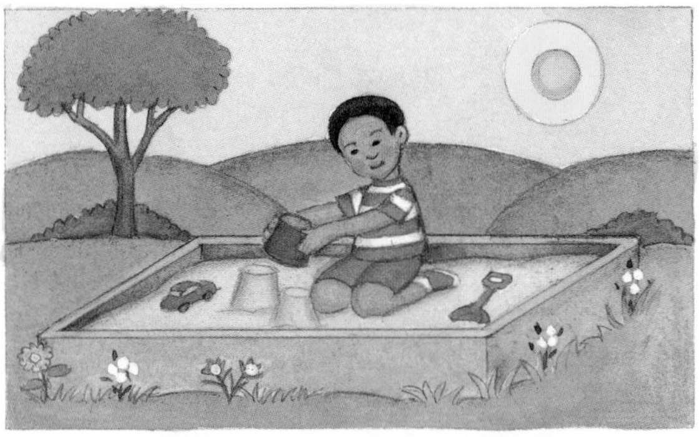

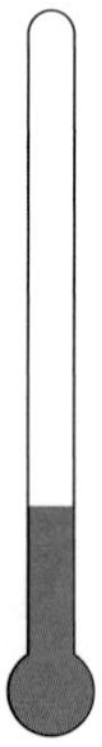

cold

| Estimate | | Measure |
|---|---|---|
| 8 |  | |

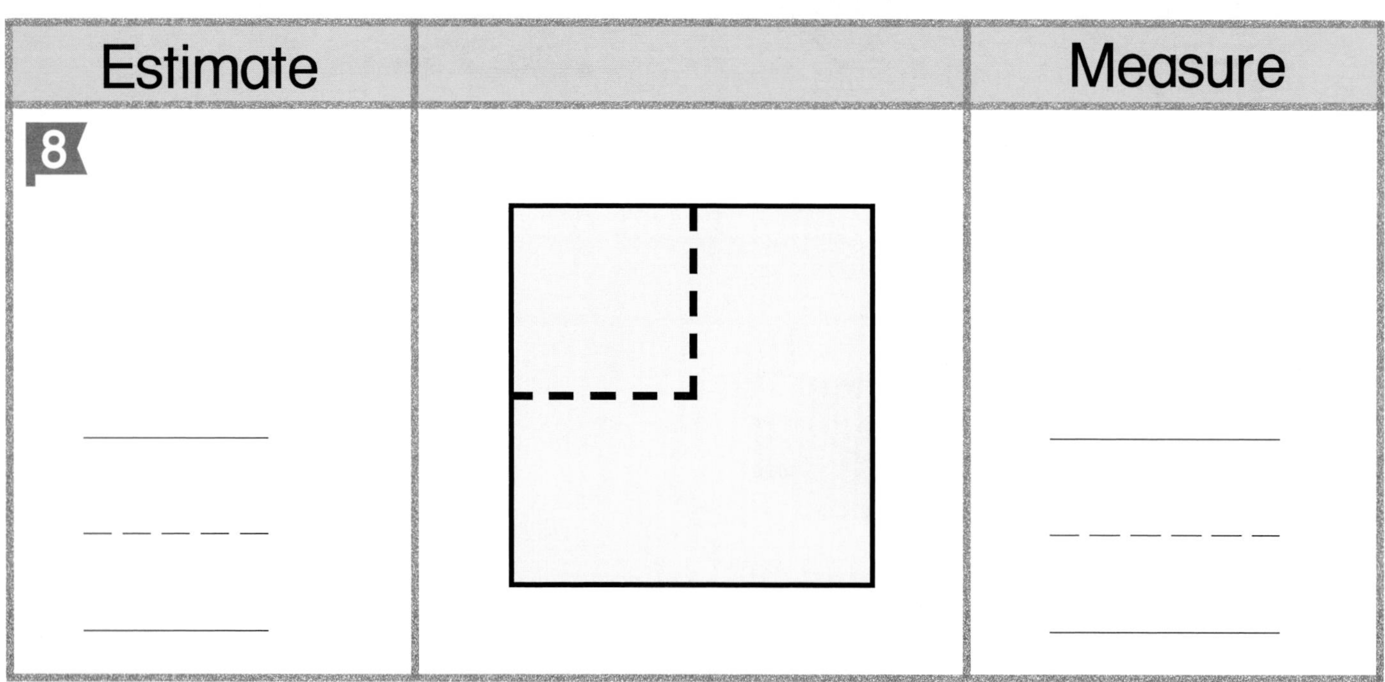

**Directions** Have children: 5. color the container that holds the most red and the one that holds the least blue; 6. circle the heaviest object and mark an *X* on the lightest; 7. circle the thermometer that shows the temperature that might go with the picture; 8. estimate and measure the number of tiles needed to cover the shape and record the numbers.

CHAPTER 7

## Time and Money

Read Together

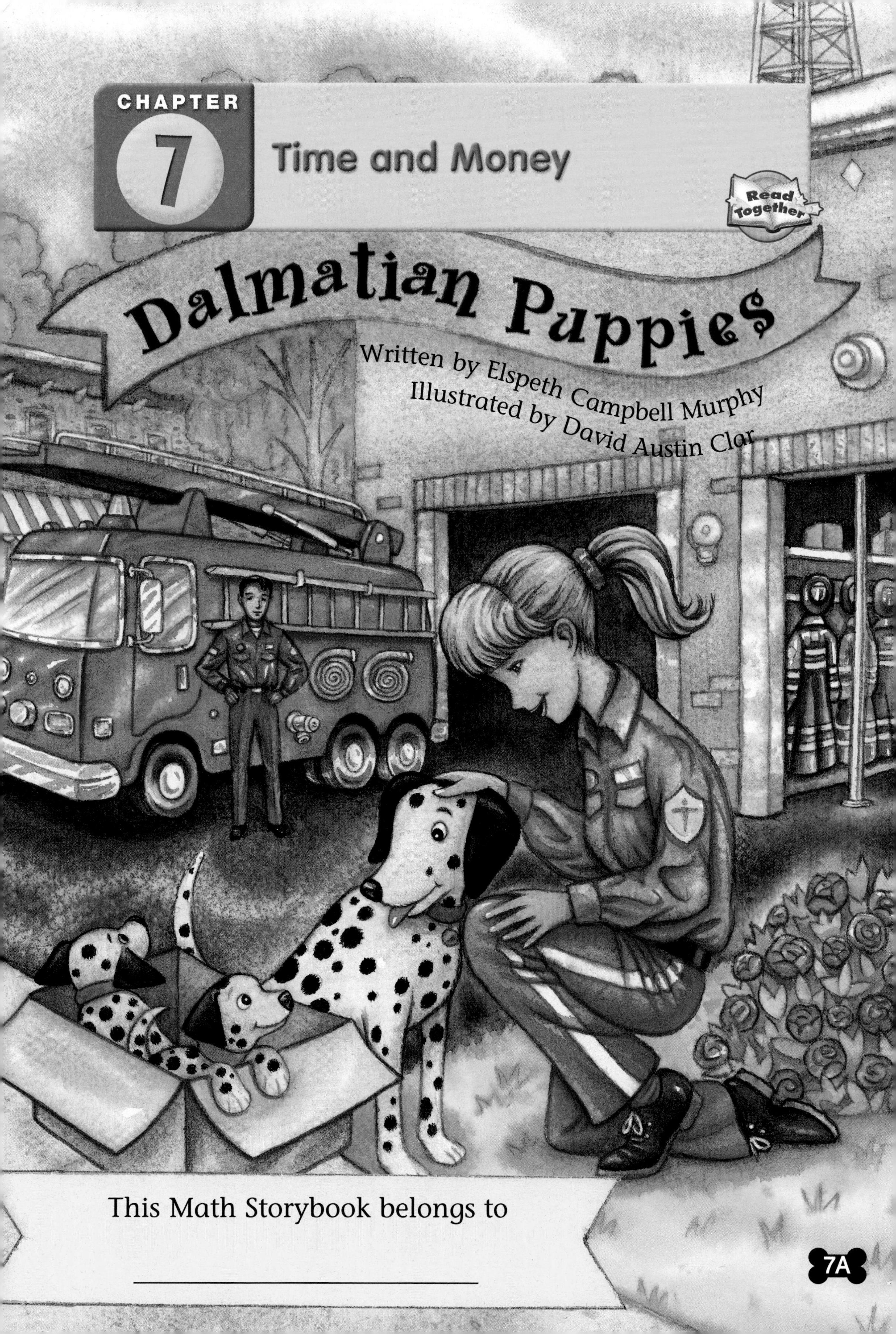

# Dalmatian Puppies

Written by Elspeth Campbell Murphy
Illustrated by David Austin Clar

This Math Storybook belongs to

______________________

Dalmatian puppies,
Come out to play!
Sunday,
Monday,
Any day.

Tuesday,
Wednesday,
Hip, hip, hooray!
Dalmatian puppies,
Lead the way!

Thursday,
Friday,
Saturday,
Every day is my favorite day

When Dalmatian puppies ...

Come out to play!

## Home-School Connection

Dear Family,

Today my class started Chapter 7, **Time and Money.** I will learn how to read a calendar, how to tell time, and how to count money. Here are some of the math words I will be learning and some things we can do to help me with my math.

Love,

_______________________________

### Math Activity to Do at Home

Play "What Time Is It?" Show 1:00 on a clock face and tell your child that when the big hand is on 12 and the little hand is on 1, it is 1 o'clock. Take turns showing 2:00 through 12:00. Talk about the difference between 2:00 "in the afternoon" and 2:00 "in the morning."

### Books to Read Together

Reading math stories reinforces concepts. Look for these titles in your local library:

***Just a Minute!***
By Teddy Slater
(Scholastic, 1996)

***Pigs Will Be Pigs: Fun with Math and Money***
By Amy Axelrod
(Simon and Schuster, 1998)

**Take It to the NET**
**More Activities**
www.scottforesman.com

### My New Math Words

**January**

| Sunday | Monday | Tuesday | Wednesday | Thursday | Friday | Saturday |
|---|---|---|---|---|---|---|
| | 1 | 2 | 3 | 4 | 5 | 6 |
| 7 | 8 | 9 | 10 | 11 | 12 | 13 |
| 14 | 15 | 16 | 17 | 18 | 19 | 20 |
| 21 | 22 | 23 | 24 | 25 | 26 | 27 |
| 28 | 29 | 30 | 31 | | | |

yesterday today tomorrow

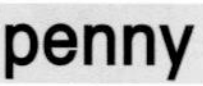

penny

nickel

dime

quarter

dollar

Name________________________________

# Dog Days

## What You Need

paper clip
pencil

## How to Play

1. Take turns spinning the spinner.
2. Say the name of the day you land on.
3. Do what the puppy is doing.
4. Put a check mark (√) on the chart.
5. The first player to check off all 7 days of the week is the winner.

| | Players | |
|---|---|---|
| | 1 | 2 |
| Sunday | | |
| Monday | | |
| Tuesday | | |
| Wednesday | | |
| Thursday | | |
| Friday | | |
| Saturday | | |

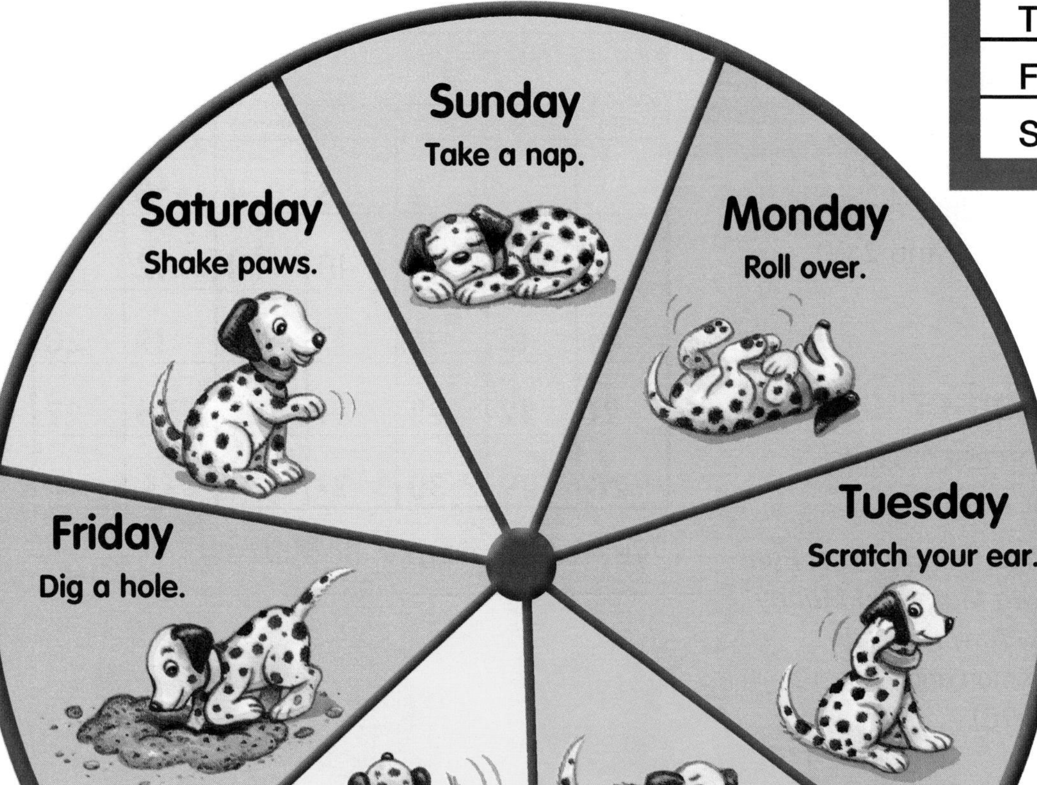

Name ______________________________

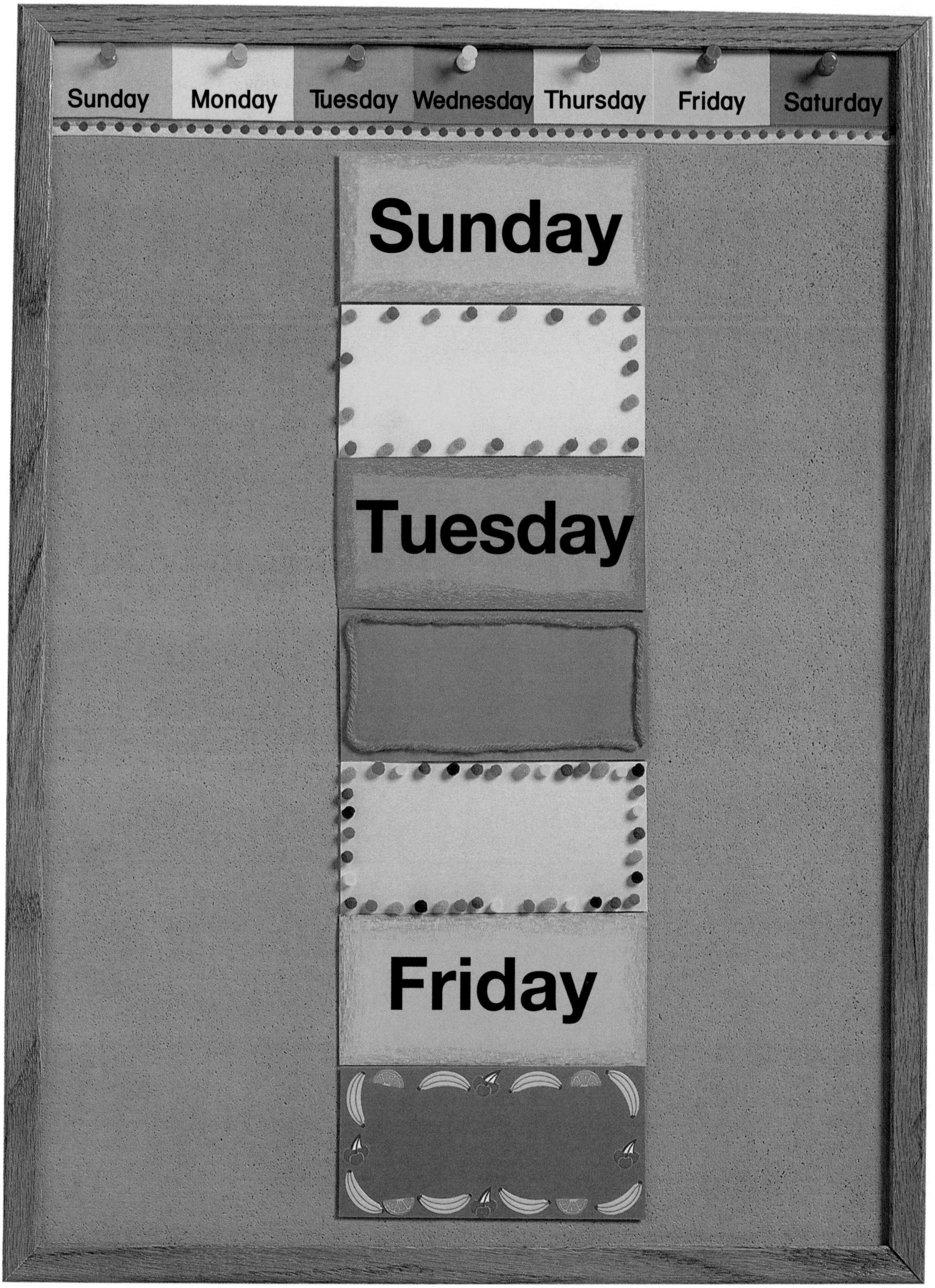

# Days of the Week

Sunday | Monday | Tuesday | Wednesday | Thursday | Friday | Saturday

Sunday

Tuesday

Friday

Saturday

Thursday

Wednesday

Monday

**Directions** Have children cut out the names of the missing days and glue them in the correct blank spaces.

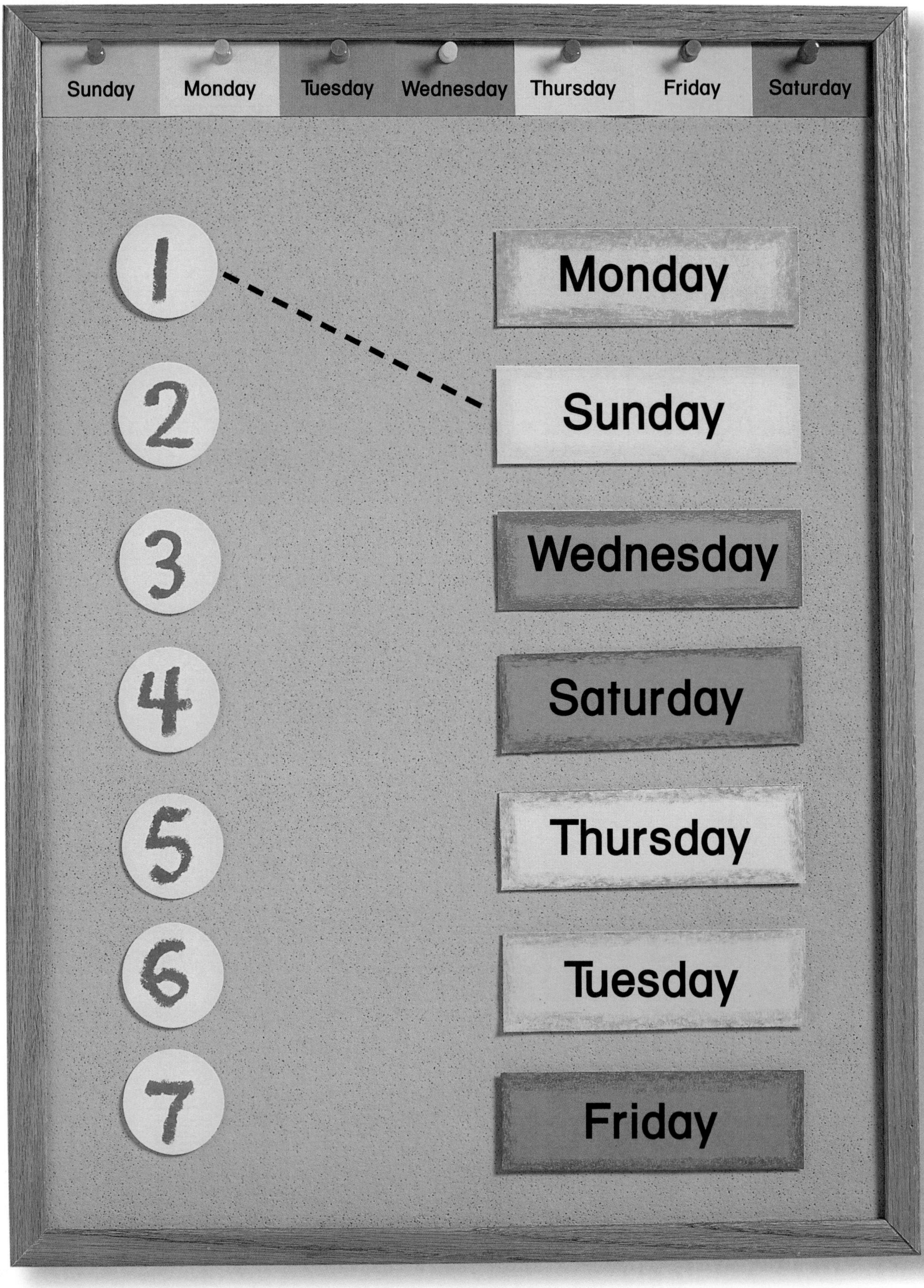

Sunday Monday Tuesday Wednesday Thursday Friday Saturday

| | |
|---|---|
| 1 | Monday |
| 2 | Sunday |
| 3 | Wednesday |
| 4 | Saturday |
| 5 | Thursday |
| 6 | Tuesday |
| 7 | Friday |

**Directions** Have children put the days of the week in order by drawing a line to match each day with a number.

**Home Activity** Show your child a calendar and have her or him point to the day of the week that is today.

Name ___________________________________

# Yesterday, Today, and Tomorrow

Sunday

Monday

Tuesday

Wednesday

Thursday

Friday

Saturday

**Directions** Have children draw a line from *today* to the correct day of the week. Have them trace the word for that day. Repeat for *yesterday* and *tomorrow*.

| Sunday | Monday | Tuesday | Wednesday | Thursday | Friday | Saturday |
|---|---|---|---|---|---|---|

# Yesterday was

________________________________.

# Today is

________________________________.

# Tomorrow will be

________________________________.

**Directions** Have children circle the day of the week that is today, mark an *X* on the day that was yesterday, and underline the day that will be tomorrow. Then have children complete the sentences.

**Home Activity** Have your child point out where he or she wrote what day today is. Read the sentences together.

Name ______________________________

| January | February | March |
| --- | --- | --- |
| April | May | June |
| July | August | September |
| October | November | December |

2

**Directions** In Exercise 1 have children circle the first month and mark an *X* on the last month. In Exercise 2 ask children to circle the picture that shows winter and mark an *X* on the picture that shows summer.

3

January

February

March

April

May

June

July

August

September

October

November

December

**Directions** In Exercise 3 have children circle their birth month and mark an *X* on the current month. In Exercise 4 have them circle their favorite season.

**Home Activity** Using a calendar, talk with your child about what is special about each month for your family.

Name ____________________



# March

| Sunday | Monday | Tuesday | Wednesday | Thursday | Friday | Saturday |
|---|---|---|---|---|---|---|
| | 1 | 2 | 3 | 4 | 5 | 6 |
| 7 | 8 | 9 | 10 | 11 | 12 | 13 |
| 14 | 15 | 16 | 17 | 18 | 19 | 20 |
| 21 | 22 | 23 | 24 | 25 | 26 | 27 |
| 28 | 29 | 30 | 31 | | | |

**Directions** Have children color the name of the month purple, the days of the week yellow, and these dates green: March 1, 10, 16, 25, and 30.

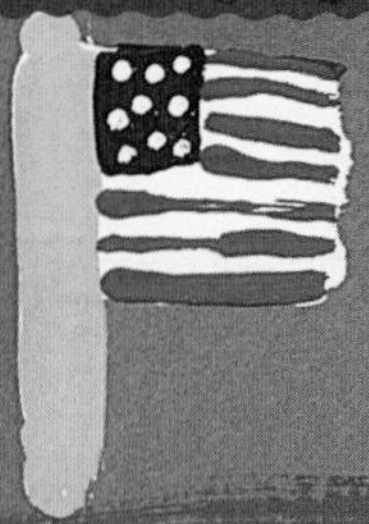

# July

| Sunday | Monday | Tuesday | Wednesday | Thursday | Friday | Saturday |
|---|---|---|---|---|---|---|
| | | | | 1 | 2 | 3 |
| 4 | | | 7 | | 9 | |
| 11 | | 13 | | 15 | | 17 |
| | 19 | 20 | | | 23 | |
| 25 | | | 28 | 29 | | 31 |

**Directions** Have children trace the name of the month and the dates on the calendar. Then have children fill in the missing dates and circle the days of the week.

**Home Activity** Show your child the calendar for this month and together circle any important dates.

Name ______________________________

**Directions** In each exercise have children draw a line to the picture that shows what happens next.

4

1

3

2

5

6

**Directions** In each exercise have children order the events from first to last using the numbers 1, 2, and 3.

**Home Activity** Talk with your child about 3 steps in getting ready for bed at night, such as: turn off the lights, brush teeth, get into bed. Ask your child to tell what happens first, next and last.

Name ________________________________________

# Time of Day

**Directions** In each exercise have children show the time of day by drawing a sun for day and a moon for evening or night.

3

morning

afternoon

evening

**Directions** In each exercise have children match the picture with the symbol for morning, afternoon, or evening.

**Home Activity** Have your child tell you what is happening in each picture on the page.

Name ______________________________

# Telling Time on an Analog Clock

3 o'clock

_____ o'clock

3

_____ o'clock

4

_____ o'clock

5

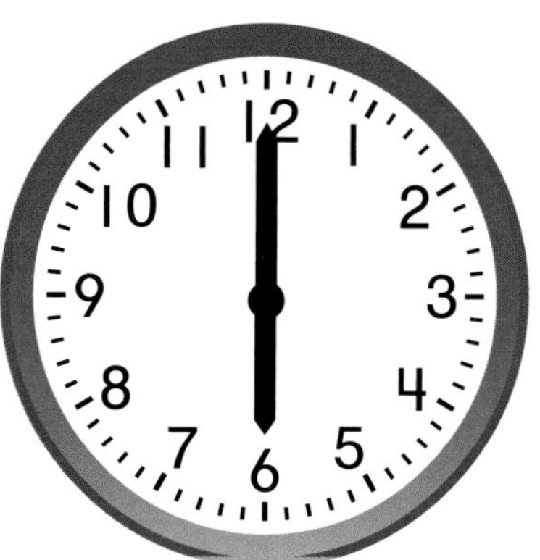

_____ o'clock

6

_____ o'clock

**Directions** Have children write the time shown on each clock.

5

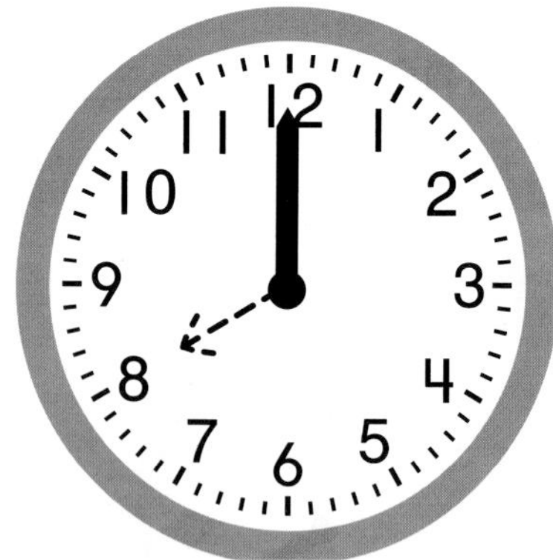

8 o'clock

6

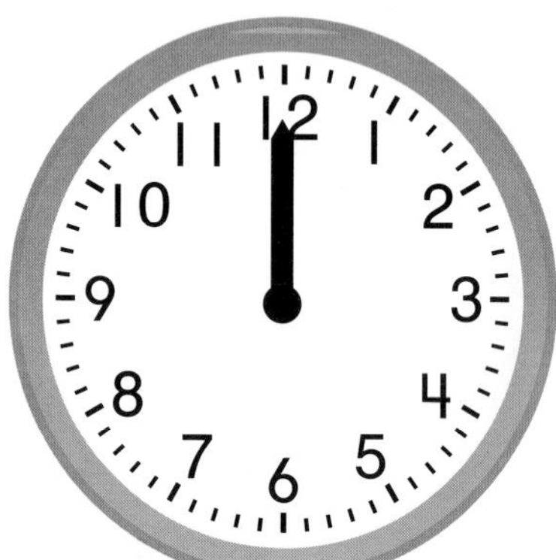

10 o'clock

7

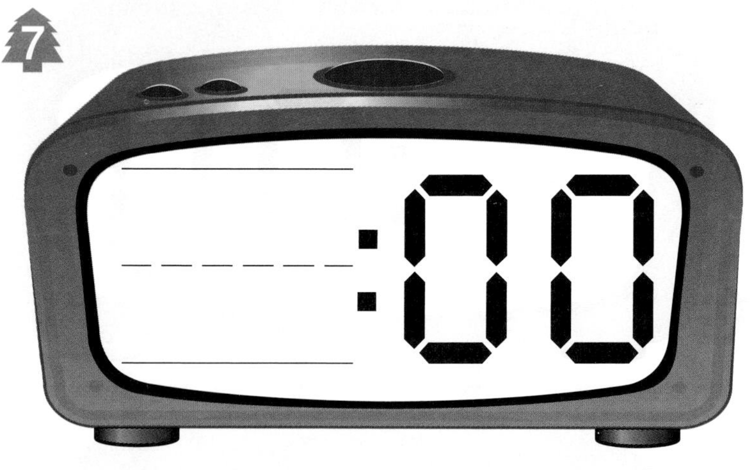

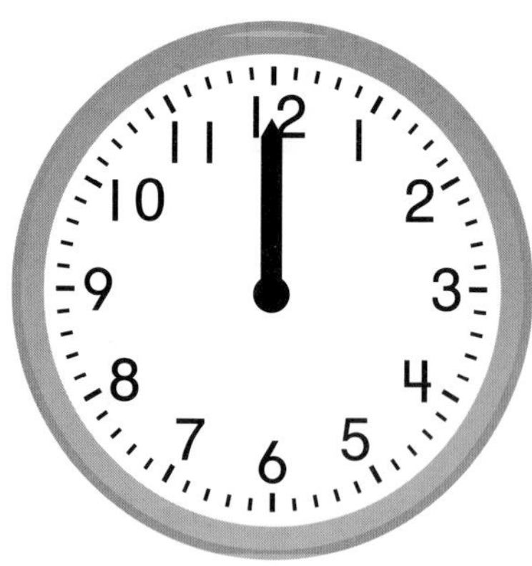

_____ o'clock

**Directions** In Exercises 5–6, have children show the time by recording a number on the digital clock and drawing the hour hand on the analog clock. In Exercise 7, have children choose a time, record it on the write-on line, and show the time on the digital and analog clocks.

**Home Activity** Ask your child to tell you how to tell time on a digital clock and on a clock with hands.

Name ___________________________________________

# More Time and Less Time

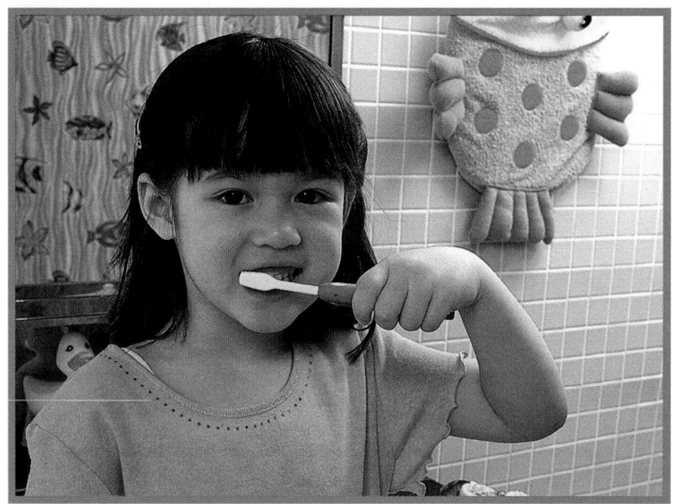

2

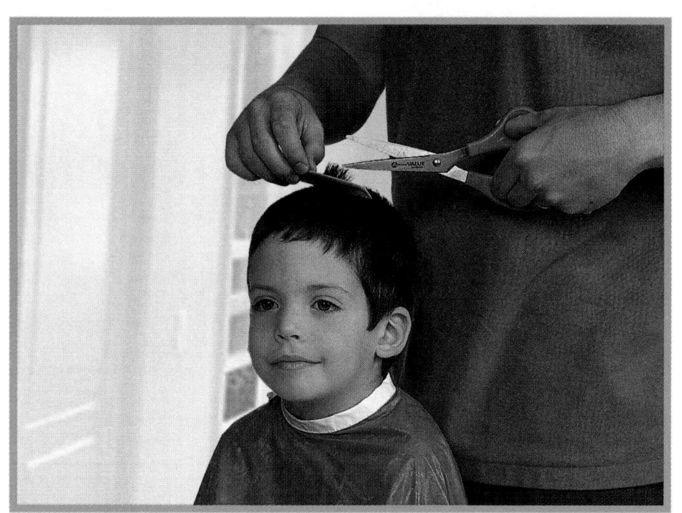

3

**Directions** In each exercise have children circle the event that takes more time.

4

**Directions** In each exercise have children mark an *X* on the event that takes less time.

**Home Activity** Ask your child whether it takes more time to flip a light switch or to eat breakfast.

Name ____________________ 



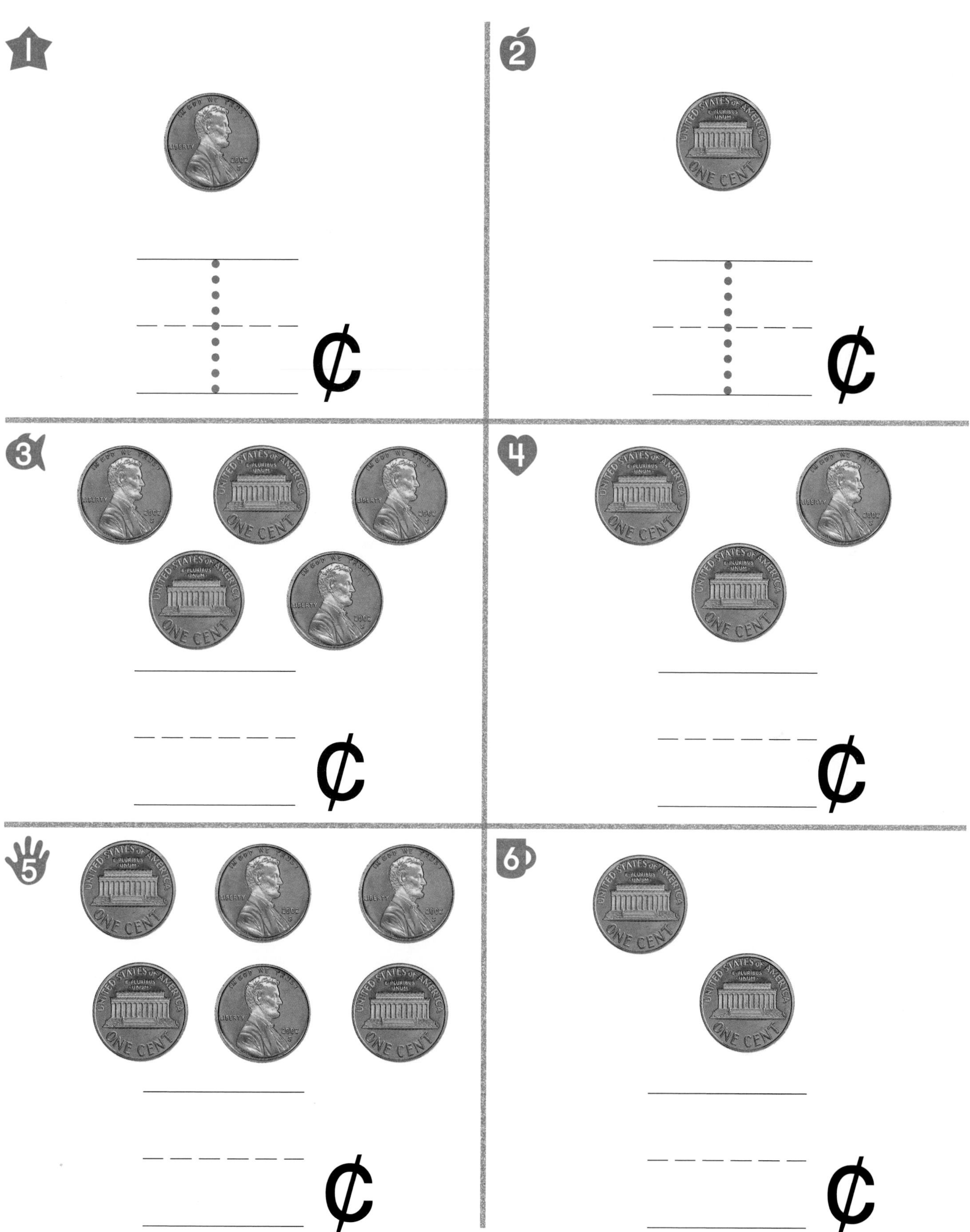

**Directions** In each exercise have children count the pennies and record the value by writing the number of cents.

7¢ 2¢ 8¢

8

6¢ 4¢ 7¢

9

7¢ 2¢ 5¢

10

8¢ 5¢ 10¢

**Directions** In each exercise have children count the pennies and circle the correct value.

**Home Activity** Give your child some pennies and ask, How many cents?

Name ______________________________ **Nickel**

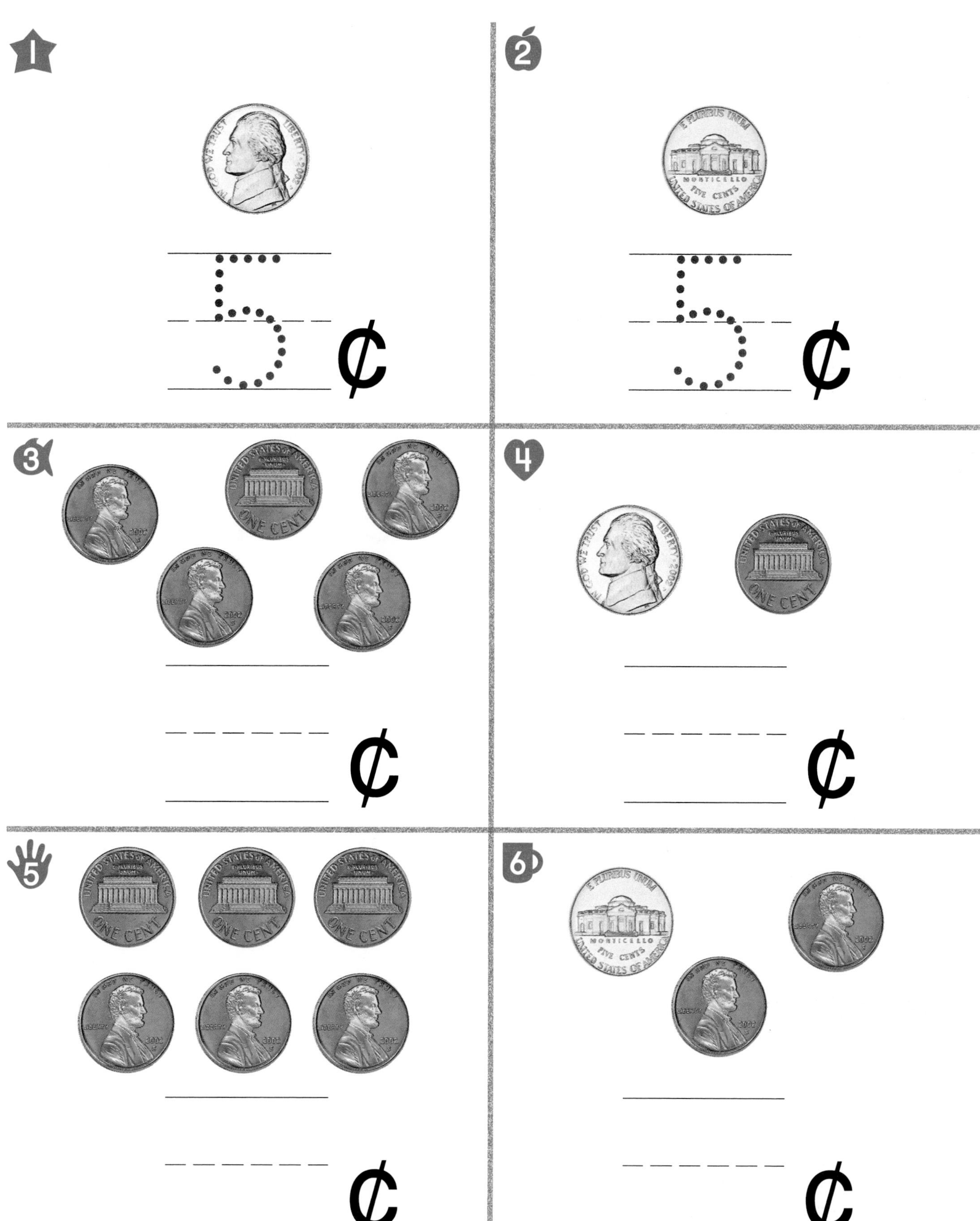

**Directions** Have children figure out the value of each group of coins and record the number of cents.

4¢ 8¢ 5¢

8

5¢ 4¢ 9¢

10¢ 5¢ 6¢

10

5¢ 10¢ 9¢

**Directions** Have children figure out the value of each group of coins and circle the correct number of cents.

**Home Activity** Give your child 9 pennies and a nickel. Have him or her show 9¢ in two different ways.

Name ____________________ **Dime**

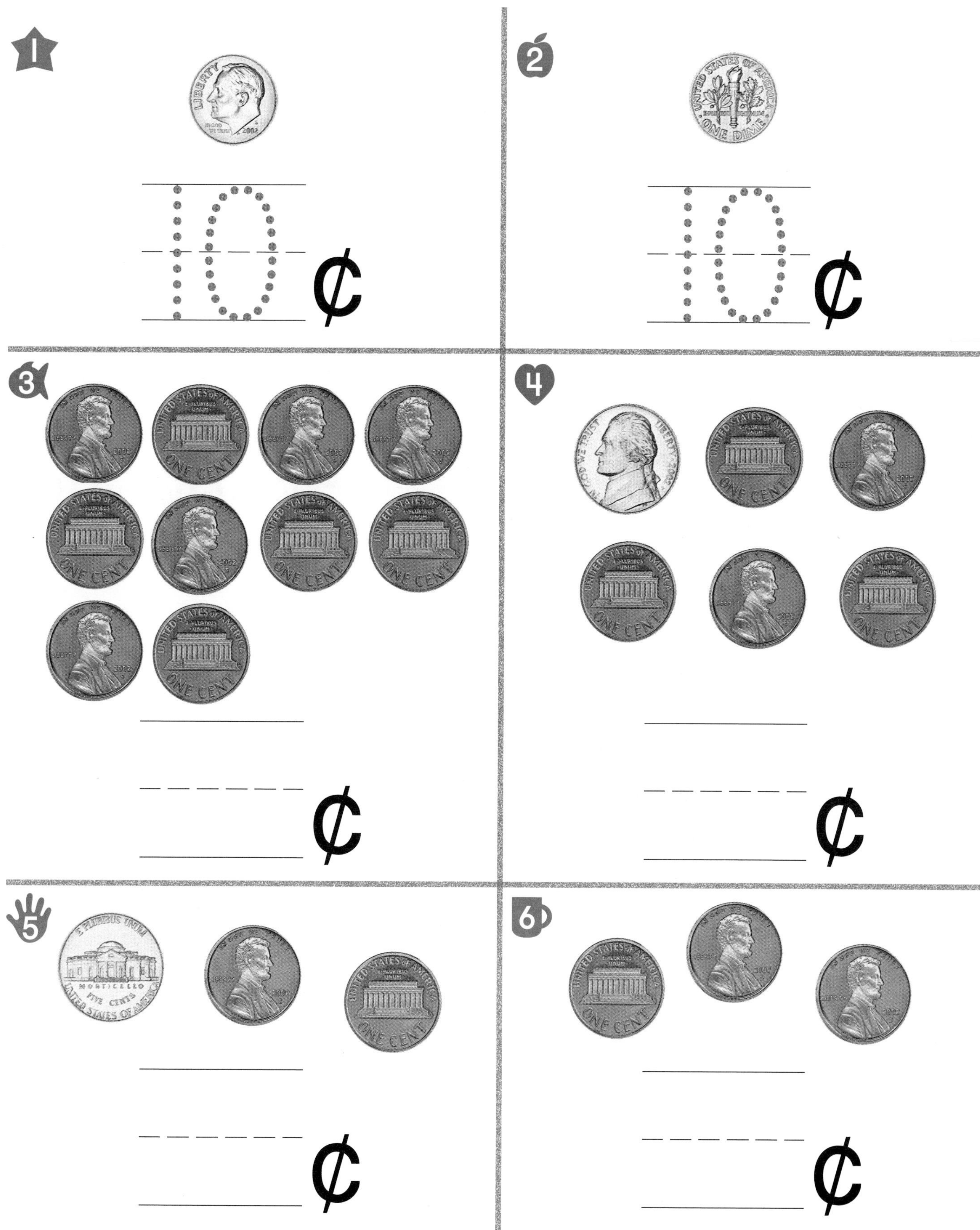

**Directions** Have children figure out the value of each group of coins and record the number of cents.

1¢ 5¢ 10¢

4¢ 8¢ 5¢

9¢ 5¢ 2¢

1¢ 10¢ 5¢

**Directions** Have children figure out the value of each group of coins and circle the correct number of cents.

**Home Activity** Give your child nickels and pennies to show 10¢ in different ways.

Name ______________________

1

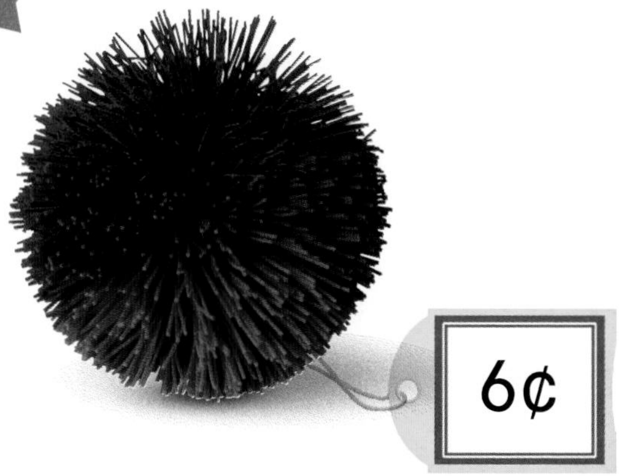

6¢

N P

2

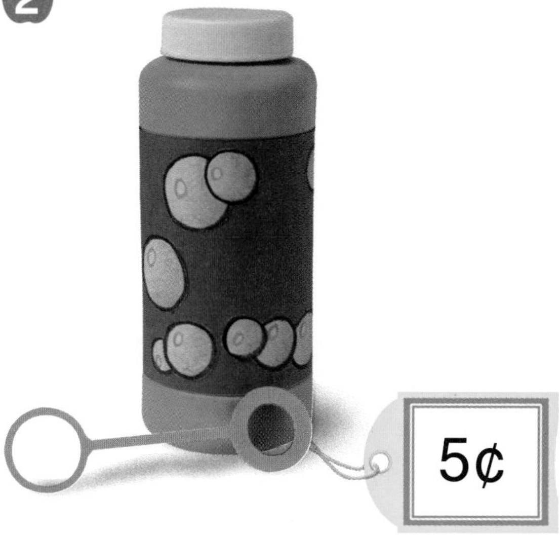

5¢

3

10¢

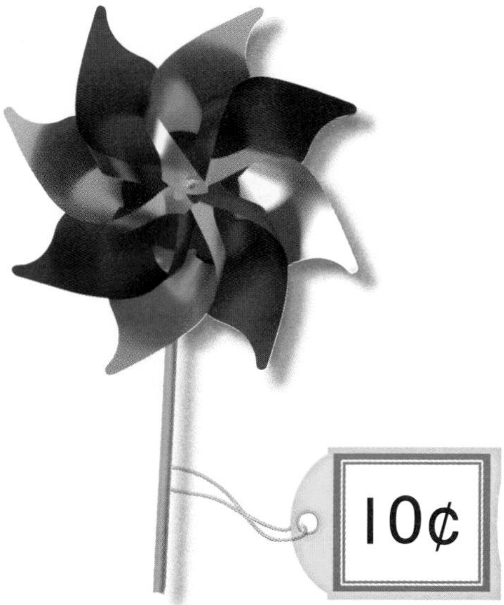

**Directions** Give children coins. Have them show the value of each item in different ways and then draw pictures of coins to show the value in one way.

4

12¢

5

7¢

6

9¢

**Directions** Give children coins. Have them show the value of each item in different ways and then draw pictures of coins to show the value in one way.

**Home Activity** Give your child a dime, 2 nickels, and 10 pennies. Have her or him show 10¢ in different ways.

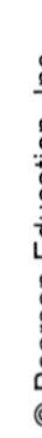

Name ______________________________

# Quarter and Dollar

**Directions** In each exercise have children identify the coins or bills on the left and circle the coin or bill on the right that belongs in the group.

**Directions** In each exercise have children identify the coins or bills on the left and circle the coin or bill on the right that belongs in the group.

**Home Activity** Give your child a penny, a nickel, a dime, a quarter, and a dollar bill. Have him or her describe them by talking about their color, size, shape, and other features.

Name ________________________________

# Comparing Values

1

2

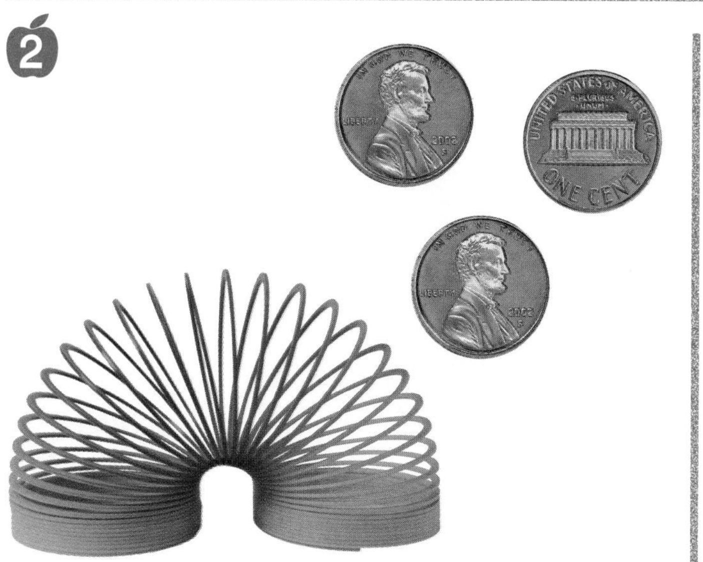

**Directions** Have children circle the item that costs more in each exercise.

4

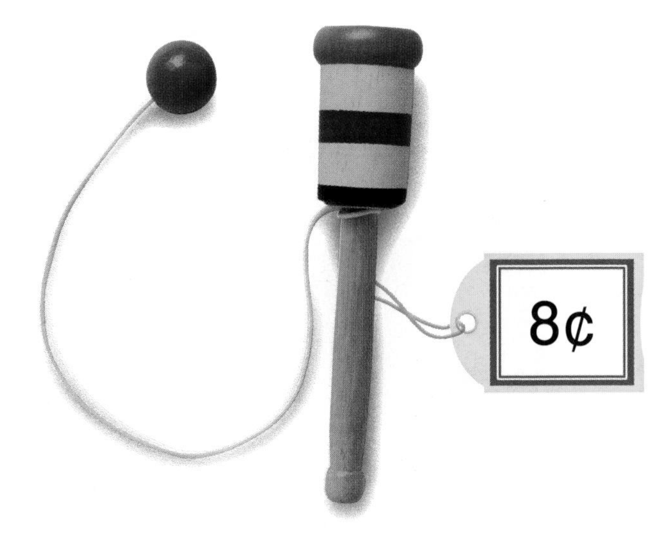


5

6

**Directions** Have children mark an *X* on the item that costs less in each exercise.

**Home Activity** Show your child 2 groups of coins and ask him or her to tell you which group has more.

Name ______________________



# Time to Play

**Directions** Tell children that some friends came to the park at 10 o'clock. Ask children to circle the clock that shows that time. Then have children draw a line under the time that the friends had lunch and mark an *X* on the time that the friends left the park. Talk about the activities shown and the time of year.

# Flea Market

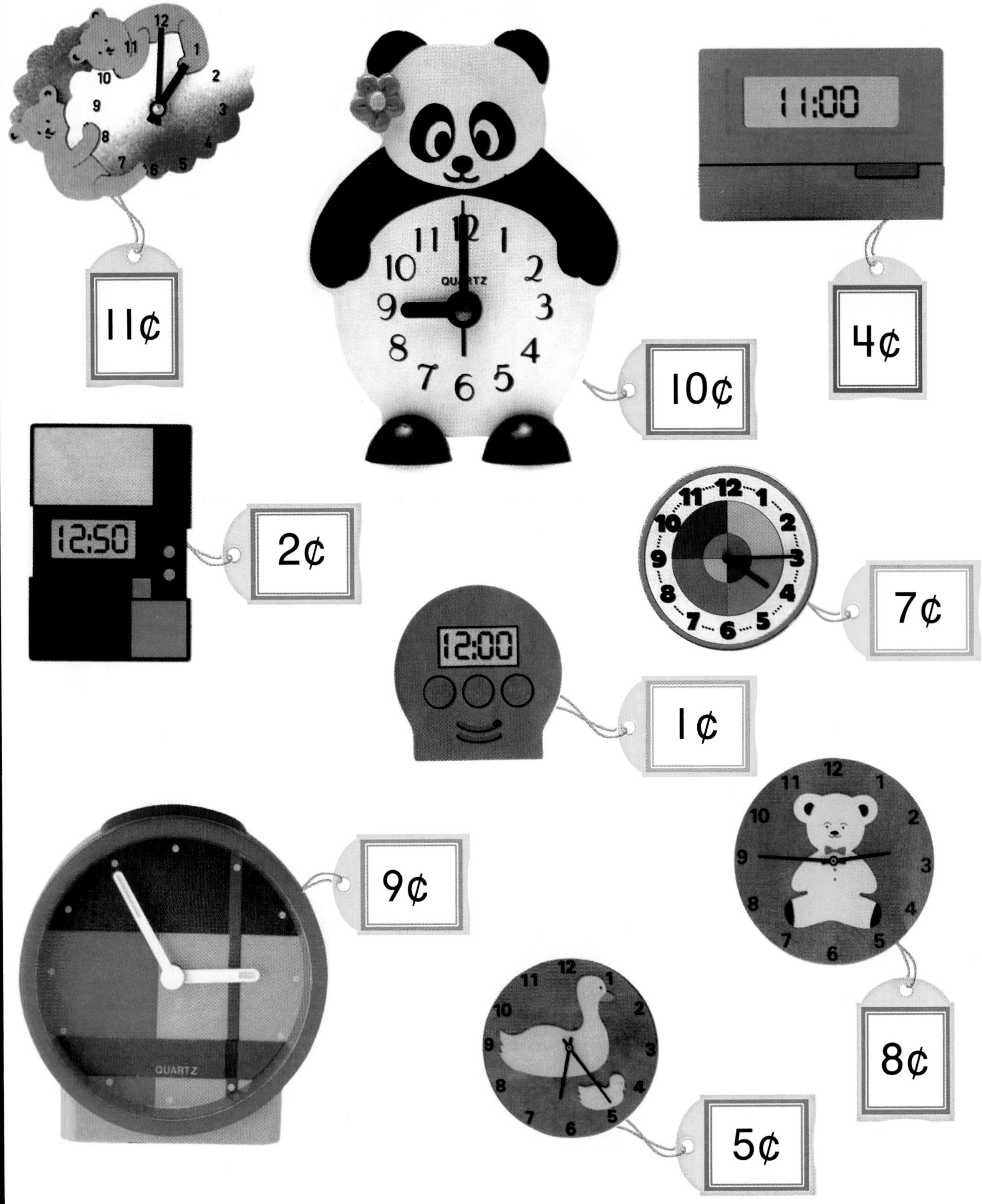

11¢

10¢

4¢

2¢

7¢

1¢

9¢

8¢

5¢

**Directions** Have children talk about the clocks for sale at the flea market. Then have children circle the clocks they could buy using only 1 coin.

**Home Activity** Talk with your child about the pictures on these two pages. Have your child tell you how he or she solved problems to complete the pages.

Name ____________________

Test

# March

| Sunday | Monday | Tuesday | Wednesday | Thursday | Friday | Saturday |
|---|---|---|---|---|---|---|
| | | 1 | 2 | 3 | 4 | 5 |
| 6 | 7 | 8 | 9 | 10 | 11 | 12 |

**Directions** Have children: 1. circle the day of the week that is today, mark an *X* on the day that was yesterday, and color March 8 green; 2. write 1, 2, and 3 to order the events; 3. circle the coin that is worth 10¢ and mark an *X* on the coin that is worth 1¢.

4

:00

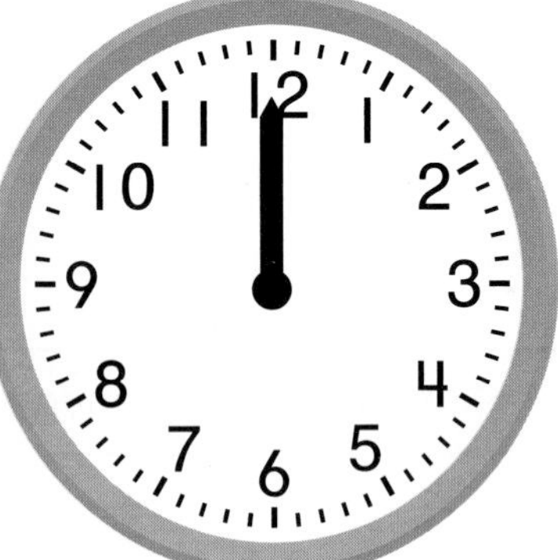


5 o'clock

5

¢

¢

6

**Directions** Have children: 4. show 5 o'clock by writing a number on the digital clock and drawing the hour hand on the analog clock; 5. write the value of the coins and circle the toy that costs more; 6. circle the picture that shows summer.

Geometry and Fractions

# Round Is a Pancake

Adapted from a Story by Joan Sullivan

Illustrated by Russell Benfanti

This Math Storybook belongs to

____________________________

**Round is a pancake.**
**Round is a plum.**

Round is a baseball.
Round is a drum.

**Round is a lemon.**
**Round is a lime.**

Round is a nickel.
Round is a dime.

**Look all around,
on the ground,
in the air.
You will find round things
EVERYWHERE!**

# Home-School Connection

Dear Family,

Today my class started Chapter 8, **Geometry and Fractions.** I will learn about solid shapes, plane shapes, and fractions. Here are some of the math words I will be learning and some things we can do to help me with my math.

Love,

______________________________

## Math Activity to Do at Home

Cut out magazine pictures of things such as a ball and a sandwich that are symmetrical, or have two parts that are alike. Then cut each of the pictures in half. Paste one half on paper. Ask your child to draw the missing half.

## Books to Read Together

Reading math stories reinforces concepts. Look for these titles in your local library:

***The Greedy Triangle***
By Marilyn Burns
(Scholastic, 1995)

***So Many Circles, So Many Squares***
By Tana Hoban
(Greenwillow Books, 1998)

**Take It to the NET**
**More Activities**
www.scottforesman.com

## My New Math Words

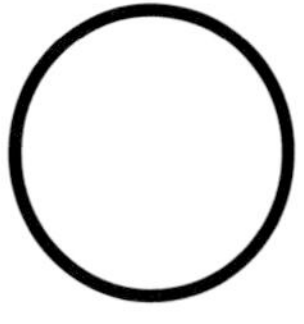

circle

rectangle

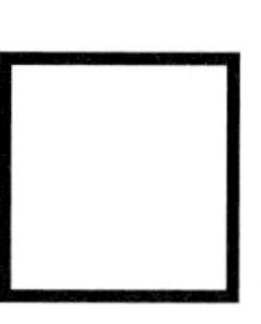

square

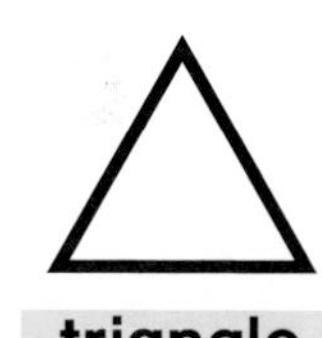

triangle

sphere

cylinder

cube

cone

Name________________________________ Practice Game

# Pancake Pathway

**What You Need**

paper clip
pencil
2 small game markers

## How to Play

1. Play with a partner.
2. Place your markers on START.
3. Take turns spinning the spinner.
4. Move your marker to the first picture that matches. Keep taking turns.
5. The first person to reach the table wins the game. Enjoy those pancakes! (And share some with your partner!)

START

FINISH

Name ________________________________

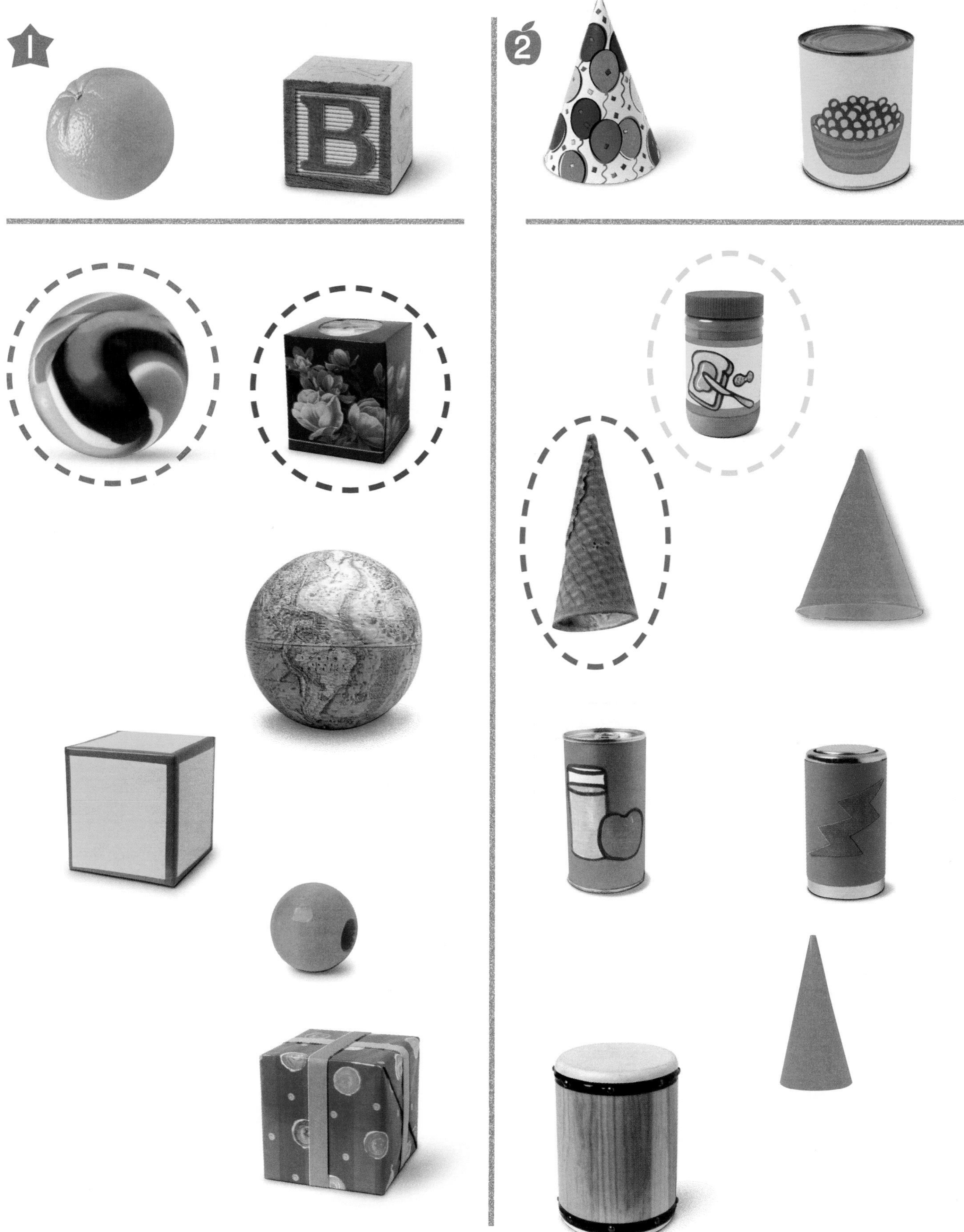


**Directions** Exercise 1: Have children use a red crayon to circle the shapes that match the orange at the top of the page and a blue crayon to circle the shapes that match the block. Exercise 2: Have children use a green crayon to circle the shapes that match the party hat and a yellow crayon to circle the shapes that match the can.

3

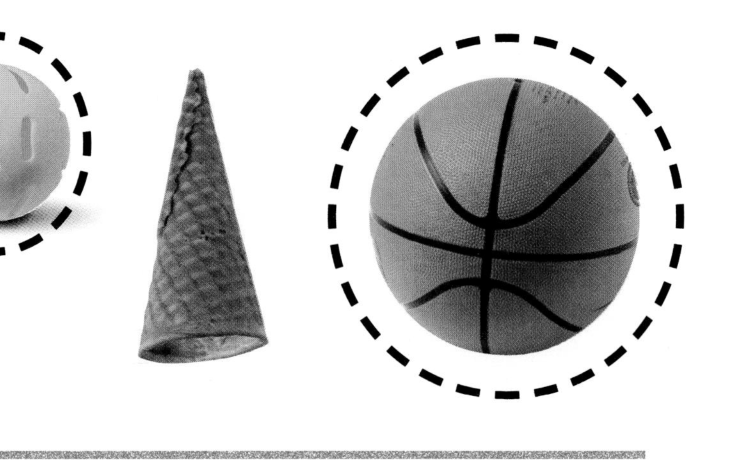

4

5

6

**Directions** In each exercise have children name the solid figure on the left and circle the everyday objects that have the same shape as the solid figure.

**Home Activity** Ask your child to point out different household objects that have the same shape as some of the objects pictured on the page.

Name ______________________________

# Comparing Solid Figures

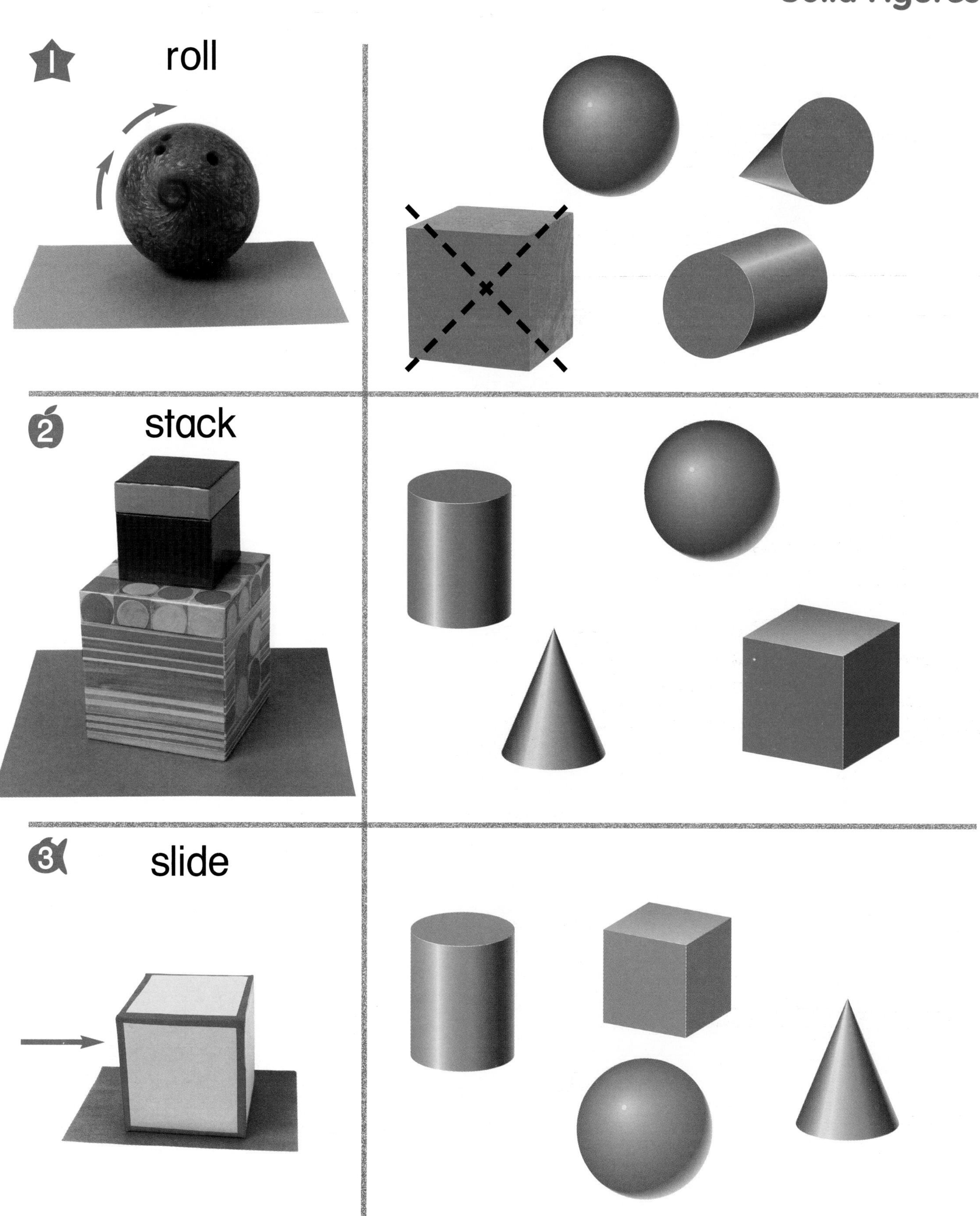


**Directions** Have children mark an *X* on the solid figure that does not roll in Exercise 1, the solid figures that do not stack in Exercise 2, and the solid figure that does not slide in Exercise 3.

4

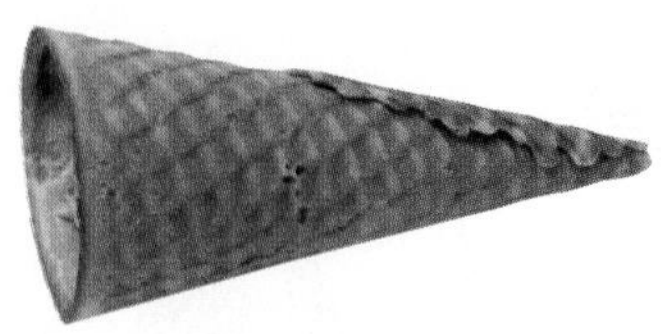

**Directions** Have children circle each item that can roll. Then have them mark an *X* on each item that can stack. Point out that some items that are circled should also be marked with an *X*.

**Home Activity** Give your child several cans of soup or other canned foods. Ask him or her to tell you why the objects can stack and why they can roll.

Name ___________________________

# Flat Surfaces on Solid Figures

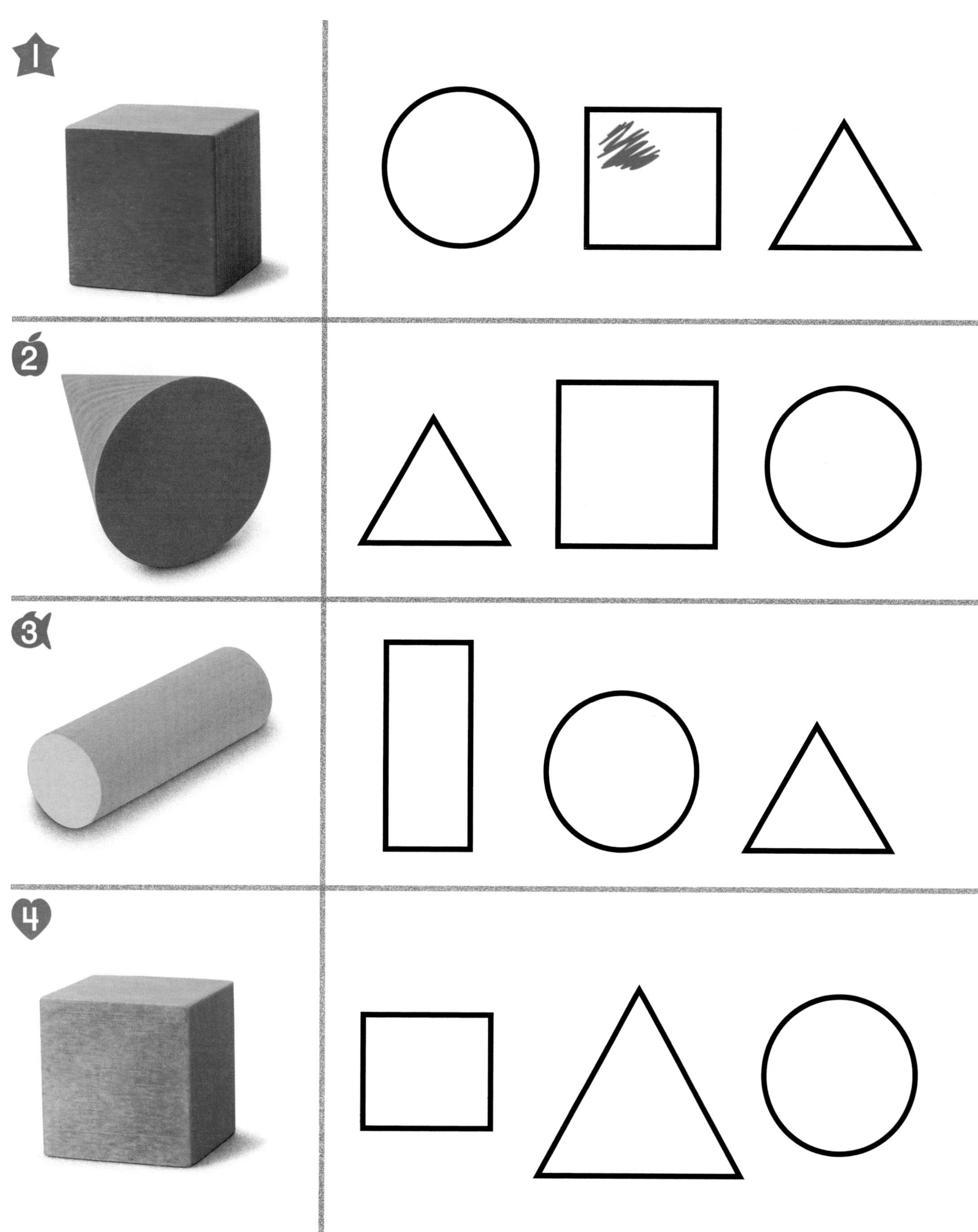

**Directions** In each exercise have children find the matching flat surface of the solid figure on the left and color it to match the color of the flat surface.

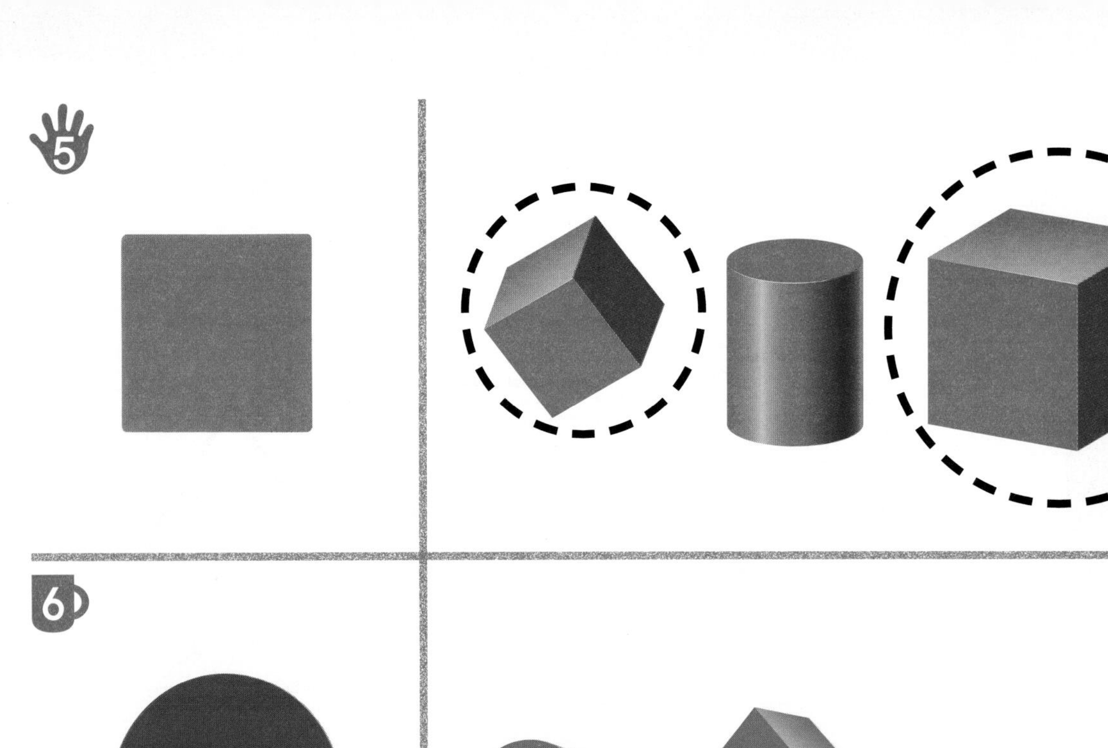

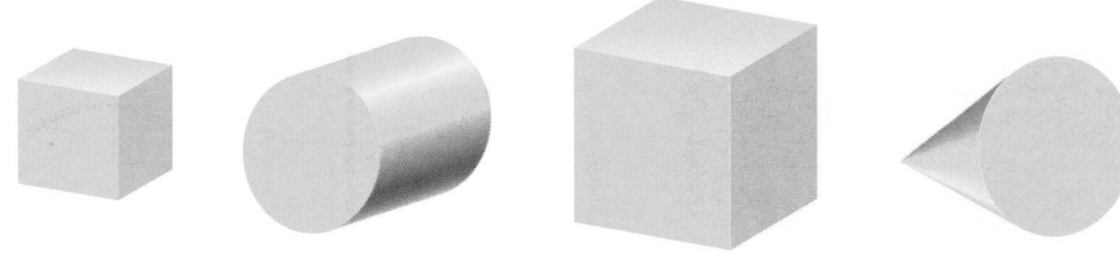

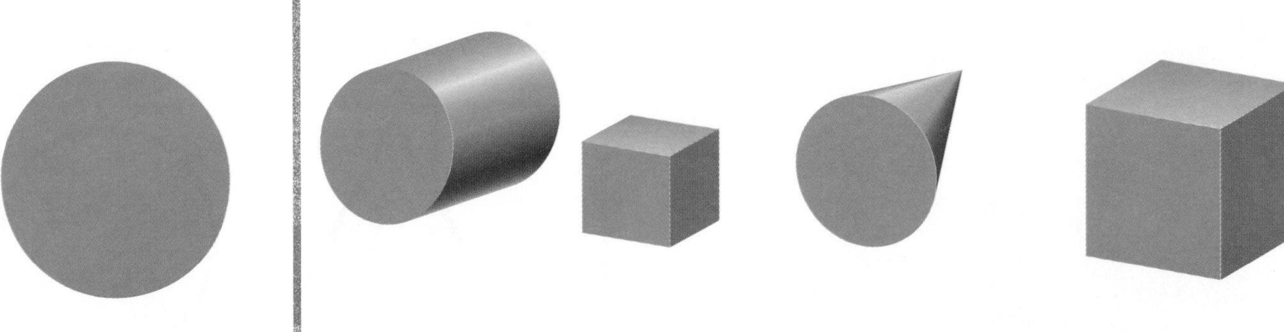

8

**Directions** In each exercise have children circle the solid figures with a flat surface that matches the shape on the left.

**Home Activity** Have your child show you the flat surface of a can or a box and describe the shape.

Name ______________________________

# Squares and Other Rectangles

**Directions** Have children circle all the rectangles. Then have children mark an *X* on all the rectangles that are squares.

2

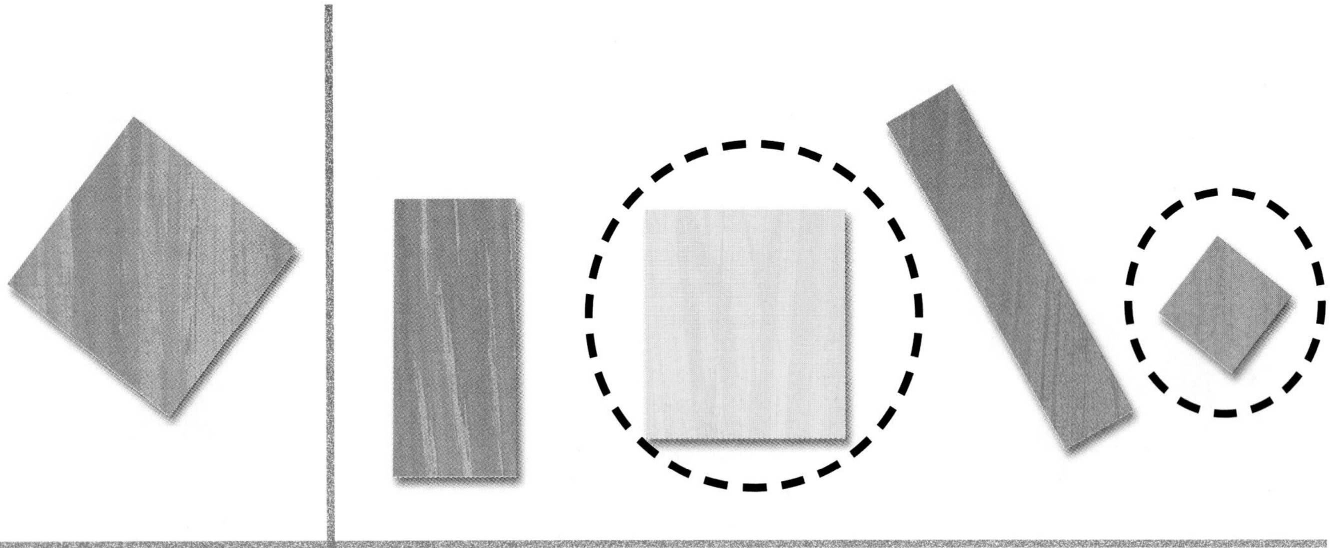

3

4

5

**Directions** In each exercise have children circle the shapes on the right that match the shape on the left.

**Home Activity** Have your child point out rectangles in your home and tell you what makes each object a rectangle.

Name ____________________

# Circles and Triangles

1

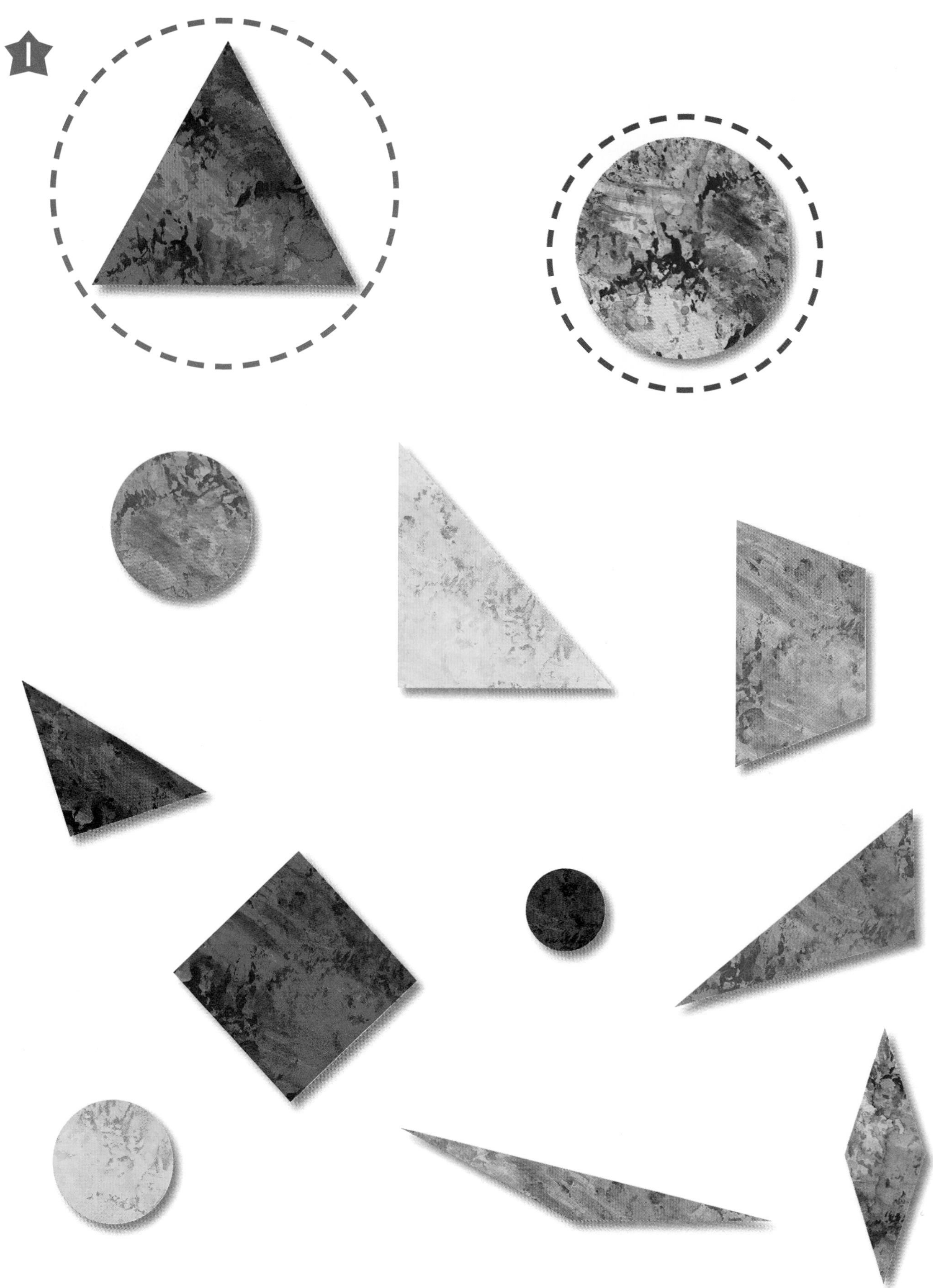

**Directions** Have children circle all the triangles with a red crayon and all the circles with a blue crayon.

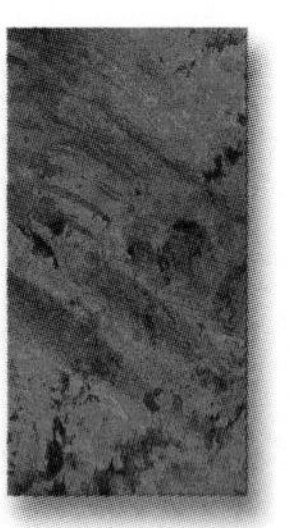

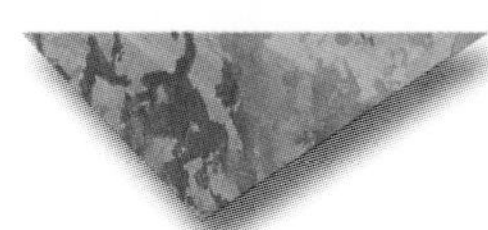

**Directions** In each exercise have children circle the shapes that match the shape on the left.

**Home Activity** During a car or a bus ride with your child, ask him or her to look around and find objects that are shaped like triangles and circles.

Name ______________________________

# Slides, Flips, and Turns

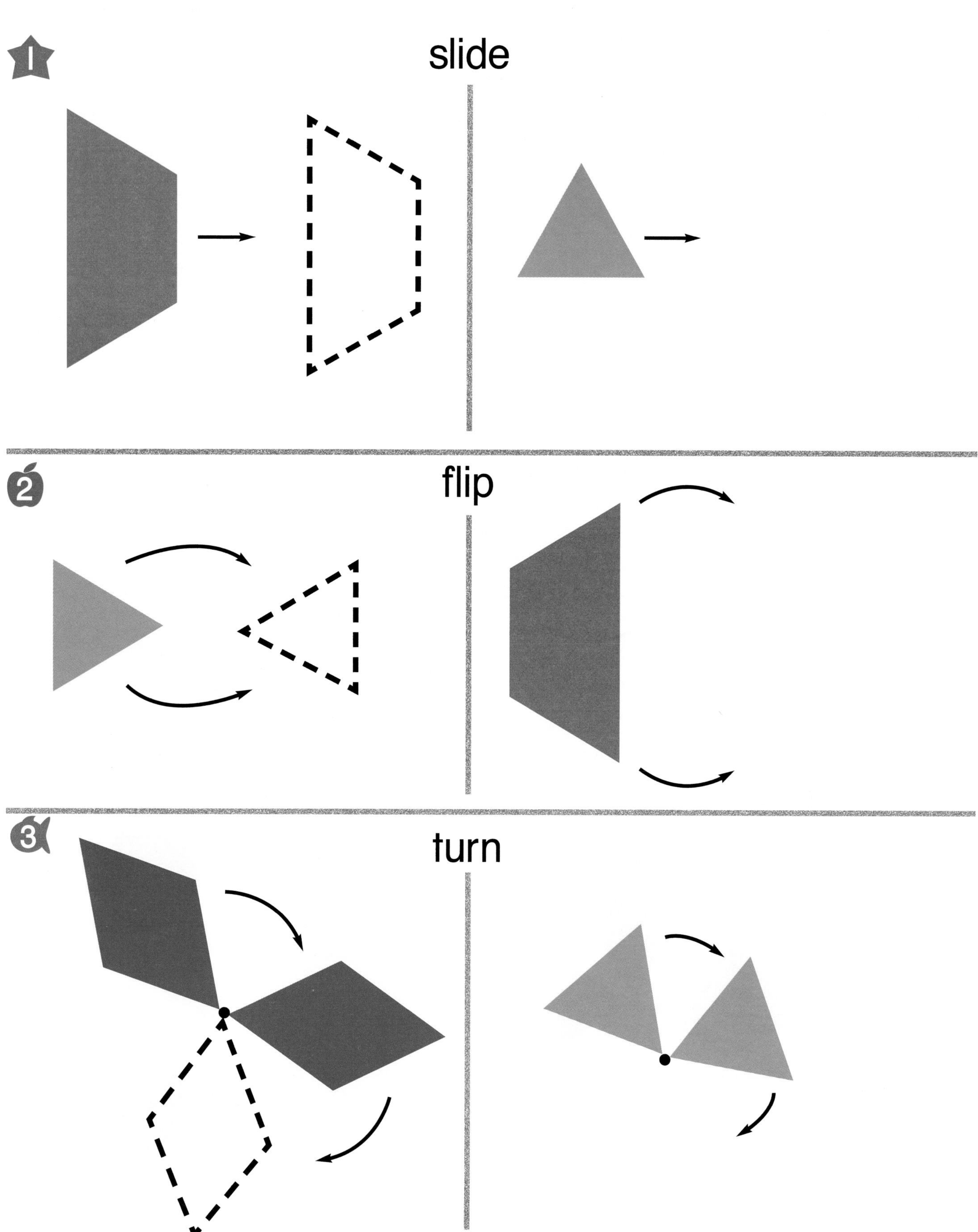


**Directions** In Exercise 1 have children place a pattern block on top of the red block and slide it to the dashed shape. Then have children slide a green block and show the slide by drawing the block to the right of the arrow. Have children follow a similar procedure to flip blocks in Exercise 2 and turn blocks in Exercise 3.

4

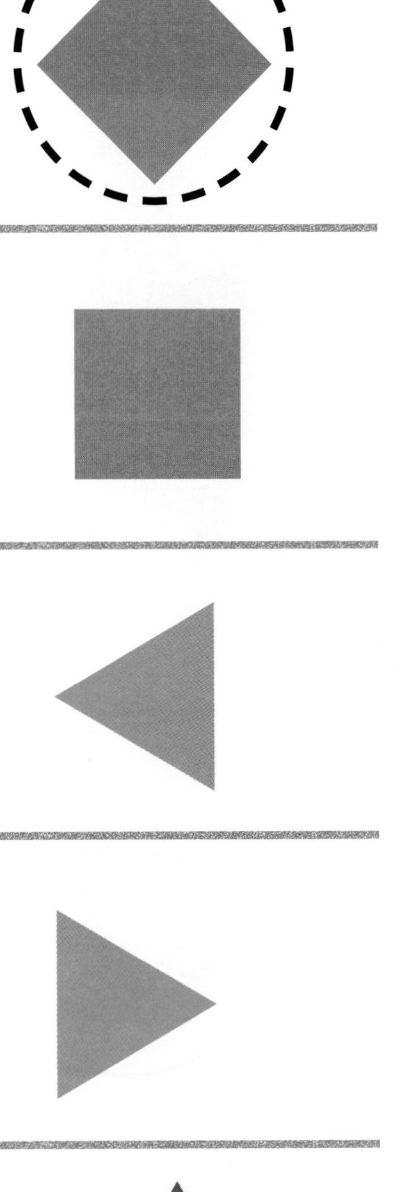

5

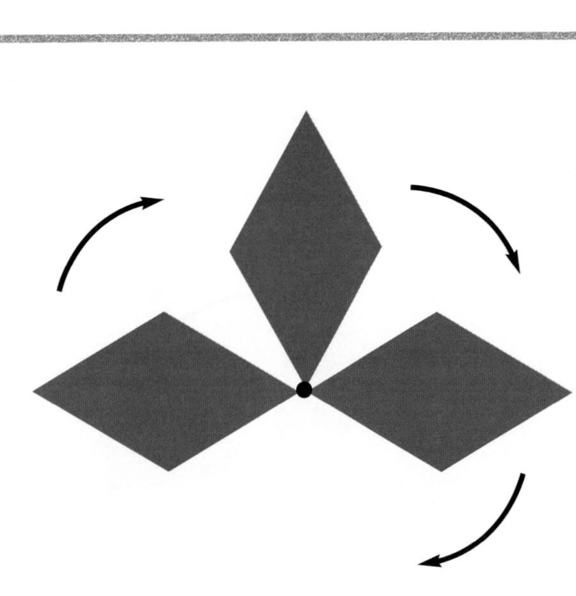

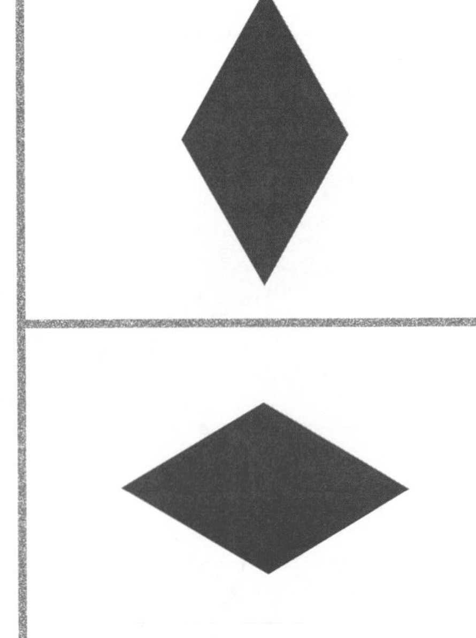

6

**Directions** In Exercise 4 have children circle the block that comes next when you slide it. In Exercise 5 have children circle the block that comes next when you flip it. In Exercise 6 have children circle the block that comes next when you turn it.

**Home Activity** Have your child show you how a block moves when you slide it, flip it, and turn it.

Name ______________________

# Combining and Separating Shapes

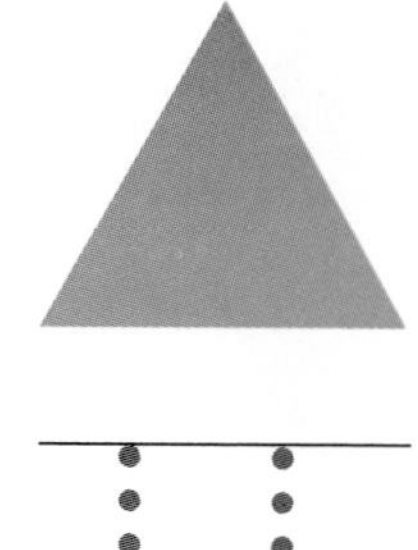

4

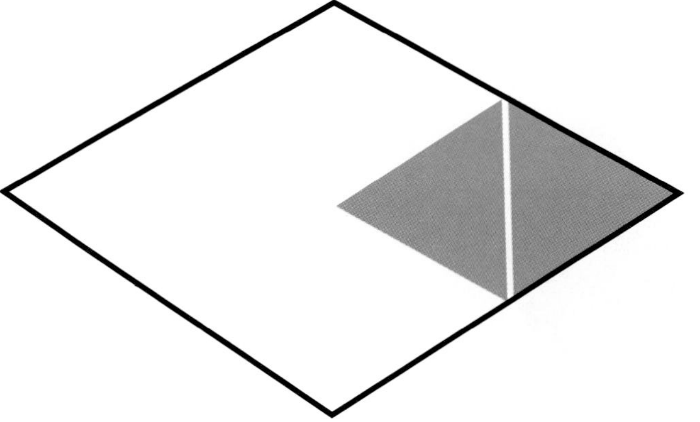

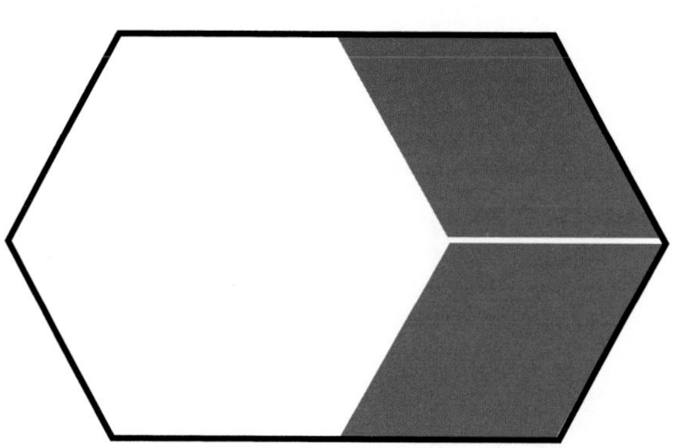

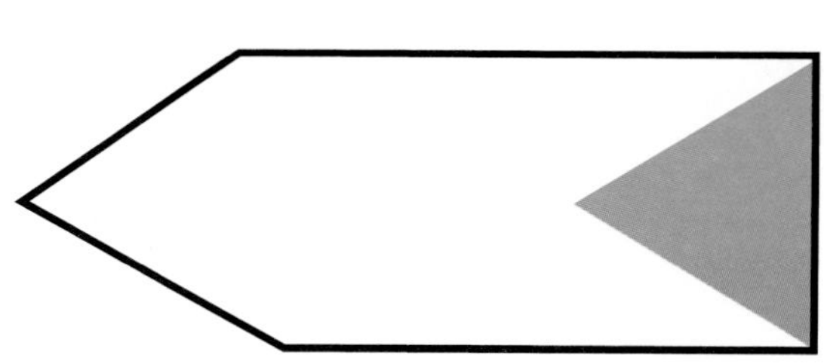

**Directions** In each exercise have children build the rest of the shape by covering the empty part with the kind of pattern block shown on the right. Have children record the number of blocks they used.

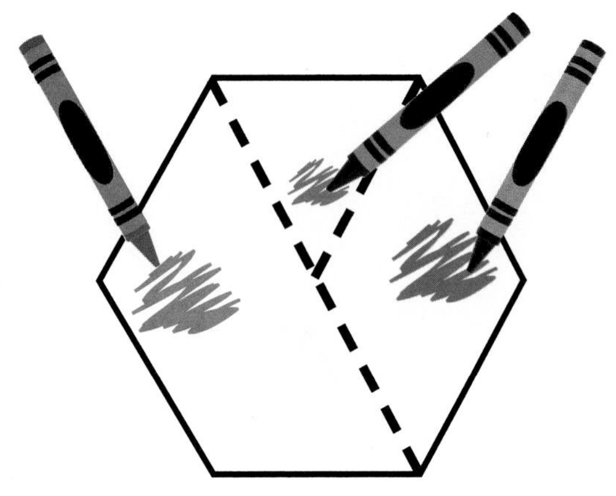

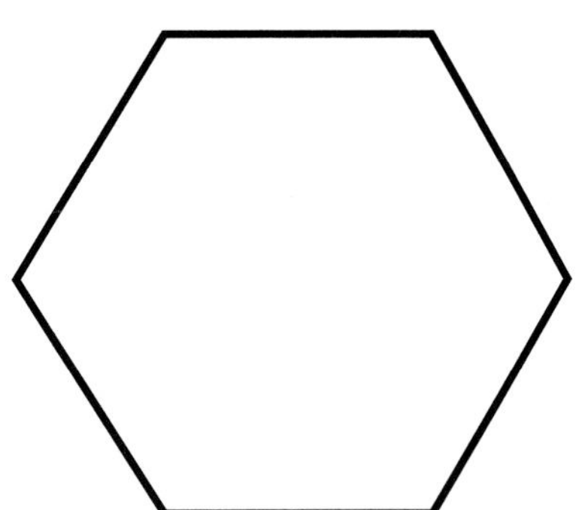

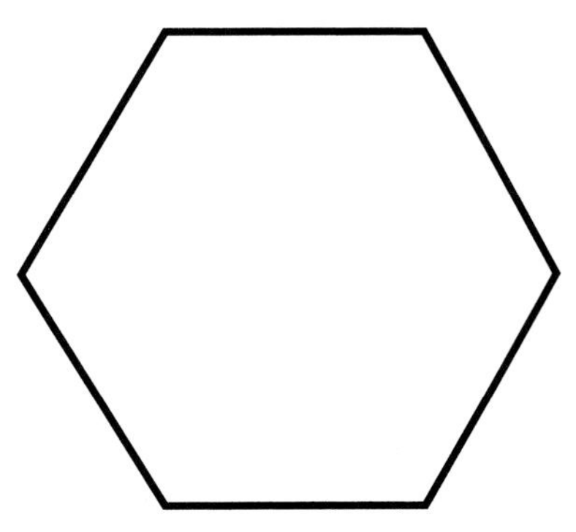

**Directions** Have children use the pattern blocks on the left to cover the larger shape on the right. Have them draw and color the pattern blocks to show how they covered the larger shape.

**Home Activity** Help your child choose a picture from a magazine, cut it into puzzle pieces, and put it back together.

Name ____________________



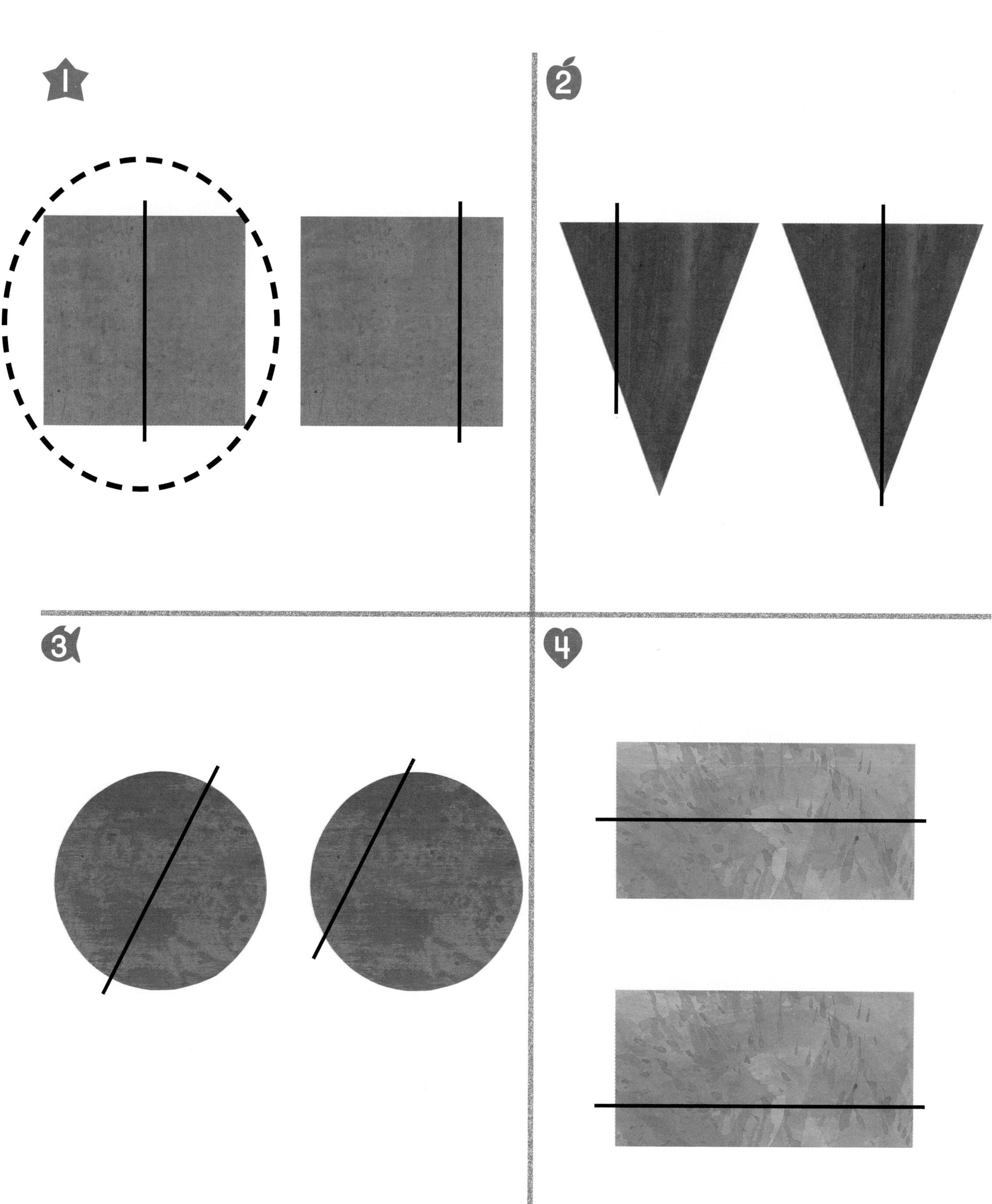

**Directions** In each exercise have children circle the shape that shows matching parts.

5

6

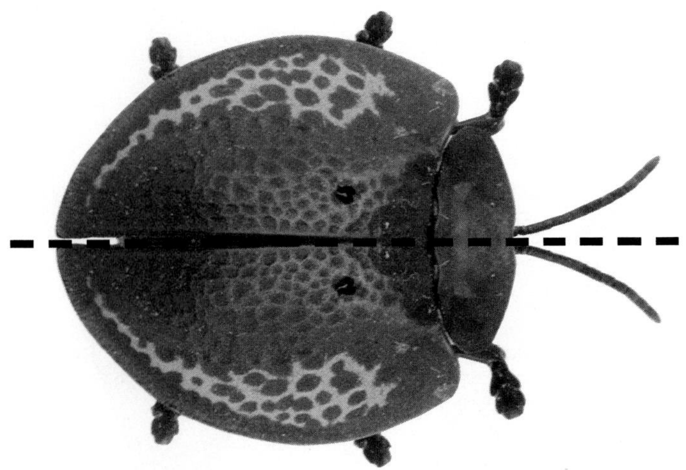

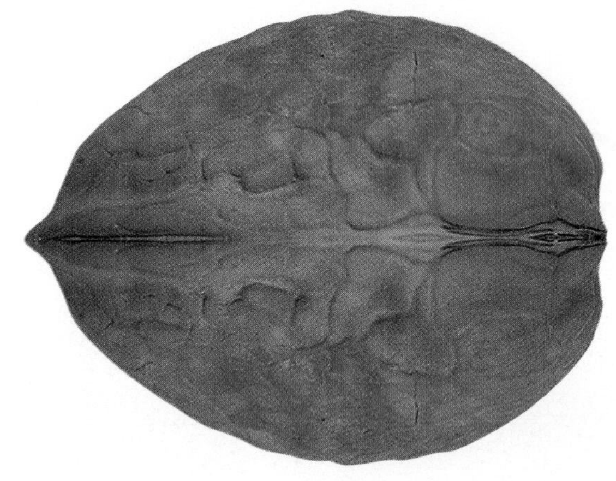

7

8

**Directions** Have children draw a line through each item to show matching parts.

**Home Activity** Fold a sheet of paper in half and then open it. Ask your child to talk about the two parts and tell you how they are the same.

Name ___________________________ 

# Equal Parts

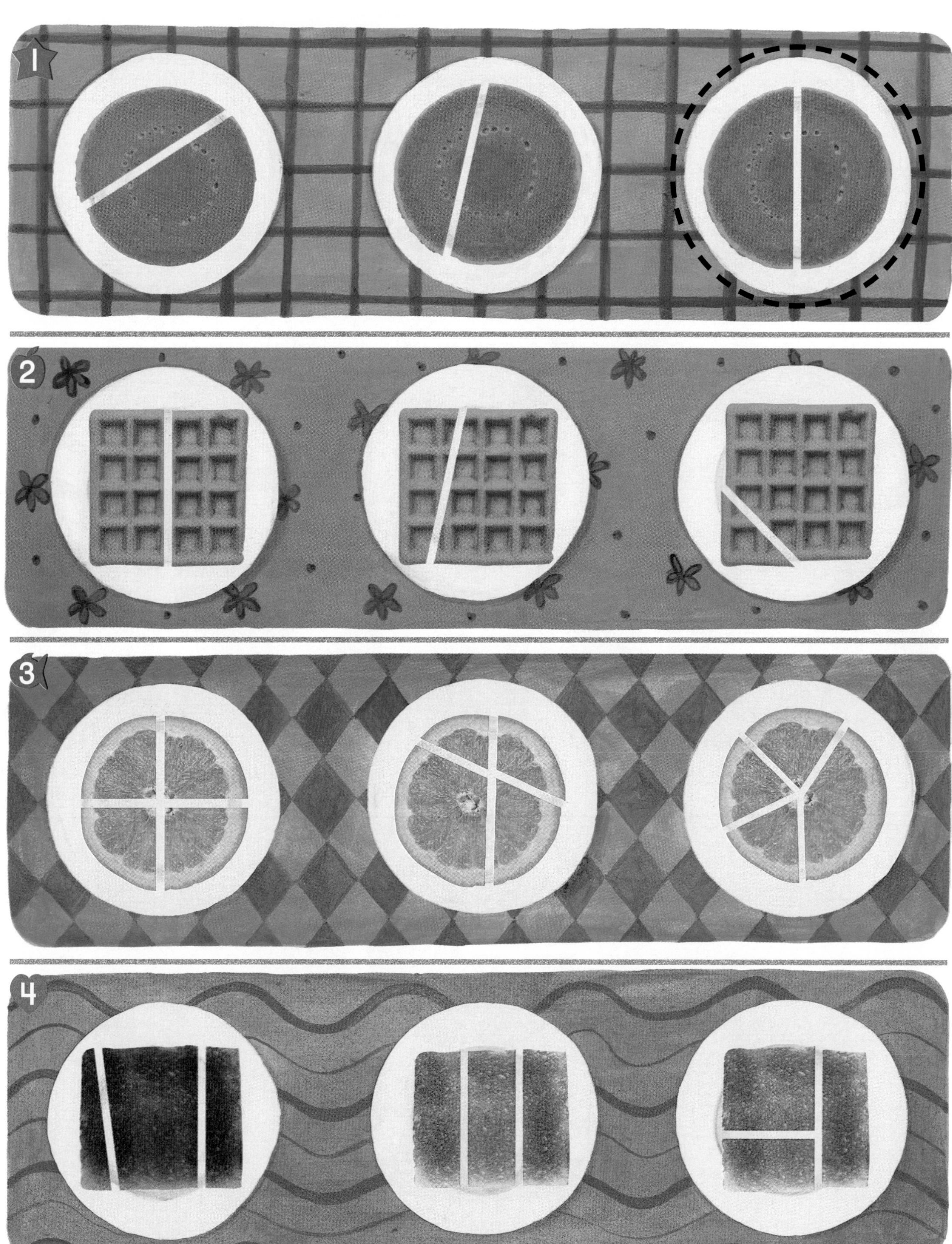


**Directions** Have children circle the item in each exercise that is cut into equal parts.

5

**Directions** Have children circle the items that are cut into equal parts.

**Home Activity** Help your child cut a sandwich into equal parts. Talk about why the parts are equal.



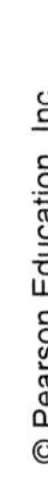

Name ______________________________

# Halves and Fourths

1

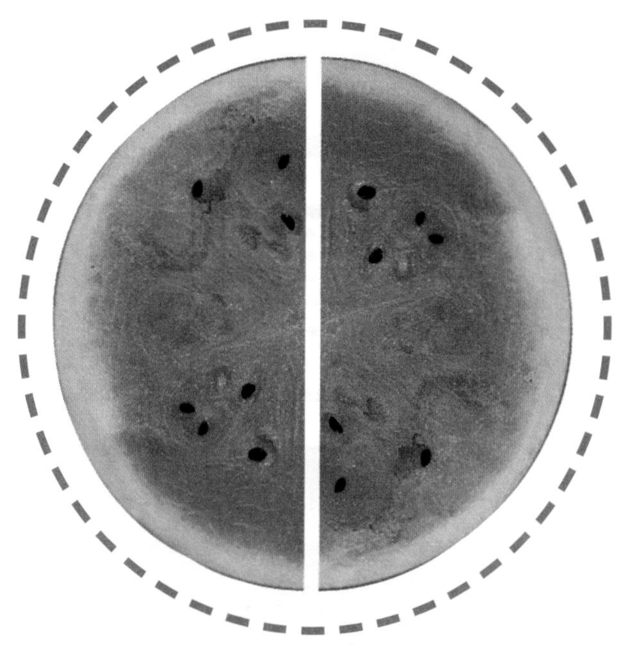

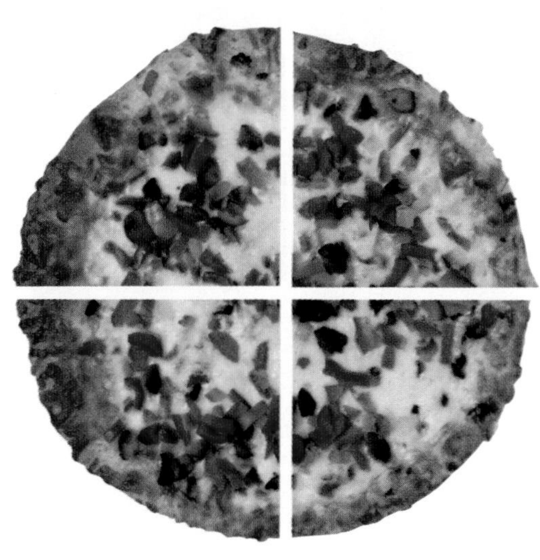

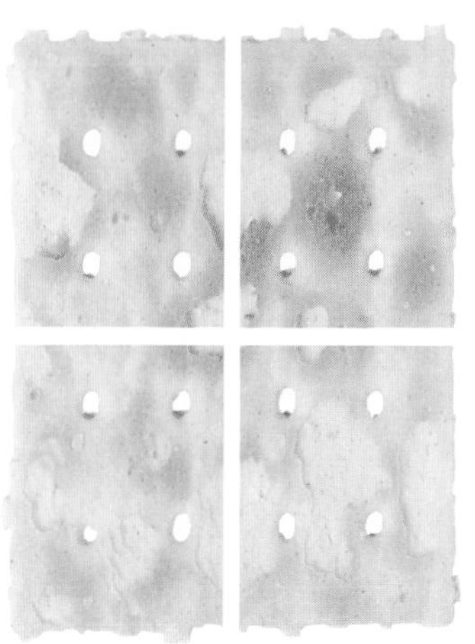

**Directions** Have children use a red crayon to circle the items that show 2 equal shares, or halves. Have them use a blue crayon to circle the items that show 4 equal shares, or fourths.

4

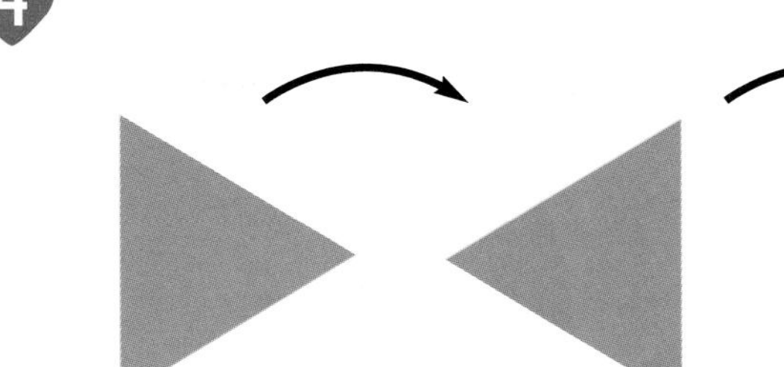
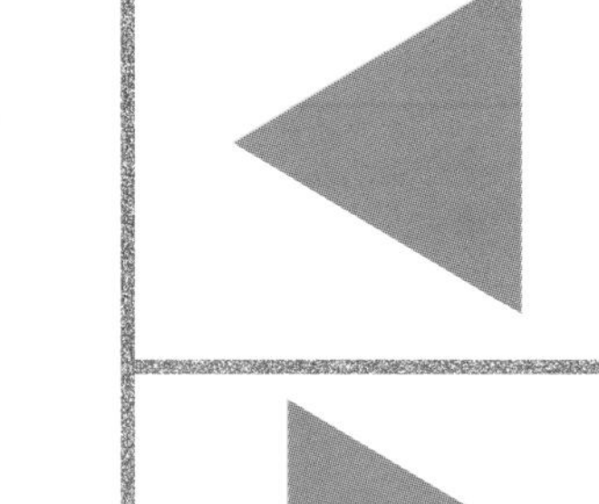

5

6

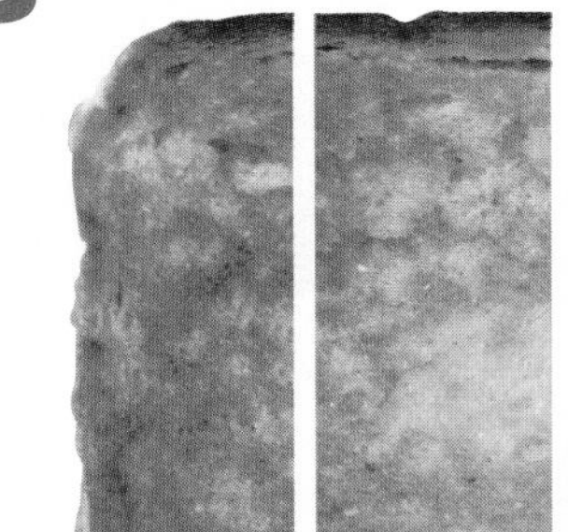

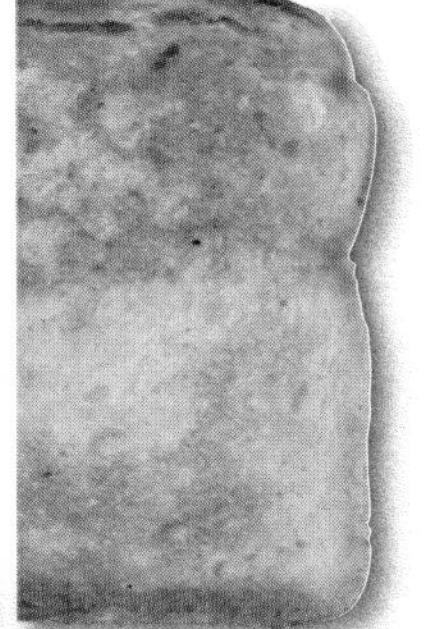
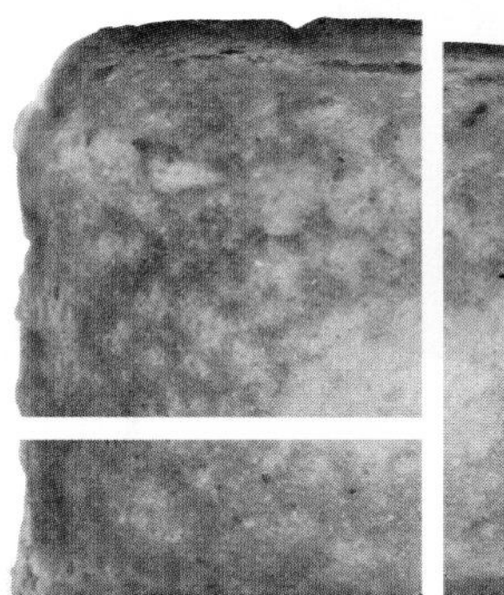
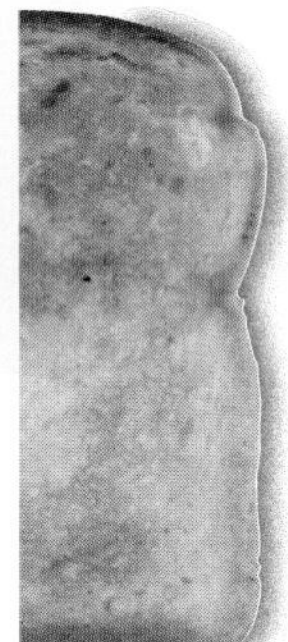

7

Dire
the r
item

**Directions** Have children: 4. circle the triangle that comes next when you flip it; 5. circle the shape that has matching parts; 6. circle the slice of toast that is cut into halves; 7. make equal shares of balls for the children shown and write the numbers.

So the **2** pigs came back with **4** of their friends.

"There are **2** of us," said Penny Pig.
"And there are **4** of us," said Rocky Raccoon.

"OK, that makes **6** customers in all,"
said Bessy Bear.

"One **BIG** pie coming right up!"

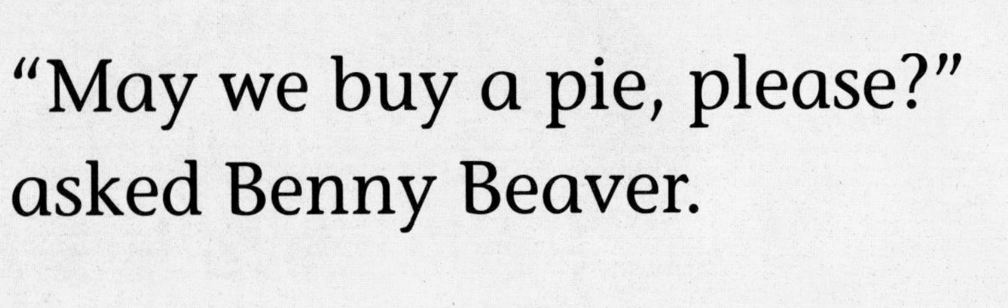

"May we buy a pie, please?"
asked Benny Beaver.

"Now, Benny," said Bessy Bear. "You know that it takes **6** customers to finish one of my pies. Go find some friends to join you."

**REMEMBER:**
**Each pie feeds 6!**

So the **3** beavers came back
with **3** of their friends.

"There are **3** of us," said Benny Beaver.
"And there are **3** of us," said Skippy Squirrel.

"OK, that makes **6** customers in all,"
said Bessy Bear.

"One **BIG** pie coming right up!"

"May we buy **6** pies, please?"
asked Honey Hippo. "There are **5** of us."

"And there is **1** of me," said Ellie Elephant.

"OK, that makes **6 BIG** customers in all,"
said Bessy Bear.

"**6 BIG** pies coming right up!"

Sometimes one customer **CAN** eat a whole pie!

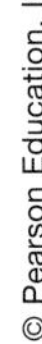

## Home-School Connection

Dear Family,

Today my class started Chapter 9, **Readiness for Addition and Subtraction.** I will learn different ways to make numbers. And I will learn how to compare different amounts. Here are some of the math words I will be learning and some things we can do to help me with my math.

Love,

______________________

### Math Activity to Do at Home

Draw or cut out pictures to show different ways to make 5. For example, you can use 3 birds and 2 cats or 4 birds and 1 cat to make 5. Have your child count the pictures. Then help your child draw an addition picture that looks something like this:

### Books to Read Together

Reading math stories reinforces concepts. Look for these titles in your local library:

***More Than One***
By Tana Hoban
(Greenwillow Books, 1996)

***Ten Flashing Fireflies***
By Philemon Sturges
(North-South Books, 1995)

### My New Math Words

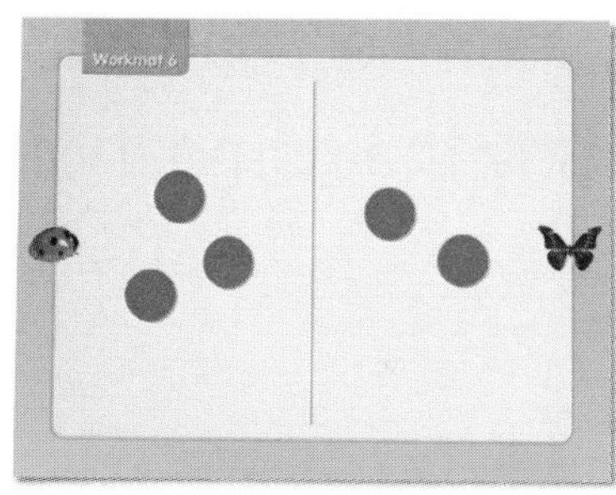

We use our **part-part mats** to show ways to make numbers.

I count **one more** blue triangle.
I count **one fewer** orange triangle.

I count **two more** green squares.
I count **two fewer** yellow squares.

Name ________________________________

# Sky-High Pie

**What You Need**

1 dot cube

30 small game markers

## How to Play

1. To help Miss Bessie make her pie, place markers on all of the peanuts and pickles.
2. Toss the cube. Count the dots. Say the number.
3. Then, take away 1 **fewer** marker than the number on the cube. Say the number of markers you are taking away.
4. Keep playing until you have taken away all of the markers.
5. Play again. This time put all of the markers in a pile. Toss the cube, say the number, and add 1 **more** marker than the number on the cube. Say the number of markers you are adding.

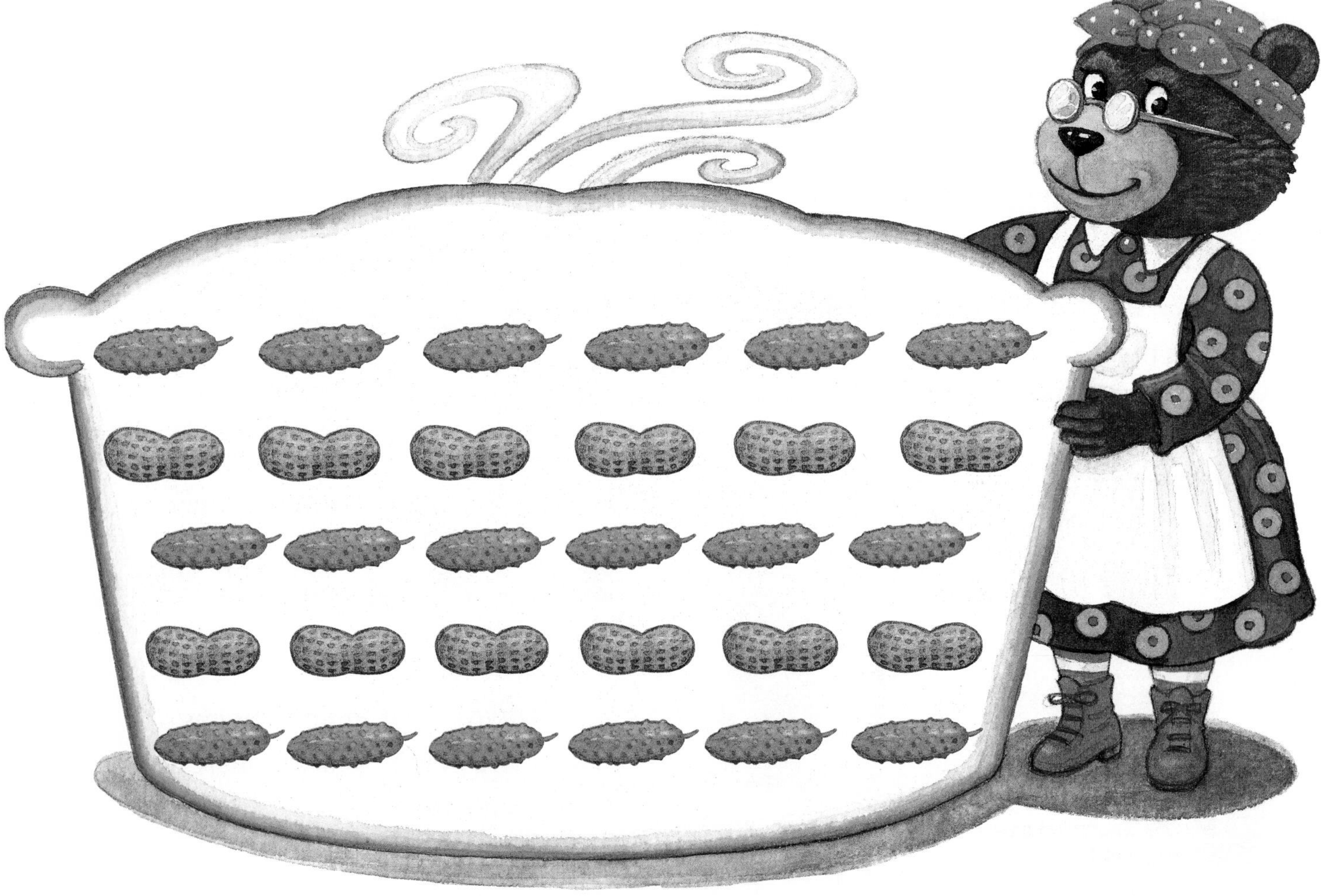

Name ______________________

# Ways to Make 4 and 5

4

1

2 and 2

2

and

3

and

**Directions** Have children show ways to make 4 by placing matching counters in Exercises 1 and 2 and recording the numbers of red and yellow counters. In Exercise 3 have children use red and yellow counters to show 4 in another way. Have them color the outlines to match the counters and record the number of each color.

5

4

2 and 3

5

and

6

and

7

and

**Directions** Have children place matching counters in Exercises 4–6 and record the number of each color. In Exercise 7 have children use counters to show 5 in another way. Have them color the outlines to match the counters and record the number of each color.

**Home Activity** Ask your child to gently toss 5 pennies and record the number of heads and tails that make up the group of 5 pennies. Ask your child to toss the pennies again. Talk about why the new combination of heads and tails still shows 5.

Name ______________________

# Ways to Make 6 and 7

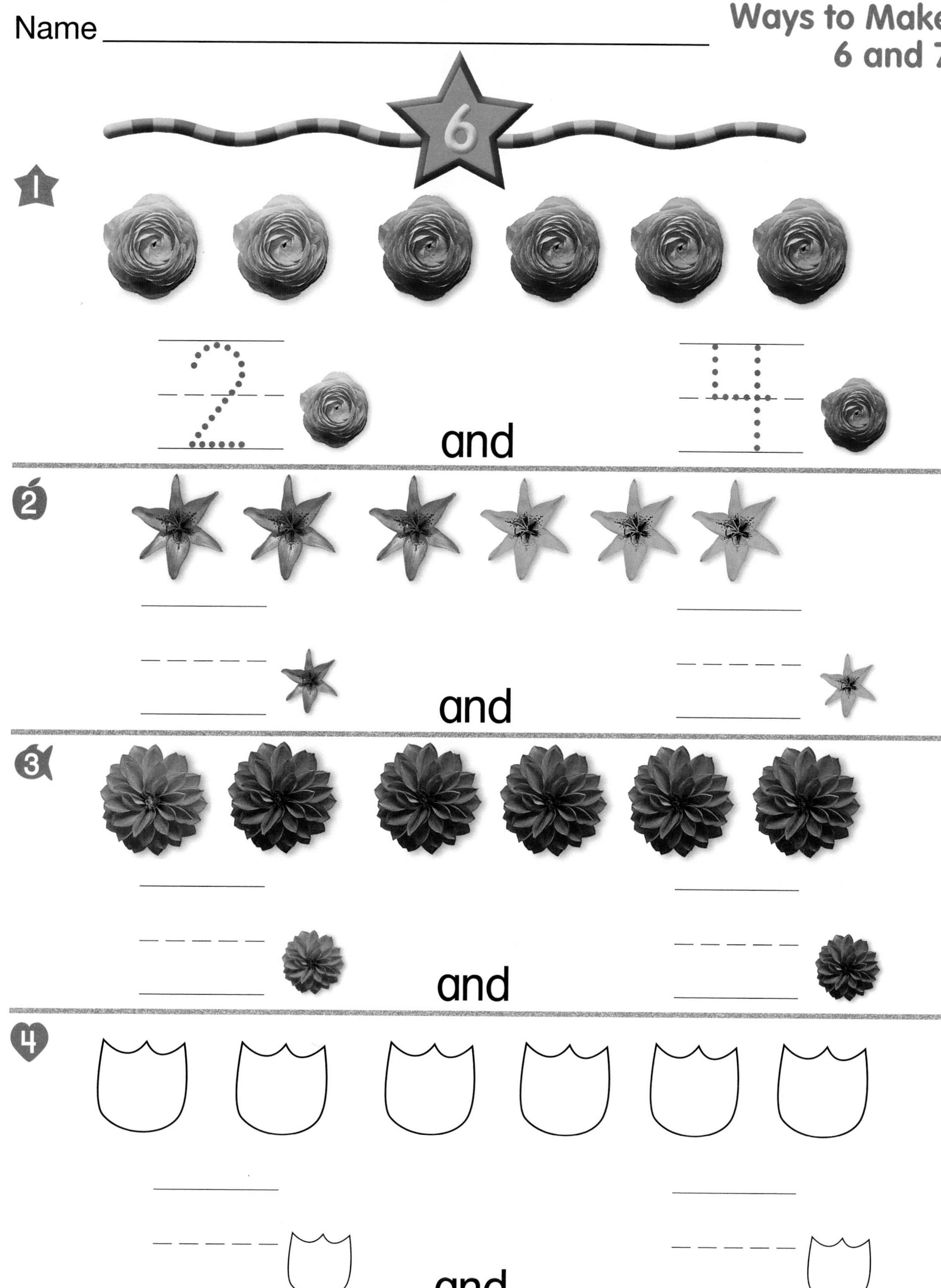


**Directions** In Exercises 1–3 have children count the flowers of each color and write the numbers. In Exercise 4 have children color to show a group of 6 flowers in two colors and write the numbers to show how many of each color.

7

5

3  and 4

6

and

7

and

8

and

**Directions** In Exercises 5–7 have children count the flowers of each color and write the numbers. In Exercise 8 have children color to show a group of 7 flowers in two colors and write the numbers to show how many of each color.

**Home Activity** Give your child socks of two colors. Have him or her make different groups of 7 socks using both colors. Ask your child to explain why the groups look different but still show 7.

Name ______________________

# Ways to Make 8 and 9

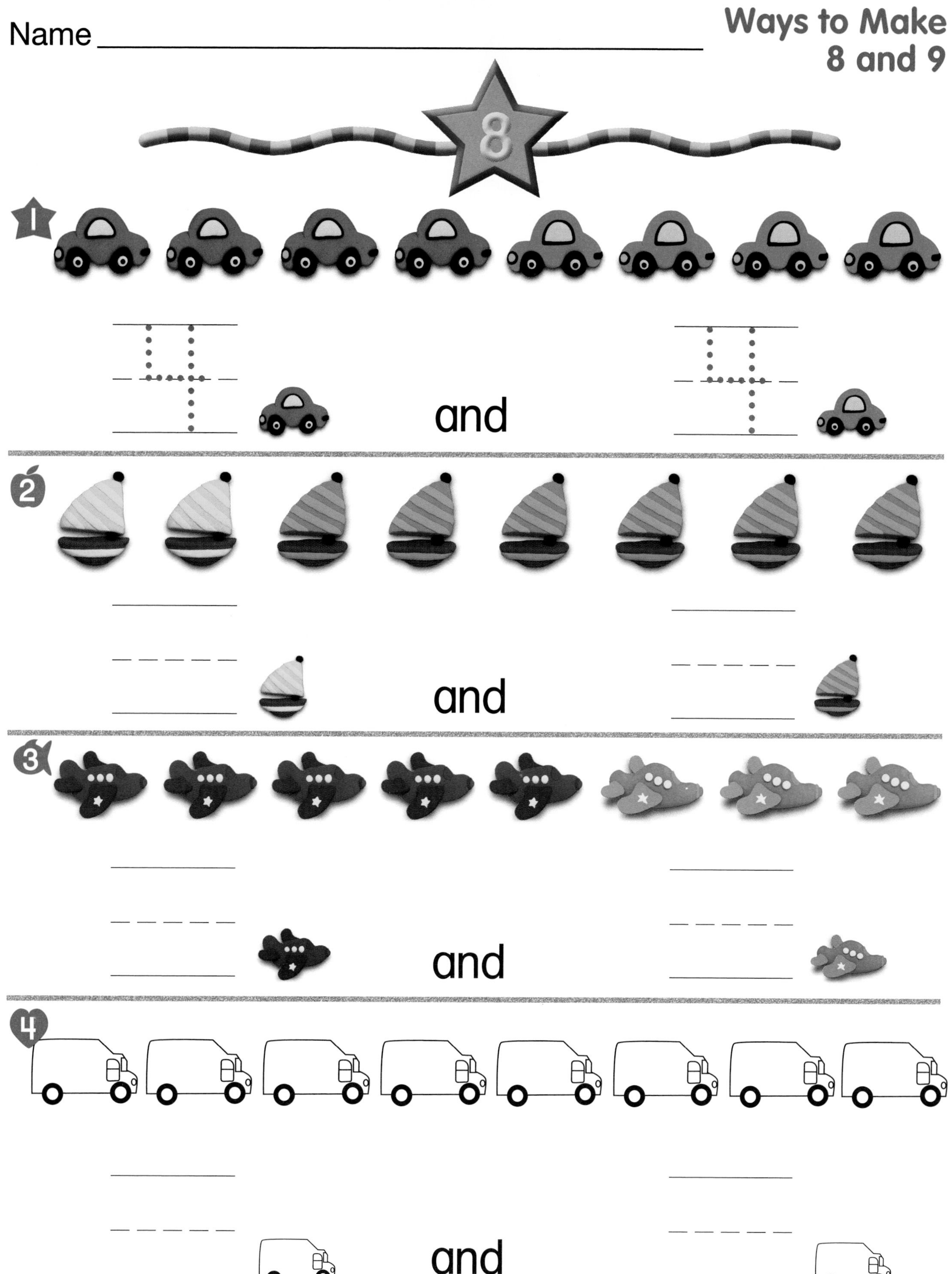


**Directions** In Exercise 1–3 have children count the items of each color and write the numbers. In Exercise 4 have children color to show a group of 8 trucks in two colors and write the numbers to show how many of each color.

9

5

4  and 5

6

and

7

and

8

and

Directions In Exercises 5–7 have children count the items of each color and write the numbers. In Exercise 8 have children color to show a group of 9 balloons in two colors and write the numbers to show how many of each color.

**Home Activity** Have your child show several different groups of large spoons and small spoons that together make 9.

Name ______________________

# Ways to Make 10

10

1

4 and 6

2

and

3

and

**Directions** In Exercises 1–2 have children count the counters and record the number of each color. In Exercise 3 have children show 10 in another way by coloring the counters red and yellow and recording the number of each color.

4

2 and 8

5

and

6

and

7

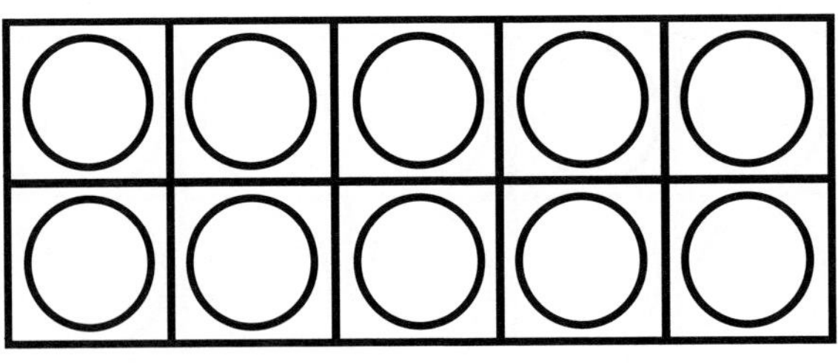

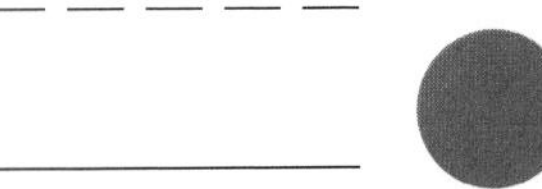

and

**Directions** In Exercises 4–6 have children count the counters and record the number of each color. In Exercise 7 have children show 10 in another way by coloring the counters red and yellow and recording the number of each color.

**Home Activity** Give your child 10 pennies and arrange them heads and tails up. Have your child count the heads and tails and tell the numbers that make 10. Repeat the activity several times. Talk about the different combinations.

Name ______________________



# Make an Organized List

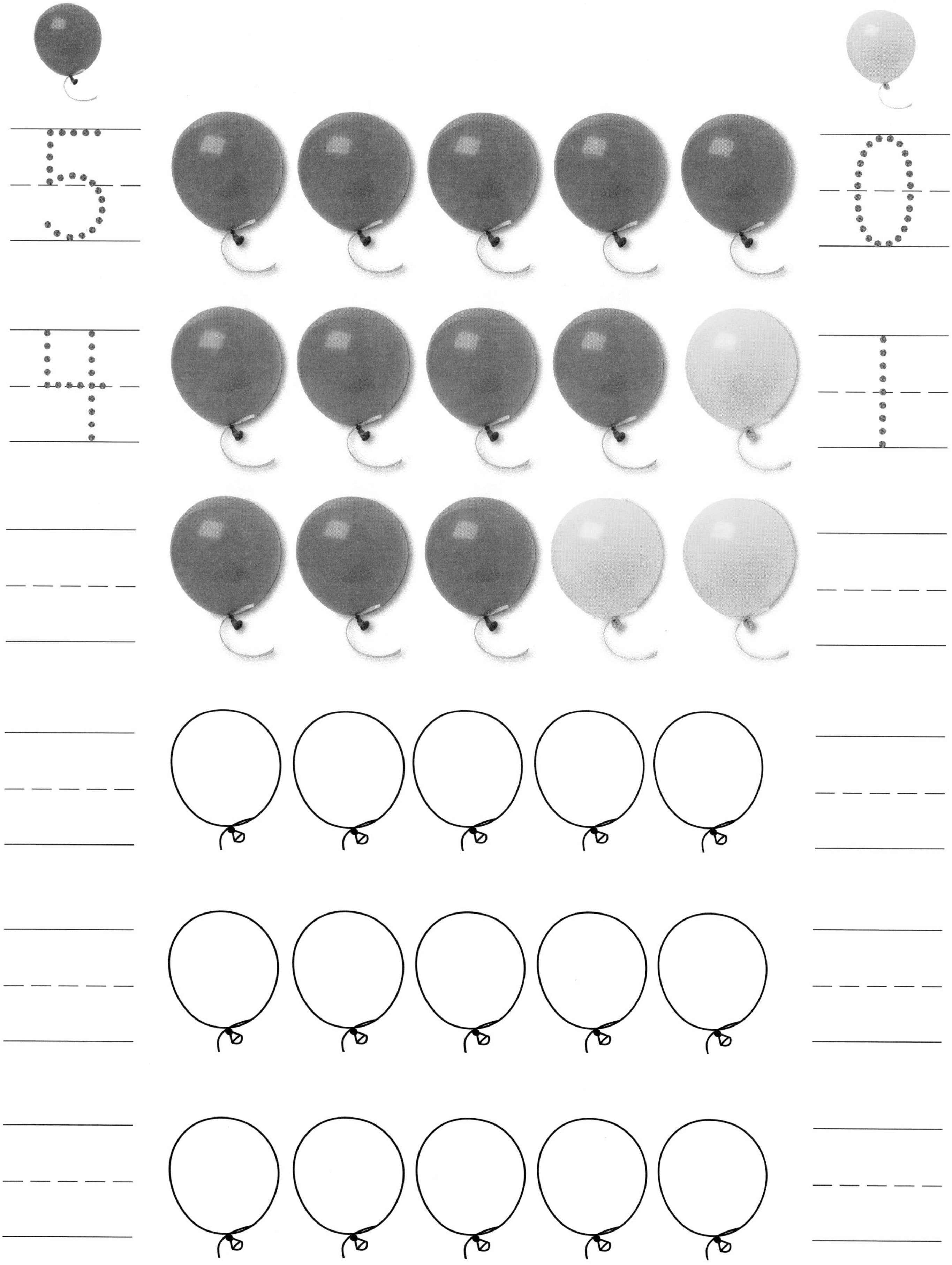

5 0

4 1

**Directions** Have children count each group of balloons and record the number of red and yellow balloons in each group. Have them continue the pattern of red and yellow by coloring balloons and writing the number of each color.

10 0

9 1

**Directions** Have children count each group of crayons and record the number of crayons in each group. Have them continue the pattern of blue and red by coloring the crayons and writing the number of each color.

**Home Activity** Ask your child to tell you how each row of crayons changes and then tell what another row of crayons would look like.

Name ______________________________

# 1 More and 2 More

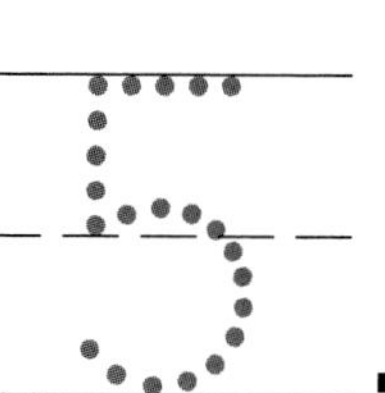

4 and 1 more is 5.

2

3 and 1 more is ____.

3

5 and 1 more is ____.

4

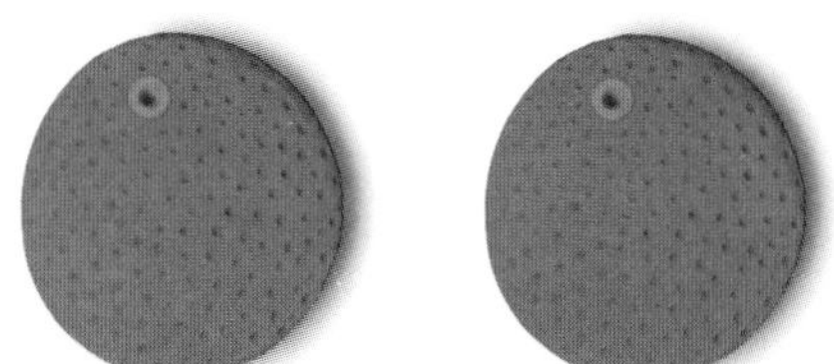

2 and 1 more is ____.

**Directions** Have children draw 1 more object in each exercise and record the number of objects in the group.

 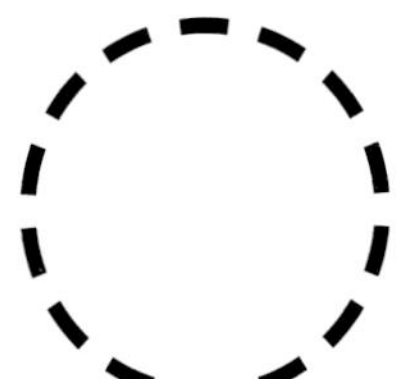 

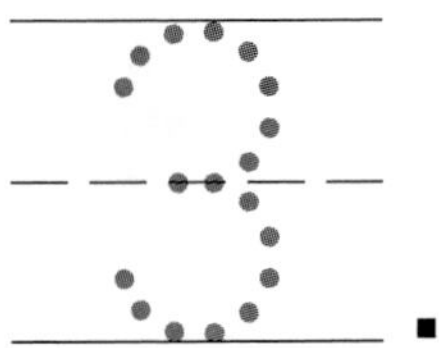

1 and 2 more is ___.

3 and 2 more is ___.

2 and 2 more is ___.

8

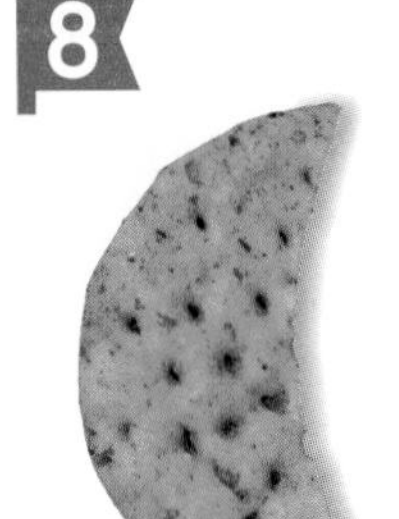 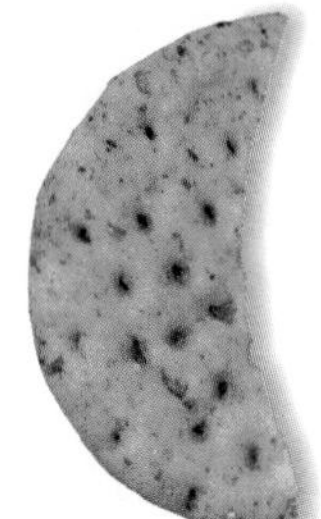 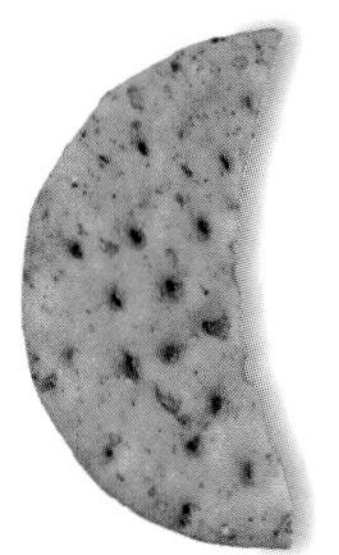 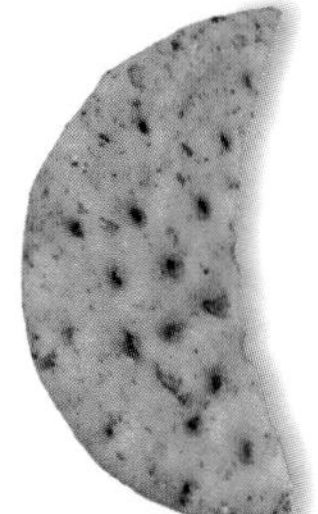

4 and 2 more is ___.

**Directions** Have children draw 2 more objects in each exercise and record the number of objects in the group.

**Home Activity** Have your child give you 2 toys and then 2 more toys. Ask your child to count and tell how many toys there are. Repeat the activity a few times, having your child give you several toys and then 2 more toys each time.

Name ____________________

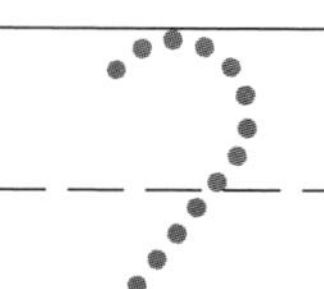

1 fewer than 3 is 2.

2

1 fewer than 5 is ____.

3

1 fewer than 4 is ____.

4

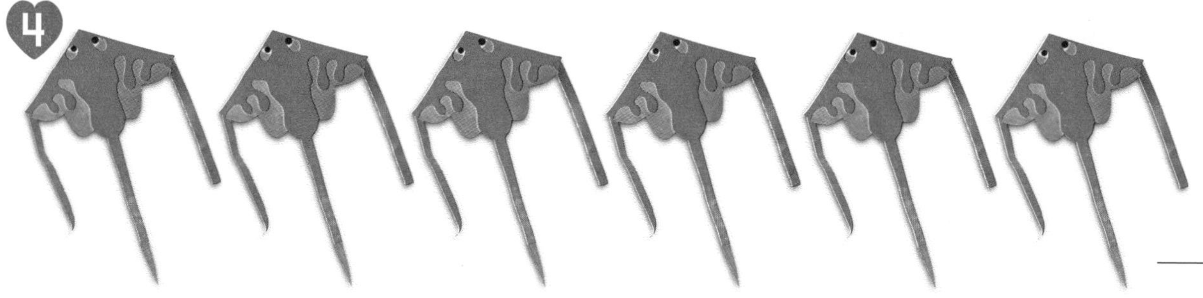

1 fewer than 6 is ____.

**Directions** Have children mark an *X* on one of the kites in each group, count how many are left, and write the number.

 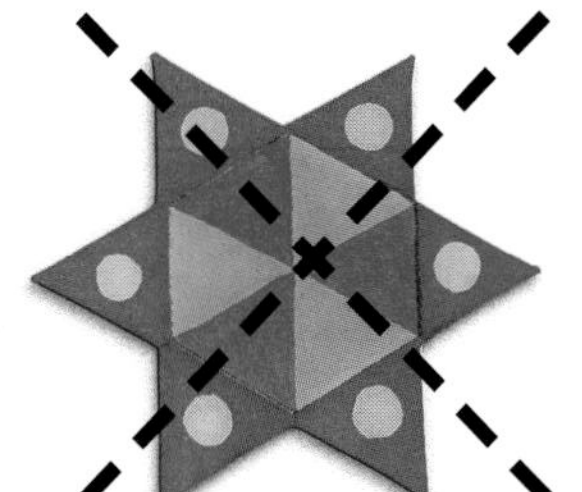 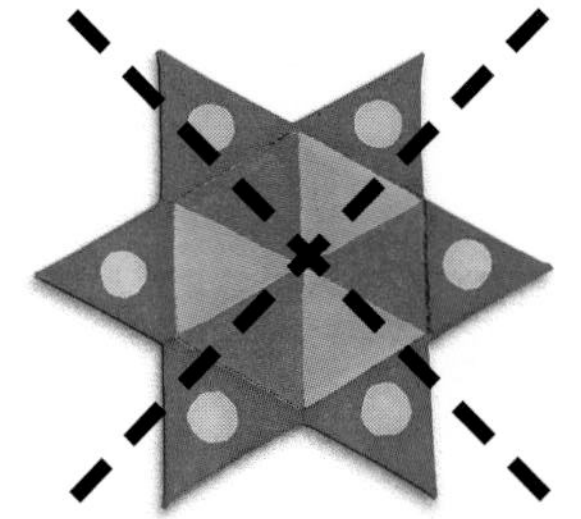

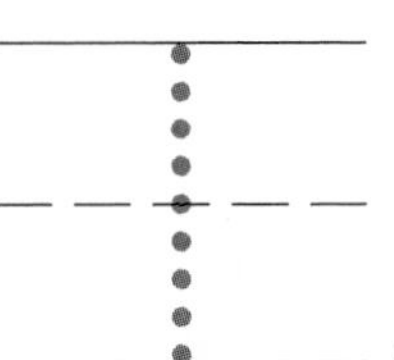

2 fewer than 3 is ______.

6

2 fewer than 5 is ______.

 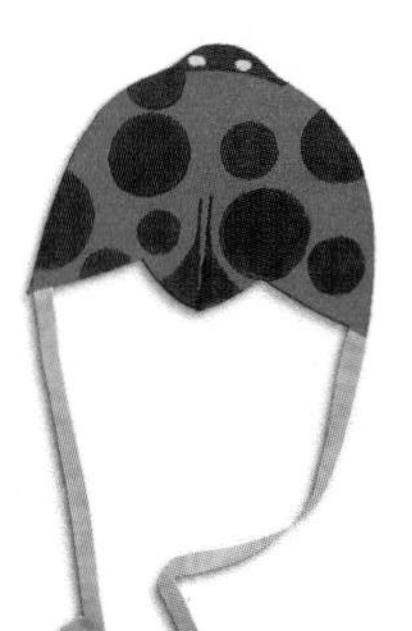 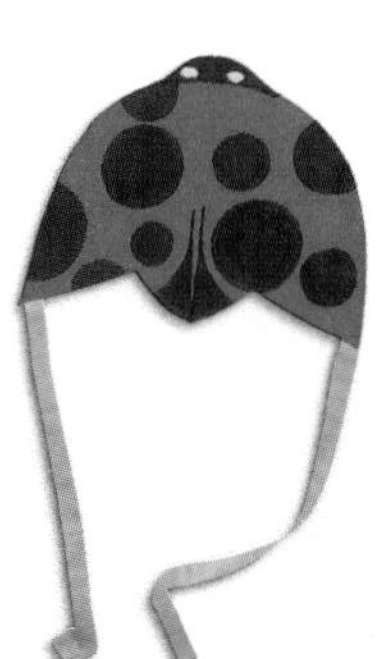 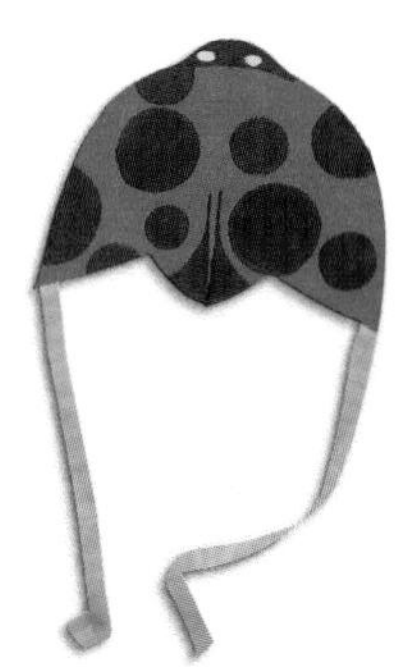

2 fewer than 4 is ______.

8

2 fewer than 6 is ______.

**Directions** Have children mark an *X* on two of the kites in each group, count how many are left, and write the number.

**Home Activity** Give your child 8 spoons. Have him or her remove 2 spoons, count the ones still in the group, and tell how many are left. Repeat the activity with other groups of spoons, having your child take away 2 spoons each time.

Name ____________________



## Visit, Look, and Learn

**Directions** Ask children which family of farm animals has more animals. Then ask children to figure out which family has more baby animals. Have them count the number of adult and baby animals in each group and record the number. Have children compare the numbers of baby animals and circle the number that is more.

2 fewer than 6 is ______.

**Directions** Tell children: Pretend you are visiting a tropical fish store where you see these 6 fish. Tell children to choose their favorite 2 fish for a classroom aquarium. Have them mark an *X* on each of these 2 fish. Then ask children to count how many fish are left and record the number.

**Home Activity** Talk with your child about the pictures on these two pages. Have your child tell you how he or she solved problems to complete the pages.

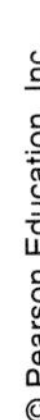

Name ________________

Test

1

5

____ and ____

2

10

____ and ____

3

9 0

Directions Have children: 1. count the blue and red sneakers and write the numbers; 2. write the numbers of red and yellow counters that make 10; 3. write the number of yellow and blue balls in each group and continue the pattern by coloring balls and by writing the number of each color.

4

3 and 1 more is ______.

5

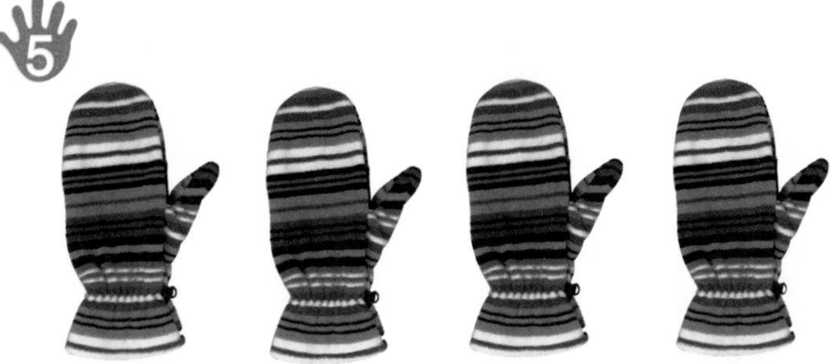

4 and 2 more is ______.

6

1 fewer than 5 is ______.

2 fewer than 4 is ______.

**Directions** Have children: 4. draw 1 more sock and write the number of socks in the group; 5. draw 2 more mittens and write the number of mittens in the group; 6. mark an *X* on 1 of the shorts, count how many are left, and write the number; 7. mark an *X* on 2 shirts, count how many are left, and write the number.

CHAPTER 10 Understanding Addition

Read Together

# Allie Gator's Elevator

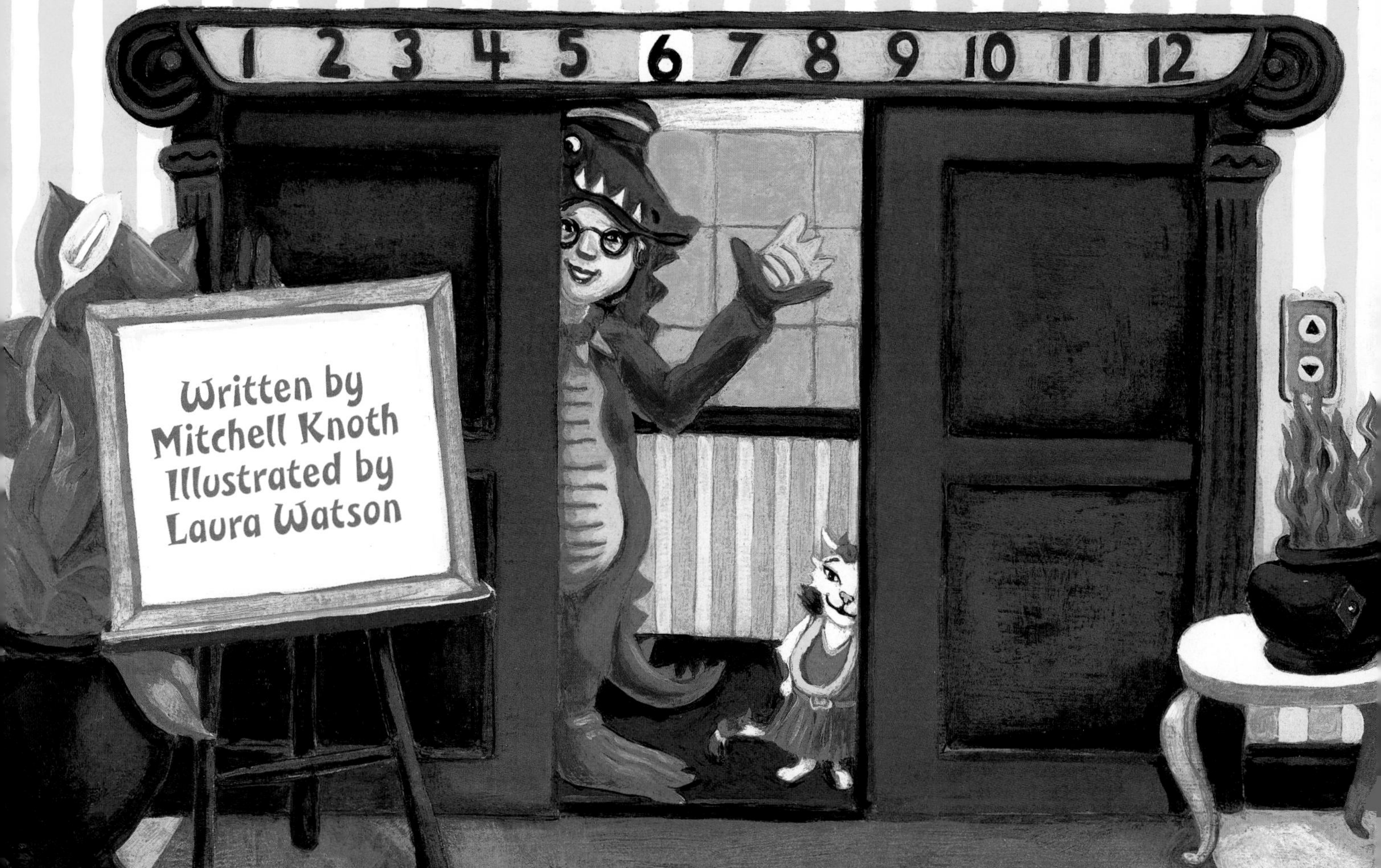
1 2 3 4 5 6 7 8 9 10 11 12
Written by
Mitchell Knoth
Illustrated by
Laura Watson

This Math Storybook belongs to

______________________________

Look! The elevator doors are opening wide.
And guess who's going for a ride.

Why, it's Miss Allie Gator in that elevator!

"Going up?" asks Miss Gator. "Which floor?"
"To the top!" roars a group of **4**.

But before the door closes,
here come **2** clowns with red noses!

"Going up?" asks Miss Gator. "Which floor?"

"To the top!" laugh the clowns
as they squeeze through the door.

"Up we go, my **6** funny friends," says Miss Gator.

Look! The elevator doors are opening wide.
Now who's going for a ride?

Why, it's **3** cowgirls!

"Going up?" asks Miss Gator. "Which floor?"

"To the top! Yahoo!" shout the girls
as they squeeze through the door.

"Up we go, my **9** funny friends," says Miss Gator.

Look! The elevator doors are opening wide.
Now who's going for a ride?

Why, it's a pirate!

"Going up?" asks Miss Gator. "Which floor?"

"To the top! Ahoy!" shouts the pirate
as he squeezes through the door.

"Up we go, my **10** funny friends," says Miss Gator.

"Next stop, the very top," says Miss Gator.

Look! The elevator doors are opening wide.
And guess who's finished with this ride.

**4** lions, **2** clowns, **3** cowgirls,
and **1** pirate—that's who!

Miss Gator has brought them all upstairs
to the Costume Contest in the Party Room!

Who do you think will win?

## Home-School Connection

Dear Family,

Today my class started Chapter 10, **Understanding Addition.** I will learn about joining groups of things together. I will also learn how to write addition sentences. Here are some of the math words I will be learning and some things we can do to help me with my math.

Love,

_______________________________

### Math Activity to Do at Home

Play "Storytelling Math." Invite your child to use stuffed toys to tell a joining story. Say, for example, "There are 3 animals playing in the grass. Then 2 more animals join them. How many animals are there now?" Ask your child to act out the story using the stuffed toys.

### Books to Read Together

Reading math stories reinforces concepts. Look for these titles in your local library:

***Addition Annie***
By David Gisler
(Children's Press, 2002)

***Domino Addition***
By Lynette Long
(Charlesbridge, 1996)

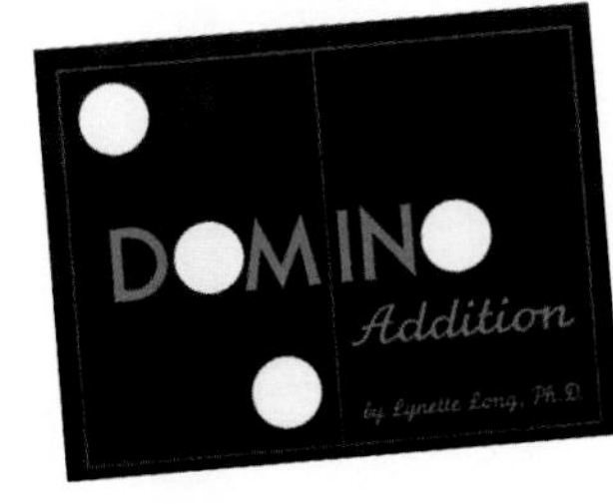

**Take It to the NET**
**More Activities**
www.scottforesman.com

### My New Math Words

2 and 2 is 4.

part part whole

2¢ + 2¢ = 4¢

plus sign equals sum

Name________________________

# Going Up? Going Down?

**What You Need**

2 dot cubes

12 small game markers

## How to Play

1. Toss the cubes. Join both sets of dots to find out how many dots there are in all.
2. Pretend that you ride the elevator to that floor. **Then** you go one floor **up** or one floor **down.** Which floor are you on now?
3. Place a marker over the elevator button that shows where you are.
4. Play until all of the buttons have been covered.

1 2 3

4 5 6

7 8 9

10 11 12

Name ______________________________

# Stories About Joining

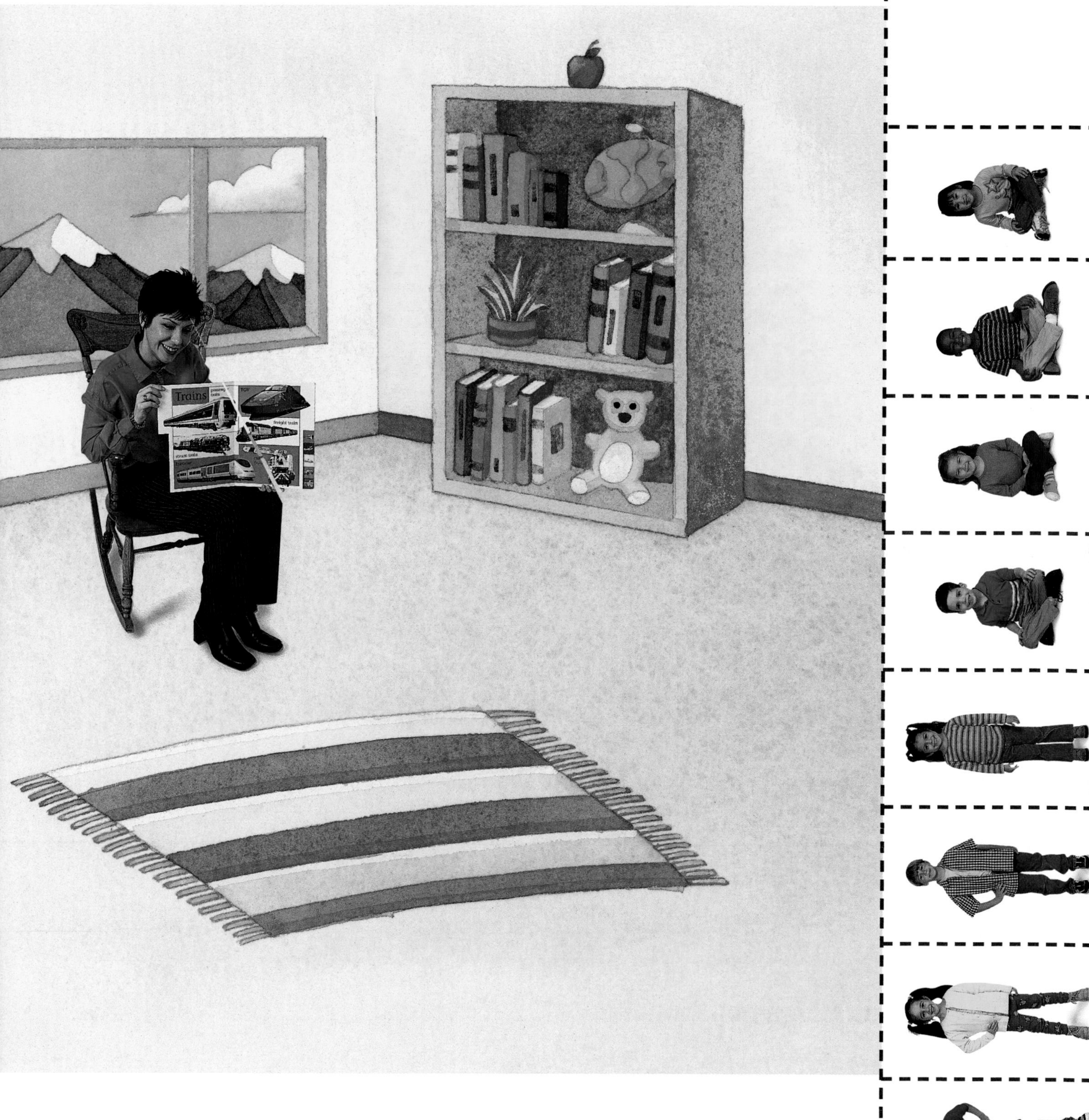


______ and ______ is ______.

**Directions** Have children cut out the pictures and act out the stories from the Teacher's Guide. Then have children glue cutouts to show one story and record a sentence that tells their story.

_____ and _____ is _____.

**Directions** Have children listen to the story from the Teacher's Guide. Have them color the small balls orange, the big balls blue, and write the number of each color. Then have children complete the sentence by writing the number of balls in all.

**Home Activity** Ask your child to tell you about the stories on these two pages and to explain how the numbers tell the stories.

Name ____________________

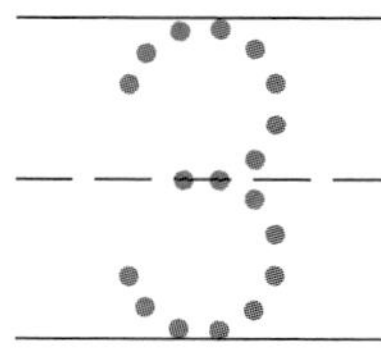 and 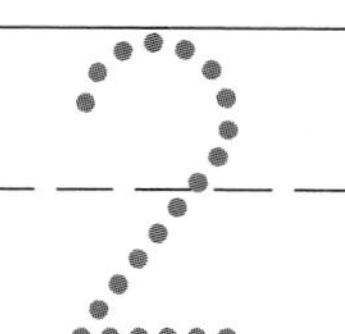 is 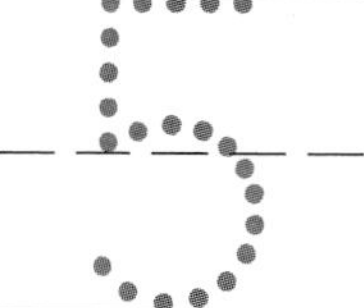.

2

______ and ______ is ______.

3

______ and ______ is ______.

**Directions** In each exercise have children write how many children there are in each group. Then have them circle the 2 groups and record how many there are altogether.

4

3 and 1 is 4.

5

____ and ____ is ____.

6

____ and ____ is ____.

**Directions** In each exercise have children write how many children there are in each group. Then have them circle the 2 groups and record how many there are altogether.

**Home Activity** Give your child two groups of objects, such as 2 books and 3 books. Ask your child to tell how many books there are altogether. Encourage your child to tell a number story about the books, such as: "There are 2 small books and 3 big books. There are 5 books altogether."

Name ____________________

PROBLEM-SOLVING STRATEGY
## Draw a Picture

1

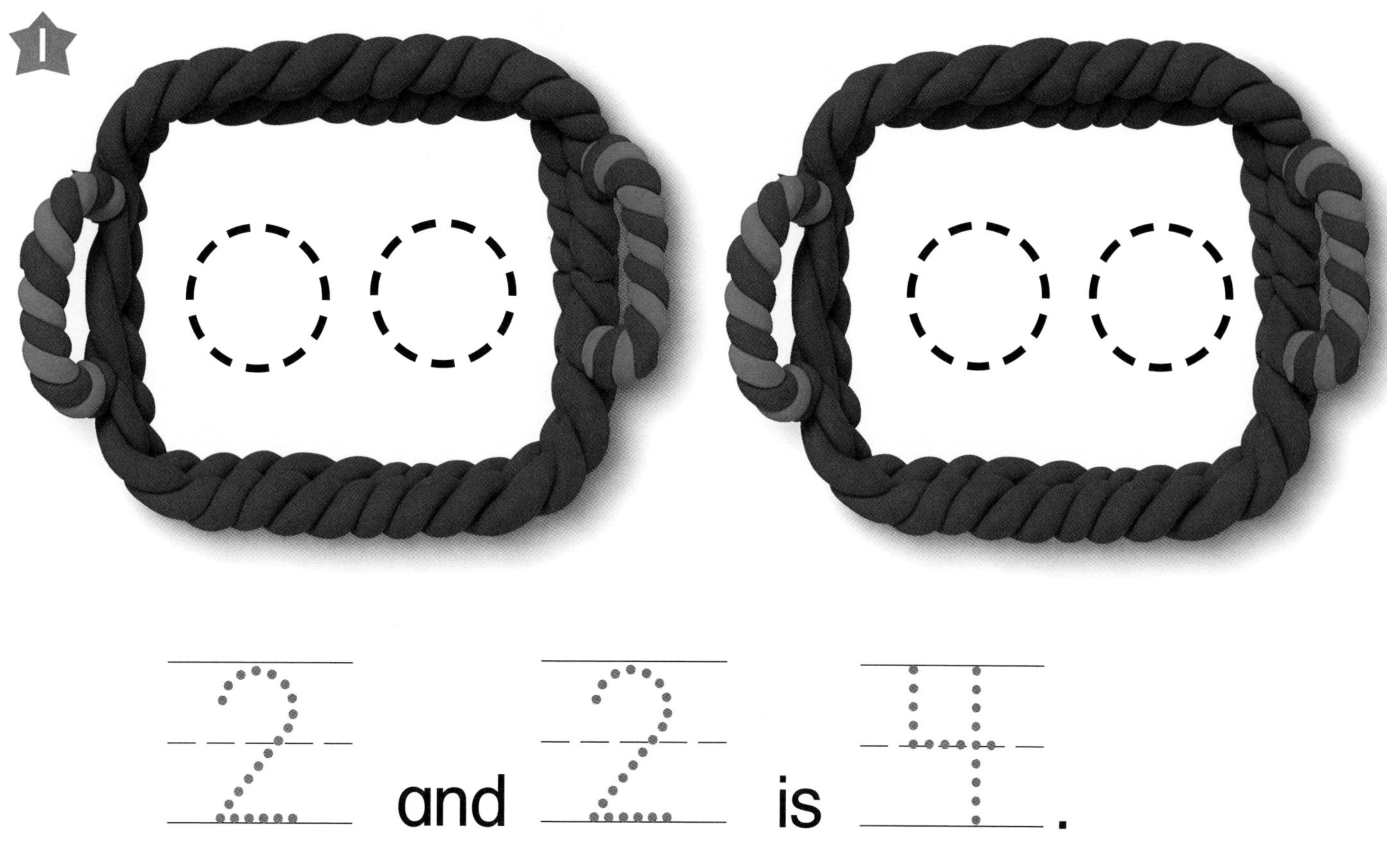

2 and 2 is 4.

2

____ and ____ is ____.

**Directions** Have children listen to the problems from the Teacher's Guide and draw pictures to solve the problems. Ask children to write the numbers that tell how many there are in each group and how many there are altogether.

3

_____ and _____ is _____.

4

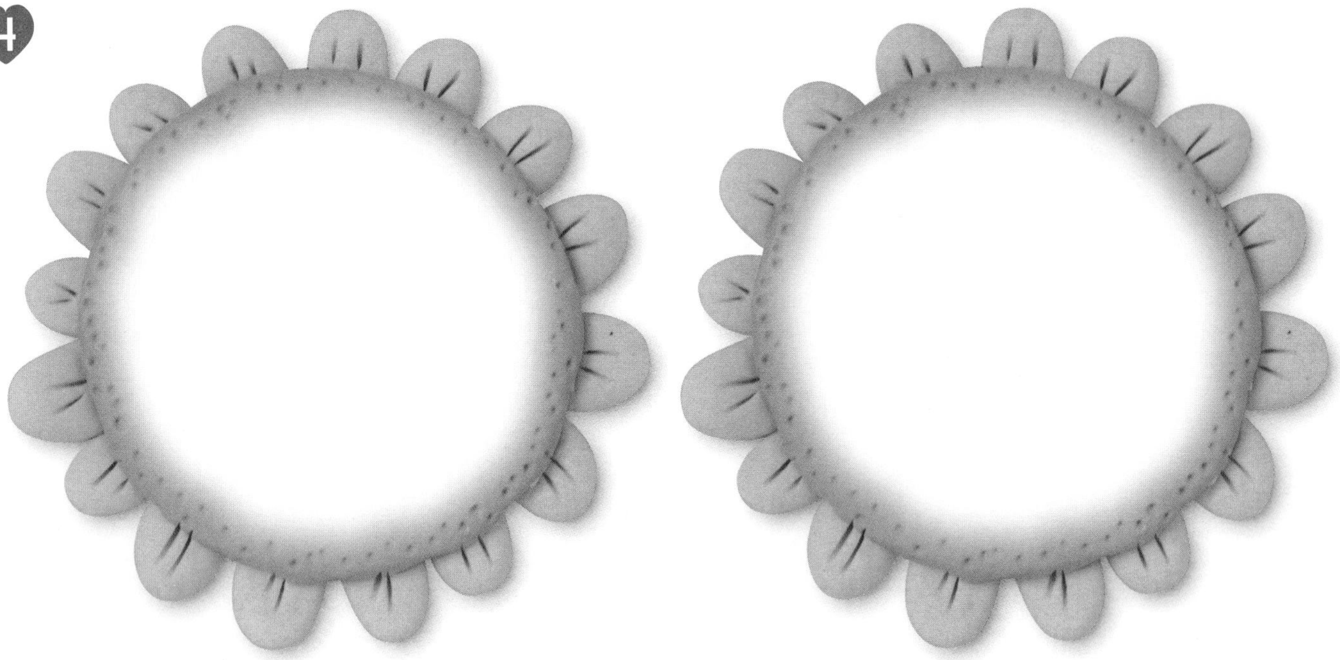

_____ and _____ is _____.

**Directions** Have children listen to the problems from the Teacher's Guide and draw pictures to solve the problems. Ask children to write the numbers that tell how many there are in each group and how many there are altogether.

**Home Activity** Have your child tell you about the pictures he or she drew. Ask your child to explain how drawing pictures helps solve problems.

Name ________________________________

# Using the Plus Sign

1

2 and 3

2 + 3

2

2 and 2

___ + ___

3

4 and 2

___ + ___

**Directions** In each exercise have children write how many animals there are in each group and circle the two groups to join them. Then have children write the plus sign and tell how many there are in all.

4

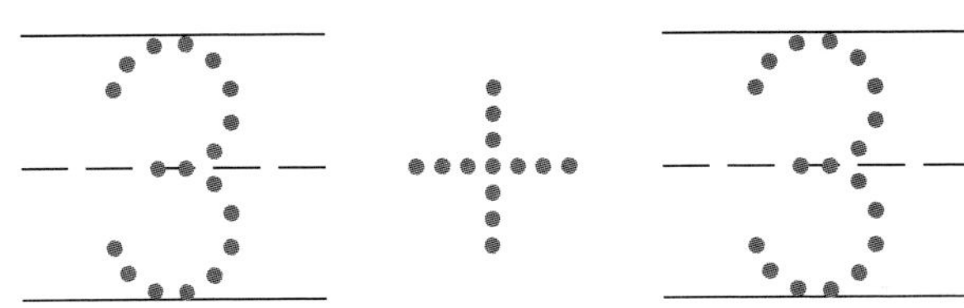

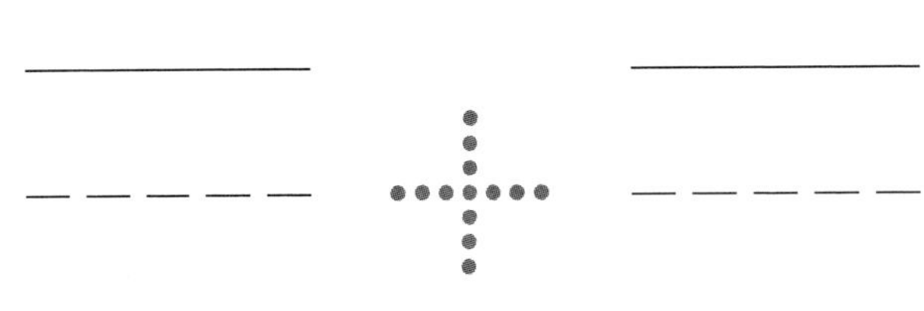

**Directions** In each exercise have children write how many animals there are in each group and circle the two groups to join them. Then have children write the plus sign and tell how many there are in all.

**Home Activity** Show your child two groups of objects, such as 1 sock and 3 socks. Help your child write a plus sign on paper and put it between the two groups. Talk with your child about what a plus sign means. Then have your child tell how many objects there are in all.

Name ____________________



1

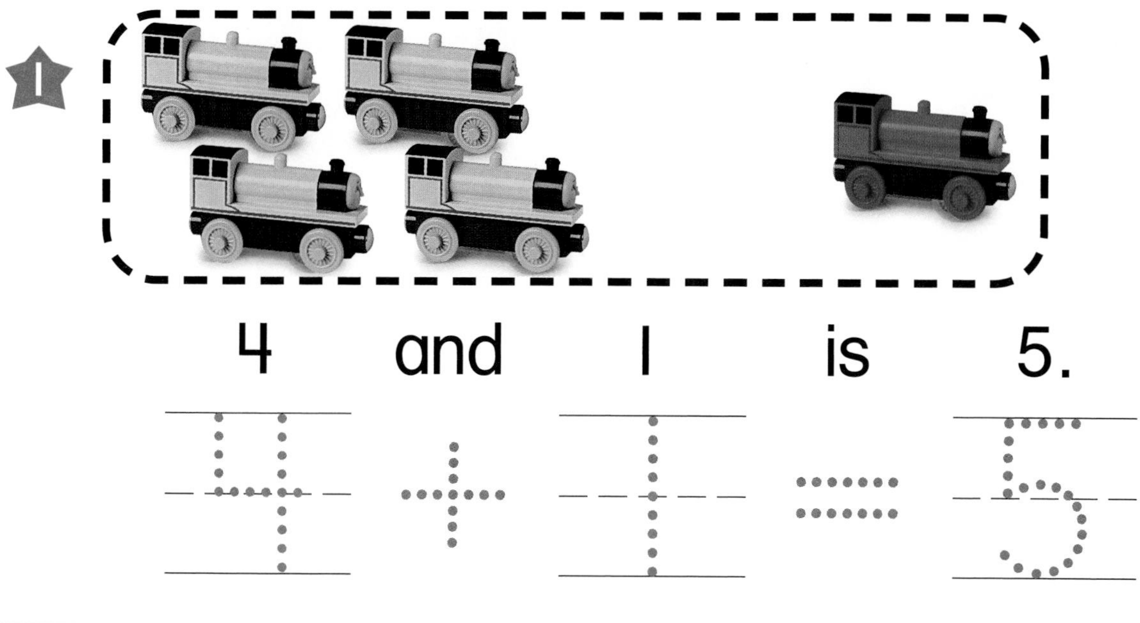

4 and 1 is 5.

4 + 1 = 5

2

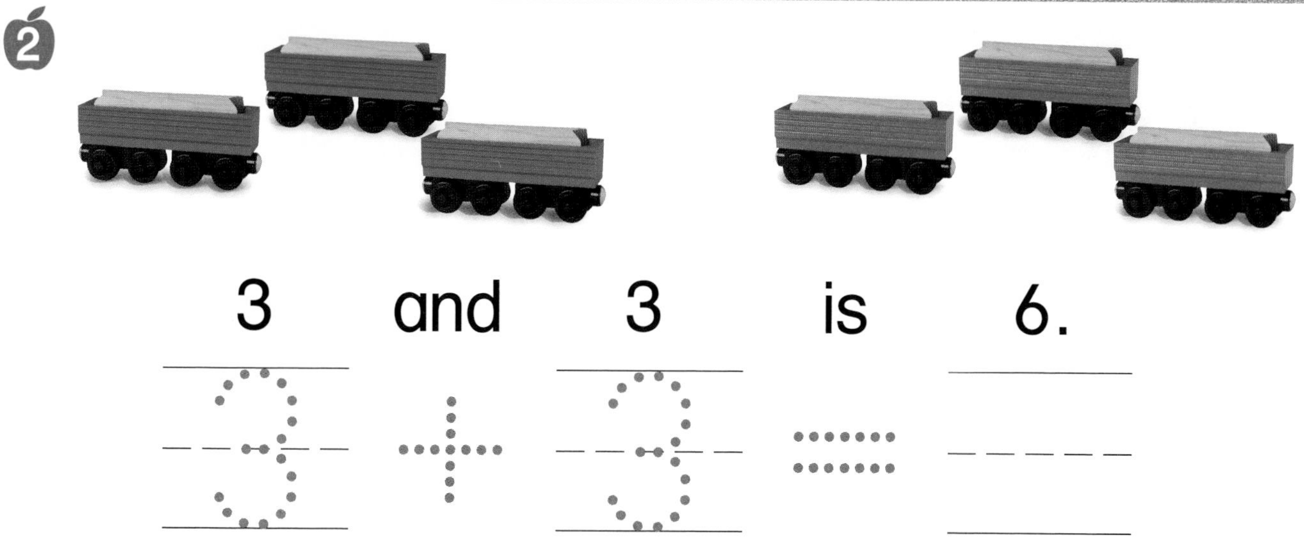

3 and 3 is 6.

3 + 3 = ___

3

2 and 1 is 3.

2 + 1 = ___

**Directions** In each exercise have children write how many there are in each group and circle the two groups to join them. Then have children write the plus and equal signs and record the sum.

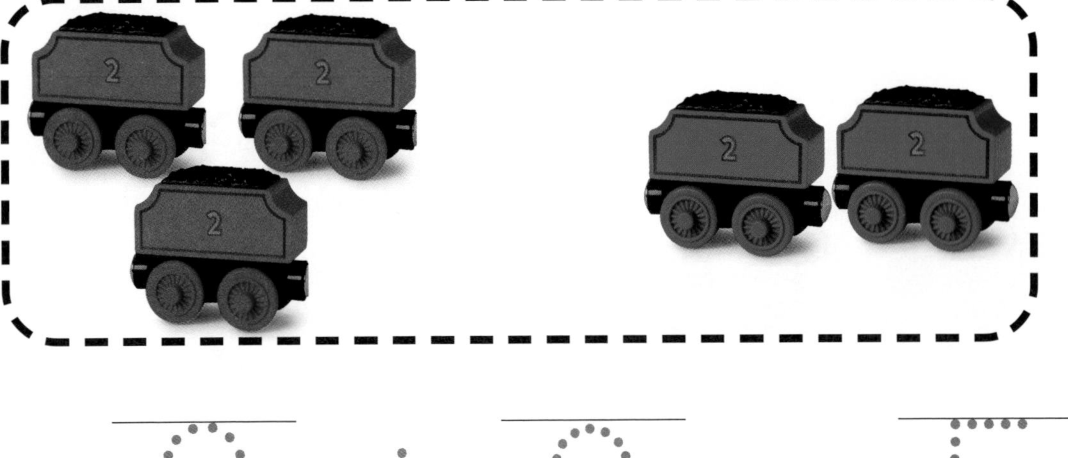

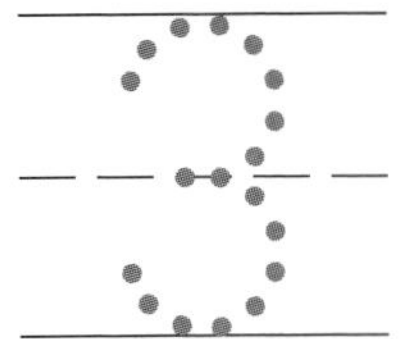 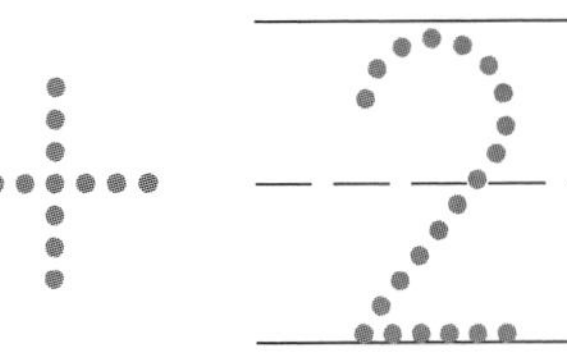 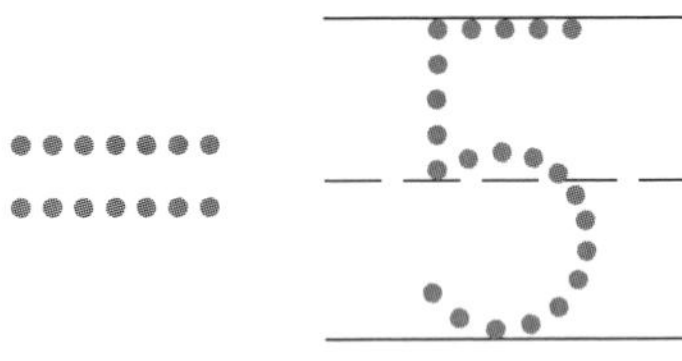

3 + 2 = 5

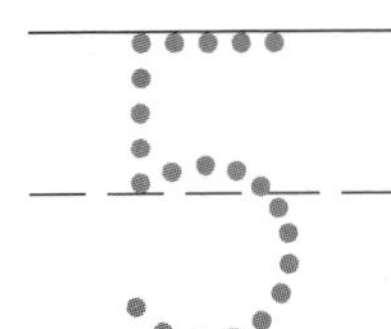 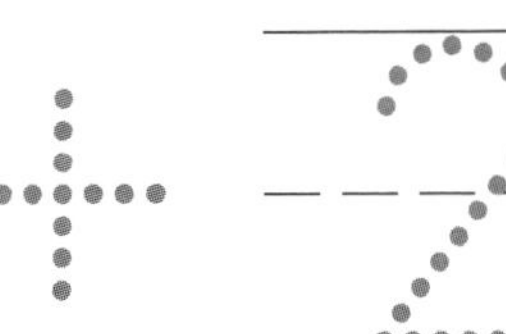 

5 + 2 =

6

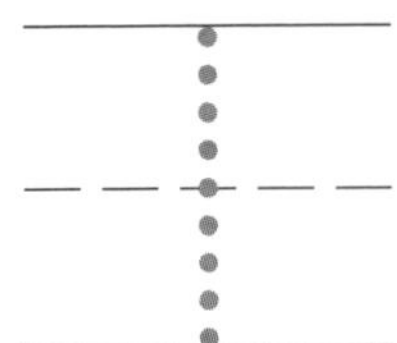 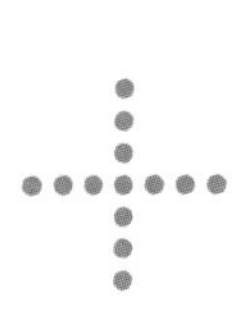 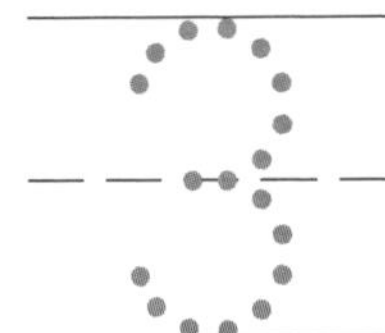 

1 + 3 =

**Directions** In each exercise have children write how many there are in each group and circle the two groups to join them. Then have children write the plus and equal signs and record the sum.

**Home Activity** Show your child a group of 2 spoons and a group of 3 spoons. Help your child write how many there are in all, using the plus and equal signs.

Name ______________________

# Addition Sentences

**Algebra**

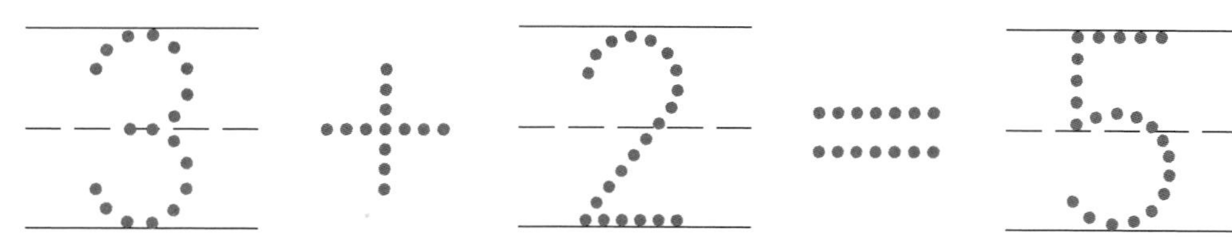

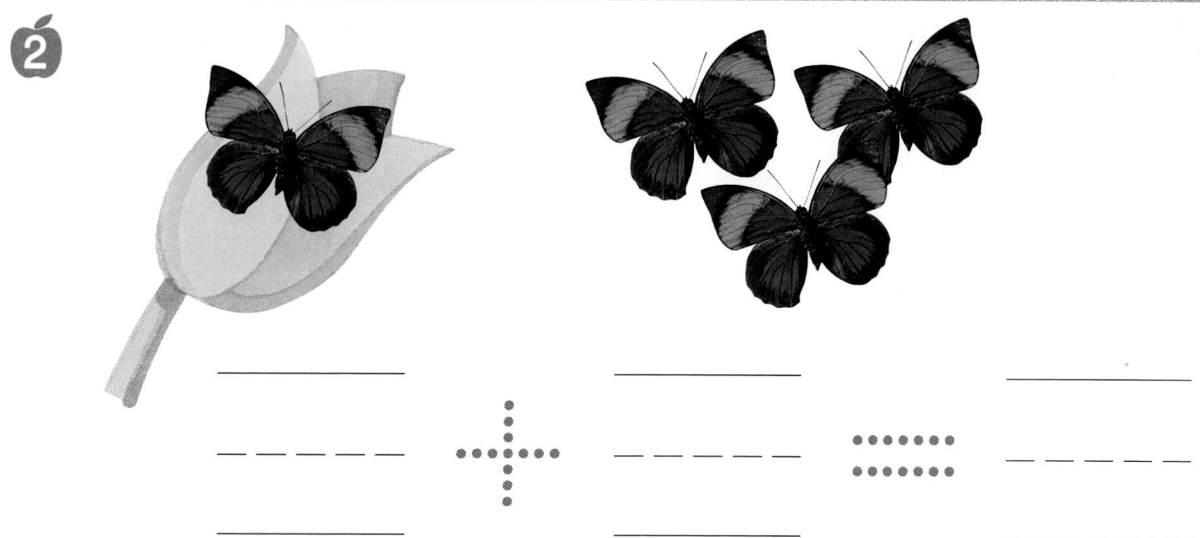

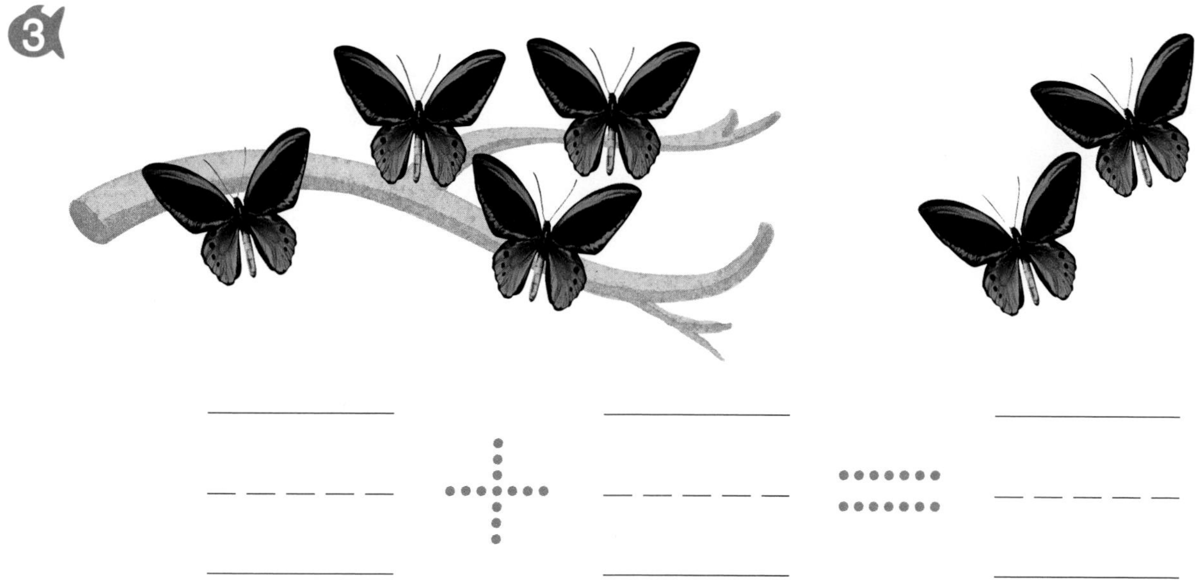

**Directions** In each exercise have children write how many butterflies there are in each group and circle the two groups to join them. Then have children complete the addition sentence by writing the plus and equal signs and recording the sum.

4

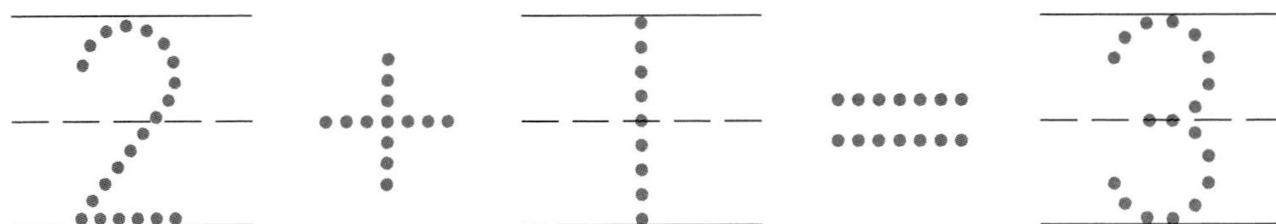

2 + 1 = 3

5

___ + ___ = ___

6

___ + ___ = ___

**Directions** In each exercise have children write how many butterflies there are in each group and circle the two groups to join them. Then have children complete the addition sentence by writing the plus and equal signs and recording the sum.

**Home Activity** Ask your child to write the addition sentence $1 + 2 = 3$ and draw a picture to show the sentence. Have your child talk about the picture and tell why it shows $1 + 2 = 3$.

Name ______________________

# Adding Pennies

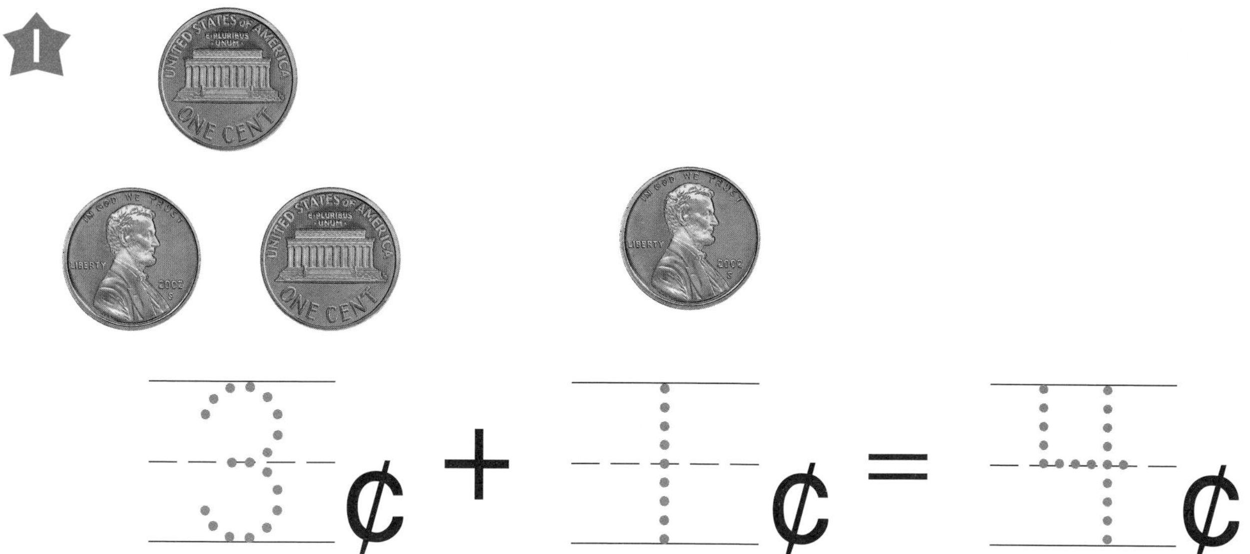

3 ¢ + 1 ¢ = 4 ¢

___ ¢ + ___ ¢ = ___ ¢

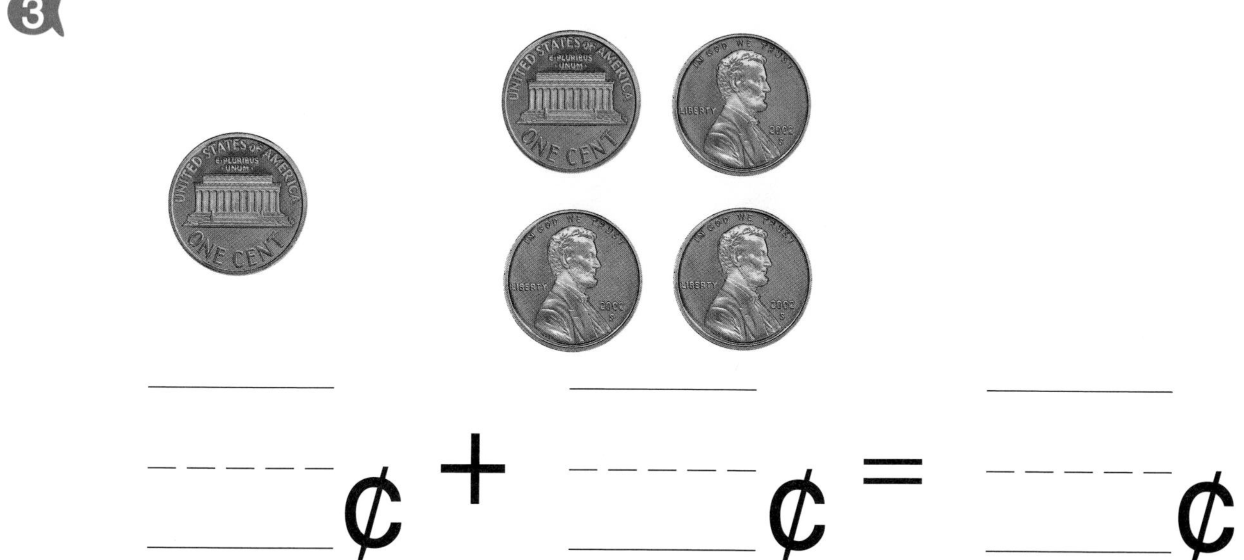

___ ¢ + ___ ¢ = ___ ¢

**Directions** In each exercise have children write how many pennies there are in each group, add the pennies, and complete the addition sentence by writing how many pennies there are in all.

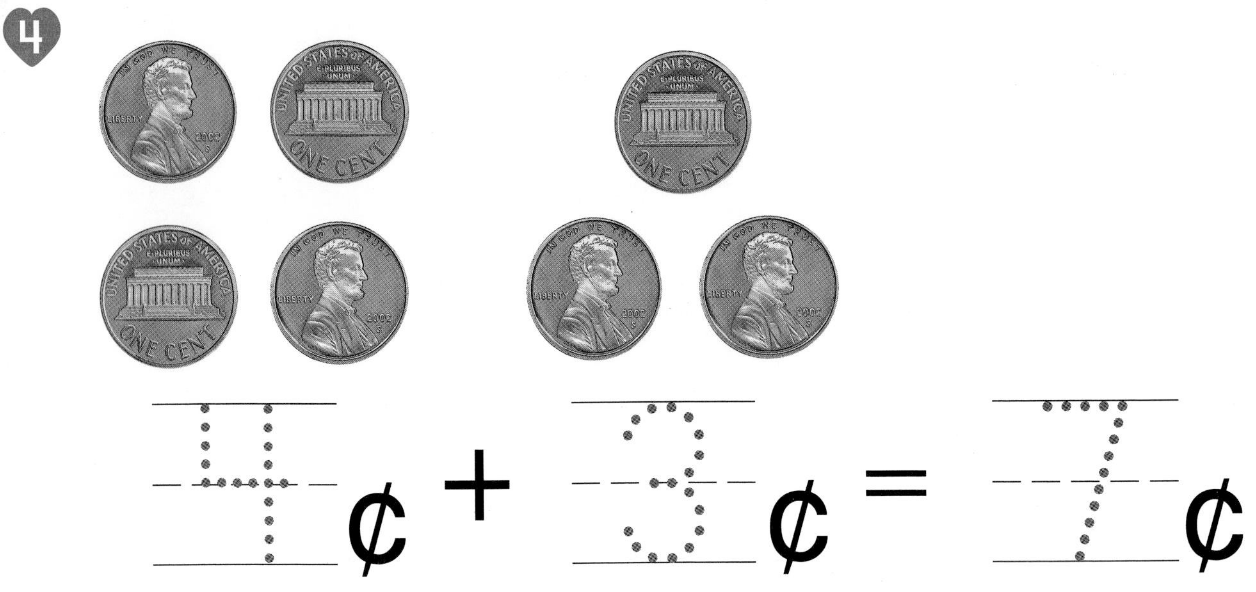

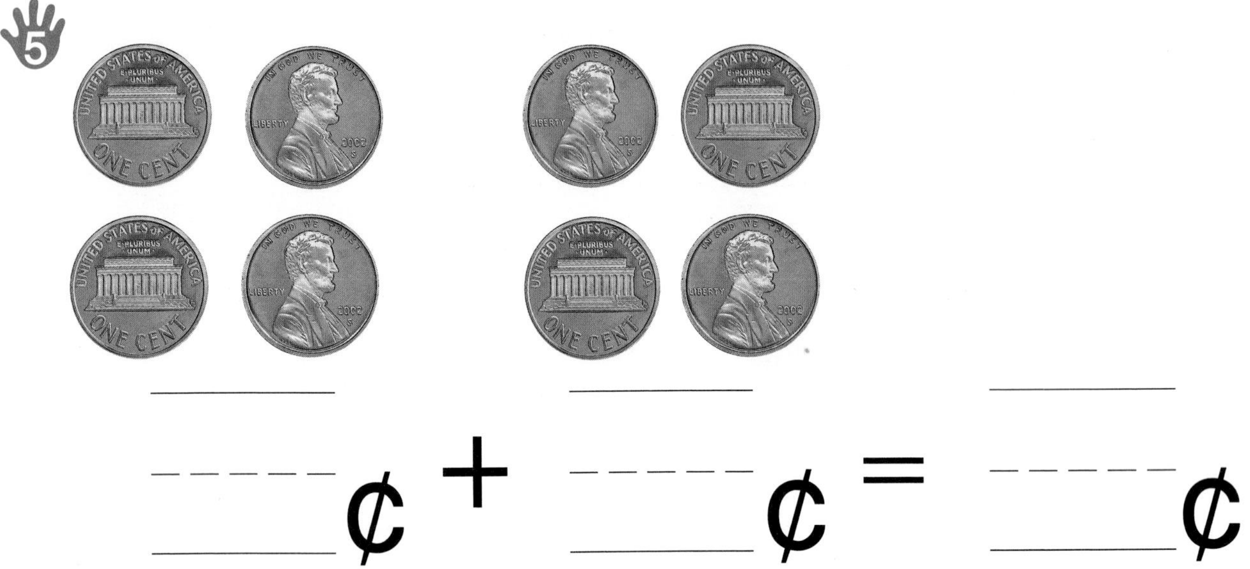

**Directions** In each exercise have children write how many pennies there are in each group, add the pennies, and complete the addition sentence by writing how many pennies there are in all.

**Home Activity** Give your child 7 pennies. Ask him or her to sort the heads and tails into 2 groups and write an addition sentence that tells how many pennies there are in all. Flip some pennies and have your child sort them again. Ask him or her to tell how the addition sentence changes and how it stays the same.

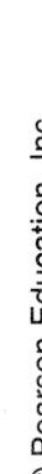

Name ______________________



# Look Alikes

**Directions** Have children describe ways in which the dogs are alike and different. Challenge them to figure out 2 different ways to sort the dogs into 2 groups. (*Small/large or white/black*) Have each child choose one way to sort the dogs and write the addition sentence that shows how many dogs there are in all.

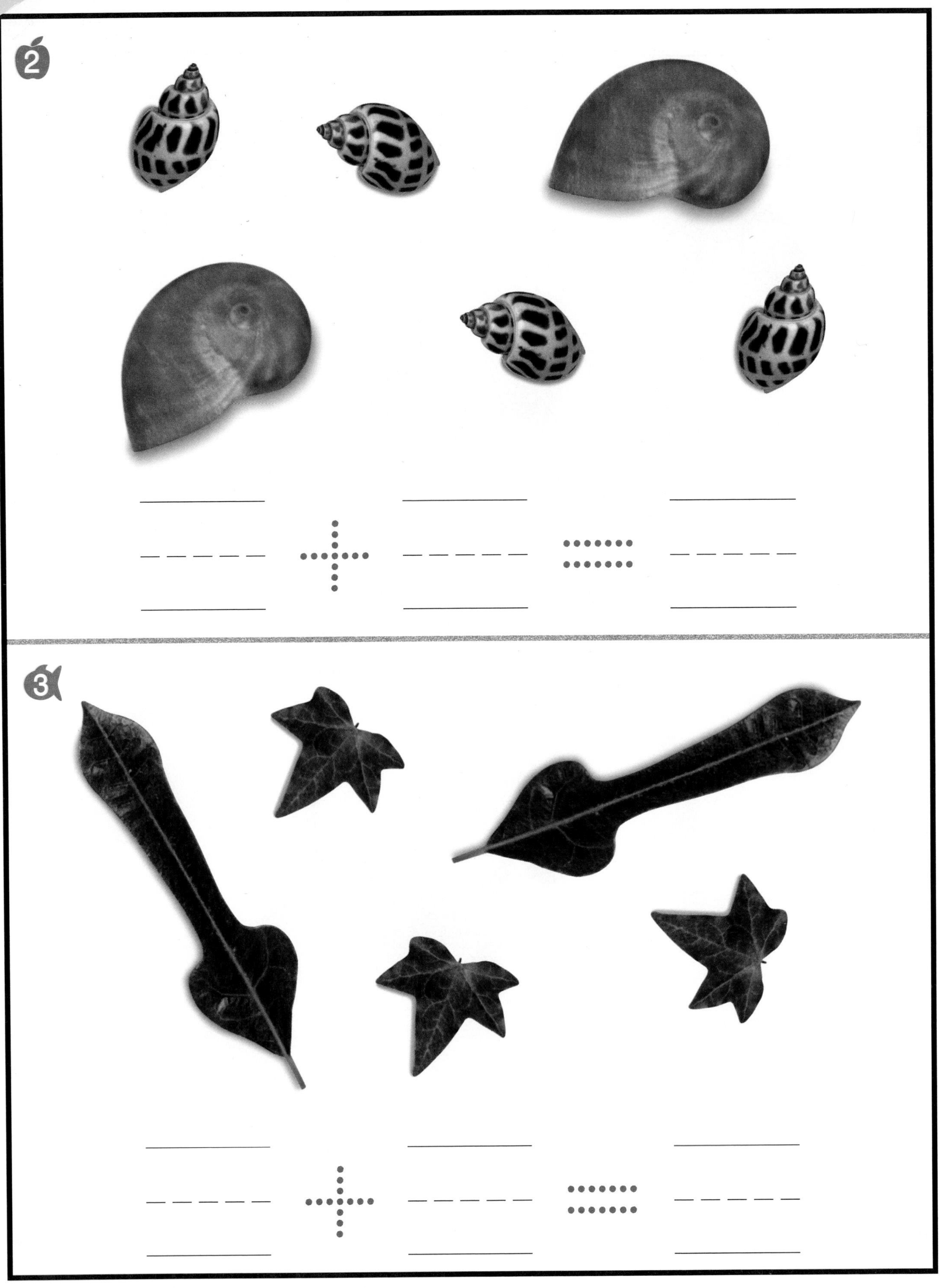

**Directions** In Exercise 2, talk with children about the different shells and ask them to figure out how to sort the shells into 2 groups. Have children add the groups and write the addition sentence. In Exercise 3, have children describe the leaves and figure out how to sort the leaves into 2 groups. Have children add the groups and write the addition sentence.

Name ______________________________

 Test

1

_____ _____ _____

_____ and _____ is _____.

2

_____ _____ _____

_____ and _____ is _____.

**Directions** Have children: 1. write how many there are in each group, circle the two groups, and record how many there are altogether; 2. draw pictures and complete the sentence to solve this problem: **There are 2 fish in one bowl and 3 fish in another bowl. How many fish are there altogether?**

3

2 + 2 = ____

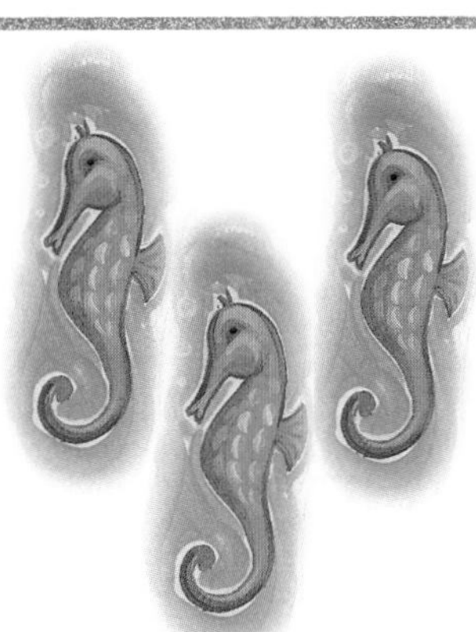

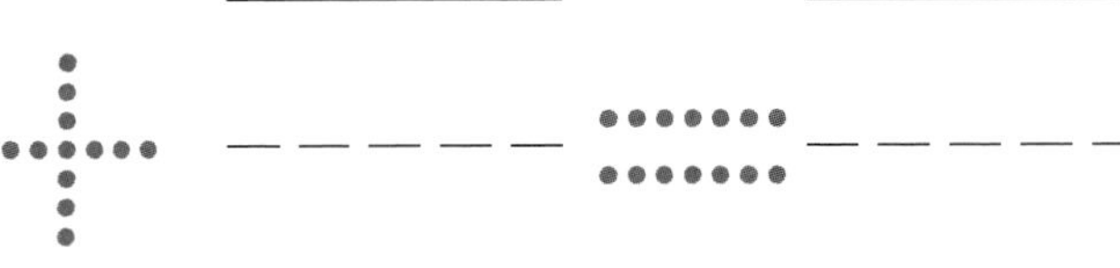

____ + ____ = ____

5

____ ¢ + ____ ¢ = ____ ¢

**Directions** Have children: 3. write how many fish there are in each group, circle the two groups, write the plus and equal signs, and record the sum; 4. write how many sea horses there are in each group, circle the two groups, and complete the addition sentence by writing the plus and equal signs and recording the sum; 5. write how many pennies there are in each group, add the pennies, and write how many pennies there are in all.

CHAPTER 11

# Understanding Subtraction

# The Mystery of the Missing Meatballs

Written by Bryce Santos
Illustrated by Lynne Chapman

This Math Storybook belongs to

______________________________

Leo and his dog Max lived on a houseboat. One night, Leo made spaghetti and meatballs. Leo thought about eating the **5** meatballs one by one.

Leo sat down to eat his dinner.
But Leo did not have a fork.
He went to get one.

Just then the wind blew.
The boat rocked.
And Max grunted and chewed his bone.

When Leo came back with a fork,
he saw only **4** meatballs!

"Hey! Where did my meatball go?" asked Leo.
It was not on his chair.
It was not on the floor.

"Oh, well," he said.
"Maybe I made a mistake when I counted."

Leo sat down to eat his dinner.
But Leo did not have a knife.
He went to get one.

Just then the wind blew.
The boat rocked.
And Max grunted and chewed his bone.

When Leo came back with a knife,
he saw only **2** meatballs!

"Oh, well," Leo said.
"Maybe I made a BIG mistake
when I counted."

Leo sat down to eat his dinner.
But Leo did not have any cheese.
He went to get some.

Just then the wind blew.
The boat rocked.
And Max grunted and chewed his bone.

When Leo came back with the cheese,
he saw only **1** meatball!

"What is going on here?" shouted Leo.
"I have only **1** meatball left!"

Just then the wind blew.
The boat rocked.
And the last meatball rolled off the spaghetti
and landed right inside the dog's mouth!

Max grunted and chewed his bone.

# Home-School Connection

Dear Family,

Today my class started Chapter 11, **Understanding Subtraction.** I will learn about separating groups and about comparing groups. Here are some of the math words I will be learning and some things we can do to help me with my math.

Love,

______________________________

## Math Activity to Do at Home

Play "Bunches of Bananas." Invite your child to count the bananas in a bunch. Then remove 1 banana and sing, "___ bananas in a bunch, in a bunch, in a bunch. Take 1 away and eat it for lunch. How many bananas are left in the bunch?"

## Books to Read Together

Reading math stories reinforces concepts. Look for these titles in your local library:

***Monster Musical Chairs: Subtracting One***
By Stuart J. Murphy
(HarperTrophy, 2000)

***Ten Little Mice***
By Joyce Dunbar
(Harcourt, 1999)

Take It to the NET
More Activities
www.scottforesman.com

## My New Math Words

If you take 3 blocks away from 5 blocks, you have 2 blocks left.

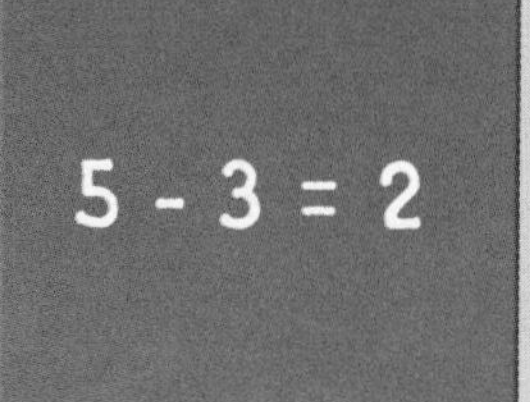



A **separating** story

5 is 2 more than 3.

A **comparing** story

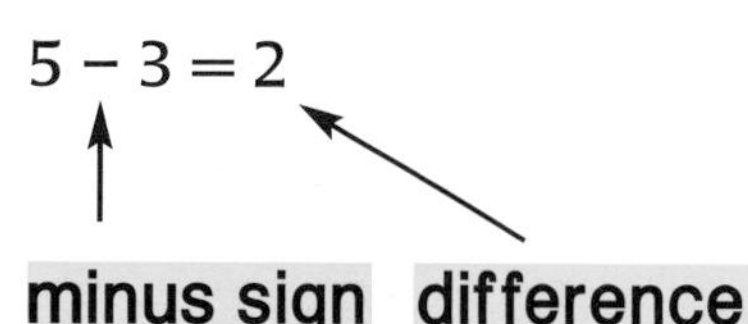

$5 - 3 = 2$

**minus sign** **difference**

Name ___________________________



# Meatball Take Away

### What You Need

1 dot cube
10 small markers

## How to Play

1. Pretend that your markers are meatballs! Put them in the dog's dish.
2. Toss the cube. Say the number.
3. Take away that many meatballs and put them inside the dog's mouth!
4. Say what you are doing, like this: "There were 10 meatballs in the dish. I took away 2 of them. Now there are only 8 meatballs in the dish."
5. Keep playing until the dish is empty!

Name ____________________

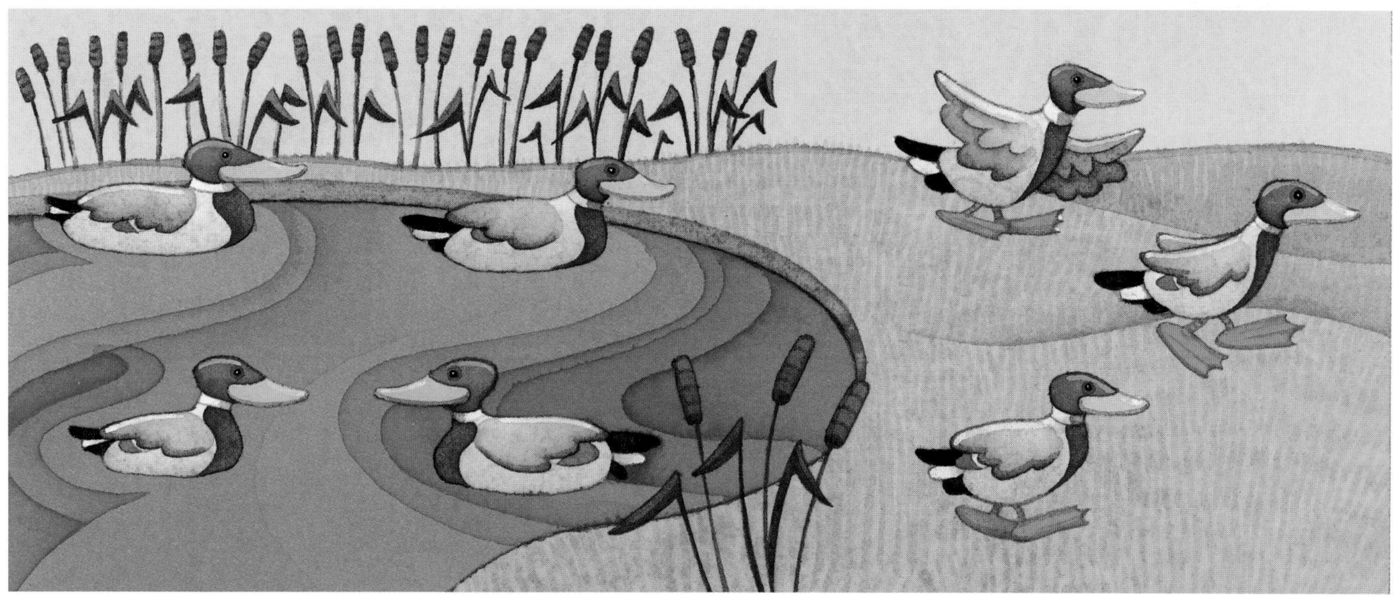

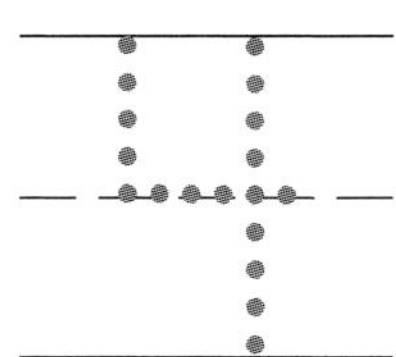 are left.

______ are left.

**Directions** In each exercise have children place a counter on each bird in both groups and count how many there are in all. Have children remove counters for the group that is leaving, count how many are left, and record the number.

3

_____

_____

_____ are left.

4

_____

_____

_____ are left.

**Directions** In each exercise have children place a counter on each bird in both groups and count how many there are in all. Have children remove counters for the group that is leaving, count how many are left, and record the number. Have partners tell each other stories about the pictures.

**Home Activity** Place 5 toys in front of your child and have him or her tell you how many toys there are. Ask your child to move 2 of the toys to the side and tell how many toys are left. Talk about what happened.

Name ____________________



1

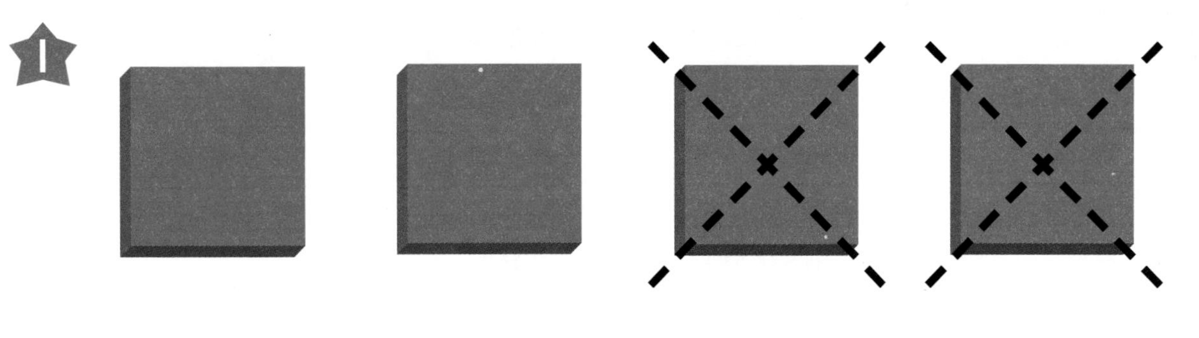

4 take away 2 is 2.

2

____ take away 3 is ____.

3

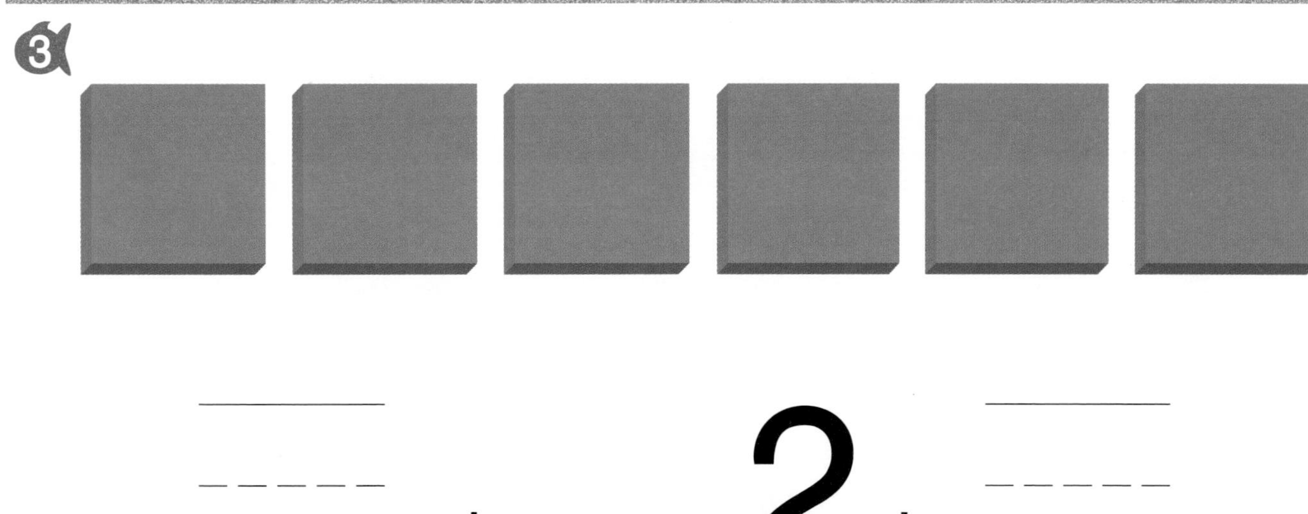

____ take away 2 is ____.

**Directions** Have children place matching tiles in Exercise 1 and write how many there are in all. Have them mark *X*s as they take away 2 tiles. Then have children write how many are left. Repeat, having children take away 3 tiles in Exercise 2 and 2 tiles in Exercise 3.

4

5 take away 1 is 4.

5

___ take away 3 is ___.

6

___ take away 4 is ___.

7

___ take away 2 is ___.

**Directions** In Exercise 4 have children write how many tiles there are in all, mark an *X* to take away 1 tile, and record how many are left. Repeat, having children take away 3 tiles in Exercise 5, 4 tiles in Exercise 6, and 2 tiles in Exercise 7.

**Home Activity** Have your child set out 6 napkins. Tell him or her to take away 3 napkins. Then ask your child to tell you how many are left. Repeat the activity using other numbers of napkins.

Name ____________________

# Comparing

1

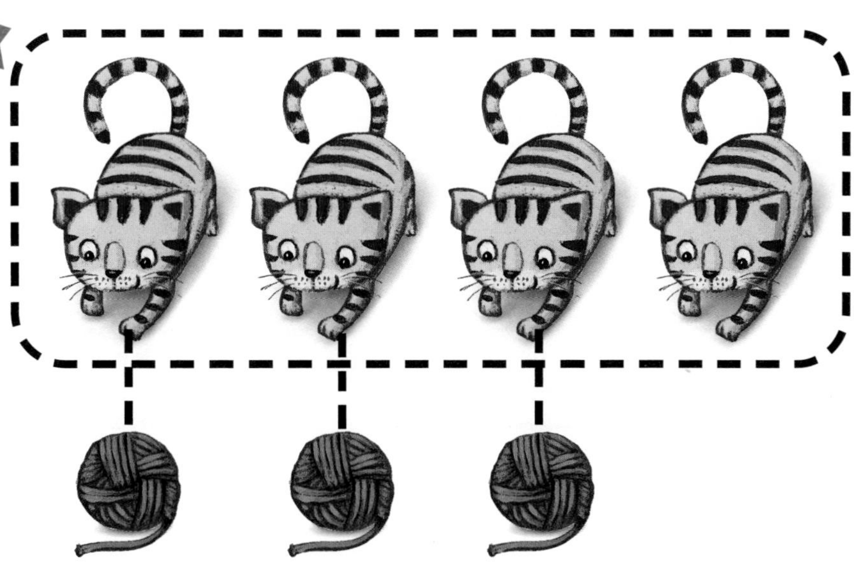

______ more 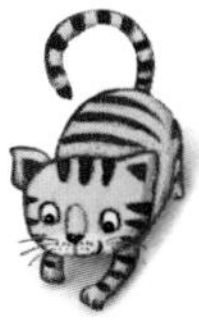

2

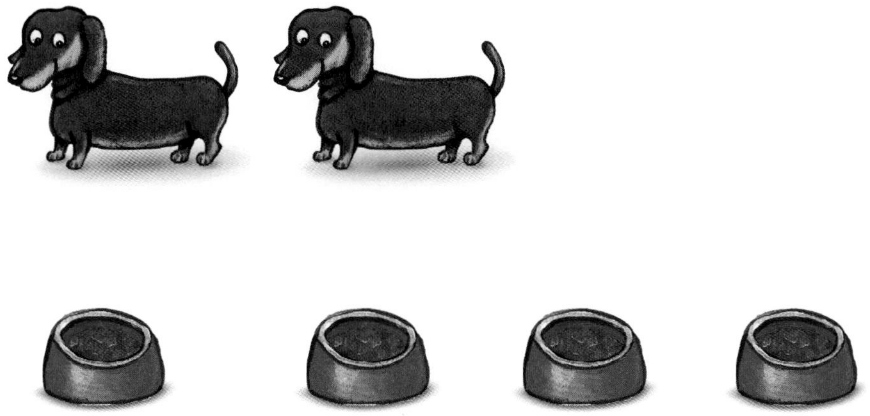

______ more 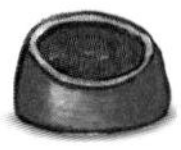

3

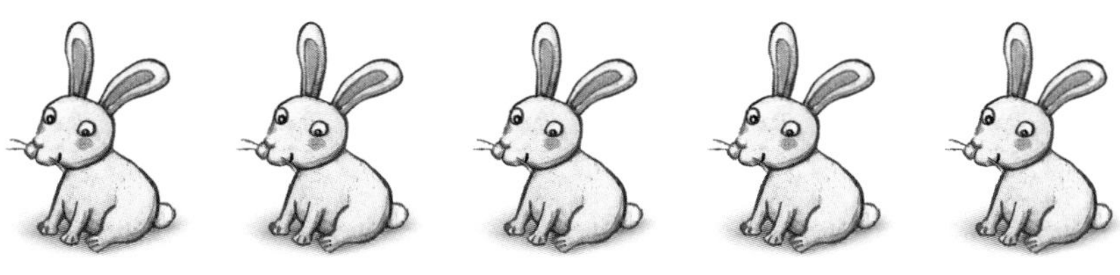

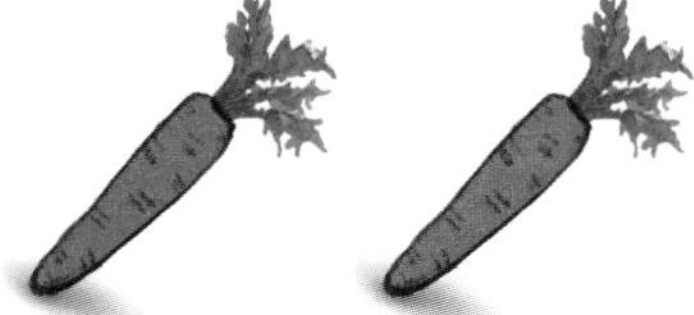

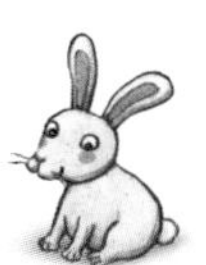

______ more 

**Directions** In each exercise have children draw a line to match each animal in one group to each item in the other group. Have them compare the groups, circle the group with more, and record how many more.

4

2 fewer

5

fewer

6

fewer

**Directions** In each exercise have children draw a line to match each animal in one group to each item in the other group. Have them compare the groups, circle the group with fewer, and record how many fewer.

**Home Activity** Have your child compare a group of 2 shoes and a group of 4 socks. Have him or her tell which group has fewer and how many fewer there are in this group. Ask your child to explain how to compare objects in two groups. Repeat the activity with other groups.

Name ______________________

5 take away 3

5 — 3

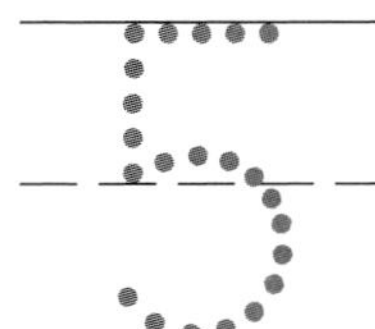

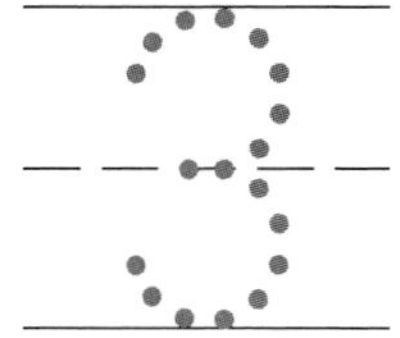

4 take away 1

____ — ____

6 take away 2

____ — ____

**Directions** In Exercise 1 have children write how many toys there are in all and mark *X*s to take away 3. Then have children write the minus sign, record the number taken away, and tell how many are left. Repeat, having children take away 1 in Exercise 2 and take away 2 in Exercise 3.

4

3 - 2

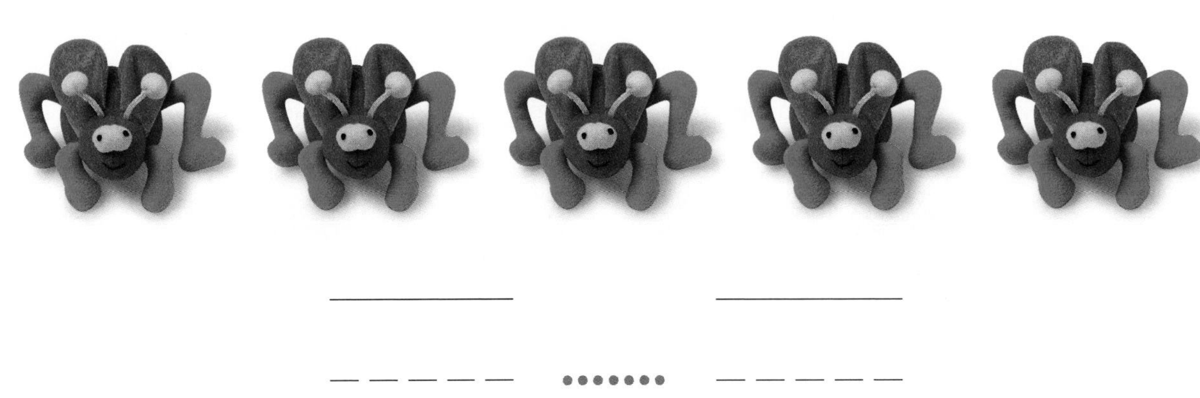

6

**Directions** In Exercise 4 have children write how many toys there are in all and mark *X*s to take away 2. Then have children write the minus sign, record the number taken away, and tell how many are left. Repeat, having children take away 1 in Exercise 5 and take away 3 in Exercise 6.

**Home Activity** Have your child point out a minus sign on the page and explain what the minus sign means. Talk about the pictures and have your child tell you why he or she marked some of the pictures with an *X*. Encourage your child to tell some stories that involve "take away" or the minus sign.

Name ____________________

## Finding the Difference

1

6 take away 2 is 4.

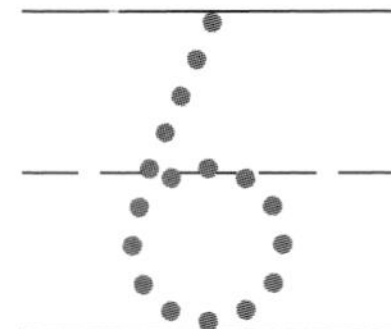 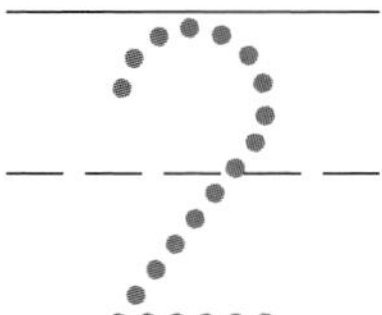  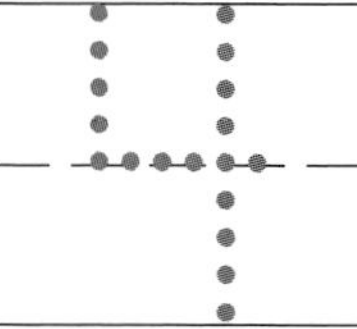

2

4 take away 1 is 3.

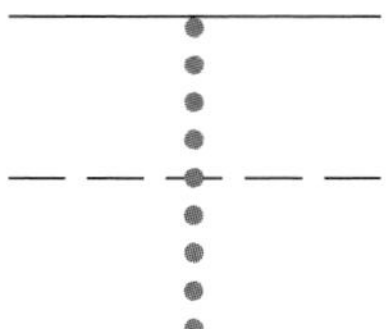 

3

5 take away 3 is 2.

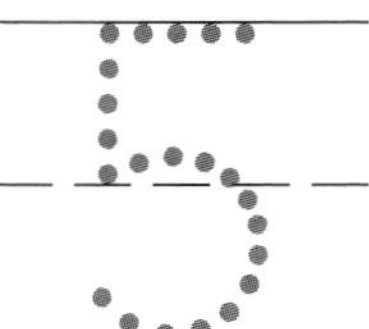 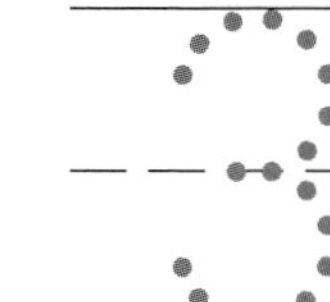  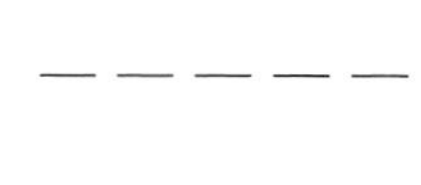

**Directions** In Exercise 1 have children write how many boats there are in all and mark *X*s to take away 2. Have children write the minus sign and record the number taken away. Then have children write the equal sign and record the difference. Repeat, having children take away 1 in Exercise 2 and take away 3 in Exercise 3.

4

7 − 3 = 4

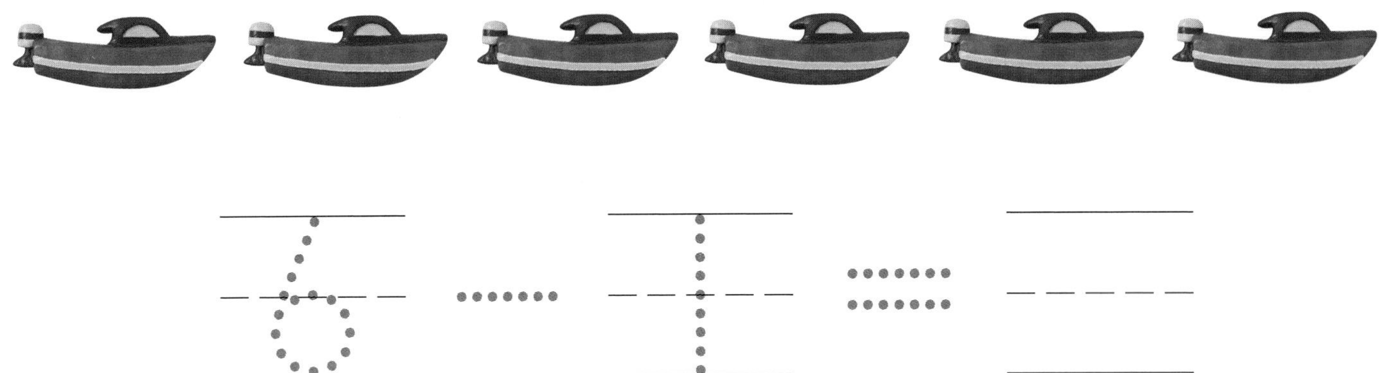

6 − 1 = ___

6

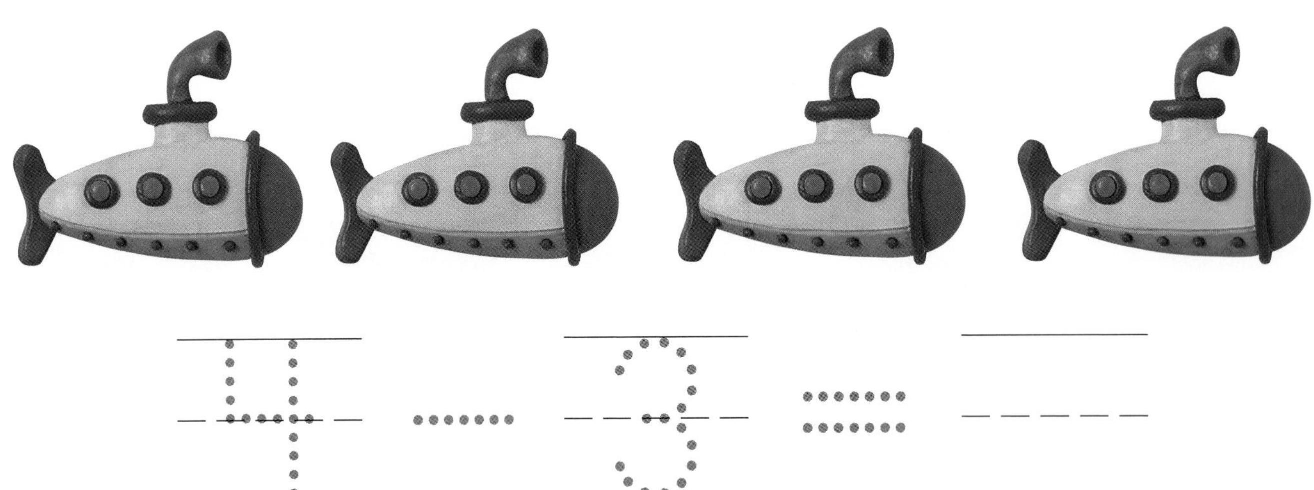

4 − 3 = ___

**Directions** In Exercise 4 have children write how many boats there are in all and mark *X*s to take away 3. Have children write the minus sign and record the number taken away. Then have children write the equal sign and record the difference. Repeat, having children take away 1 in Exercise 5 and take away 3 in Exercise 6.

**Home Activity** Ask your child to tell you about the pictures using sentences such as "7 boats take away 3 boats equals 4 boats." Encourage your child to tell different sentences for the same picture.

Name ______________________



**Algebra**

1

4 − 2 = 2

2

___ ··· ___ = ___

3

___ ··· ___ = ___

**Directions** In Exercise 1 have children write how many there are in all and mark *X*s to take away 2. Have children write the minus sign and record the number taken away. Then have children complete the subtraction sentence by writing the equal sign and recording the difference. Repeat, having children take away 3 in Exercise 2 and take away 1 in Exercise 3.

4

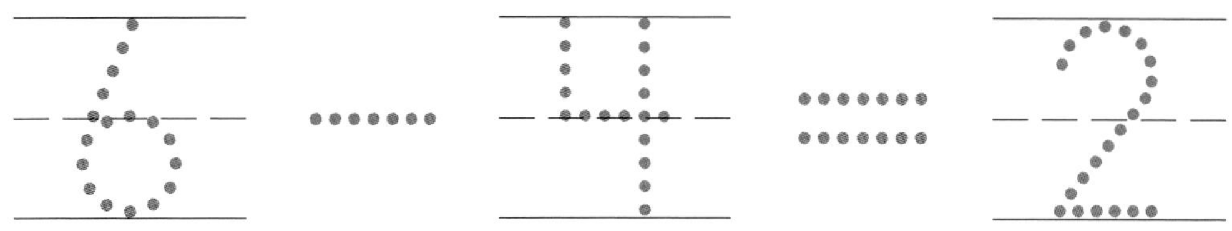

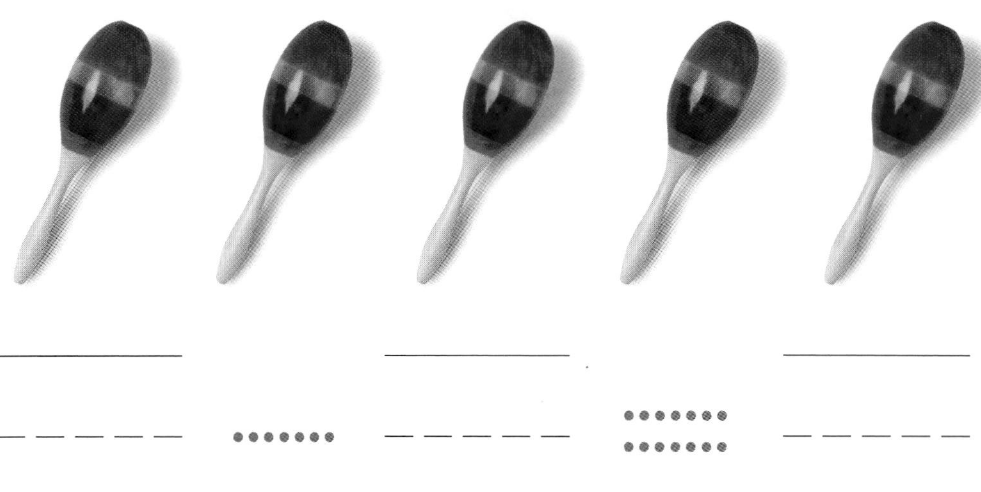

6

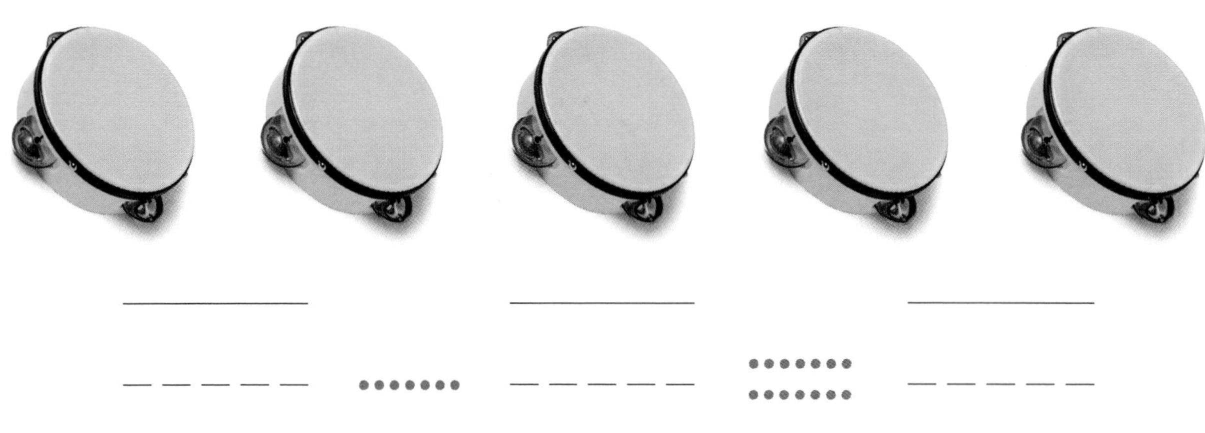

**Directions** In Exercise 4 have children write how many there are in all and mark *X*s to take away 4. Have children write the minus sign and record the number taken away. Then have children complete the subtraction sentence by writing the equal sign and recording the difference. Repeat, having children take away 2 in Exercise 5 and take away 1 in Exercise 6.

**Home Activity** Give your child 6 small objects and ask him or her to give you 4 of the objects. Ask your child to tell what he or she did and to write the subtraction sentence. *(6 − 4 = 2)* Repeat the activity using other subtraction situations.

Name ______________________

# Subtracting Pennies

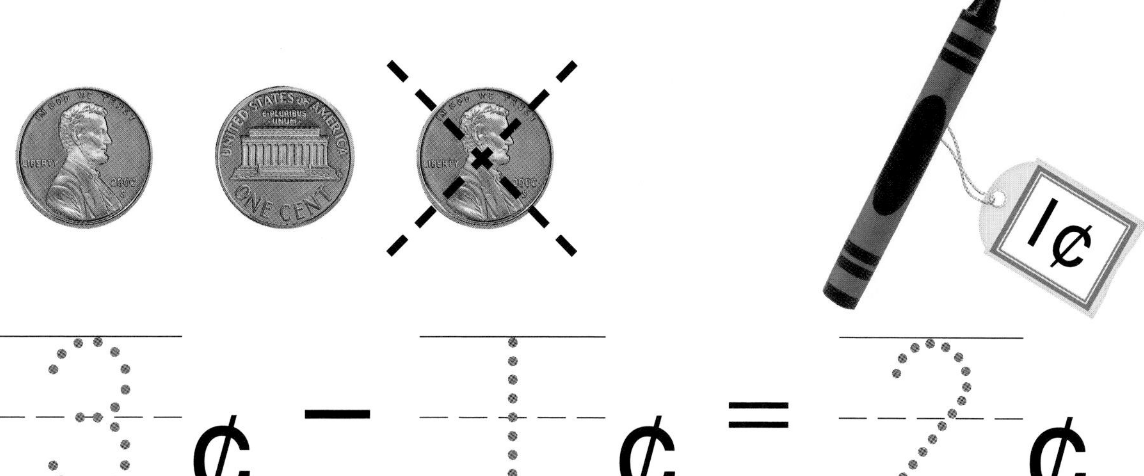


3 ¢ − 1 ¢ = 2 ¢

2

____ ¢ − ____ ¢ = ____ ¢

3

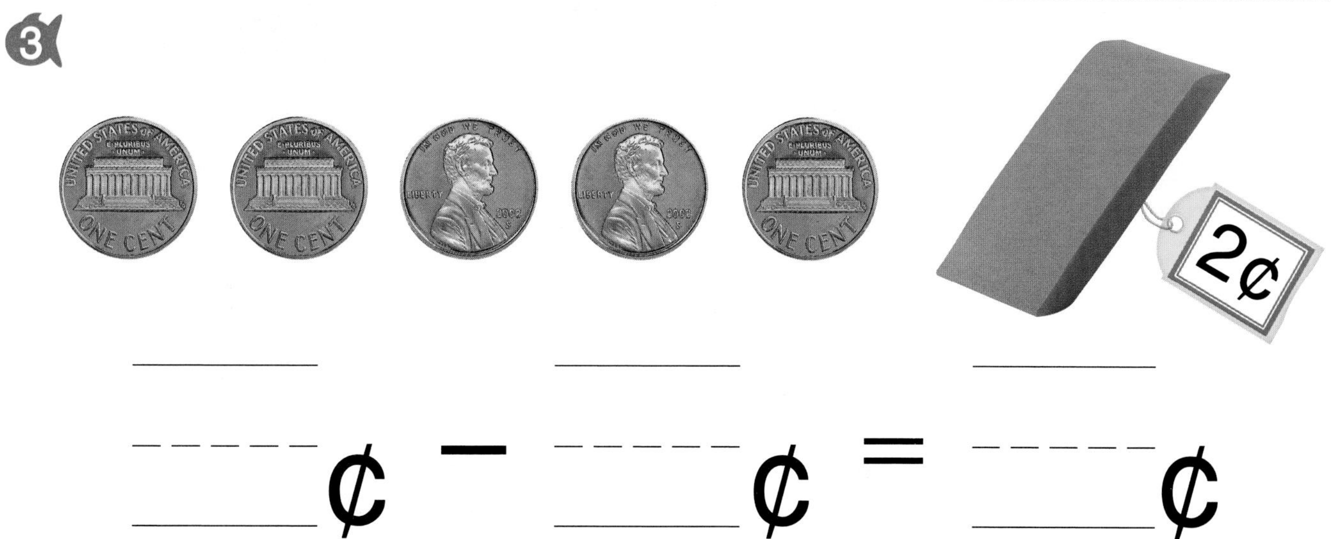


____ ¢ − ____ ¢ = ____ ¢

**Directions** In each exercise have children write how many pennies there are in all and mark *X*s to show how many pennies they would use to buy the item. Then have children complete the subtraction sentence.

4

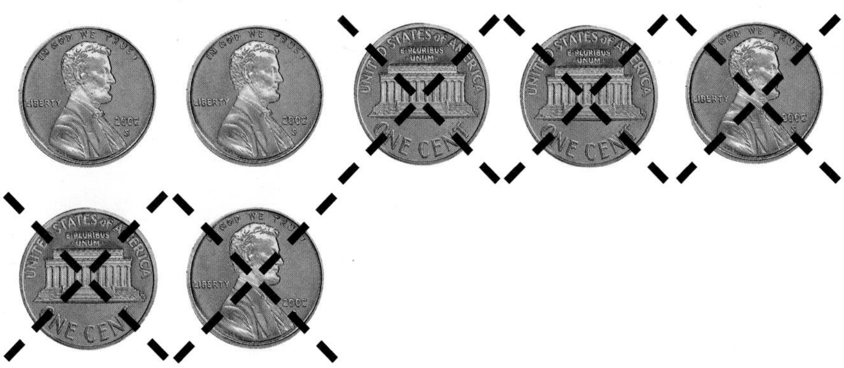

7 ¢ − 5 ¢ = 2 ¢

5¢

5

___ ¢ − ___ ¢ = ___ ¢

2¢

6

___ ¢ − ___ ¢ = ___ ¢

4¢

**Directions** In each exercise have children write how many pennies there are in all and mark *X*s to show how many pennies they would use to buy the item. Then have children complete the subtraction sentence.

**Home Activity** Give your child 6 pennies. Show a small object and tell your child to pretend that it costs 3 pennies. Have your child "buy" the object by giving you the correct number of pennies. Ask your child how many pennies are left.

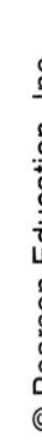

Name ______________________



# Choose an Operation

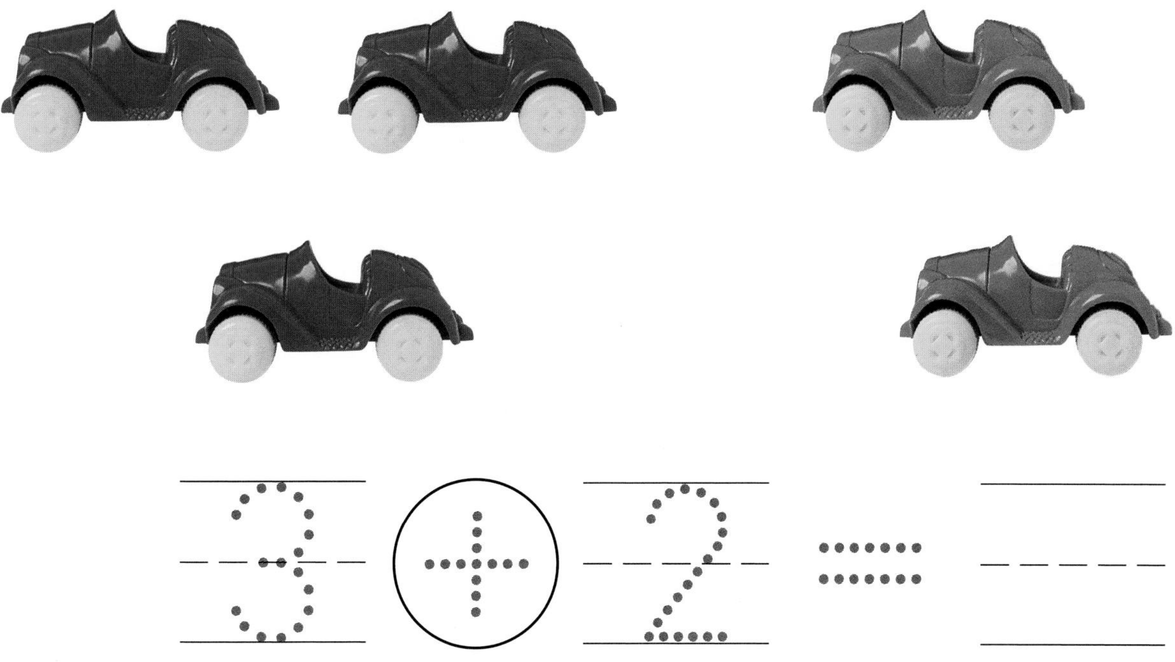

3 + 2 = ____

2

3 − 1 = ____

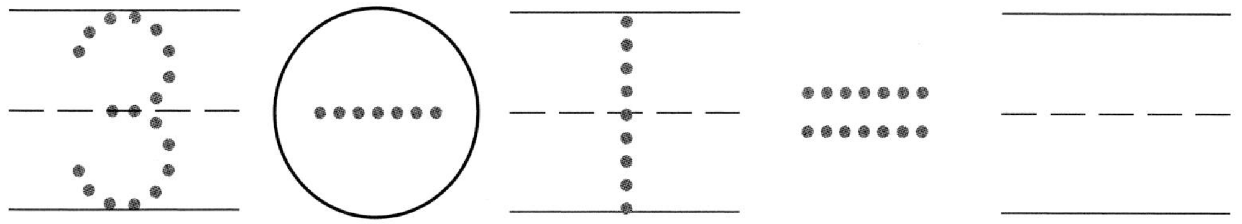

**Directions** In each exercise have children listen to the problem from the Teacher's Guide and decide whether to add or subtract. Then have children complete the addition or subtraction sentence.

3

4 + 1 = 5

4

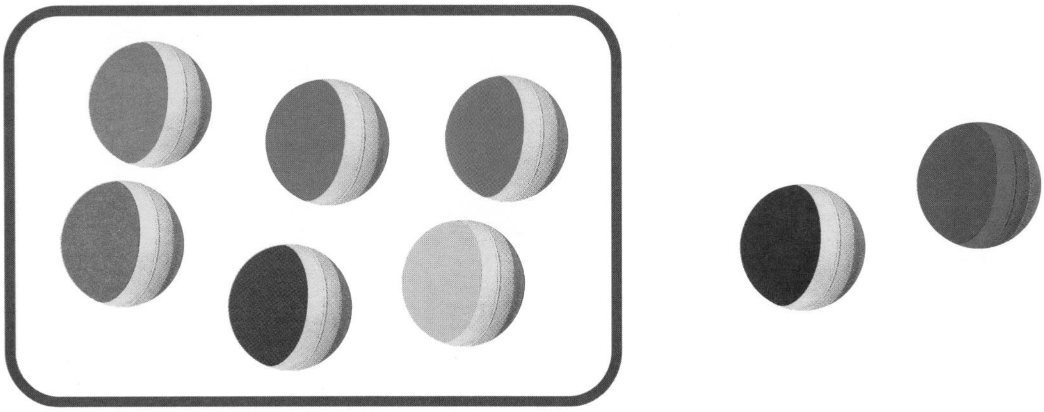

5

**Directions** In each exercise have children listen to the problem from the Teacher's Guide and decide whether to add or subtract. Then have children complete the addition or subtraction sentence.

**Home Activity** Ask your child to explain how he or she decided whether to add or subtract to solve each problem. Together, make up stories that involve adding or subtracting.

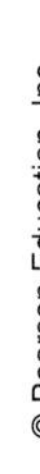

Name ______________________



# Walk, Swim, or Fly

**Directions** Talk with children about the pictures, pointing out that some of the animals walk on 4 legs and some walk or hop on 2 legs. Tell children: **There are 5 animals in all. 3 animals walk on 4 legs. How many of the animals walk on 2 legs?** Guide children to write the subtraction sentence that answers the question.

2

**Directions** Talk with children about the pictures, pointing out that some of the animals swim while others fly. Tell children: **There are 7 animals in all. 4 animals fly. How many of the animals swim?** Guide children to write the subtraction sentence that answers the question.

**Home Activity** Talk with your child about the pictures on these two pages. Have your child tell you how he or she solved problems to complete the pages.

Name ______________________ Test

_____ are left.

_____ take away 3 is _____.

_____ more

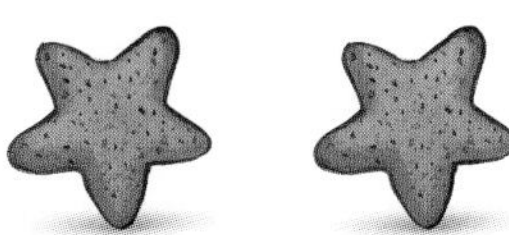

_____ fewer

**Directions** Have children: 1. record how many are left if 2 snails leave; 2. write how many tiles there are in all, mark *X*s to take away 3 tiles, and write how many are left; 3. draw a line to match each fish in one group to each seashell in the other group, circle the group with more, and record how many more; 4. draw a line to match each starfish in one group to each sea horse in the other group, circle the group with fewer, and record how many fewer.

6

7

¢ – ¢ = ¢

**Directions** Have children: 5. write how many boats there are in all, mark *X*s to take away 2, and complete the subtraction sentence; 6. listen to the problem and complete the number sentence: **There are 2 red bells and 3 green bells. How many bells are there in all?** 7. write how many pennies there are in all, mark *X*s to show how many pennies they would use to buy the item, and complete the subtraction sentence.

# Counting and Number Patterns to 100

# The Space Guy with 100 Eyes

Written by Barbara Herzic

Illustrated by Jimmy Pickering

This Math Storybook belongs to

______________________________

Orbie Orbit is from a far-out place.
She searches for treasures in outer space.

Right now she's searching for a VERY big prize—
The Space Guy with 100 Eyes!

Orbie's space jet is fast—zip, zippy, zoom!
She grabs 10 rocks as she flies by the moon.

Look! Over there! Is that Orbie's prize?
No, that's not The Guy with 100 Eyes!
Or is it?

**It's a race in space to the planet Mars.**
**Orbie holds out a net and catches 20 stars!**

**Look! Over there! Is that Orbie's prize?**
**No, that's not The Guy with 100 Eyes!**
**Or is it?**

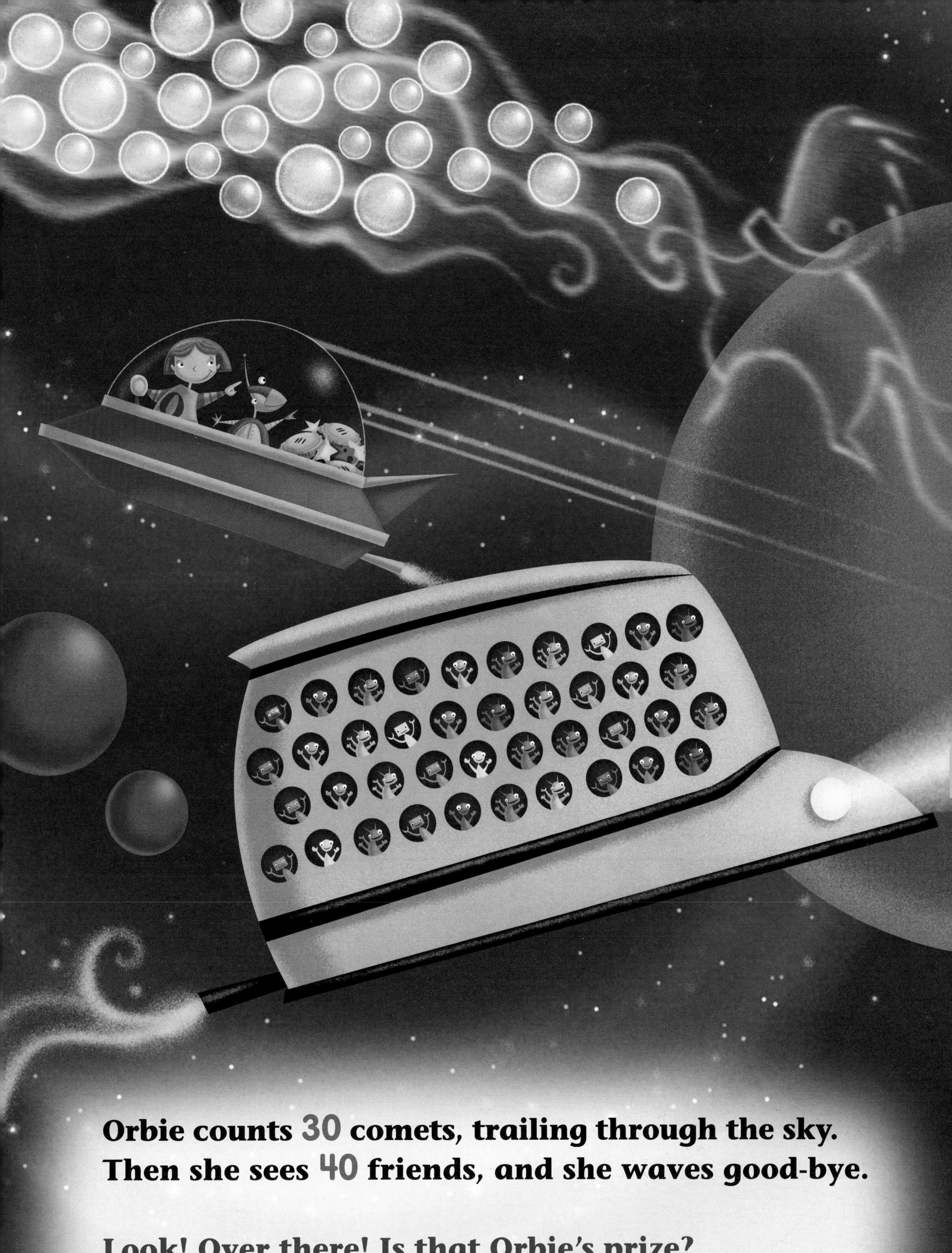

**Orbie counts 30 comets, trailing through the sky.**
**Then she sees 40 friends, and she waves good-bye.**

**Look! Over there! Is that Orbie's prize?**
**No, that's not The Guy with 100 Eyes!**
**Or is it?**

**Orbie jumps off her jet with her 50 moon pies. Now where is The Space Guy with 100 Eyes?**

## Home-School Connection

Dear Family,

Today my class started Chapter 12, **Counting and Number Patterns to 100.** I will learn how to count, write, and recognize patterns in larger numbers. Here are some of the math words I will be learning and some things we can do to help me with my math.

Love,

______________________________

## Math Activity to Do at Home

Play "Give Me Five!" Group together 5, 10, 15, and 20 pieces of cereal or pasta. Point to a group and ask, "How many 5s are in this group?" Work together to count by 5s and to place the correct number of hands (1, 2, 3, or 4 hands with fingers spread apart) in front of each group.

## Books to Read Together

Reading math stories reinforces concepts. Look for these titles in your local library:

***From One to One Hundred***
By Teri Sloat
(Puffin Books, 1995)

***The Wolf's Chicken Stew***
By Keiko Kasza
(Putnam, 1996)

## My New Math Words

**hundred chart** I can use it to explore number patterns, such as **ten more** and **ten less**.

| 1 | 2 | 3 | 4 | 5 | 6 | 7 | 8 | 9 | 10 |
|---|---|---|---|---|---|---|---|---|---|
| 11 | 12 | 13 | 14 | 15 | 16 | 17 | 18 | 19 | 20 |
| 21 | 22 | 23 | 24 | 25 | 26 | 27 | 28 | 29 | 30 |
| 31 | 32 | 33 | 34 | 35 | 36 | 37 | 38 | 39 | 40 |
| 41 | 42 | 43 | 44 | 45 | 46 | 47 | 48 | 49 | 50 |
| 51 | 52 | 53 | 54 | 55 | 56 | 57 | 58 | 59 | 60 |
| 61 | 62 | 63 | 64 | 65 | 66 | 67 | 68 | 69 | 70 |
| 71 | 72 | 73 | 74 | 75 | 76 | 77 | 78 | 79 | 80 |
| 81 | 82 | 83 | 84 | 85 | 86 | 87 | 88 | 89 | 90 |
| 91 | 92 | 93 | 94 | 95 | 96 | 97 | 98 | 99 | 100 |

**skip counting** I can skip count by 2s, 5s, 10s, and other numbers.

I can count by 2s all the way to 20!

I can count by 5s all the way to 50!

I can count by 10s all the way to 100!

Name ______________________

Practice Game

# 10s in Outer Space

**What You Need**

2 dot cubes

5 small game markers for each player

## How to Play

1. Play with a partner.
2. Count the stars on your rocket by 10s. Say the total.
3. Toss both cubes. If the sum of the two numbers is 10, place a marker over one group of 10 stars.
4. The first player to get to the top of his or her rocket is the winner. BLAST OFF!

Player 1

FINISH

START

Player 2

FINISH

START

Name ______________________________

# Counting Groups of 10

1

10

20

50

100

**Directions** Have children count the groups of 10 fingers and write the numbers.

2

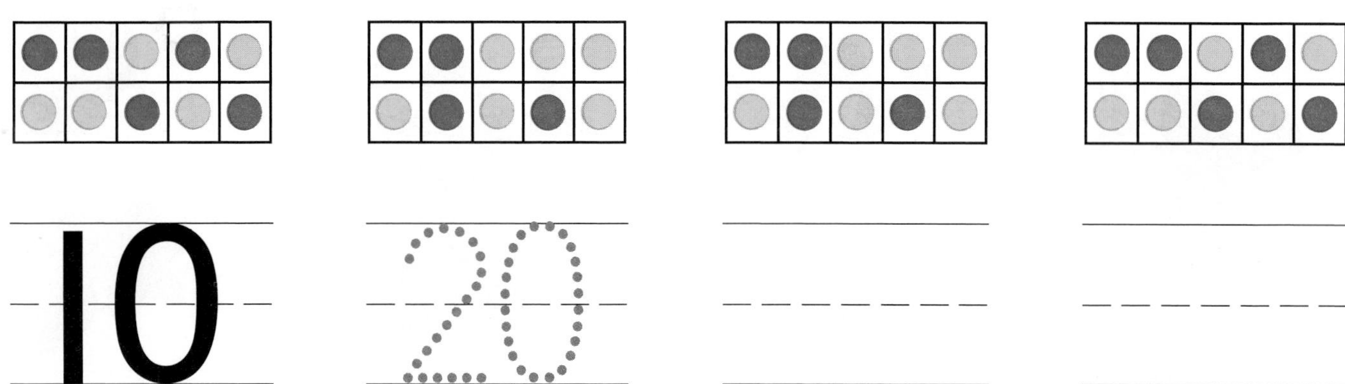

10 20

3

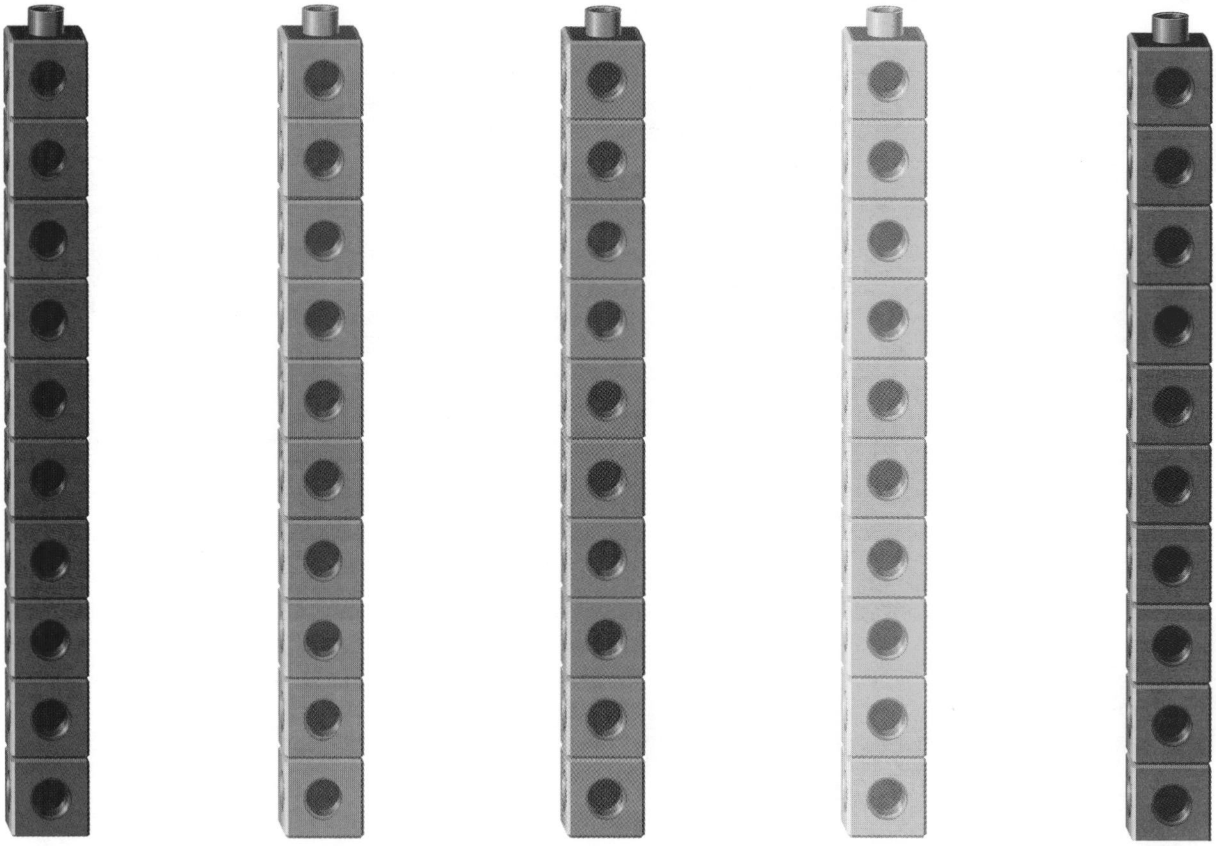

10 20

Directions In each exercise have children count the groups of 10 and write the numbers.

**Home Activity** Set out 4 groups of 10 small objects, such as pasta pieces or dried beans. Have your child count the groups and tell how many objects there are. Ask your child to talk about how she or he counted by 10s.

Name ______________________________

| 1 | 2 | 3 | 4 | 5 | 6 | 7 | 8 | 9 | 10 |
|---|---|---|---|---|---|---|---|---|---|
| 11 | 12 | 13 | 14 | 15 | 16 | 17 | 18 | 19 | 20 |
| 21 | 22 | 23 | 24 | 25 | 26 | 27 | 28 | 29 | 30 |
| 31 | 32 | 33 | 34 | 35 | 36 | 37 | 38 | 39 | 40 |
| 41 | 42 | 43 | | 45 | 46 | 47 | 48 | | 50 |
| | 52 | 53 | 54 | 55 | 56 | | 58 | 59 | 60 |
| 61 | 62 | | 64 | | 66 | 67 | 68 | 69 | 70 |
| 71 | | 73 | 74 | 75 | 76 | 77 | 78 | 79 | |
| 81 | 82 | 83 | | 85 | 86 | 87 | | 89 | 90 |
| | 92 | 93 | 94 | 95 | 96 | 97 | 98 | | 100 |

**Directions** Have children count to 100 on the hundred chart and write the missing numbers. Talk with children about different patterns on the hundred chart.

| 1 | 2 | 3 | 4 | 5 | 6 | 7 | 8 | 9 | 10 |
|---|---|---|---|---|---|---|---|---|---|
| 11 | 12 | 13 | 14 | 15 | 16 | 17 | 18 | 19 | 20 |
| 21 | | 23 | 24 | 25 | 26 | 27 | 28 | | 30 |
| 31 | 32 | | 34 | 35 | | 37 | 38 | 39 | 40 |
| 41 | 42 | 43 | 44 | | 46 | 47 | 48 | 49 | |
| 51 | | 53 | 54 | 55 | 56 | | 58 | 59 | 60 |
| | 62 | 63 | | 65 | 66 | 67 | 68 | 69 | 70 |
| 71 | 72 | 73 | 74 | 75 | 76 | 77 | | | 80 |
| 81 | 82 | | 84 | 85 | 86 | 87 | 88 | 89 | |
| | 92 | 93 | 94 | | 96 | 97 | 98 | 99 | 100 |

**Directions** Have children count to 100 on the hundred chart and write the missing numbers.

**Home Activity** Practice reading numbers on the hundred chart with your child. Together, count along several rows as he or she points to each number. Say a number and have your child find it on the chart. Repeat for other numbers.

Name ______________________

# Counting Large Quantities

1

How many? ________

**Directions** Ask children to count the groups of 10 beads and then count on the remaining beads. Have children record how many beads there are.

2

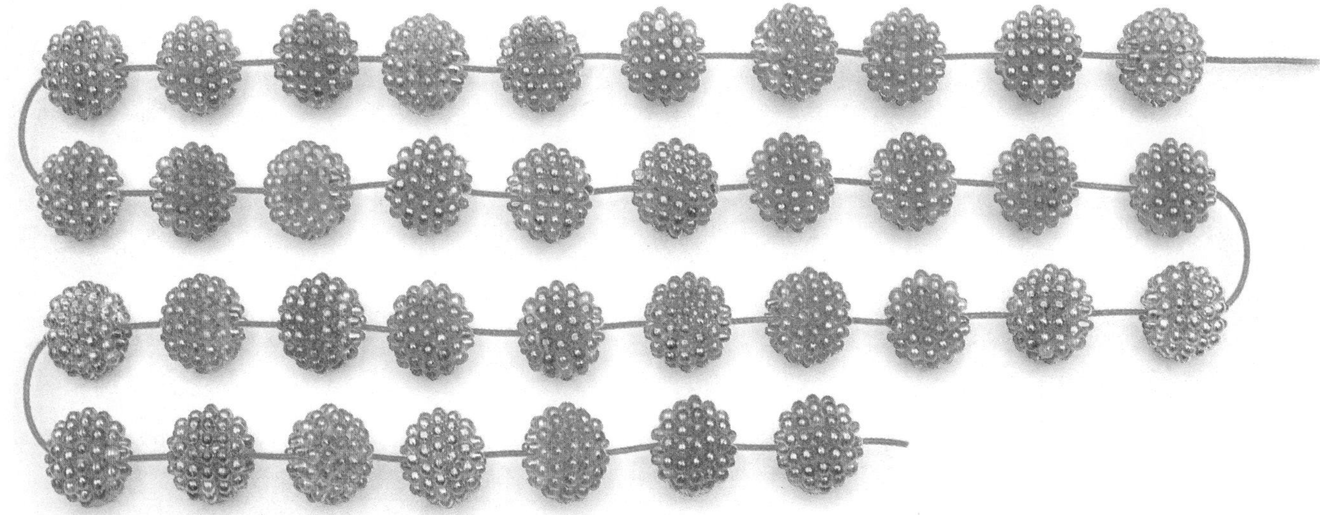

How many? ______

3

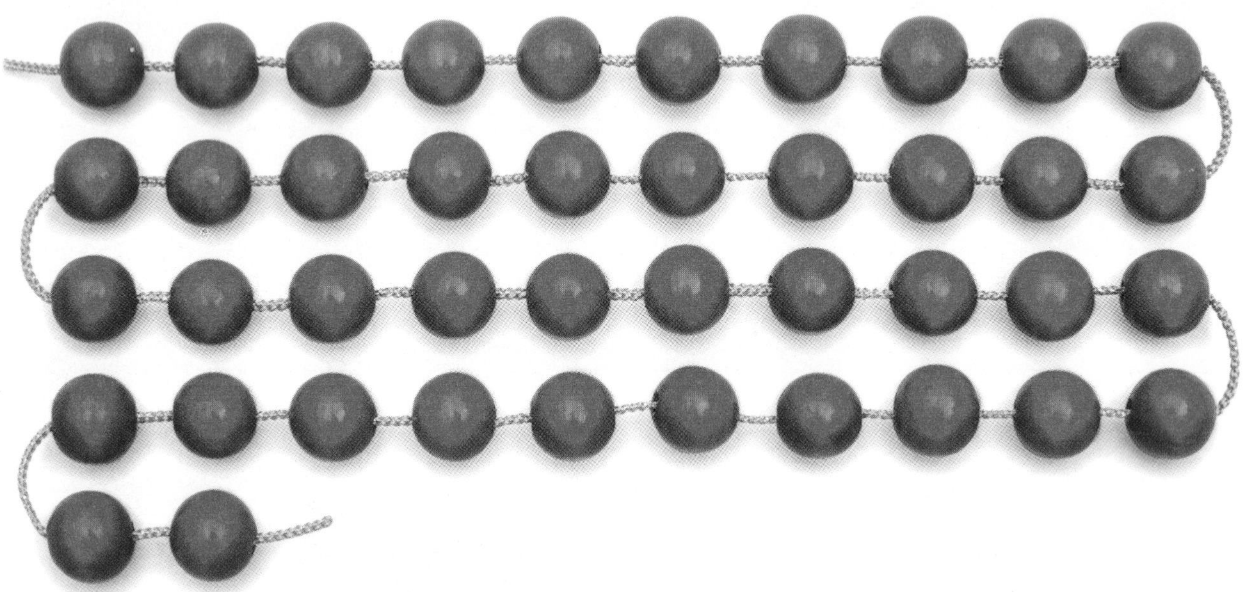

How many? ______

**Directions** In each exercise ask children to count the groups of 10 beads and then count on the remaining beads. Have children record how many beads there are.

**Home Activity** Place 30 pennies or other small objects on a table and have your child make groups of 10. Place 4 more pennies on the table. Have your child count all the pennies and tell how many there are. Talk about how to count the pennies. Repeat with other objects.

Name ____________________

**Algebra**

# 2s, 5s, and 10s on the Hundred Chart

| | | | | | | | | | |
|---|---|---|---|---|---|---|---|---|---|
| 1 | 2 | 3 | 4 | 5 | 6 | 7 | 8 | 9 | 10 |
| 11 | 12 | 13 | 14 | 15 | 16 | 17 | 18 | 19 | 20 |
| 21 | 22 | 23 | 24 | 25 | 26 | 27 | 28 | 29 | 30 |
| 31 | 32 | 33 | 34 | 35 | 36 | 37 | 38 | 39 | 40 |
| 41 | 42 | 43 | 44 | 45 | 46 | 47 | 48 | 49 | 50 |
| 51 | 52 | 53 | 54 | 55 | 56 | 57 | 58 | 59 | 60 |
| 61 | 62 | 63 | 64 | 65 | 66 | 67 | 68 | 69 | 70 |
| 71 | 72 | 73 | 74 | 75 | 76 | 77 | 78 | 79 | 80 |
| 81 | 82 | 83 | 84 | 85 | 86 | 87 | 88 | 89 | 90 |
| 91 | 92 | 93 | 94 | 95 | 96 | 97 | 98 | 99 | 100 |

**Directions** Have children count by 2s on the hundred chart and use a yellow crayon to color the numbers.

| 1 | 2 | 3 | 4 | 5 | 6 | 7 | 8 | 9 | 10 |
|---|---|---|---|---|---|---|---|---|---|
| 11 | 12 | 13 | 14 | 15 | 16 | 17 | 18 | 19 | 20 |
| 21 | 22 | 23 | 24 | | 26 | 27 | 28 | 29 | |
| 31 | 32 | 33 | 34 | | 36 | 37 | 38 | 39 | |
| 41 | 42 | 43 | 44 | | 46 | 47 | 48 | 49 | |
| 51 | 52 | 53 | 54 | | 56 | 57 | 58 | 59 | |
| 61 | 62 | 63 | 64 | | 66 | 67 | 68 | 69 | |
| 71 | 72 | 73 | 74 | | 76 | 77 | 78 | 79 | |
| 81 | 82 | 83 | 84 | | 86 | 87 | 88 | 89 | |
| 91 | 92 | 93 | 94 | | 96 | 97 | 98 | 99 | |

**Directions** Have children count by 5s on the hundred chart and write the numbers. Then have children count by 10s and use a yellow crayon to color the numbers.

**Home Activity** Ask your child to explain the hundred chart to you and tell how he or she counted by 5s and by 10s.

Name ______________________



**Algebra**

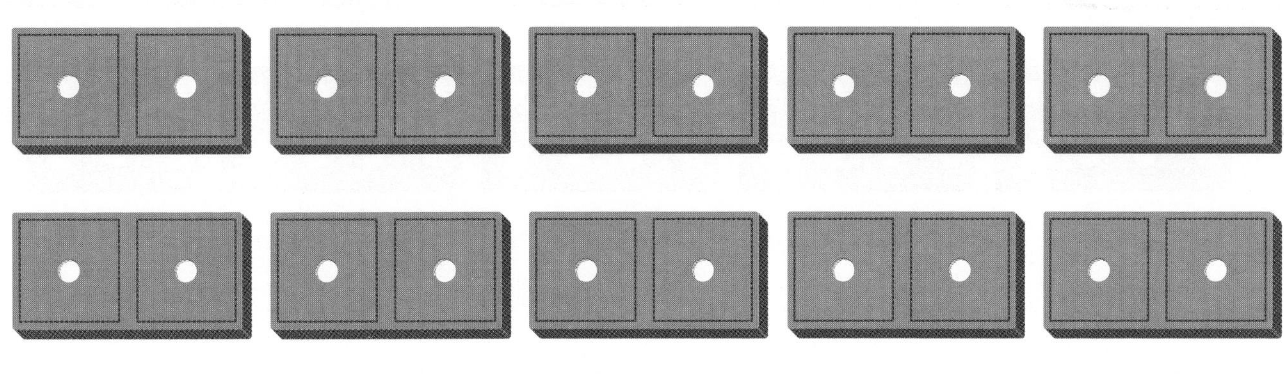

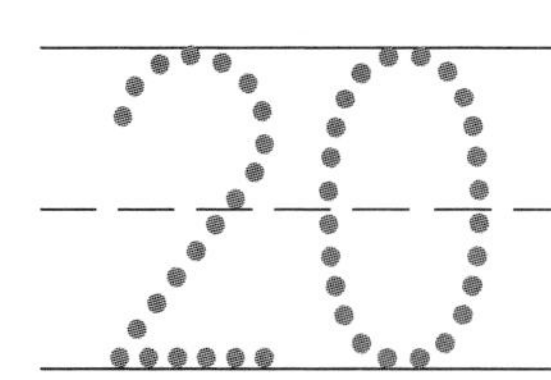

How many? 20

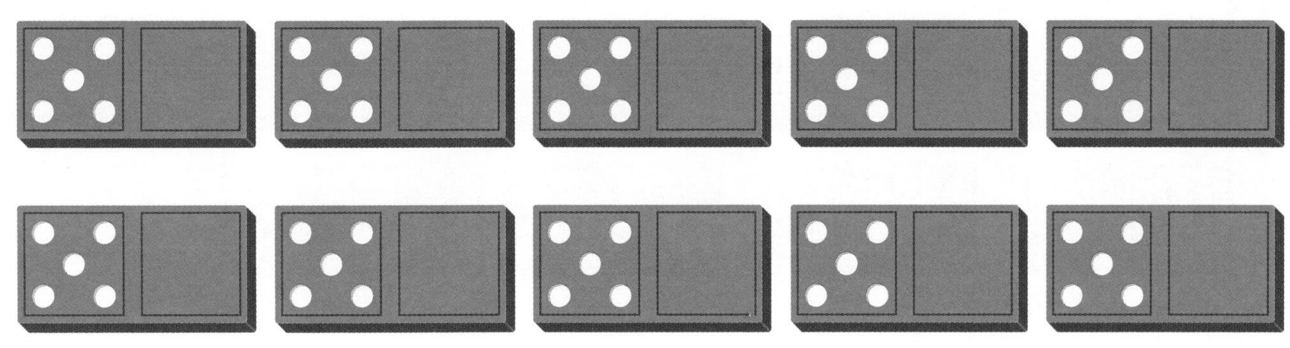

How many? ______

3

How many? ______

**Directions** In Exercise 1 have children count by 2s and record how many. In Exercise 2 have children count by 5s and record how many. In Exercise 3 have children count by 10s and record how many.

4

How many? ________

5

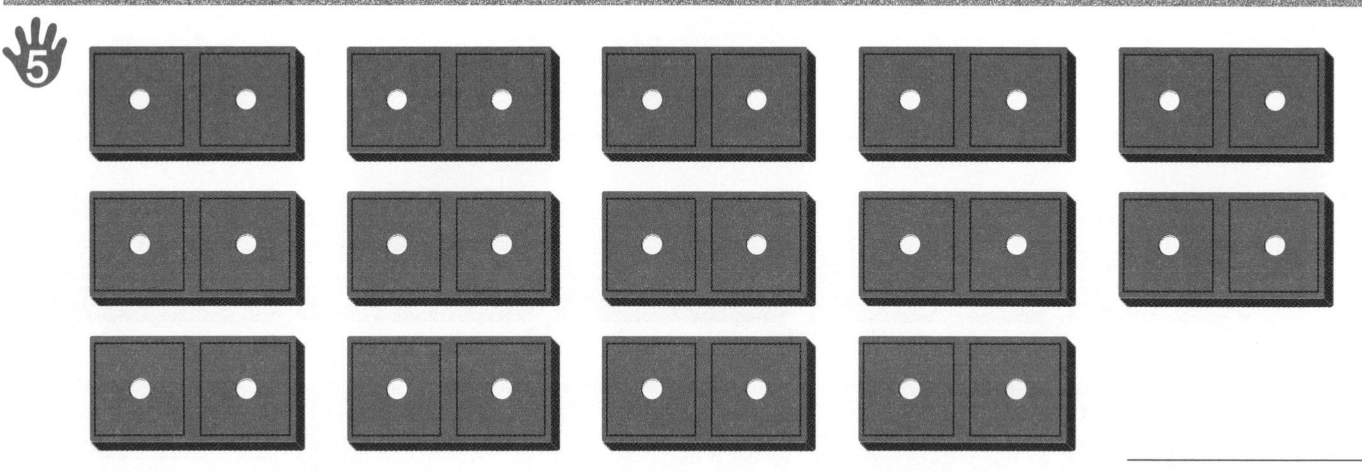

How many? ________

6

How many? ________

**Directions** In Exercise 4 have children count by 10s and record how many. In Exercise 5 have children count by 2s and record how many. In Exercise 6 have children count by 5s and record how many.

**Home Activity** Give your child 30 small objects, such as dried beans or pennies. Have him or her count them by 2s, 5s, and 10s.

Name ____________________

# Look for a Pattern

## Algebra

2

3

**Directions** In each exercise have children identify the number pattern and then continue the pattern by writing the missing numbers.

4

5

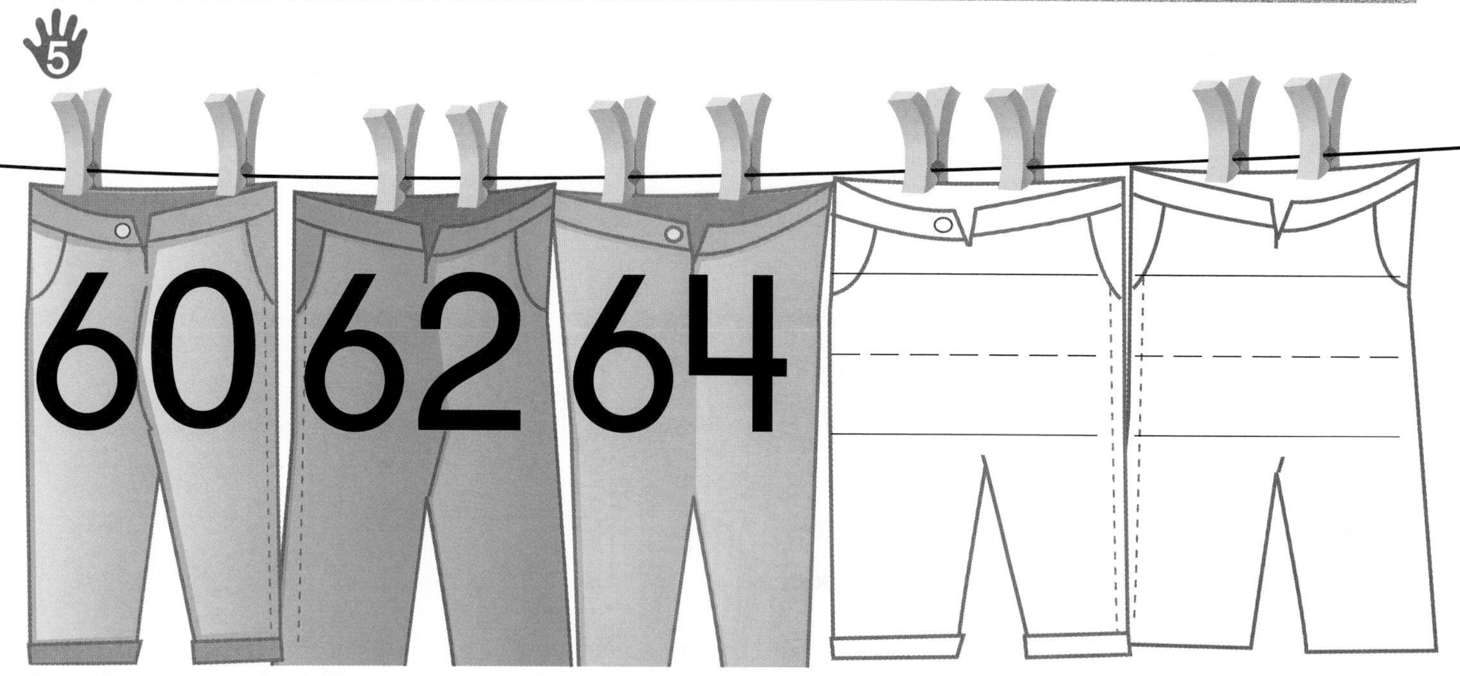


6

**Directions** In each exercise have children identify the number pattern and then continue the pattern by writing the missing numbers.

**Home Activity** Talk with your child about the number patterns shown on this page. Ask your child to explain why he or she wrote the numbers to continue the patterns.

Name ______________________

PROBLEM-SOLVING APPLICATIONS

# Nature Walk

How many? ________

**Directions** Tell children that a kindergarten class made a bulletin board display of leaves that shows groups of 10. Ask children how they can figure out how many leaves there are on the bulletin board. Then have children count the groups and write how many.

4 legs

legs

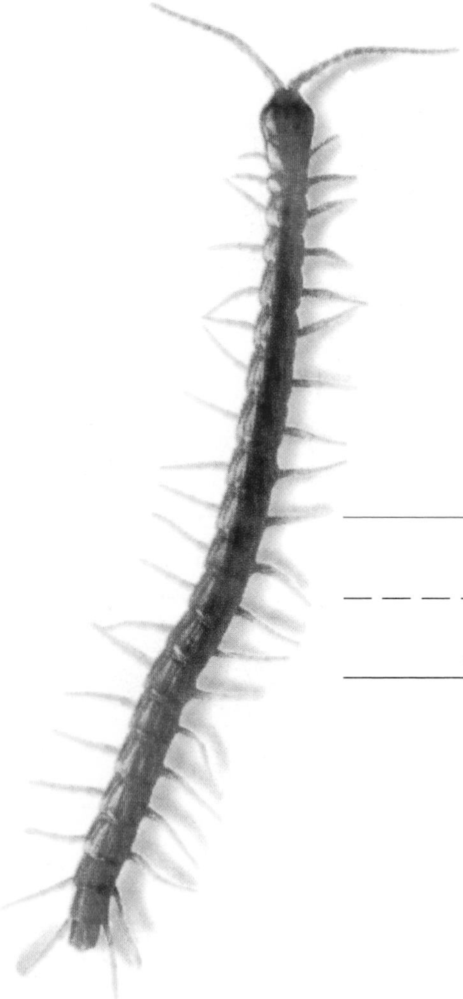

legs

legs

legs

**Directions** Talk about the pictures, pointing out that some animals have legs and some animals do not have legs. **How many legs do these animals have?** Ask children to count legs, write the numbers, and tell how they counted.

**Home Activity** Talk with your child about the pictures on these two pages. Have your child tell you how he or she solved problems to complete the pages.

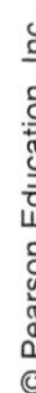

Name ______________________

Test

1

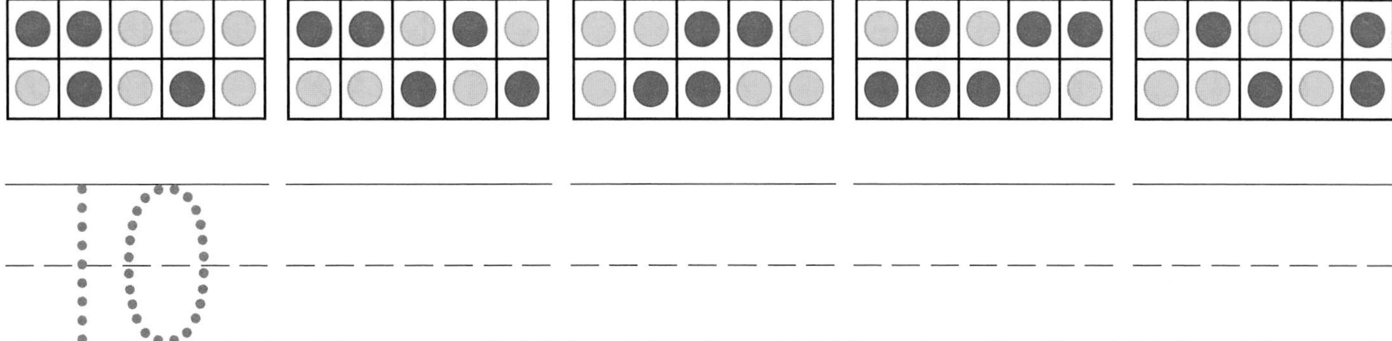

10

2

How many? ______

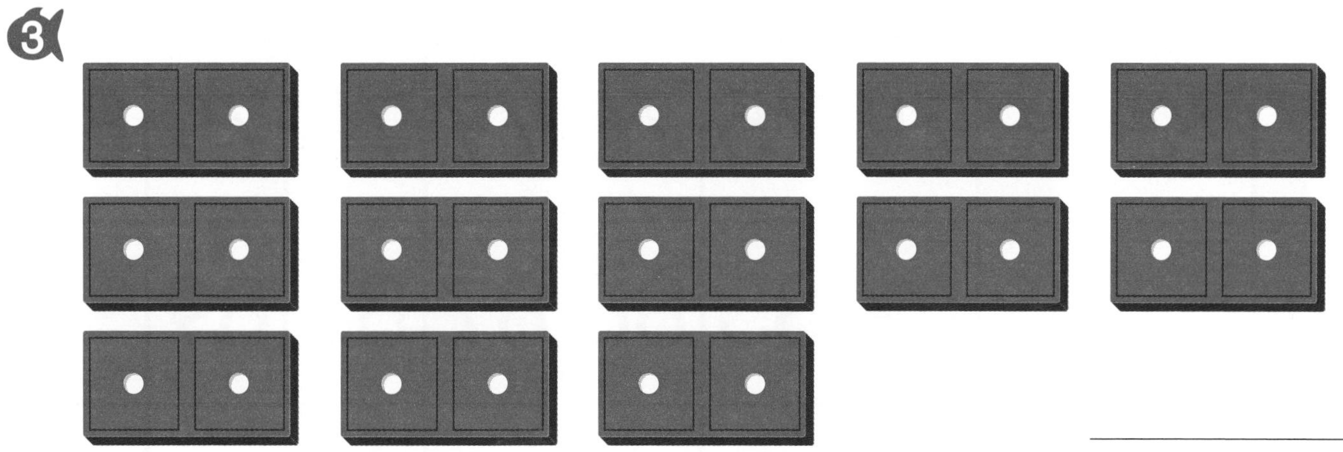

How many? ______

**Directions** Have children: 1. count the groups of 10 and write the numbers; 2. count the groups of 10 beads, count on the remaining beads, and record how many beads there are; 3. count by 2s and record how many.

4

| 1 | 2 | 3 | 4 | 5 | 6 | 7 | 8 | 9 | 10 |
|---|---|---|---|---|---|---|---|---|---|
| 11 | 12 | 13 | 14 | 15 | 16 | 17 | 18 |  | 20 |
| 21 | 22 |  | 24 | 25 | 26 |  | 28 | 29 | 30 |
|  | 32 | 33 | 34 | 35 | 36 | 37 | 38 | 39 |  |
| 41 |  | 43 | 44 | 45 | 46 | 47 |  | 49 | 50 |
| 51 | 52 | 53 |  | 55 | 56 | 57 | 58 |  | 60 |
| 61 | 62 | 63 | 64 |  | 66 |  | 68 | 69 | 70 |
|  | 72 |  | 74 | 75 | 76 | 77 | 78 | 79 | 80 |
| 81 |  | 83 | 84 | 85 | 86 | 87 | 88 | 89 |  |
| 91 | 92 | 93 |  | 95 |  | 97 | 98 | 99 | 100 |

**Directions** Have children: 4. write the missing numbers on the hundred chart; count by 5s to 100 on the chart and use a yellow crayon to color the numbers.

# Credits

## Cover:

Illustration: **Larry Moore**
Photograph: **Getty Images**

## Text:

Dorling Kindersley (DK) is an international publishing company specializing in the creation of high-quality reference content for books, CD-ROMs, online materials, and video. The hallmark of DK content is its unique combination of educational value and strong visual style. This combination allows DK to deliver appealing, accessible, and engaging educational content that delights children, parents, and teachers around the world. Scott Foresman is delighted to have been able to use selected extracts of DK content within this Scott Foresman Math program.

21–22: *My First Number Book* by Marie Heinst. Copyright ©1992, 1999 by Dorling Kindersley Limited; 47–48: *My First Math Book* by David and Wendy Clemson. Copyright ©1994 by Dorling Kindersley Limited; 71–72: *My Very First Colors, Shapes, Sizes, and Opposites Book* by Angela Wilkes. Copyright ©1993 by Dorling Kindersley Limited; 97–98: *My First Number Lift-the-Flap Board Book*. Copyright ©2001 by Dorling Kindersley Limited; 127–128: *The Lifesize Animal Counting Book*. Copyright ©1994 by Dorling Kindersley Limited; 155–156: *My First Word Board Book* by Angela Wilkes. Copyright ©1997, 1999 by Dorling Kindersley Limited; 191–192: *My First Book of Time* by Claire Llewellyn. Copyright ©1992 by Dorling Kindersley Limited; 219–220: *My First Look at Shapes*. Copyright ©2001 by Dorling Kindersley Limited; 239–240: *My First Animal Book*. Copyright ©2002 by Dorling Kindersley Limited; 259–260: *My First Number Board Book*. Copyright ©1999 by Dorling Kindersley Limited; 281–282: *My First Animal Board Book*. Copyright ©1998, 1999 by Dorling Kindersley Limited; 299–300: *Baby's Book of Nature* by Roger Priddy. Copyright ©1995 by Dorling Kindersley Limited.

## Illustrations:

1R **Amy Vangsgard;**
3R **Steve Henry;**
4R **Jayoung Cho;**
1A, 1B, 1C, 1D, 1E, 1F, 2, 3, 7, 11, 12, 15, 18, 19, 171 **Jason Wolff;**
1 **Karen Stormer Brooks;**
2A, 2B, 2C, 2D, 2E, 2F, 25, 26, 27, 29, 34, 40, 41, 45 **Donna Catanese;**
3A, 3B, 3C, 3D, 3F, 51, 52, 57, 58, 61, 65, 67 **Marisol Sarrazin;**
3, 66, 69, 71 **Reggie Holladay;**
4A, 4B, 4C, 4D, 4E, 4F, 8, 9, 10, 75, 76, 77, 79, 85, 89, 90, 92, 96, 100 **Drew Rose;**
4, 5 **Steven Boswick;**
5A, 5B, 5C, 5D, 5E, 5F, 101, 102, 103, 105, 109, 115, 116, 125, 126 **Laura Ovresat;**
6A, 6B, 6C, 6D, 6E, 6F, 131, 132, 135, 136, 140, 143, 144, 151 **Grace Lin;**
6 **Robert Masheris;**
7A, 7B, 7C, 7D, 7E, 7F, 159, 160, 165 **David Austin Clar;**
8A, 8B, 8C, 8D, 8E, 8F, 195, 196 **Russel Benfanti;**
9A, 9B, 9C, 9D, 9E, 9F, 223, 224 **Kathi Ember;**
9, 11, 31 **Steve Henry;**
10A, 10B, 10C, 10D, 10E, 10F, 243, 244 **Laura Watson;**
11A, 11B, 11C, 11D, 11F, 263, 264 **Lynne Chapman;**
12A, 12B, 12C, 12D, 12E, 12F, 285, 286 **Jimmy Pickering;**
23 **Bernard Adnet;**
24 **Jennifer Beck Harris;**
29, 30, 32 **Mindy Pierce;**
49, 59, 64, 74 **Steve Cox;**
53, 54, 146 **Janet Skiles;**
62 **Gary Colby;**
63, 94 **Lyn Martin;**
73 **Tim Huhn;**
93, 113 **Carly Castillon;**
99, 154, 216, 273, 274 **Amy Vangsgard;**
123, 124 **Sally Jo Vitsky;**
153, 158 **Carolyn Croll;**
166, 194 **Thomas Taylor;**
170, 193 **Kate Flanagan;**
171, 172 **John Sandford;**
213, 214, 218 **Jayoung Cho;**
229, 230, 235, 236, 249, 250, 261 **Jill Meyerhoff;**
245, 246, 255, 256, 265, 266, 283 **Peter Grosshauser;**
251, 252, 262, 297, 298 **Don Tate;**
269, 270, 283 **Keiko Motoyama;**

## Photographs:

Every effort has been made to secure permission and provide appropriate credit for photographic material. The publisher deeply regrets any omission and pledges to correct errors called to its attention in subsequent editions.

Unless otherwise acknowledged, all photographs are the property of Scott Foresman, a division of Pearson Education.

Photo locators denoted as follows:
Top (T), Center (C), Bottom (B), Left (L), Right (R), Background (Bkgd)

iii Jason Wolff
iv Donna Catanese
v Marisol Sarrazin
vi Drew Rose
vii Laura Ovresat
viii Grace Lin
ix David Austin Clar
x Russel Benfanti
xiA Kathi Ember
xiiA Laura Watson
xiiiA Lynne Chapman
xiv Jimmy Pickering
3 Getty Images
4 ©Comstock Inc.
21, 22, 47, 48, 71, 72, 128, 155, 156, 191, 192, 239, 240, 259, 260, 281, 282, 299, 300 ©Dorling Kindersley
55 (TC) ©David Frazier/Corbis, (TR, TL) ©G. K. and Vikki Hart/Getty Images
56 (BL, CL) Getty Images, (TCL) Corbis, (TL) ©Siede Preis/Getty Images, (C) ©G. K. and Vikki Hart/Getty Images
87 (T, TCL) ©Siede Preis/Getty Images, (C, CL) Getty Images, (B, BCL) Corbis
88 (CR) ©Siede Preis/Getty Images, (TR, TCL, B) Corbis, (TL, BCL) Getty Images
105 (TL) ©Steve Grubman/Getty Images, (TR) ©Lawrence Lawry/Getty Images
106 (T) ©Geostock/Getty Images, (TCL, C) ©Siede Preis/Getty Images, (B) Getty Images
127 Natural History Museum/©Dorling Kindersley
135 Mark Goebel/Painet Stock Photo Agency
150 Robert Harding World Imagery/Alamy.com
219 Natural History Museum/©Dorling Kindersley, Stephen Oliver/©Dorling Kindersley
220 Stephen Oliver/©Dorling Kindersley
227, 228 Getty Images
255, 256 Burke/Triolo/Brand X Pictures
261 (B) Hemera Technologies
300 Booth Museum of Natural History/©Dorling Kindersley
Work Mat 1 (Bkgd), Work Mat 3 Getty Images
Work Mat 3 (R, L) ©Dorling Kindersley